Sacred Texts of the World

Grant Hardy, Ph.D.

THE
GREAT
COURSES®

PUBLISHED BY:

THE GREAT COURSES
Corporate Headquarters
4840 Westfields Boulevard, Suite 500
Chantilly, Virginia 20151-2299
Phone: 1-800-832-2412
Fax: 703-378-3819
www.thegreatcourses.com

Copyright © The Teaching Company, 2014

Printed in the United States of America

This book is in copyright. All rights reserved.

Without limiting the rights under copyright reserved above, no part of this publication may be reproduced, stored in or introduced into a retrieval system, or transmitted, in any form, or by any means (electronic, mechanical, photocopying, recording, or otherwise), without the prior written permission of The Teaching Company.

Grant Hardy, Ph.D.

Professor of History and Religious Studies
University of North Carolina at Asheville

Professor Grant Hardy is Professor of History and Religious Studies at the University of North Carolina at Asheville (UNC Asheville). After serving two terms as the chair of the Department of History, he is currently the director of the Humanities Program. He has a B.A. in Ancient Greek from Brigham Young University (BYU) and a Ph.D. in Chinese Language and Literature from Yale University.

Dr. Hardy is the author or editor of six books, including *Worlds of Bronze and Bamboo: Sima Qian's Conquest of History*; *The Establishment of the Han Empire and Imperial China*, coauthored with Anne Kinney of the University of Virginia; and *Understanding the Book of Mormon: A Reader's Guide*. His most recent book is the first volume of the *Oxford History of Historical Writing*, coedited with Andrew Feldherr of Princeton University.

Professor Hardy won UNC Asheville's 2002 Distinguished Teaching Award for Humanities and was named to a Ruth and Leon Feldman Professorship for Outstanding Service for 2009–2010. He has participated in scholarly symposia on Sima Qian and early Chinese historiography at the University of Wisconsin–Madison, Harvard University, and Heidelberg University. He also received a research grant from the National Endowment for the Humanities.

Professor Hardy was raised in northern California and has taught at BYU, BYU–Hawaii, Elmira College, and UNC Asheville. He lived in Taiwan for two years in the 1980s. He and his wife, Heather, have two children. One of his proudest achievements is that he has written or rewritten most of the articles on imperial China for *The World Book Encyclopedia*; thus, his name is in every elementary school library in the country. ■

Table of Contents

INTRODUCTION

Professor Biography i
Course Scope 1

LECTURE GUIDES

LECTURE 19
Related Traditions—Jain Scriptures 4

LECTURE 20
Five Confucian Classics 23

LECTURE 21
Four Books of Neo-Confucianism 43

LECTURE 22
Daoism and the Daodejing 62

LECTURE 23
The Three Caverns of Daoist Scriptures 81

LECTURE 24
Related Traditions—Shinto and Tenrikyo 100

LECTURE 25
Christian Testaments Old and New 119

LECTURE 26
Gospels and Acts 138

LECTURE 27
Letters and Apocalypse 156

LECTURE 28
Apocryphal Gospels 174

Table of Contents

LECTURE 29
Related Traditions—Mormon Scriptures 193

LECTURE 30
Islam and Scriptural Recitation 212

LECTURE 31
Holy Qur'an 230

LECTURE 32
Hadith and Sufism 250

LECTURE 33
Related Traditions—Baha'i Scriptures 268

LECTURE 34
Abandoned Scriptures—Egyptian and Mayan 287

LECTURE 35
Secular Scripture—U.S. Constitution 306

LECTURE 36
Heavenly Books, Earthly Connections 324

SUPPLEMENTAL MATERIAL

Recommended Texts and Translations 342
Bibliography 346

Sacred Texts of the World

Scope:

Religious texts are, in many cases, the best way to learn about the faith traditions of others. Authoritative and widely available, they offer a window into a new world of ideas and practices. In our rapidly shrinking world, where cultural traditions are converging at an ever-increasing rate, the value of mutual understanding cannot be overstated.

But it would be far too simple to suggest that we can easily discover some universal truth or common ground by a cursory read of another faith's sacred writings. These texts exhibit tremendous variety in content, form, use, and origins. We must approach these texts with an open mind and great care. In so doing, we may find that we learn as much about ourselves and our own beliefs as we do about others'.

The library of world scriptures is huge, and sacred texts can be studied and pondered for a lifetime. Thus, this course will focus on a specific selection of texts. The course provides an overview of the sacred writings of seven major religious traditions, basically in chronological order of the religions' founding, along with descriptions of holy books from another half dozen lesser-known or smaller faiths.

We begin by discussing how to approach reading these texts, then start our journey with the sacred works of the Hindus. Among the many great opportunities here will be a chance to broaden the definition of *text*, for many of these texts defy Western ideas about scripture. We will also look at the related faith of Sikhism, whose relatively recent sacred text occupies a unique role in world religions.

Next, we will study Jewish scripture, including the Tanakh (also called the Hebrew Bible, or the Old Testament by Christians), the Apocrypha, and the Dead Sea Scrolls. We will look at the formerly oral traditions now written down in the Mishnah and Talmud, and we will see why the Jewish relationship to their scripture rightly earns them the title "people of the book." Before moving on, we will also consider the ancient Near Eastern monotheistic religion of Zoroastrianism; its text, the Avesta; and some interesting parallels between this faith and the three great Abrahamic faiths.

The Buddhist canon is the largest in the world, containing about 100,000 pages. We will consider the Tripitaka, or "Three Baskets," of the Buddhist scriptural tradition: the Vinaya (rules for monks and nuns), the Sutras (discourses of the Buddha), and the Abhidharma (works of systematic philosophy) from all of the major Buddhist traditions. After this, we will look at the Jain faith, which arose in a similar time and place as Buddhism. This faith is in the unique position of sharing many of its core principles among its different sects but not sharing its core scriptures.

Confucianism is often thought of as a philosophy rather than a religion, but its texts discuss morality, principles for living in harmony with the universe, rituals for dealing with unseen beings, divination, and temple ceremonies, much like the other scriptures in this course. We will see, however, that although the contents of the Confucian Classics are much like that of other scriptures, their uses are rather different, with a decidedly this-worldly, even political, focus.

Daoism is another great faith of Chinese origin, and its history is entwined with that of Confucianism. Its most famous text, the Daodejing, is fairly well known in the West, but it is only a small section of a much larger canon with a complicated history of development.

We will consider both of these traditions, then turn to Japan for a brief look at two of its native faiths, Shinto and Tenrikyo. One has no official scripture beyond the ancient histories of Japan; the other is a modern faith based in the ideas and the beautiful poetry of its founder.

To most students of this course, Christian scriptures will be among the most familiar, either as part of their faith's own tradition or through the deep influence of these scriptures on Western literature. We will attempt, however, to view these works through fresh eyes as we consider the development and canonization of the Gospels, the letters of Paul and the audience who first read them, and the Apocryphal and Gnostic books that did not make it into the orthodox Christian canon. Then we will look at a late attempt to expand the Christian canon through the addition of the Book of Mormon.

Muslims consider the Qur'an to be the complete and final revelation of God, but it is not the only Muslim text we will consider in this course. In addition to this central and most revered text of Islam, we will look at the legal interpretations of Islamic law passed down through the Hadith, as well as the mystical poetry of Sufism. We will also look at the Baha'i faith, a 19th-century religion that came out of the context of Shia Islam and has its own unique scriptures.

We will end the course with some unusual cases and questions. First, we will ask what happens to a sacred text when the religion it represents is no longer practiced; specifically, we will consider two cases: the Egyptian Book of the Dead and the Mayan Popol Vuh. We will next ask whether explicitly secular writing can take on aspects of the sacred by looking at the place of the U.S. Constitution and the Declaration of Independence in American culture. Finally, we will close with a consideration of how the comparative study of sacred texts might make a difference in our lives as individuals, as members of faith communities, and as citizens of the world. ∎

Related Traditions—Jain Scriptures
Lecture 19

Jainism and Buddhism are sister religions—much like Judaism and Christianity. The two Indian traditions share many foundational concepts and come out of the same social environment. And like Judaism and Christianity, they followed different paths, with one becoming a successful missionary religion, and the other, arguably the more demanding of the two, maintaining a vibrant religious and intellectual presence yet remaining relatively small. Today there are some 500 million Buddhists in the world, and only about 4 million Jains. Despite the size differential, Jainism is an ancient religious tradition that is well worth studying; in this lecture, we'll see how Jainism upends some of our common assumptions about scripture.

Jainism and Buddhism

- It's not exactly clear when Buddha and Mahavira, the founder of Jainism, lived. Traditional dates are in the 6th century B.C.E., though scholars now lean more toward the 5th century. Either way, Buddha and Mahavira seem to have been contemporaries or near-contemporaries.

- Both were raised as princes in the Kshatriya (warrior) caste in northern India. Both left home at the age of 30 to find spiritual fulfillment through asceticism and meditation. After six years, the Buddha dropped his severe fasting and then became enlightened under a bodhi tree. In contrast, Mahavira never gave up his ascetic practices, and after 12 years, he achieved his own sort of enlightenment and became a Jina, or "Conqueror."

- Jains are those who follow the Jinas. Mahavira is not regarded as the founder of the religion; rather, he is the last of a series of 24 Tirthankaras in this world era. *Tirthankara* means "maker of a ford"—someone who gains liberation and can teach others the way across the oceans of suffering and samsara. Actually, even Mahavira is a title—"Great Hero"; his name was Vardhamana.

- For the next three or four decades after enlightenment, both Buddha and Mahavira taught the truths they had discovered. They gained lay followers and ordained monks and nuns, who left behind all worldly connections and devoted themselves exclusively to salvation. Their teachings were passed down orally for several centuries before they were transcribed in written form.

Basic Principles of Jainism

- As you may recall, Hindus believed that humans, animals, and gods all had a soul, or *atman*, while the Buddha proclaimed that nothing had a soul. Mahavira taught that everything has a soul—not just people and animals but plants, rocks, drops of water, gusts of wind, and flames of fire.
    - The world is divided into two types of phenomena—*jiva* (living beings, or the life principle within things) and *ajiva* (insentient matter, time, and space).

    - There is no creator god or creation; *jiva* have been entangled with material elements from eternity, but even without a beginning, there can nevertheless be an end, and existence as a human being offers the best chance at this.

    - Once a *jiva* is freed from the corrupting influence of matter, it attains infinite knowledge, perception, bliss, and energy. But it remains distinct; it isn't subsumed into *brahman* (as in Hinduism), and it doesn't dissipate into nonexistence (Buddhism.)

- In all three religions, living a good life to attain a better rebirth is a good thing, but the ultimate goal is to escape from the cycle of rebirth altogether.
    - In Hinduism, this is done when one's *atman* merges with *brahman* (ultimate reality), through the ways of knowledge, works, or devotion. In Buddhism, liberation comes with the realization that there was never any self to begin with, and like Hinduism, it develops the notion of savior figures—bodhisattvas—who can assist in this process.

- o In Jainism, however, liberation comes only through one's own efforts, by ridding oneself of karma, which is thought of as a subtle form of matter that sticks to *jiva* and weighs them down. Escaping karma can be done through ascetic renunciation, with the preeminent virtue being ahimsa, or nonviolence. Jains believe it is far better to suffer oneself than to cause suffering to other living beings.

- All Jains accept the five vows: no injuring other living beings, no lying or deceit, no taking what is not given, no sexual immorality, and no attachment. For ordinary Jains, this means living simple lives of kindness, integrity, and generosity. Sexual relations are restricted to marriage, and possessions are kept to a minimum. When Jains pray (or, more accurately, chant mantras), they show respect for those who have achieved liberation, but they are not allowed to ask for blessings or material benefits.

- The requirements for monks and nuns are much stricter, because they hope to attain moksha, or liberation, in this lifetime by ridding themselves of all karmic residues. They give up home, family, and nearly all possessions and eat only what is given to them. Jain monks and nuns are not allowed to use vehicles and must walk barefoot everywhere. Their lives are devoted to meditation, preaching, and scholarship, and the greatest spiritual achievement is to gradually stop eating or drinking anything and fast to death.

- There are several subsects of Jains, but the major division is between Shvetambara and Digambara Jains, which split sometime around the 4th or 5th centuries C.E. The main differences are that Digambara ("Sky-clad") monks wear nothing whatsoever, while Shvetambara ("White-clad") monks and nuns wear plain white robes.

Jain Scriptures
- In most world religions, scripture is at the core of religious identity, but in Jainism, Shvetambaras and Digambaras for the most part reject each other's scriptures as forgeries. They are clearly in the

same religious tradition, and their beliefs are quite similar, but there are almost no shared textual resources.

- Shvetambaras and Digambaras both agree that Mahavira taught 14 texts called Purvas, which were identical to those taught by all the preceding Tirthankaras. These communicated the eternal truths of omniscient beings. Mahavira's first followers came from the Brahman caste, and those disciples memorized the Purvas, but ultimately, all the Purvas were lost, with only fragments or paraphrases remaining.

- Over several centuries, the Shvetambaras developed replacement scriptures that captured some of the traditions associated with Mahavira and were written in the Ardhamagadhi language—a more vernacular dialect than Sanskrit, though it became a literary, scriptural language.
    - Most Shvetambaras accept 45 texts as authoritative, most of which go by the name of sutras: 12 Angas ("limbs"), dealing with basic doctrines, moral prescriptions for monks and laypersons, cosmology, and narratives of Mahavira, Jina, and pious believers; 12 Upangas ("subordinate limbs"), treating ontological, cosmological, and epistemological matters; 6 Cheda-sutras ("separate") , having to do with disciplinary issues; 4 Mula-sutras ("basic") that were typically studied by new monks and nuns, 10 miscellaneous texts on astrology and ascetic ritual; and 2 appendices that offer summaries and explanations.

    - This Shvetambara canon was written down on palm-leaf manuscripts about the 5th century C.E. after a series of councils, yet even today, there is not complete agreement on exactly which texts belong in the collection of 45, and some Shvetambara subsects reject as many as 13 of them.

- Digambara Jains also believe that the 14 original Purvas were lost, but they reject all the Shvetambara scriptures. Instead, they view as authoritative two doctrinal synopses written by monks in the 2nd century C.E.: the Scripture of Six Parts and the Treatise on the Passions. The Digambara scriptures are written in a different vernacular language, called Jaina Sauraseni.

- In both traditions, laypersons don't really read or study the scriptures; instead, they learn some of their contents through sermons or short summaries written by monks. Nevertheless, the Jains have a rich tradition of scholarship, commentaries, philosophy, and literature.

Examples of Jain Texts
- Hermann Jacobi, a German scholar, translated four Jain texts for Max Müller's Sacred Books of the East: the Acaranga Sutra, the Uttaradhyayana, the Kritanga Sutra, and the Kalpa Sutra.

- Jacobi began with the first of the 12 Angas, the Acaranga Sutra, which is often regarded as the oldest item in the Jain scriptures and includes rules for monks and nuns regarding food, clothing, and lodging, as well as the earliest account of Mahavira's life. This sutra also includes the Five Great Vows undertaken by all Jains.

- The Uttaradhyayana, one of the four Mula-sutras, is more specific about what the vows mean for renunciants. For instance: "If a layperson abuses a monk he should not grow angry against him; because he would be like a child, a monk should not grow angry."

- Jacobi also translated the second Anga, the Kritanga Sutra, which offers an introduction to Jain teachings, as well as a critical examination of competing doctrines at the time of Mahavira. According to the Kritanga Sutra, "These three classes of living beings have been declared by the Jinas: (1) earth, water, fire, wind; (2) grass, trees, and plants; and (3) the moving beings, both the egg-bearing and those that bear live offspring, those generated from dirt and those generated in fluids. Know and understand that they all desire happiness."

- And finally, Jacobi translated the Kalpa Sutra, which retells the story of Mahavira's life with more legendary details than what is found in the Acaranga Sutra, along with narratives from the biographies of a few other Tirthankaras. This text is from one of the Cheda-sutras, but it gained its prominence from the fact that it is read aloud every year during the eight-day Paryushana (rainy season festival)—the most important event in the Shvetambara ritual calendar, when Jains fast, confess their sins, and ask forgiveness.

- The Digambaras also celebrate Paryushana, but instead of the Kalpa Sutra, they recite the Tattvartha Sutra ("That Which Is"), the first systematic exposition of Jain doctrines written in Sanskrit, which was composed by the 2nd-century monk Umasvati. In 250 terse aphorisms, it covers Jain epistemology, metaphysics, cosmology, and ethics.
  - Although it is not exactly scriptural, the Tattvartha Sutra is nevertheless the only Jain text that is held in high respect by both Shvetambaras and Digambaras.
  - The form is similar to that of Hindu sutras, and it quickly moves through lists of the seven categories of truth, five varieties of knowledge, eight types of karma, different types of beings, various spatial realms, enumerations of vows and moral precepts, karmic obstacles, and the process of liberation.

- What's striking about Jainism is not just the desire to escape perpetual suffering but the desire to avoid any entanglement in causing or even benefiting from the use and exploitation of other living creatures, both animate and inanimate. The Uttaradhyayana in particular offers a powerful, even startling vision of empathy and compassion.

Suggested Reading

Dundas, *The Jains*.

Jacobi, trans., *Jaina Sutras*.

Jaini, *The Jaina Path of Purification*.

Tatia, trans., *Tattvartha Sutra*.

Questions to Consider

1. What does it mean for a religion when the sacred texts associated with a founding figure have all been lost?

2. How is it that the two major branches of Jainism have virtually no scriptures in common?

3. How do Jain sacred texts emphasize the concept of ahimsa, or nonviolence?

Related Traditions—Jain Scriptures
Lecture 19—Transcript

We've finished our lectures on Buddhism, and now we're going to move to a related tradition that's a little bit smaller: Jainism (actually a lot smaller).

Jainism and Buddhism are sister religions, much like Judaism and Christianity, as we'll see in Lecture 25. The two Indian traditions share many foundational concepts, and they come out of the same social environment; and like Judaism and Christianity, they followed different paths, with one of those religions becoming a successful missionary religion and the other, arguably the more demanding of the two, maintaining a vibrant religious and intellectual presence, yet remaining relatively small. Today there are some 500 million Buddhists in the world and only about 4 million Jains. But despite the size differential, Jainism is an ancient religious tradition well worth studying. For instance, before the end of this lecture, we'll see how Jainism upends some of our common assumptions about scripture.

It's often said that the Buddhist sangha—that's the community of monks and nuns—is the oldest continuously-existing social organization in the world. That's probably true since monks have been ordaining younger monks in a generational succession that goes back some 2,500 years to the Buddha himself. But Jain monks and nuns might also be in the running. It's not exactly clear when Buddha and Mahavira, the founder of Jainism, lived. Traditional dates are in the sixth B.C.E., though scholars now lean more toward the 5th century, a little bit later. Either way, Buddha and Mahavira seem to have been contemporaries, or near-contemporaries; so this succession of Jain monks and nuns also goes back some 2,500 years.

Both Buddha and Mahavira were raised as princes in the Kshatriya caste, the warrior caste, in northern India. Both left home at the age of 30 to find spiritual fulfillment through asceticism and meditation. You'll recall that after six years, the Buddha dropped his severe fasting and then became enlightened under a bodhi tree (so the title "Buddha" means "the awakened one"; his regular name was Siddhartha Gautama). By contrast, after Mahavira left home, he never gave up his ascetic practices; and after 12 years, he achieved his own sort of enlightenment and he became a Jina, or a conqueror, though that term refers to spiritual rather than military conquest. That's an important transition because the Buddha and Mahavira are both from the warrior caste, and they're now redefining or repurposing that martial prowess, dedication, and focus that used to be used for conquering other peoples to now conquering the self or towards spiritual conquests. So Jains are those who follow the Jinas. Mahavira isn't regarded as the founder of the religion; rather, he's thought to be the last of a series of 24 Tirthankaras. Tirthankaras means the "maker of a ford," so someone something that gets you across a body of water. A Tirthankara is someone who gains liberation and then can teach others the way across the oceans of suffering and samsara. Actually, even the word *Mahavira* is a title; it means "Great Hero." This man's name originally was Vardhamana.

For the next three or four decades after their enlightenments, both the Buddha and Mahavira taught the truths that they'd discovered. They gained lay followers as well as ordaining monks and nuns who left behind all worldly connections and devoted themselves exclusively to salvation. Then their teachings were passed down orally for several centuries before they were transcribed in written form. In addition, Buddha and Mahavira both tapped into ideas that had been recently formulated by the sages of the Upanishads; remember the ideas of samsara (of reincarnation), karma, dharma, and moksha.

There were, however, a few critical differences in what Buddha and Mahavira taught, and then also what the Upanishads taught as well. Where Hindus believed that humans, animals, and gods all had a soul, or *atman*, which could be reborn into any one of those three types of bodies, the Buddha proclaimed that nothing had a soul. He said there's no such thing as an eternal, unchanging, independently-existing self; rather, we're made up of temporary bundles of various aspects of personality and matter. You may remember the five *skandas*; that we're made up of a body, sensations, perceptions, psychic disposition, and consciousness. Mahavira, by contrast, taught that everything has a soul; so not just animals, people, and heavenly beings, but also plants, rocks, drops of water, gusts of wind, and flames of fire, they all have souls. The Jain scriptures talk of earth-bodies, water-bodies, wind-bodies, and fire-bodies. When I teach this in class I sometimes ask if there's anybody who has a lighter in class; and I ask them to flick their lighter and then a flame comes up, and then when they release their thumb it disappears, and I tell them in Jain thought that flame was a soul that was born into a fire-body and then has now died, has extinguished, and may be reborn to be a person someday.

In Jainism, the world is divided into two types of phenomena: There are *jiva*, and that means living beings, or it's the life principle within beings; and then *ajiva*, which is insentient matter, or time and space. Jains use the term *jiva* rather than *atman* to make this distinction between what they believe and what Hindus assume. In Jainism, there's no creator god or creation. *Jiva* have been entangled with material elements from eternity, but even though there's no beginning, there can nevertheless be an end; and existence as a human being offers the best chance at this, the best chance of moksha, of liberation. Once a *jiva* is freed from the corrupting influence of matter, it attains infinite knowledge, infinite perception, bliss, and energy. But it remains distinct; it isn't subsumed into *brahman* (as in Hinduism, the great over-soul, the great world being), and it doesn't dissipate into nonexistence (as in Buddhism). Actually, that's not quite right because nirvana isn't exactly nonexistence and it isn't exactly existence, but it some kind of extinguishing, some sort of snuffing out.

In all three of these religions, living a good life to attain a better rebirth is a good thing; but the ultimate goal is to escape from the cycle of rebirth altogether. In Hinduism, this is done when one's *atman* merges with *brahman* (that ultimate reality) through the ways of knowledge, the way of works, or the way of devotion. In Buddhism, liberation comes with the realization that there was never any self to begin with; and like Hinduism, it develops the notion of savior figures, remember bodhisattvas, who can assist in this process. That's especially the case in Mahayana Buddhism. In Jainism, however, liberation comes only through one's own efforts by ridding oneself of karma, which is thought of as a subtle form of matter that sticks to *jiva* and then weighs them down. Escaping karma can be done through ascetic renunciation, with the preeminent virtue being ahimsa, or nonviolence. Jains believe it's far better to suffer oneself than to cause suffering to other living beings; you sort of work off the residues of a lifetime of karma by self-sacrificing behavior.

All Jains accept the five great vows: No injuring other living beings, no lying or deceit, no taking what isn't given, no sexual immorality, and no attachment. You may remember that that sounds like the five vows of Buddhists, except the last one in Buddhism is no intoxicants and in Jains it's no attachments. For ordinary Jains, this means living simple lives of kindness, integrity, and generosity. Sexual relations are restricted to marriage, though monks and nuns are going to be completely celibate, of course; and possessions are kept to a minimum. When Jains pray—or more accurately, they chant mantras—they show respect for those who've achieved liberation, for Jinas; but they're not allowed to ask for blessings or for material benefits from the gods. In fact, Jains don't worship the gods; those are celestial beings whose good karma entitles them to eons of bliss because the gods, too, will someday have to be reborn as humans in order to attain moksha. Even in the heavens they're still entwined in the world of passions and attachments.

Think about the implications of combining strict nonviolence with a cosmology in which the whole world is alive; so even plants, rocks, and things. Jains are vegetarians, but even vegetables have souls; and so it's better to eat as little as possible. Since the plants from which clothing is made have souls, one should dress as simply as possible. Jains aren't exactly vegans because they consume dairy products, but not eggs. Devout Jains limit their travel; they filter drinking water so they don't accidentally drink in little creatures; they try not to eat at night, where you can't see exactly what you're eating; and they don't consume root vegetables, which are thought to have complex souls.

Jains undertake regular periods of fasting and self-denial, and they avoid farming, which they consider to be a violent occupation. Think not just of harvesting the plants, but think about killing pests or even plowing; that you'd pull a plow through the ground, and break up the dirt, and cause all kinds of pain to the earth and to the rocks. Perhaps ironically, when Jains left their lives of farming, they went into trade and banking—I'm not exactly sure that banking is exactly nonviolent; my relationship with banks have not always been without suffering—but nevertheless, as merchants and bankers, Jains were more successful than their Hindu farming neighbors; and so although Jainism never really spread beyond its country of origin, it's nevertheless maintained a constant presence in India, unlike Buddhism, which actually died out in India and then went to East Asia. Today, there are millions of Jains still, and the business ethics of that particular community are legendary; they're thought to be absolutely honest and having perfect integrity.

Monks and nuns, however, have stricter requirements, since these are people who hope to attain not just a better life in the next go-round, but they want to achieve moksha or liberation in this lifetime by ridding themselves of all karmic residues. They give up home, family, and nearly all possessions, except for a begging bowl and a small broom to sweep insects out of their path as they walk along. They eat only what's given to them, though it has to be leftovers; they're not allowed to ask people to cook something for them, and it's not the point to have people prepare a special meal for them. They just take whatever's left over. Jain monks and nuns aren't allowed to use vehicles, and must walk barefoot everywhere.

Rather than shave their heads like the Buddhists, Jains clergy pull out their hair in small clumps; as you can see, it's sort of more difficult and more disciplined. Their lives are devoted to meditation, preaching, and scholarship, and the greatest spiritual achievement is to gradually stop eating and drinking anything and to fast to death, although this practice is actually rather rare. From such a description, it might be easier to see how Buddhism thinks of itself as the middle way between Hinduism and then the sort of extreme asceticism that the Jains practice.

There are several sub-sects of Jains. For instance, some orders of monks and nuns wear small rectangular pieces of cloth over their mouths to avoid breathing in tiny creatures; and some Jains reject the use of temples and images in worship, not because of divine disproval as with the case of Judaism or Islam, but because of the violence done in carving wood or stone. But the major division is between Shvetambara and Digambara Jains, who split sometime around the 4th or the 5th centuries C.E. The main difference is that Digambara monks (and *Digambara* means "sky-clad") wear nothing whatsoever, they wear air basically; while Shvetambara monks and nuns wear a plain white robe (*Shvetambara* means "white-clad"). For practical reasons, Digambara nuns have never been allowed to live completely naked; it's believed that they must be reborn as a male to complete the process of liberation, perhaps in the next life. By contrast, Shvetambara Jains hold that women can achieve full liberation in this lifetime; and indeed, one of the 23 Tirthankaras that preceded Mahavira was a woman, at least in the Shvetambara tradition. There are many more Shvetambara Jains than Digambara; about 3 million to 1 million. In the stricter Digambara sect, monks aren't allowed to own anything other than a whisk made of peacock feathers—and those are feathers that have fallen out naturally that they pick up from the ground—and they have a small water pot for cleaning themselves. They're not even allowed a begging bowl, so they have to receive any offerings of food into their bare hands and then they consume them without utensils.

Think for a moment about what it would be like to live without any clothes. You'd have to drop all sense of embarrassment or self-consciousness, and you'd be so obviously vulnerable to everything. It's hard to imagine a more powerful statement of renunciation or a shaper demarcation from ordinary life. It seems clear when we look at monks and nuns in the Buddhist tradition now that shaving your head makes a difference; but being naked is so much more so. Shvetambaras and Digambaras also have different traditions about the life of Mahavira, and they have somewhat different rituals, but their basic beliefs are quite similar; more similar, say, than Theravada and Mahayana Buddhists.

Jainism is a fascinating religious tradition, but in this course we're particularly interested in sacred texts; and here's where things get a little strange. In most world religions, scripture is at the core of a religious identity. There are different types of Jews, but they all accept the Torah as somehow distinct from other books. It's similar for Muslims and the Qur'an, or Hindus and the Vedas, or Christians and the Bible, with a few minor differences between Catholic and Protestant Bibles. Buddhists and Daoists may regard some sacred books as being more significant or more advanced than others, but they tend to accept the entire canon, as large as it is. Yet in Jainism, Shvetambaras and Digambaras for the most part reject each other's scriptures as forgeries. They're clearly in the same religious tradition, and the beliefs of those two sects are quite similar, but there are almost no shared textual resources.

It's true that in late Second Temple Judaism and early Christianity, there were sectarian communities that used very different collections of scripture—think about the Dead Sea Scrolls or the Nag Hammadi Codices—but the situation proved unstable and canons were eventually established to bring unity and cohesion to the faith. By contrast, Jains have never had an agreed upon, cohesive list of sacred texts; yet they've been able to keep their distinct tradition going for centuries or even millennia. What's going on here? Shvetambaras and Digambaras both agree that Mahavira taught 14 texts called Purvas, which were identical to those taught by all the preceding Tirthankaras. These texts communicated the eternal truths of omniscient beings. Mahavira's first followers came from the Brahman class—remember that's the priestly caste from Hinduism, and that social makes sense because oftentimes there was a Kshatriya king surrounded by Brahman advisors; in this case Mahavira is a Kshatriya caste and then he has Brahmans around him who then follow him and accept his teachings—and those Brahman disciples memorized the Purvas; remember that's something that Brahmans do with the Vedas and other Hindu scriptures. Similarly, early Buddhists and Hindus passed on their sacred texts orally; but in the Jain case, all the Purvas were lost, with only fragments or paraphrases remaining.

Over several centuries, the Shvetambara developed replacement scriptures that captured some of the traditions associated with Mahavira and that were written in the Ardhamagadhi language; that's a more vernacular dialect than Sanskrit, though Ardhamagadhi, like the Pali of Theravada Buddhism, eventually became a literary, scriptural language. Most Shvetambaras accept 45 texts as authoritative, and most of those go by the name of Sutras: There are 12 Angas (that means "limbs") dealing with basic doctrines, moral prescriptions for monks and laypersons, cosmology, and narratives of Mahavira, of other Jina, and pious believers, though the 12th of those Anga has since been lost; and then the next section are 12 Upangas (those are "subordinate limbs"), and those treat ontological, cosmological, and epistemological matters (more philosophical); then there are six Cheda Sutras (that word means "separate"), and those have to do with disciplinary issues; there are four Mula Sutras (*Mula* means "basic" sutras) that were typically studied by new monks and nuns; then 10 short Miscellaneous texts on astrology and on ascetic ritual; and finally, two Appendices that offer summaries and explanations.

This Shvetambara canon was written down on palm-leaf manuscripts in about the 5th century C.E. after a series of councils, so long after Mahavira lived; yet even today, there's not complete agreement on exactly which texts belong in the collection of 45, and some Shvetambara sub-sects reject as many as 13 of those. Digambara Jains also believe that the 14 original Purvas were lost, but they reject all of the Shvetambara scriptures. Instead, they view as authoritative two doctrinal synopses that were written by monks in the 2nd century C.E., and those synopses are the Scripture of Six Parts and the Treatise on the Passions. The Digambara scriptures are written in a different vernacular language called Jaina Saurasseni. In both traditions, laypersons don't really read or study the scriptures; instead, they learn some of their contents through the sermons or short summaries written by monks. Nevertheless, the Jains have a rich tradition of scholarship, commentaries, philosophy, and literature. They're probably the most widely-literate population in India, and their libraries are the oldest on the subcontinent.

All in all, Jainism is somewhat unique among world religions for its keen awareness of the loss and vulnerability of sacred texts, particularly during the many centuries when the strict prohibition of monks owning property meant that books and writing implements were forbidden to them. Jains recovered what they could, but sacred texts have never been the primary basis for the faith; yet they're still worth taking a look at.

The study of Jain scripture still owes a tremendous debt to Max Müller's Sacred Books of the East. Hermann Jacobi, a German scholar with expertise in Sanskrit as well as Indian mathematics and science, chose four Jain texts to translate for the series, and those four texts appeared in two volumes, one in 1884 and the other in 1895. As the most recent edition of the massive *Encyclopedia of Religion* states, Jacobi's "pioneering translations of the Acaranga Sutra, the Kalpa Sutra, the [Kritanga Sutra], and the Uttaradhyayana Sutra ... though outdated in many ways, have never been adequately replaced." Because they're old, because they belong to this Sacred Books of the East series, they're online; you can see them there, but let me just give you a few examples from each to give you a flavor of Jain sacred texts.

Jacobi began his translations with the first of the 12 Angas, the Acaranga Sutra, which is often regarded as the oldest item in the Jain scriptures. This includes rules for monks and nuns regarding food, clothing, and lodging, as well as the earliest account of Mahavira's life, where we read the following:

> Neglecting his body, the Venerable Ascetic Mahavira meditated on his Self, in blameless lodgings, in blameless wandering, in restraint, kindness, avoidance of sinful influence, chaste life, in patience, freedom from passion, contentment; control, circumspectness, practicing religious postures and acts; walking the path of Nirvana and liberation, which is the fruit of good conduct. Living thus he with equanimity bore, endured, sustained, and suffered all calamities arising from divine powers, men, and animals, with undisturbed and unafflicted mind, careful of body, speech and mind.

Then it goes on to tell some stories about how other ascetics used to carry around staffs to protect themselves from dogs or other creatures, and Mahavira just let mosquitoes bite him and he didn't fight off attackers, he just let his body be a sacrifice as it may be.

Then in that Sutra comes the Five Great Vows undertaken by all Jains, beginning with nonviolence; and these are the words from the Sutra:

> I renounce all killing of living beings, whether subtle or gross, whether movable or immovable. Nor shall I myself kill living beings (nor cause others to do it, nor consent to it). As long as I live, I confess and blame, repent and exempt myself of these sins in the thrice threefold way, in mind, speech, and body.

Detailed explanations of each of those clauses are then given, along with the four other vows of truthfulness, not stealing, no sexual immorality, and nonattachment.

The second text that was translated by Jacobi, the Uttaradhyayana, one of the four Mula Sutras or basic texts, was used to train monks and nuns and it's more specific about what these vows mean for renunciants. For example, it says:

> If a layperson abuses a monk he should not grow angry against him; because he would be like a child, a monk should not grow angry. If a monk hears bad words, cruel and rankling ones, he should silently overlook them and not take them to heart. A monk should not grow angry if beaten, nor should he therefore entertain sinful thoughts; knowing patience to be the highest good, a monk should meditate on the Law. If someone strikes a restrained, resigned [monk] somewhere, he should think: [It could be worse], 'I have not lost my life.'"

Jacobi also translated the second Anga, the Kritanga Sutra, which offers an introduction to Jain teachings as well as a critical examination of competing doctrines at the time of Mahavira; so other ascetics at the time or spiritual teachers were teaching things such as fatalism, agnosticism, non-action, eternalism, annihilationism, and all of those are rejected in the Jain scriptures as being limited, partial, or one-sided. Jains eventually developed an elaborate epistemology based on the notion that all human viewpoints are partial and limited.

According to the Kritanga Sutra:

> These three classes of living beings have been declared by the Jinas: 1) earth, water, fire, wind; 2) grass, trees, and plants, and 3) the moving beings, both the egg-bearing and those that bear live offspring, those generated from dirt and those generated in fluids [that's the category that would include human being]. Know and understand that they all desire happiness. By hurting these beings, people do harm to their own souls and will repeatedly be born as one of them.

So some guidance there about what ahimsa means; about the kinds of beings to be aware of. Even the little invisible beings that are so small we can't see them, we still have duties or we owe obligations to them to not cause suffering to them.

Finally, Jacobi translated the Kalpa Sutra, which retells the story of Mahavira's life with more legendary details than what's found in the Acaranga Sutra, along with narratives from the biographies of a few other Tirthankaras. This text is from one of the Cheda Sutras, but it gained its prominence from the fact that it's read aloud every year during the eight-day Paryushana or Rainy Season Festival; that's the most important event in the Shvetambara ritual calendar, and that's the time when Jains fast, they confess their sins, and ask forgiveness. They also write apologetic letters to friends or business associates whom they can't talk to in person. In some places, the Kalpa Sutra is read over the course of the first 7 days in the ancient Ardhamagadhi language, with explanations in the contemporary tongue; and then on the 8th day, the whole thing is recited quickly in Ardhamagadhi, with lavish illustrations that are brought out for display.

The Digambaras celebrate Paryushana in 10 days, but they don't recite the Kalpa Sutra, since they don't regard it as scripture. Instead, they recite the 10 chapters of the Tattvartha Sutra (that means "That Which Is"), and this is the first systematic exposition of Jain doctrines written in Sanskrit. It was composed by the 2nd-century monk Umasvati. In 250 terse aphorisms, it covers Jain epistemology, metaphysics, cosmology, and ethics. Although it's not exactly scriptural, the Tattvartha Sutra is nevertheless the only Jain text that's held in high respect by both Shvetambaras and Digambaras. The form of that text is similar to Hindu sutras, and it quickly moves through lists of the seven categories of truth, the five varieties of knowledge, the eight types of karma, different types of beings, the various spatial realms, enumerations of vows and moral precepts, karmic obstacles, and the process of liberation; remember that like the Hindu Sutras, these are lots of lists that are made from memorization. The Tattvartha Sutra is comprehensive, but it's a bit on the dry side.

For greater insight into the spiritual impulses that fuel this demanding religion, we can return to the Uttaradhyayana Sutra, where we read of Prince Balasri, who was asking permission from his royal parents to leave palace life and embark on the path of a Jain ascetic:

> O mother, O father, I have enjoyed pleasures which are like poisonous fruit: their consequences are painful, as they entail

> continuous suffering. This body is not permanent, it is impure and of impure origin; it is but a transitory residence of the soul and a miserable vessel of suffering. I take no delight in this transitory body which one must leave sooner or later, and which is like foam or a bubble.

And then this passage, reflecting on the infinite cycles of reincarnation; and then imagine as I recite this, as I read this, how it feels to think of an ongoing, almost infinite succession of lives in which painfulness, sorrow, and suffering is mostly what you've been exposed to. The passage says:

> As [a deer] I have, against my will, been caught, bound, and fastened in snares and traps, and frequently I have been killed. As a fish I have, against my will, been caught with hooks and in bow-nets; I have therein been scraped, slit, and killed, an infinite number of times. As a bird I have been caught by hawks, trapped in nets, and bound with bird-lime, and I have been killed, an infinite number of times. As a tree I have been felled, slit, sawn into planks, and stripped of the bark by carpenters with axes, hatchets, etc., an infinite number of times. As iron I have been malleated, cut, torn, and filed by blacksmiths, an infinite number of times.

What's striking in that passage isn't just incredible awareness of suffering and the kind of suffering that we cause through our action, but also the desire to escape those perpetual rounds of agony and to avoid any entanglement in causing or even benefitting from the use and exploitation of other living creatures, both animate and inanimate. Jainism offers a powerful, even startling, vision of empathy and compassion.

Five Confucian Classics
Lecture 20

In the last lecture, we saw that Jainism seems to undermine some common assumptions; it's clearly a religion, but unlike most of the other traditions we will encounter in this course, Jain identity is not primarily based on an established, widely accepted set of sacred texts. In this lecture, we are faced with nearly the opposite situation; Confucianism has a well-defined canon (in fact, two of them: the Five Classics and the Four Books), but it is often thought of as more of a philosophy than a religion. In this lecture, we'll explore possible explanations for this distinction and look in detail at four of the Five Classics.

Defining Confucianism
- Confucianism is a system of thought that originated in ancient China with Confucius (551–479 B.C.E.). The Chinese call this system of thought *rujia* ("the school of scholars") or *rujiao* ("teachings of the scholars"). Confucius was the inheritor and transmitter of an earlier cultural heritage, much of which was contained in the Five Classics.
    o When we think about religion in the West, we often have in mind social groups that share in a broad family of characteristics, such as belief in a god or gods, rituals, prayer, a moral code, and so on. Not every religion has all these features, yet we tend to think that we can fairly easily distinguish religion from, say, philosophy.

    o Confucianism contains traces of most of the common elements of religion, but the emphases are different than we might expect.

    o For example, Confucianism has a concept of an impersonal moral force called Heaven that is not exactly a god yet sometimes rewards and punishes human behavior. At the same time, the basic religion in China from its earliest period has been ancestor worship. The ceremonies of ancestor worship were incorporated into Confucian living, though they were not elaborated upon theologically.

- Confucianism offers a strong moral code, a vision for living in harmony with the universe, and rituals for dealing with unseen beings, but many of its tenets seem rather practical and this-worldly, with an emphasis on family and politics. For these reasons, it has been viewed as both a philosophy and a religion.

Religion or Philosophy?
- In the 17th century, Jesuit missionaries to China admired Confucianism and treated it as a philosophy or an ethical system that was compatible with Christianity. Thus, Chinese Christians could continue to study the Confucian classics and participate in Confucian rituals.

Confucianism encompasses many of the elements of religion, including temples where offerings are made to the sage himself.

- The Jesuits made considerable progress and even gained positions in the imperial court, but Dominicans and Franciscans insisted that the rites honoring Confucius and ancient ancestors were religious, and Chinese converts had to choose between Christianity and Confucianism.

- The Rites Controversy went on for nearly a century, but the result was that Chinese Catholics were forbidden to participate in Confucian rites, which almost brought Catholic missionary work in China to an end.

- In the 19th century, at a time when China was much weaker compared to European societies, Protestant missionaries were less accommodating, though Western scholars were beginning to develop the idea of world religions and view Confucianism within that category, as something worthy of respect.
  - One key individual—both a missionary and a scholar—was James Legge. A Scotsman who served as the head of a Christian college in Hong Kong for nearly 30 years, Legge began translating and publishing the Confucian Classics while in China, and then, in 1876, he was appointed as the first chair of Chinese Language and Literature at Oxford. Four years later, Legge published *The Religions of China: Confucianism and Taoism Described*, which put the teachings of Confucius firmly within the religion camp.

  - During his 20 years at Oxford, Legge continued to revise and enlarge the scope of his translations. At Oxford, he met Max Müller, and together, they published some of Legge's translations of Confucian and Daoist classics as part of the Sacred Books of the East. This, as much as anything, contributed to the notion that Confucianism could be considered on an equal footing with Hinduism, Buddhism, and Islam.

- In the 20th century, Chinese scholars themselves started writing in English about Confucian texts, and they tended to treat them more as philosophy than religion. This was probably an attempt to make the ideas more attractive to Westerners, but it also reflected attitudes in China, where successive governments did not count Confucianism as one of the five recognized religions.

- Eventually, Western scholars began to split the difference. One important study was titled *Confucius: The Secular as Sacred*, and textbooks often use such terms as "religious humanism" to describe the tradition.

The *Odes* and *Documents*

- One of the ways in which Confucianism is most like more familiar religions is in its use of sacred texts. From earliest times, Confucian scholars have been devoted to a collection of ancient writings that they regarded as profound, comprehensive, and uniquely authoritative. These were the Five Classics: the *Odes*, the *Documents*, the *Rites*, the *Changes*, and the *Spring and Autumn Annals*.
    - These texts all preceded Confucius, and even though later scholars regarded Confucius as the editor or commentator on these books, he probably did not have a direct role in their production. Indeed, the canonical forms of the texts were not established until several centuries after his death.

    - In the 1st century C.E., during the Han dynasty, the Five Classics became the basis for Chinese civil service exams and the foundation of state ideology.

- The *Odes*, also known as the *Book of Poetry*, consists of 305 poems dating from the 10th to the 7th centuries B.C.E. The poems are divided into four sections: Airs of the States, Lesser Odes, Greater Odes, and Temple Hymns.
    - The poems include a number of sacrificial and ceremonial hymns, often praising royal ancestors, but the most interesting poems for modern readers are probably those in the Airs. Many of these are folk songs about courtship, marriage, agriculture, military conscription, or oppressive officials.

- o The tradition is that Confucius selected these songs from a much larger collection. Consequently, Chinese scholars have long looked for the hidden moral meaning that would have attracted Confucius's attention.

- The *Documents* is a collection of 58 speeches or edicts from the mythical sage kings Yao and Yu through the first three Chinese dynasties (roughly the 23rd to the 3rd centuries B.C.E.). The *Documents* treats matters of statecraft, including the notion of the Mandate of Heaven. The idea here is that Heaven, as an impersonal moral force, can grant its seal of approval to a virtuous ruler and, if necessary, later transfer that approval to a more worthy family, thereby authorizing rebellion and the foundation of a new dynasty.

- Both the *Odes* and the *Documents* were targeted by the first emperor of China in the famous burning of the books in 213 B.C.E. Later, copies of these texts were discovered, known as the New Text and the Old Text according to the style of writing used. In the mid-18th century, Chinese scholars proved that the Old Text chapters were 4th-century forgeries.

The *Rites* and *Annals*
- The third of the Five Classics is the *Rites*, which is a collection of three texts, the Ceremonials, the Zhou Rites, and the Records of Rites. These are compilations of traditions attributed to the early Zhou dynasty of proper government functions, ceremonies, and decorum, along with interpretations of the meaning of various rituals.
    - o For example, in the Records of Rites, we find rules governing social visits, interviews with government authorities, and family interactions, along with rituals for coming of age, marriages, funerals, and so on. This information is presented through systematic descriptions, essays, dialogues, and historical narratives.

    - o The *Rites* texts present an idealized version of social interactions during the time of the sage kings and were probably compiled many centuries after the golden years of the early Zhou dynasty.

- The *Spring and Autumn Annals* consists of short notices of events that were recorded in Confucius's home state of Lu between 722 and 481 B.C.E. These texts are mostly notes about changes of rulers, marriages, deaths, diplomatic visits, and battles between the numerous feudal lords in the centuries immediately preceding Confucius.
  - What makes the *Spring and Autumn Annals* wonderful is its earliest commentary, compiled about 300 B.C.E. and attributed to Zuo Qiuming. This *Zuo Commentary* provides detailed historical narratives that explain the notices in the *Annals*.

  - The *Zuo Commentary* is a sort of encyclopedia of ancient China, with details about politics and warfare, family life, gender relations, ethics, ghosts, omens, and ancestral spirits.

  - The *Commentary* probably dates to the 3rd century B.C.E. and may have originally been an independent history, but because it covered basically the same time period and events as the *Spring and Autumn Annals*, it was reorganized as a commentary and immortalized by its association with Confucius.

Classics versus Scripture
- The Five Classics is an eclectic mix, but all its genres can also be found in the Hebrew Bible. Why, then, do we generally refer to the sacred texts of ancient Israel as "scripture" and the sacred texts of Confucianism as "classics"?
  - First, even though the Confucian Classics often mention Heaven, spirits, sacrifices, divination, and so forth, they are not as directly focused on a god or gods as the Hebrew Bible.

  - Second, the texts of Confucianism don't claim to be revealed; they were always regarded as the writings of ancient sages.

- o Third, as far back as the 2nd century B.C.E., the Confucian Classics were intimately connected with state orthodoxy, imperial sponsorship, government education, and the civil service exams—precisely the sorts of worldly connections that we in the West tend to treat as political rather than spiritual.

- Yet part of the problem also seems to be a simple matter of translation. The five primary texts of Confucianism began to be known as *jing* ("classics") in the Han dynasty. The word *jing* refers to the vertical threads, or warp, on a weaving loom and, hence, carries the connotations of basic guidelines, rules, or norms. A *jing* is a text that is deemed authoritative and orthodox.
  - o When Buddhist sutras were translated into Chinese, they were labeled *jing*. Indeed, the fact that Buddhism entered China in the 1st century C.E. with authoritative texts probably made it more acceptable to the Chinese, who were already used to the idea of a written canon.
  - o The scriptures of other faiths were also categorized as *jing*, such as the Daoist Daodejing, the Bible, and the Qur'an.
  - o The word *jing* is the same in Chinese, and whether we translate it as "classic" or "scripture" is mostly a matter of habit.

Suggested Reading

Legge, trans. *The Chinese Classics*.

———, trans. *The Li Ki*.

Littlejohn, *Confucianism*.

Nylan, *The Five "Confucian" Classics*.

Watson, trans. *The Tso Chuan*.

Waley, trans. *The Book of Songs*.

Questions to Consider

1. Is Confucianism more of a religion or a philosophy? And how does that affect the way we read its primary texts?

2. What themes are shared by Confucian Classics in the different genres of poetry, history, and ritual?

Five Confucian Classics
Lecture 20—Transcript

We're moving on now to the sacred texts of East Asia. In the previous lecture, we saw how Jainism seems to undermine some common assumptions: It's clearly a religion; but unlike most of the other traditions we'll encounter in this course, Jain identity isn't primarily based upon an established, widely-accepted set of sacred texts. In this lecture, we're faced with nearly the opposite situation: Confucianism has a well-defined canon—in fact, it has two of them, the Five Classics and the Four Books—but Confucianism is often thought of as more of a philosophy than a religion; so perhaps we should begin with some definitions.

Confucianism is a system of thought—how's that for a vague term—which originated in ancient China with Confucius, who lived from 551–479 B.C.E. However the English term *Confucianism* wasn't used until the 19th century and it's not a direct translation from the Chinese. The Chinese don't name this thought after its founder, after Confucius, but they use the term *rujia*, which means "the school of scholars," or they may call it *rujiao*, the "teachings of the scholars." Confucius is an exemplary figure, but things don't exactly start with him; he was an inheritor and a transmitter of an earlier cultural heritage, much of which was contained in the Five Classics.

When we think about religion in the West, we often have in mind social groups that share in a broad family of characteristics, such as belief in a god or gods; revelation; a sense of the sacred; concepts of ultimate reality, especially if they include a supernatural realm; rituals, prayer, a moral code; and some notion of an afterlife and salvation. Not every religion has all of these—for instance, early Judaism had a relatively undeveloped idea about the afterlife; and although Jainism accepts the existence of gods, they're irrelevant to one's spiritual progress—yet nevertheless, we tend to think that we can fairly easily distinguish religion from, say, philosophy.

Confucianism, however, presents something of a puzzle. It contains traces of most of the common elements of religion, but the emphases are different than what we might expect, making it seem like Epicureanism or Stoicism, which were two of the most prevalent philosophies in the Roman Empire;

they both taught that happiness could be attained by limiting or restricting one's passions and desires. (We think of Stoicism and Epicureanism as philosophies now, but in ancient Rome, those were the people most likely to try to grab you in the marketplace, missionary-like, for a conversation about the meaning of life.) Confucianism has a concept of an impersonal moral force called Heaven, which isn't exactly a god, yet which sometimes rewards and punishes human behavior. At the same time, however, the basic religion in China from the earliest period has been ancestor worship, in which people pray to, they make offerings to, and they seek favors from their deceased parents, grandparents, and great-parents. The ceremonies of ancestor worship were incorporated into Confucian living, though they weren't elaborated on theologically. For example, in a famous exchange, one of Confucius' students once asked about the worship of the ghosts and the spirits, and Confucius replied, "We don't know yet how to serve men; how can we know about serving the spirits?" The student pressed forward, "What about death?" Confucius said, "We don't know yet about life; how can we know about death?"

So Confucianism offers a strong moral code, a vision for living in harmony with the universe, rituals for dealing with unseen beings, divination, opportunities for awe and reverence, and even Confucian temples where offerings are made to the Sage himself; but many of its tenets seem rather practical and this-worldly, with an emphasis on family and politics, they don't talk a lot about spirits and the afterworld. So is it a religion or a philosophy? It could sort of go either way, which is exactly what happened.

In the 17th century, Jesuit missionaries to China admired Confucianism and treated it as a philosophy or an ethical system that was compatible with Christianity; thus, Chinese Christians continued to study the Confucian classics and continued to participate in its rituals. The Jesuits regarded ancestor worship not as idolatry, but as a means of honoring one's father and mother, as in the Ten Commandments. The Jesuits made considerable progress and even gained positions in the imperial court. On the other hand, Dominicans and Franciscans said, "No, wait a minute, those are religious rites," and they insisted that Chinese converts had to choose between Christianity and Confucianism. The Rites Controversy, as it's called, went on for nearly a century, with several popes weighing in as well as the Chinese emperor; but the end result was that Chinese Catholics were forbidden to participate in Confucian rites and forbidden to participate in ancestor worship, which just about brought Catholic missionary work in China to an end.

Then, in the 19th century, at a time when China was much weaker compared relatively to European societies, Protestant missionaries were less accommodating—less accommodating than the Jesuits certainly—though Western scholars were beginning to develop the idea of world religions and view Confucianism within that category, as something worthy of respect. One key individual, both a missionary and a scholar, was James Legge. Legge was a Scotsman who served as the head of a Christian college in Hong Kong for nearly 30 years, Legge began translating and publishing the Confucian classics while in China; and then in 1876, he was appointed as the first Chair of Chinese Language and Literature at Oxford University. Four years later, Legge published a book called *The Religions of China: Confucianism and Taoism Described*, which put the teachings of Confucius firmly within the religion camp. During his 20 years at Oxford, Legge continued to revise and enlarge the scope of his translations; it was truly a stupendous achievement, and more than a century later his versions of the Confucian classics are still widely used. At Oxford, Legge met another professor there, our old friend Max Müller, and together they decided to publish some of Legge's translations of Confucian and Daoist classics as part of the Sacred Books of the East. This, as much as anything, contributed to the notion that Confucianism could be considered on an equal footing with Hinduism, Buddhism, and Islam. Legge eventually contributed 6 of the 50 volumes in Sacred Books of the East; so that's more than any other single translator.

In the 20th century, Chinese scholars themselves started writing in English about Confucian texts, and they tended to treat them more as philosophy than religion; so it's going to switch over a little bit. This was probably an attempt make those ideas of Chinese civilization, of Confucianism, more attractive to Westerners; but it also reflected attitudes in China, where successive governments in the 20th century didn't count Confucianism as one of the five recognized religions: Daoism, Buddhism, Protestantism, Catholicism, and Islam. Yet eventually, Western scholars began to split the difference; one important study was titled *Confucius: The Secular as Sacred*—it's written by a scholar named Herbert Fingarette, it's a sort of classic in sinology; it's not a very long book, it's actually well worth reading—and then Western textbooks also use terms like "religious humanism" to describe the tradition of Confucianism.

Confucianism can certainly function like a religion, giving transcendent meaning and guidance to people's lives; and I'm comfortable calling it a religion, with a suitably expansive definition. Keep in mind that in Asia, religions are not always mutually exclusive. People can adopt Confucian precepts and rituals for some aspects of their lives, while being Daoist or even Buddhist at other times. It's a different notion of religiosity than in the Abrahamic religions, where it would be impossible to simultaneously be Muslim and Jewish, or even Catholic and Protestant. One of the ways in which Confucianism is like what we might call a religion is in its use of sacred texts. From earliest times, Confucian scholars have been devoted to a collection of ancient writings that they regarded as profound, comprehensive, and uniquely authoritative, in which every word was significant; and these texts were the Five Classics (Five Confucian Classics, they're often called): Those are the *Odes*, the *Documents*, the *Rites*, the *Changes*, and the *Spring and Autumn Annals*. These texts all preceded Confucius—along with a sixth classic on music, which was subsequently lost—and even though later scholars regarded Confucius as the editor or the commentator on these books, he probably didn't have a direct role in their production; it's just part of the cultural heritage of China that he was part of and he and his school specialized in this. Indeed, the final canonical forms of the Five Classics weren't established until several centuries after Confucius's death. But in 1st century C.E., during the Han Dynasty, the Five Classics became the basis for the Chinese civil service exams and thus became the foundation of state ideology.

We'll begin with the first one, the *Odes*, which is also known as *The Book of Poetry*. This consists of 305 poems dating from the 10th to the 7th centuries B.C.E. They're divided into four sections: Airs of the States, Lesser Odes, Greater Odes, and Temple Hymns. These include a number of sacrificial and ceremonial hymns, often praising royal ancestors; but the most interesting poems for modern readers are probably those in the Airs section, many of which are folksongs about courtship, marriage, and agriculture, or they're songs that complain about military conscription and oppressive officials. The poems are generally in rhyming four-character lines, and they're rich in metaphor and nature imagery.

The tradition is that Confucius selected these 300 or so songs from a much larger collection of 3,000—it's probably not true; but for a long time, this is what the Chinese saw as the connection between the book of *Odes* and Confucius—and consequently, Chinese scholars have long looked for the hidden moral meanings that would've attracted Confucius's attention. Take for instance this ode, which seems clearly to be a love poem. It says:

> That the mere glimpse of a plain cap
> Could harry me with such longing
> Cause pain so dire.
> That the mere glimpse of a plain coat
> Could stab my heart with grief. Enough! Take me with you to your home.

Clearly, it's a female voice and she's smitten by a dashing young man in his handsome clothes. Generations of Confucian scholars, however, have read that poem and interpreted the emotion expressed there as anguish caused by the sight of someone dressed in inappropriate clothes during the time they should be mourning for their parents; so they're going to work in these moral principles of filial piety.

The *Documents*, the second of these Five Classics, is a collection of 58 speeches or edicts from the mythical sage kings Yao and Yu through the first three Chinese dynasties; so roughly from the 23rd to the 3rd centuries B.C.E. The *Documents* addresses matters of statecraft, including the notion of the Mandate of Heaven: that Heaven—remember that's that impersonal moral force that sort of oversees the world—can grant its seal of approval to a virtuous ruler; and then when his descendants over time become corrupt or oppressive, Heaven will transfer its approval to a more worthy family thereby authorizing them to rebel and start a new dynasty. But there are generally warning signs that come to that old, decrepit dynasty on the edge, and those warning signs come in the form of natural disasters like floods, famines, or eclipses; and those indicate when a royal house is starting to lose the Mandate.

One of the most famous episodes in the *Documents* is the story of the metal-bound coffer. In the late 11th century B.C.E., the admirable founder of the Zhou Dynasty, King Wu, one of the great sage kings in Confucianism, fell terribly ill. In response, his younger brother, known as the Duke of Zhou, secretly prayed to the ancestors that they'd take his own life rather than taking the life of the king. The Duke of Zhou had his petition sealed up in a metal-bound coffer, but in the end the ancestral spirits spared both men. Five years later, however, the king did die and his 13-year-old son ascended to the throne. There were rumors that the Duke of Zhou—this is now uncle of the young monarch—would try to take advantage of his nephew's weak position and usurp the throne, so the Duke voluntarily withdrew for a period of three years. Heaven, however, indicated that something was amiss with a great storm that destroyed fields and overthrew trees; this is the way that Heaven can send its messages. The court officers, who saw these disasters, were looking around for an explanation and eventually they came upon and opened that metal-bound coffer, and inside they found the written evidence of the Duke of Zhou's self-sacrificing attitude many years before. They realized that he'd been a good guy all along, and he was recalled to court where relationships were repaired, and the Duke of Zhou has ever since been held up as a model of loyal service. Those are the kinds of moral lessons that we might read in the *Documents*.

Both the *Odes* and the *Documents* were targeted by the First Emperor of China in the famous Burning of the Books in 213 B.C.E. The First Emperor, Qin Shi Huangdi, is the one whose tomb in the city of Xi'an housed those 7,000 life-sized terracotta soldiers that you may have seen pictures of or may have even visited. Apparently, the First Emperor was tired of being unfavorably compared to the [illustrious sage-kings of the past], and therefore the First Emperor wanted to get rid of all of the works of history, literature, and philosophy so that history would begin with him. This at least is the story of that Confucians told of their darkest hour, when the First Emperor sort of rounded up all those texts, had them burned, and even had some scholars who tried to protect them buried alive; at least this is the myth. The reality is probably a bit more complicated, but many copies of the *Documents* and the *Odes* were indeed destroyed at that time.

When a new dynasty, the Han Dynasty, came to power in 202 B.C.E, a copy of the *Documents* came to light that had been hidden by a scholar in the wall of his home; and this had been written in the contemporary style of Chinese script (the New Text, they called it). One of the things that the First Emperor did during his short reign was he revised and standardized all of the Chinese characters that were used; so this text is written in these new, standard characters. There was also a copy of the documents that had been found in Confucius's old home—that also had been walled up or hidden there—and that was written in ancient-style characters; so it was called the Old Text, the characters before the script reform of the Qin Dynasty, of the First Emperor. During the Han Dynasty—and as I said it begins in 202 B.C.E. and then it goes to 220 C.E.; so about 400 years—the New Text School, with its more religious ideas of Confucius as a miracle-working uncrowned king, was dominant and the Old Text fell into disuse, only to be rediscovered again in the 4th century C.E. Eventually, the standard edition of the *Documents* consisted of 33 New Text chapters and 25 Old Text chapters; they sort of split the difference and combined what they could.

If one of the marks of scripture is its ability to provoke crises of faith, the *Documents* qualifies. In the mid-18th century, brilliant Chinese textual scholars used the tools of philology to definitively prove that the Old Text chapters of the *Documents*—which had been accepted as authoritative canon for 1,500 years—were actually 4th-century forgeries, and it came as a terrible shock to Chinese culture to try to figure out what that might mean for Confucianism or even for Chinese civilization as a whole.

We'll move on now to the third of the Five Classics, and that's the *Rites*. This is a collection of three texts: the Ceremonials, the Zhou Rites, and the Records of Rites. All of these are compilations of traditions attributed to the early Zhou Dynasty concerning proper government functions, ceremonies, decorum, and etiquette, along with interpretations of the meanings of various rituals. To take the Records of Rites, for example, we find rules governing social visits, interviews with government authorities, and family interactions, along with rituals for coming of age ceremonies, marriages, funerals, mourning periods, sacrifices, banquets, and archery contests. There are also instructions for appropriate clothing, seasonal activities, education, and court protocol. This information is presented through systematic descriptions, essays, dialogues, and historical narratives; so there's a lot there about how at least the governing class ought to act in their everyday lives, in their official capacities. The *Rites* texts present an idealized version of social interactions during the time of the sage-kings, and they were probably compiled many centuries after the golden years of the early Zhou Dynasty. By the way, fragments from the lost Classic of Music seem to have been preserved as one of the chapters in the Records of Rites.

To give you a sense of what all this might sound like, here are the opening lines from the Records of Rites. It says: "Always and in everything let there be reverence; with the deportment grave as when one is thinking deeply, and with speech composed and definite. This will make the people tranquil. Pride should not be allowed to grow; the desires should not be indulged; the will should not be gratified to the full; pleasure should not be carried to excess." You can see a message there of moderation in general, and then these texts give lots of specific actions and expectations for social interactions.

Some of the details of the *Rites* texts were things that were only appropriate to ancient China; yet there are also bits of timeless wisdom. I like the following model presented in the chapter on education where it says: "In his teaching, he leads and does not drag; he strengthens and does not discourage; he opens the way but does not conduct to the end," and I think what that last bit means is that a good teacher has to allow his students some space so they can take some initiative themselves; that's where the best learning might happen.

We'll talk much more about two particular chapters from the Records of Rites in the next lecture, since they become eventually two of the Four Books. Stay tuned for that a little bit later.

Confucius, the master teacher of early China, once said, "Find inspiration in the Odes, take your place through ritual, and achieve perfection with music"; and remember *Music* is a lost classic there. The Five Classics—or rather the early versions of the books that we now know as the Five Classics—were Confucius's primary textbooks. So far, we've talked about the *Odes*, the

Documents, and the *Rites*. We have time in this lecture for one more, the *Spring and Autumn Annals*; and then we'll have to save the last of the five, the classic of *Changes*, for the next lecture.

As a historian, the *Spring and Autumn Annals* is, oddly enough, both my favorite and my least favorite of the Five Classics. The *Annals* itself isn't particularly appealing. It consists of short notices of events that were recorded in the small state of Lu—which is Confucius's home state—between 722 and 481 B.C.E., and they're often dated by season; so that's the "Spring and Autumn" part (I guess actually it would be the *Spring and Summer and Autumn and Winter Annals*, but they shortened it down to just those two, *Spring and Autumn Annals*). These are mostly quick notes about changes of rulers, marriages, deaths, diplomatic visits, and battles between numerous feudal lords in the centuries immediately preceding Confucius.

For instance, the first three entries in the *Annals*, dated to first year of the reign of Duke Yin of Lu (so in 722 B.C.E.), read, in their entirety: First, "It was his first year, the spring, the king's first month." Number two: "In the third month, the Duke and Yifu of Zhu made a covenant at Mie" (a covenant is a treaty they signed.) Third entry: "In summer, in the fifth month, the Earl of Zheng overcame Duan in Yan." That's it; there's not much there.

There are, however, some commentaries. There are two early commentaries, the Guliang and the Gongyang, which tried to decipher the moral judgments that they assumed Confucius had hidden within the text by analyzing exact terms that he used. But what makes the *Spring and Autumn Annals* wonderful is its earliest commentary, compiled about 300 B.C.E. and attributed to Zuo Qiuming; he was a court writer who supposedly lived about the time of Confucius. Mr. Zuo's *Commentary* (this is what it's called) provides detailed historical narratives that explain the terse notices in the *Annals*; and this is where all the interest comes from.

To return again to the first year where it says, "In the summer, in the fifth month, the Earl of Zheng overcame Duan in Yan," the *Zuo Commentary* has a long story about two princes, the older of whom was hated by his mother, apparently because there was a difficult childbirth—I'm not sure why you'd blame a child for that, but she never really forgives him for that pain and agony that she went through—so she hated the older son and she doted upon the younger prince. When the eldest son inherited the kingdom of Zheng and then became the duke there, his mother plotted with her younger son, Duan, to overthrow the duke, the older brother; and she herself offered to open the gates of the capital city to the rebel army. There was a civil war, with the Earl of Zheng (I guess he was an earl, not a duke) overcoming Duan; and when his younger brother was safely out of the way, the earl then banished his mother and he made a vow that he'd never see her again until they'd meet in the Yellow Springs (which is in the underworld; it was thought to be the place under the earth where the dead went).

After a while, however, the earl regretted his vow; respect for parents, or filial piety, is a big deal in Chinese culture. When a guard at a banquet asked for the equivalent of a doggie bag so that he could share some of that delicious court food with his mother, the duke said (I guess he's a duke and an earl here), "You have a mother to take things to; alas, I alone have none." When the guard heard the story of the vow, he said, "Why don't you dig a tunnel into the earth until you reach the springs [the Yellow Springs, underneath] and then you could fulfill your oath by meeting your mother there?"

The grateful duke did just that; and as he passed through the tunnel that had just been dug, he sang a few lines of a song, and then his mother sang a few lines, and then they were happily reunited. One of my graduate professors once suggested that the duke may have been symbolically reenacting his passage through the birth canal, with happier results this time.

There are hundreds of such stories in the *Zuo Commentary*, which becomes sort of an encyclopedia of ancient China, with details not only about politics and warfare, but also about family life, gender relations, ethics, ghosts, omens, and ancestral spirits. The commentary probably dates to the late 4th century B.C.E., and may have originally been an independent history; but since it basically covered the same time period and the same events as the *Spring and Autumn Annals*, it looks like it was reorganized as a commentary on that book—so these events were attached to entries in the *Spring and Autumn Annals*—and then consequently was immortalized by its association with one of the Confucian Classics and studied intently by scholars and would-be candidates for the exam system ever after.

So far, in the Five Classics, we've seen poetry, history, ritual, rules for living, and explorations of morality. It's an eclectic mix; but then again, all of these genres can also be found in the Hebrew Bible. So why then do we generally refer to the sacred texts of ancient Israel as scripture and the sacred texts of Confucianism as classics?

Three explanations come quickly to mind: The first is that even though the Confucian Classics often mention Heaven, spirits, sacrifices, divination, and so forth, they're not as directly focused on a god or gods. Second, the texts of Confucianism don't claim to be revealed; they were always regarded as the writings of ancient sages, men remarkably in tune with the patterns and harmonies of the cosmos, to be sure, but still human beings. Third, as far back as the 2nd century B.C.E., the Confucian Classics were intimately connected with state orthodoxy, imperial sponsorship, government education, and the civil service exams; precisely the sorts of worldly connections that we in the West tend to treat as political rather than spiritual.

Yet part of the problem is surely a simple matter of translation. The five primary texts of Confucianism began to be known as Classics or *jing* in the Han Dynasty. The word *jing* refers to the vertical threads or the warp on a weaving loom, and hence carries the basic connotations of guidelines, rules, norms, continuity; a *jing* is a text that's deemed authoritative and orthodox. When Buddhist sutras were translated into Chinese they were labeled *jing*, as with the Lotus Sutra, which in Chinese is *fǎhuá jīng*. Indeed, the fact that Buddhism entered China in the 1st century C.E. with authoritative texts probably made it more acceptable to the Chinese, who were already used to idea of a written canon. The scriptures of other faiths were also categorized as *jing*, such as the Daoist Daodejing, and the Bible, which in Chinese is known as the *shèng jīng*, or the Holy Scripture, and the Qur'an, which is transliterated as the *gǔ lán jīng* (*gǔlán* is supposed to sound a little bit like Qur'an). The word *jing* is the same in Chinese, and whether we translate it in English as "classic" or "scripture" is mostly a matter of habit.

Be prepared for some paradoxes as we continue the next time by talking about the fifth of the Five Classics, the *Changes*, or the *Yijing*, which definitely starts as a religious handbook of divination and then is transformed into a philosophical treatise; while two of the Four Books, the *Analects* and the *Mencius*, are philosophical works that get redirected toward religious purposes by the Neo-Confucians of the 10th century. Classics or scripture; religion or philosophy? Chinese sacred texts challenge all sorts of Western assumptions, which is partly what makes them so interesting.

Four Books of Neo-Confucianism
Lecture 21

We begin this lecture with the last of the Five Confucian Classics, the *Changes*, or *Yijing* (*I-Ching*), which the Chinese considered the oldest and holiest of the Classics and which is by far the best known in the West. We will then turn to the canonization of the Five Classics, along with several other texts, and the development of Neo-Confucianism. As we'll see, the influential Neo-Confucian scholar Zhu Xi urged his students to concentrate their efforts on learning the Four Books: the *Analects*, the *Mencius*, the *Great Learning*, and the *Constant Mean*. We will explore these texts and Zhu Xi's metaphysical theory of *li* ("principle") and *qi* ("vital energy").

The *Yijing*

- The *Yijing* is an ancient manual of divination. The user manipulates milfoil stalks or, much later, coins to indicate a particular hexagram to predict the future or find clues about how a dynamic situation might change. The core text consists of 64 graphs of six stacked horizontal lines—some broken and some unbroken—along with a title and a short statement for each. There is also a series of brief judgments on each of six lines of the 64 graphs, which are useful when specific lines are determined to be particularly powerful or unstable.

- The solid lines in a hexagram are thought of as yang, while the broken lines represent yin, in accordance with the ancient Chinese notion that the cosmos consists of two opposing forces that are manifest in all things.

- The Chinese have long ascribed the hexagrams, statements, and line texts to the founders of the Zhou dynasty, in the 11th century B.C.E., and in fact, the book seems to be a compilation of divination lore from several centuries before Confucius. Yet the *Changes* is more than just a divination manual.

- Eventually, there were 10 appendices, or "wings," that were added to the core text. These were commentaries, traditionally ascribed to Confucius, that explored cosmic patterns of change and transformation and even suggested that the *Yijing* contained within its hexagrams all possible states of transition and, hence, was a textual model or microcosm of the universe.

- By learning to distinguish significant from trivial change, careful readers could prioritize their concerns and efforts and learn to live in harmony with the inevitable ebbs and flows of the cosmos.

Neo-Confucianism

- With the canonization of the Five Classics in the Han dynasty, there came a need to establish, preserve, and transmit authoritative versions of the texts. Unlike in Hinduism, where there were rigorous methods of memorization, or in Judaism, with the amazing scribal quality control of the Masoretes, in China, canonization came about by carving the classics into stone.

- In 172 C.E., the emperor ordered a complete set of stone classics for the imperial academy. Seven Classics (the standard five, plus the *Analects of Confucius* and the brief Classic of Filial Piety) were carved onto 46 steles, each a little over eight feet high and three feet wide. Students could take rubbings from the stone texts on paper.

- After the collapse of the Han dynasty in the 3rd century C.E., Confucianism, which had been closely associated with the imperial government, fell into decline, while Daoism and Buddhism became more prominent. In the Tang dynasty, with the reunification of China under centralized rule, Confucianism began to make a comeback, and the Five Classics were again carved into stone in 837, along with several supplemental classics. From the 12th century on, it became common to talk about the Thirteen Classics of Confucianism.

- But Confucianism in the Tang dynasty and the succeeding Song dynasty (10th–13th centuries) was not quite the same as that of the Han dynasty. Buddhism had influenced Chinese sensibilities, and the new Confucianism (Neo-Confucianism) was much more interested in the ultimate nature of reality and humanity. It was also aimed at pursuing a program of self-cultivation and inner spirituality, rather than gaining the historical knowledge necessary to pass exams and become a government official.

- The most influential figure in Neo-Confucianism was a scholar named Zhu Xi (1130–1200). He championed a metaphysical theory in which everything is a combination of *li* ("principle") and *qi* ("vital energy," which in its heavier forms is matter). There is a principle, then a sort of ideal blueprint for being a ruler, a mother, or even a mountain or river. Actual rulers or mountains are all different because of the particular *qi* of which they are made.
    - This theory is important for two reasons: (1) It offers an analysis of the nature of the cosmos that could compete with Buddhist philosophy, and (2) it provides an ethical program for living; one can purify one's actions and emotions to bring them into harmony with the near-perfect principle that is within us all.

    - Human nature is inherently good, and it's our job to recapture that innate goodness through study, self-discipline, and "quiet-sitting." By so doing, one can follow the Way (the Dao) of Heaven.

- Zhu Xi claimed to have recovered the long-lost original meanings of Confucian texts, though rather than the Five Classics, he urged his students and followers to concentrate their efforts on the Four Books: the *Analects*, the *Mencius*, the *Great Learning*, and the *Constant Mean*.
    - Mastery of one or two of the Five Classics had long been a path to success in the civil service exams and government office, but Zhu Xi realized that the Four Books were shorter, easier to read, and more directly applicable to personal moral improvement and inner spirituality.

- His elevation of these texts was controversial during his lifetime, but in 1315, more than a century after Zhu Xi's death, the Mongols, who were trying to recruit Chinese to work as officials under them, restored the civil service exams and started testing students on their knowledge of the Four Books and Zhu Xi's commentaries.

- For the next 700 years, until the abolition of the state exams in 1905, the Four Books were the foundation of the official curriculum. The exams were the primary route to social mobility and respectability, and every exam candidate, along with nearly every schoolchild, had to memorize the Four Books. As the Five Classics declined in importance in late imperial China, the Four Books were widely studied in Japan, Korea, and Vietnam. In other words, Neo-Confucianism became an international movement.

The *Great Learning* and the *Analects*

- The *Great Learning* is the shortest and simplest of the Four Books. It begins with a few paragraphs attributed to Confucius, followed by 10 short passages of commentary credited to Zengzi, one of Confucius's first disciples. The *Great Learning* advocates a spiritual goal and an organized plan for one's studies; the crux is the "investigation of things," which Zhu Xi defined as examining the principle (*li*) that one was meant to fulfill.

- The next text in Zhu Xi's streamlined educational curriculum was the *Analects*. This text consists of 20 chapters of aphorisms attributed to Confucius, brief dialogues, or anecdotes about his life. The book seems to have had its origin with his students, who recorded some of their favorite sayings or stories about their beloved teacher after his death.

- Confucius's engaging, inspiring personality seems to come through in his debates with students and government officials about education, ritual, literature, history, wealth and poverty, statecraft, friendship, and ethical behavior. He is generally enthusiastic and generous, yet there are also times when he is frustrated at his inability to secure appropriate employment, and he is nearly in despair at the death of his favorite student.

- In the *Analects*, Confucius develops the technical terms of humaneness, refinement, righteousness, filial piety, the noble person, moral force, and the Way but not in a systematic fashion. The reported conversations seem to be in random order, and Confucius explains his ideas in different ways to different students. He also tends to offer examples and illustrations rather than rigorous definitions.

The enthusiastic and generous personality of Confucius emerges in the *Analects*.

- Later readers have tried to get at the heart of Confucius's teachings, which has given rise to a great body of commentary and competing interpretations. But the fact that Confucian thought can be reconstituted in a variety of ways has allowed it to be continuously relevant in widely differing eras. Students who read the *Analects* as a moral guide come away with respect for authority, reverence for the past, a love of learning, preference for nonviolent reform, moral courage, and exactness in dealing with others.

Mencius and the *Constant Mean*

- The third of the Four Books is the *Mencius*, which is both the name of a book and the name of Confucius's most prominent successor, who lived from 372 to 289 B.C.E. The book has seven chapters, each divided into two parts. It presents extended discourses and reports of advice that Mencius gave to rulers or debates he had with philosophical opponents. As a result, this later text clarifies many points that had been left somewhat vague by Confucius.

- For instance, Mencius argues at length that human nature is inherently good and that evil comes when people ignore their basic impulses of compassion, righteousness, propriety, and wisdom.

- One of his most famous illustrations is his observation that people instinctively feel alarm or distress when they see a child about to fall into a well. Not everyone runs to the rescue—it's possible to suppress those feelings—but that sort of compassion comes naturally to human beings.

- Because physical and social surroundings are crucial in nurturing the ability to follow good impulses, Mencius emphasizes education, the family, and good government. And he regularly chides rulers who do not lay the economic groundwork necessary for a basic level of well-being for their subjects.

• The *Constant Mean*, or *Doctrine of the Mean*, is another relatively short chapter from the Records of Rites, and it was considered the most subtle and profound of the Four Books. The word "mean" in this case refers to moderation and balance. And these qualities, combined with sincerity, can bring a person into harmony with other human beings and with the cosmos itself. The *Constant Mean* points the way to an almost mystical unity with heaven and earth.

Suggested Reading

Chan, Wing-tsit, trans., *A Source Book in Chinese Philosophy*.

Gardner, trans., *The Four Books*.

Lau, trans., *Confucius: The Analects*.

———, trans., *Mencius*.

Legge, trans., *The Chinese Classics*.

Leys, trans., *The Analects of Confucius*.

Nylan and Wilson, *Lives of Confucius*.

Shaughnessy, trans., *I Ching: The Classic of Changes*.

Smith, *The I Ching: A Biography*.

Wilhelm and Baynes, trans., *The I Ching or Book of Changes*.

Questions to Consider

1. How did the Four Books become the basis of the Chinese education system for 600 years?

2. Why do many Chinese believe that the Four Books offer a better introduction to Confucianism than the Five Classics?

3. In what ways are the Four Books a response to the challenge of Buddhism?

Four Books of Neo-Confucianism
Lecture 21—Transcript

We'll begin this lecture with the last of the Five Confucian Classics, the *Changes*, or the *Yijing*. Let me spell this out for you, because you may have seen it in one of two different ways. Nowadays, in Pinyin, it's *Yijing*, but you may have seen it in earlier books as *I-Ching*; both of those are ways of representing the Chinese characters *Yijing* into an English alphabet. The *Yijing* is considered by the Chinese to be the oldest and holiest of the Classics, and it's by far the best known of them in the West.

The *Yijing* is an ancient manual of divination, whereby one manipulates milfoil stalks or, much later, coins to derive a particular hexagram by which one can predict the future, or at least offer clues as to how a dynamic situation might be changing. The core text consists of 64 graphs of six stacked horizontal lines—some of those lines are broken and some of them are unbroken—and each of those graphs has a title and a short statement, and then a series of brief judgments on each of the six lines of the 64 graphs (the hexagrams), which are useful when specific lines are determined to be particularly powerful or unstable. There are 64 of these graphs, called hexagrams, since that number represents every possible combination of broken or unbroken lines that are arranged into sets of six; so it's like two to the sixth power.

In preparing for this lecture, I actually used some coins to generate an appropriate hexagram for this course; and as I threw those coins, saw how they came up, and then did the manipulations that I needed to I came up with a hexagram number 17, which is called Sui or "Following"; and it has, starting from the bottom, a solid line, and then a broken line, a broken line, solid line, solid line, and then finally at the top is a broken line. The summary statement for this hexagram is "Following has supreme success. Perseverance furthers. No blame," which seemed to suggest that if I were careful to follow somebody or something and then pushed ahead, this course might turn out okay, or at least not be a disaster. That very day, I took some of my lectures that I'd written over to a few of my colleagues with expertise in various religions for their critiques and comments; and following their advice has indeed saved me from several errors.

The solid lines in a hexagram are thought of as yang while the broken lines represent yin, in accordance with the ancient Chinese notion that the cosmos consists of two opposing forces that are manifest in all things; so yin and yang, sometimes Americans say "yin" and "yang." Notice that the relationship between yin and yang is more complementary than oppositional. It's not that one's good and the other's bad, it's more like the difference between high and low, hot and cold, or male and female; or in Chinese, the paradigmatic polarity is between heaven and earth. Both of those are necessary parts of the whole, even though they stand in contrast with each other. Notice that the Daoists aren't the only people in ancient China who were talking about yin and yang; Confucians do it, as well as do other philosophical schools.

When I cast my hexagram, the bottom line was the only one that had reached the limits of yang, so it had a score of nine—there are ways that you can determine this with the coins—so the line judgment was applicable, which says: "Nine at the beginning means: The standard is changing. Perseverance brings good fortune. To go out of the door in company produces deeds"; which, again, seemed to suggest that I not try to write these lectures all on my own. Those are all of the lines that had particular significance in the hexagram that I made; but if the next line up had been a full yin line with a score of six then the judgment on that line would've been: "Six in the second place means: If one clings to the little boy, one loses the strong man." I have no idea what that might mean. Similarly, a six at the top line would've gotten this line text: "He meets with firm allegiance and is still further bound. The king introduces him to the Western Mountain."

Perhaps this gives you some idea of what to expect from the *Changes*. There are a number of somewhat vague, cryptic sayings associated with the various hexagrams and their individual lines. The Chinese have long ascribed the hexagrams, the statements, and the line texts to the founders of the Zhou Dynasty in the 11th century B.C.E.; and, in fact, the book does seem to be a compilation of divination lore from several centuries before Confucius.

Personally, I have my doubts about whether the *Yijing* really taps into the underlying principles of the universe, but I do think that it actually works in a functional sense. There's something about focusing one's attention on a particular situation or problem and then trying to relate it to cryptic statements such as those line judgments, and that can help you see things in a different way, or it can provoke new insights or solutions as you try to match the situation at hand to these sort of odd divination instructions that are given.

Yet the *Changes* is more than just a divination manual. Eventually there were 10 appendices, or "wings," which were added to the core text. These were commentaries; they were traditionally ascribed to Confucius—probably actually not written by him—but these explored cosmic patterns of change and transformation, and even suggested that the *Yijing* contained within its 64 hexagrams all possible states of transition and hence was a textual model or microcosm of the entire universe. By learning to distinguish significant from trivial change, careful readers could prioritize their concerns and efforts, and they could learn to live in harmony with the inevitable ebbs and flows of the cosmos. These sorts of grand metaphysical claims generated intense interest throughout Chinese history, manifest in hundreds of detailed commentaries on the *Yijing*, on the Classic of *Changes*; and in the West, ever since Richard Wilhelm's German rendition caught the attention of the famous psychologist Carl Jung and was translated into English in 1950, the *Yijing* has enjoyed an almost mystical countercultural prestige. It's the only one of the Five Confucian Classics that can still be found in most American bookstores.

With the canonization of the Five Classics in the Han Dynasty, there came a need to establish, preserve, and transmit authoritative versions of the texts, exactly. *Canonization* is only an approximate term here; the selection of the Confucian texts didn't come about by church council, but instead came by government fiat when the Five Classics were made the core of the official state curriculum in 136 B.C.E. Unlike in Hinduism, where there were rigorous methods of memorization, or in Judaism with the amazing scribal quality control of the Masoretes, in China this standardization of the texts—this fixing of the exact words—was done by carving the Classics into stone. Ordinarily, Chinese texts were written on narrow vertical strips of bamboo slips that were connected together with cords, something like window shades that you might roll up; and this actually is why Chinese characters traditionally written in lines from top to bottom, because they originally fit into those bamboo slips.

In 172 C.E., the emperor ordered a complete set of stone Classics for the imperial academy. There were seven Classics—the standard five, plus the *Analects* of Confucius (we'll talk about that in a moment) and the brief Classic of Filial Piety—and those seven texts were carved onto 46 steles, each a little over eight feet high and about three feet wide. It took nine years to carve the 200,000 characters. It was thought that those steles were lost, and then in 1980, 96 fragments were discovered. Students at the imperial academy wouldn't only step outside and then consult the stone texts; they could take rubbings from them on paper, which is a process similar to that used in woodblock printing, which was invented in China in the 9th century.

After the collapse of the Han Dynasty in the 3rd century C.E., Confucianism, which had been closely associated with the imperial government, fell into decline, while Daoism and Buddhism became more prominent. In the Tang Dynasty, with the reunification of China under centralized rule, Confucianism began to make a comeback, and the Five Classics were again carved into stone in 837 along with several supplemental texts: There were two more rites texts and two more commentaries on the *Annals*, and then there was also the *Analects* of Confucius, the Filial Piety Classic, and the Erya, which was an early dictionary, making 12 texts in all. Some 650,000 characters were carved onto 114 large steles, which you can still see in the Forest of Steles Museum in Xi'an. Eventually, the book of Mencius was added to make a 13th Classic; so from the 12th century on, it was common to talk about the Thirteen Classics of Confucianism, which incorporated both the original Five Classics, and then the four books that we'll be talking about in a moment.

Confucianism in the Tang Dynasty and the succeeding Song Dynasty—so that's from the 10th to the 13th century—wasn't quite the same as that of the Han Dynasty. Buddhism had influenced Chinese sensibilities, and the new Confucianism—which Westerners have dubbed Neo-Confucianism—was much more interested in the ultimate nature of reality and humanity, and it was aimed at pursuing a program of self-cultivation and inner spirituality as much as gaining the historical knowledge necessary to pass the exams and become a government official. There was at this time a lot of interest in the cosmological interpretations of the Classic of *Changes*. Neo-Confucianism has even more of the qualities that we typically associate with religions than did the original Confucianism of the Warring States Era.

The most influential figure in Neo-Confucianism was a scholar named Zhu Xi, and he lived from 1130–1200. He championed a metaphysical theory in which everything is a combination of *li*, which is principle, and *qi*, vital energy; and this energy in its heavier forms is matter, some translations call it "congealed energy." So there's principle, a sort of an ideal blueprint for being a ruler, a mother, or even a mountain or a river. Actual rulers or mountains are all different from each other because of the particular *qi* that makes them up, though they share the same *li*, the same basic pattern. This theory is important for two reasons: It offers an analysis of the nature of the cosmos that could compete with Buddhist philosophy; it was sophisticated and had some interesting ideas about ontology and metaphysics. Then the second reason it's important is it provides an ethical program for living: One can purify one's actions and emotions in order to bring them into harmony with the near-perfect principle that's within us all. According to Neo-Confucianism, human nature is naturally good; everyone has this *li* of being a human being, this perfect pattern within them, and it's our job to recapture that innate goodness through study, self-discipline, and quiet-sitting, which is a practice that's quite similar in some ways to Buddhist meditation. By doing so doing, one can follow the Way (that is, the Dao) of Heaven. Keep in mind that Confucians talk about the Dao, just as Daoists do. In Chinese, in fact, Neo-Confucianism is known as Daoxue, the Teaching of the Way, or Lixue, the Teachings of Principle.

But given China's longstanding reverence for ancestors, and for the past, and legendary sage-kings, it was usually not effective to present one's ideas as new and revolutionary; so instead of Zhu Xi saying "Here are my ideas, they're unprecedented, they've never been heard before," he instead claimed to have recovered the long-lost original meanings of Confucian texts; though rather than the Five Classics, he urged his students and followers to concentrate their efforts on the Four Books, and the Four Books are: the *Analects*, the *Mencius*, the *Great Learning*, and the *Constant Mean*. Those last two texts were originally chapters in the records of *Rites*. Mastery of one or two of the Five Classics had long been a path to success in the civil service exams and government office, since those ancient texts were thought to hold to the keys to solving contemporary social and political processes; or actually contemporary social and political problems, and you could look to the precedents of the past and remember how it was done in the golden age of the early Zhou Dynasty. But Zhu Xi realized that the Four Books were shorter, easier to read, and more directly applicable to personal moral improvement and inner spirituality than the Five Classics had been.

Zhu Xi's elevation of those texts was controversial during his lifetime; but then in 1315, more than a century after Zhu Xi's death, the Mongols, who at the time had taken over China and were trying to recruit Chinese to work as officials under them, restored the civil service exams and started testing students on their knowledge not of the Five Classics, but of the Four Books and Zhu Xi's commentaries on them. For the next 700 years, until the abolition, the discontinuation, of the state exams in 1905, the Four Books were the foundation of the official curriculum. The exams were the primary route to social mobility and respectability, and every exam candidate, along with nearly every schoolchild, had to memorize the Four Books; so together, they comprise some 50,000 characters, making them about two-thirds the length of the Qur'an. As the Five Classics declined in importance in late imperial China and were reserved mostly for specialized scholars, the Four Books became much more important among regular, educated people and they were also widely studied in Japan, in Korea, and in Vietnam. In other words, Neo-Confucianism became an international movement.

Zhu Xi would've been delighted. He encouraged his students to recite the Four Books, to keep them continually in mind, and to strive to apply them in their lives. They were treated virtually as scripture, though the ultimate goal wasn't heaven but rather to become a sage; to become someone at peace, in harmony with the cosmos, and embodying the highest moral standards. For these reasons, Zhu Xi wanted his students to begin with the shortest and the simplest of the Four Books, the *Great Learning*, where the goal of study was clearly self-cultivation rather than success in the exams and success as an official in the government. The book—and it's actually more of a pamphlet—begins with a few paragraphs attributed to Confucius, followed by 10 short passages of commentary credited to Zengzi, one of Confucius' first disciples. So Confucius's words that start out the *Great Learning* include the following exhortations:

> Knowing where to come to rest, one becomes steadfast; being steadfast, one may find peace of mind; peace of mind may lead to inner serenity ... Things have their roots and branches; affairs have a beginning and an end. One comes near the Way in knowing what to put first and what to put last.... From the Son of Heaven [that's the emperor] on down to commoners, all without exception should regard self-cultivation as the root.

In other words, there should be a spiritual goal and an organized plan for one's studies—from beginning to the end—and the *Great Learning* goes on to provide a step-by-step strategy; so listen to these steps, and wait for the time when you're going to get to the end of all this. It says:

> The ancients who wished to illustrate illustrious virtue throughout the kingdom, first ordered well their own States.
>
> Wishing to order well their States, they first regulated their families.
>
> Wishing to regulate their families, they first cultivated their persons.
>
> Wishing to cultivate their persons, they first rectified their hearts.
>
> Wishing to rectify their hearts, they first sought to be sincere in their thoughts. [We're still waiting to get to the basis; the fundamental thing here.]
>
> Wishing to be sincere in their thoughts, they first extended to the utmost their knowledge. Such extension of knowledge lay in the investigation of things.

That's where it bottoms out; that's the basic goal, the "investigation of things"; then from that, one can work your way out to self-cultivation, and your family, and the state, and the world being put in order. That "investigation of things" was defined by Zhu Xi as examining the perfect, primordial principle, the *li*, which all of those things were meant to conform to.

The next text in Zhu Xi's streamlined educational curriculum was the *Analects* of Confucius; and he was right about putting that text at the beginning. The *Analects* is a great place to start one's study of Confucianism. It consists of 20 chapters of aphorisms attributed to Confucius, or some brief dialogues and maybe some anecdotes about his life. The book seems to have had its origin with his students, who after Confucius's death wanted to record some of their favorite sayings or stories about their beloved teacher. The English title, *Analects*, which we owe to James Legge's translation, is from a Greek word meaning "a selection"; the Chinese title, *Lunyu*, means "conversations." Confucius's engaging, inspiring personality really does seem to come through in his back and forth with students and government officials about education, ritual, literature, history, wealth and poverty, statecraft, friendship, and ethical behavior. He covers lots of topics; they're pretty much in random order as well, they're sort of all mixed up together. Confucius is generally enthusiastic and generous; yet there are also times when he's frustrated at his inability to secure appropriate employment himself—he actually had interviews with numerous rulers looking for employment and never really was able to find the kind of government job that he thought would be appropriate for himself; so he was disappointed in that—and he's nearly in despair at the death of his favorite student when that happens. You get a sense of what Confucius cares about and his sorts of highs and lows in his life.

Confucius develops the technical terms of humaneness, refinement, righteousness, filial piety, the noble person, moral force, and the Way—those are all themes or terms that come up again and again—but they're not in a systematic fashion. The reported conversations, as I said, seem to be in a random order, and ever the teacher, Confucius explains things one way to one student and differently to another student; he tailors his ideas to the capacities and temperaments of individual learners. Students may ask the same question—"Tell me about filial piety" or something—and he'll tell one thing to one student and something slightly different to another. Confucius also tends to offer examples and illustrations rather than rigorous definitions of the kind we might find in, say, Aristotle; so later readers have had to go through the texts comparing various statements on the same topics to try to get at the heart of Confucius's teachings, and that's given rise to a great body of commentary and competing interpretations. But the fact that

Confucian thought can be reconstituted in a variety of ways has allowed it to be continuously relevant in widely different eras, as Zhu Xi discovered. It's a text that you can go into and whatever your particular questions are, you can find answers to that, even as the questions change over centuries.

The *Analects* offers ideas that are for the most part practical and understandable. It's fun to read, and it's eminently quotable. I can give just a few favorites, starting with the famous opening lines:

> The Master said [and this is always Confucius], "To learn, and at due time to practice what one has learned, is that not also a pleasure? To have friends come from afar, is that not also a joy? To go unrecognized, yet without being embittered, is that not also to be a noble person?"

Another example: "The Master said, 'A clever tongue and fine appearance are rarely signs of Goodness.'" You can see the proverbial nature of these. Another: "Zigong asked about the [noble person] [what is he like?]. Confucius said, 'He acts before he speaks and then speaks according to his action.'" Another: "The Master said, 'Walking in a group of three, I am sure to have teachers. I pick out the good points and follow them and the bad points and change them in myself.'" "The Master said, 'How dare I claim to be a sage or a benevolent man? Perhaps it might be said of me that I learn without flagging and teach without growing weary.'" You can see how these just sort of stack up and you can find these relevant in many points to our own lives. I can't resist, let me give you one more: "In education there should be no class distinctions."

In the *Analects*, Confucius is clearly regarded as a role model; so there are also brief descriptions of the way that he performed ancestral sacrifices, or how he asked questions when he was in a new place, or even how he fished or how he sat on a mat. We'll see similar traditions about Muhammad in the Hadith in a later lecture, where Muslims are looking to Muhammad's own life and actions for guidelines or a model for how to act. Students who are reading the *Analects* as a moral guide—that is, as Zhu Xi recommended—will come away with a number of attitudes. In so many different ways, the Confucian *Analects* want to encourage respect for authority, whether for parents, teachers, or rulers; they want to encourage reverence for the past; a love of learning; preference for nonviolent reform; moral courage; and exactness in dealing with others.

The third of the Four Books is the *Mencius*, which is both the name of a book and also the name of a person, in this case Confucius's most prominent successor who lived from 372–289 B.C.E., nearly two centuries after Confucius or about the time of Plato. The *Mencius* has seven chapters, and each chapter is divided into two parts; and rather than the brief aphorisms and exchanges that characterized the *Analects*, the Mencius presents more extended discourses and reports of advice that Mencius gave to rulers or it reports debates that he had with his philosophical opponents. As a result, this later text clarifies many points that had been left somewhat vague by Confucius. In the *Mencius*, you really start to get philosophical argumentation. For instance, Mencius argues at length that human nature is inherently good, and that evil comes when people ignore their basic impulses of compassion, righteousness, propriety, and wisdom. Mencius's idea that human nature is naturally good, you can see how Zhu Xi grabs onto that because that seems to fit with his principle of *li*, this principle of being human.

One Mencius's most famous illustrations of the goodness of humanity is his observation that people instinctively feel alarm or distress when they see a child who's about to fall into a well; everyone will have that sort of gasp, that sort of feeling of alarm. Not everybody runs to the rescue, so it's possible to suppress those feelings; but that sort of compassion comes naturally to human beings. Or in a slightly more elaborate metaphor, Mencius tells this story; he says:

> Bull Mountain was once beautifully wooded. But, because it was close to a large city, its trees all fell to the axe. What of its beauty then? However, as the days passed things grew, and with the rains and the dews it was not without greenery. Then came the cattle and goats to graze. That is why, today, it has that scoured-like appearance. On seeing it now, people imagine that nothing ever grew there. But this is surely not the true nature of a mountain.

You can see where he's going with this: There's a mountain, but it's gotten away from its true nature. Then he puts the moral on the tale in this way:

> And so, too, with human beings. Can it be that any man's mind naturally lacks Humanity and Justice? If he loses his sense of the good, then he loses it as the mountain lost its trees. It has been hacked away at—day after day—what of its beauty then?

But, Mencius says, that original, pure heart/mind can be recovered through study and introspection. Let me talk about that term for just a minute. The word *xin* in China means what we refer to as both our heart and our mind; and sometimes in translations of the Neo-Confucian texts scholars will use this "heart/mind" to translate that one word.

Because one's physical and social surroundings are crucial in nurturing his or her ability to follow good impulses, Mencius emphasizes education, the family, and good government; and he regularly chides rulers who don't lay the economic groundwork necessary for a basic level of wellbeing for their subjects. Desperate people will do desperate things, and inept rulers must bear some of the blame for that. Mencius says:

> If [the people] have a secure livelihood, they will have a secure mind. And if they have no secure livelihood, they will not have a secure mind. And if they have no secure mind, there is nothing they will not do in the way of self-abandonment, moral deflection, depravity, and wild license. When they fall into crime, to pursue and punish them is to entrap them. How can such a thing as entrapping the people be allowed under the rule of a man of humanity?

Zhu Xi was clear about his intentions in promoting the Four Books. He said: "I want men first to read the Great Learning to fix upon the pattern of the Confucian Way; next the Analects to establish its foundations; next the Mencius to observe its development; and next [the Constant Mean] to discover the mysteries of the ancients."

We'll move now to the fourth of those four books, the *Constant Mean*; the one that was supposed to be the acme, the epitome, of this model of education. The *Constant Mean*, sometimes translated as the *Doctrine of the Mean*, is another relatively short chapter from the Records of the *Rites*, and it was considered the most subtle and profound of the Four Books. The word *mean* in this case doesn't signify an average, it refers to moderation and balance; and these qualities, combined with sincerity, can bring a person into harmony with other human beings and with the cosmos itself. The *Constant Mean* points the way to an almost mystical union with heaven and earth. It says: "Equilibrium is the great root from which grow all the human actings in the world, and Harmony is the universal path which they all should pursue. Let the states of equilibrium and harmony exist in perfection, and a happy order will prevail throughout heaven and earth, and all things will be nourished and flourish."

The Five Classics were the basis of Confucian culture from the Han to the Song dynasties. Confucianism waxed and waned during that 1,300-year period, in conjunction with imperial rule; but after Zhu Xi, the Four Books reigned supreme from the 14th until the early 20th century.

For an idea of what the sacred texts of Confucianism could mean in the life of an individual, we can turn to the Song Dynasty martyr Wén Tiānxiáng. He lived from 1236–1283. He was a scholar, an official, a poet, and a commander of Southern Song forces against the invading Mongols. When he was captured, the Mongols attempted to win him over with offers of an official position in the new Yuan Dynasty, but he stubbornly refused to compromise his loyalty to the Song regime. Wén Tiānxiáng would accept nothing short of death, and after four years of imprisonment he was finally executed in Beijing at the age of 46. While in prison, contemplating the right course of action, he wrote the following: "The sun of those dead heroes has long since set; but their record is before me still. And, while the wind whistles under the eaves, I open my book and read; and lo! in their presence my heart glows with a borrowed fire." That's the sort of power that these sacred texts of Confucianism hold upon those who follow them and look to them as guidelines.

Daoism and the Daodejing
Lecture 22

Many of the earliest versions we have of several important texts were recovered in the 20th century from ancient tombs. In some cases, both Confucian and Daoist texts have been discovered in the same tomb, a fact that seems to contradict the traditional view of Confucianism and Daoism as bitterly competing philosophies. In this lecture, we'll explore that traditional view and learn why scholars no longer believe it is correct. We'll also delve into the Daodejing and a book with which it has been associated, the Zhuangzi. As we'll see, both texts offer challenges to our ordinary ways of thinking.

Early Daoism
- According to the standard story, the philosophy of Daoism was founded by a man referred to as Laozi or Master Lao, an older contemporary of Confucius. After several years of teaching his ideas, Laozi became frustrated with conditions in China and set out for the western regions beyond its borders. The gatekeeper stopped him and begged him to put some of his ideas into writing so that they wouldn't be lost. Laozi thereupon wrote the Daodejing ("The Classic of the Way and Its Power") and was never heard from again.
  - Later students of Daoism adopted Laozi's ideas and created a philosophical school that competed with Confucianism. Then, after the fall of the Han dynasty in the 3rd century C.E., when Confucianism declined, Daoism became more prominent, but in the process, it turned into a religion rather than a philosophy, complete with gods, rituals, a priesthood, and a canon of scripture.

  - As a native-born religion, it provided a Chinese alternative to Buddhism. Educated Chinese continued to view Daoism primarily as a philosophy, but the common people were awed by the miracles, ceremonies, and spectacles of its religious practitioners.

- Unfortunately, not much of this familiar story of Daoism stands up to scholarly scrutiny. The Daodejing appears to be a collection of sayings and folk wisdom that accumulated over a couple of centuries, down to about 300 B.C.E. It's doubtful that it was written by one individual, let alone by a contemporary of Confucius.

- The whole notion that there were distinct philosophical schools in pre-imperial China seems to be, like Laozi's biography, a Han dynasty invention, reading contemporary divisions back into the past. The *Records of the Historian*, one of China's earliest histories, includes an essay outlining the basic beliefs of six schools, but with the exception of one (the Mohists), these schools actually represent an eclectic mix of ideas. Daoists and Confucians were not bitter rivals in early China, and it's not clear that teachers whom we today regard as Daoist would have used that term to describe themselves.

- During the Han dynasty, there emerged a sense of what "Daoists" believed, but as we saw with Confucianism, our modern Western categories of philosophy versus religion don't quite apply in ancient China. Thinkers with Daoist tendencies addressed political and ethical matters and speculated about the nature of reality, yet they also offered a path to transcendence and an escape from worldly concerns through meditation and spiritual disciplines.

The Daodejing

- The standard text of the Daodejing, also known as the Laozi, was established in the 3rd century C.E. (though its origins are much older) in a commentary by Wang Bi. The Laozi consists of two parts of roughly equal length: the Daojing ("Classic of the Way") and the Dejing ("Classic of Power or Virtue").

- The Daodejing is relatively short, with each of its 81 chapters taking up only a page or two. It is written in a terse, almost cryptic style. There are striking images, and it is wonderfully suggestive. It seems as if it means so much, even when it is difficult to put one's finger on exactly what's going on.

- The combination of brevity and profundity has made the Daodejing irresistible to commentators and translators. More than 350 Chinese commentaries are extant, and there are now more than 300 translations into English. In fact, the Daodejing is probably the best known work of Chinese culture.

- The overriding concern of the Daodejing is the Dao, or the Way, which is a transcendent order underlying all phenomena. It is somehow connected with nature, as opposed to human artifice, but ultimately, it is beyond words. According to the Daodejing, the Way is eternal, inexhaustible, and the origin of all things.

- The Daodejing is a book of wisdom; to live peacefully and fully, it advises that we need to bring our thoughts and deeds into harmony with the Dao. Or, rather, we should avoid overthinking and practice *wu wei* ("nonaction" or "effortless action"). The goal is to act spontaneously, without trying to force a situation one way or another.

- The Daodejing upends some common assumptions: It might be beneficial or even preferable to adopt more stereotypically feminine characteristics—deference, quietude, passiveness—even in circumstances where traditionally masculine virtues hold sway, such as politics. One should be wary of ambition, desires, and possessions.

- Much of the Daodejing is directed toward rulers, and Laozi informs them that rather than forceful leadership and conquest, a small state with an unobtrusive government might, in the end, yield better results. At a time of incessant conflict (the Warring States period), a ruler who kept out of the limelight and avoided direct confrontation might fare better than one who was eager to lead his people into battle.

Recent Scholarship on Daoist Texts
- For nearly two millennia, the Chinese have read and savored the Daodejing, and they have wanted to attribute its wisdom to a historical sage named Laozi. Yet modern scholars have had serious doubts about its authorship. The Daodejing seems to be a jumble

Selections from the Daodejing

On the Way:

A Way that can be followed is not a constant Way. A name that can be named is not a constant name. Nameless, it is the beginning of Heaven and earth; Named, it is the mother of the myriad creatures. (Ivanhoe, trans.)

A thing was formed murkily; she was generated before heaven and earth. Silent and vast, unique she stands and does not change; She turns full circle and is not used up. She can be the mother of the world. I do not know her name; I entitle her the Way. (Ryden, trans.)

On practicing *wu wei*:

Attain utmost emptiness. Maintain steadfast tranquility ... Be like heaven and merge with the Tao, One with the Tao, you will last long. You may die but will never perish. (Kohn, trans.)

On rulership:

The more taboos and prohibitions there are in the world, the poorer the people will be. The more sharp weapons the people have, the more troubled the state will be. The more cunning and skill man possesses, the more vicious things will appear. The more laws and orders are made prominent, the more thieves and robbers there will be. Therefore the sage says: I take no action and the people of themselves are transformed. I love tranquility and the people of themselves become correct. I engage in no activity and the people of themselves become prosperous. I have no desires and the people of themselves become simple. (Chan, trans.)

On self-cultivation:

In preserving the soul and embracing the One, can you avoid departing from them? In concentrating your qi and arriving at utmost weakness, can you be like an infant? In cleansing and purifying your profound insight, can you be without fault? In loving the people and governing the state, can you be without knowledge? In the opening and closing of the gates of Heaven, can you play the role of the female? In understanding all within the four reaches, can you do nothing (wuwei)? (Bloom, trans.)

of proverbs, paradoxes, observations, and advice, with frequent repetitions and disjunctions. It appears to have started as an oral compilation of aphorisms that was added to and rearranged over time—something like the biblical book of Proverbs—and then attributed to the Old Master.

- In the late 4th century, a version of this memorized wisdom tradition was written down. The oldest extant copy was found in a tomb at Guodian in 1993 and dated to about 300 B.C.E. It is recognizably the Daodejing that we know today, but it is only about 40 percent of the current text, and the individual sayings are not in the same order. The Guodian text may be a selection of someone's favorite lines from a more complete work, an earlier version that was added to later, or an alternative version. It does not seem to be a work that was written in close to its final form by a contemporary of Confucius.

- Two somewhat later copies were found at Mawangdui in 1973, dated to about 200 B.C.E. and 170 B.C.E. These versions are quite close to the standard 3rd-century-C.E. text of Wang Bi, although they have some variations, and most curiously, the order of the two major sections is reversed.

- As interesting as such archaeological finds are to textual scholars, historians have been anxious to understand the role of the Daodejing in Chinese culture. For his two volumes of Daoist classics in the 19th-century Sacred Books of the East, James Legge translated both the Daodejing and the Zhuangzi, a longer prose work supposedly written by a 4th-century-B.C.E. philosopher of that name. Ever since, Westerners have read the works of Laozi and Zhuangzi together as the foundational texts of Daoism. The Chinese themselves have considered Zhuangzi to have been an early follower of Laozi, but again, that assumption has not held up under close scrutiny.

- The Zhuangzi is a spectacular work of literature and philosophy, with arresting insights that challenge ordinary ways of thinking. It also overlaps with ideas of the Daodejing: Zhuangzi writes about the Dao and spontaneous action; he praises "perfected persons" who have transcended the physical and social constraints of ordinary life; and he is skeptical of human judgments and limited perspectives. Zhuangzi is perhaps most famous for dreaming he was a butterfly and then waking up and being unsure whether he wasn't now a butterfly dreaming that he was Zhuangzi.

- Yet there are also stark differences between Zhuangzi and Laozi. Zhuangzi rejects political activity outright; he doesn't discuss nonaction; and he doesn't urge the adoption of stereotypically feminine qualities. Before the Han dynasty, no one thought to categorize Zhuangzi and Laozi in the same philosophical school, and in fact, modern scholars believe that Zhuangzi came first. His core writings preceded the compilation of the Daodejing.

- The Zhuangzi has been influential in Asian culture, particularly in Zen Buddhism, and it has been justly celebrated in the West. Still, it doesn't have nearly the stature of the Daodejing, which became sacred scripture for many. During the late Han dynasty, Laozi came to be regarded as an immortal, a cosmic deity, and a savior of humankind, and reciting the Daodejing became a devotional exercise with magical possibilities.

Suggested Reading

Hendricks, trans., *Lao-Tzu: Te-Tao Ching*.

Ivanhoe, trans., *The Daodejing of Laozi*.

Kirkland, *Taoism*.

Kohn, *Introducing Daoism*.

Kohn and LaFargue, eds., *Lao-tzu and the Tao-te-ching*.

Lao, trans., *Lao Tzu: Tao Te Ching*.

Mair, trans., *Tao Te Ching*.

Palmer, trans., *The Book of Chuang Tzu*.

Watson, trans., *The Complete Works of Chuang Tzu*.

Questions to Consider

1. If the Dao is so important, why is it so hard to talk about?

2. What do archeological finds of the last 40 years add to our understanding of the Daodejing?

Daoism and the Daodejing
Lecture 22—Transcript

Hello, it's good to be back with you. In the very first lecture, when we were talking about the value of sacred texts, I asked: If there were a fire in your home, which books, if any, would you try to save? As we continue our overview of Chinese scripture, I could ask another variant of that question: Which books, if any, would you consider being buried with?

This was a real question in ancient China, because many of the earliest versions we have of several important texts were recovered in the 20th century from tombs. For example, in 1973, three adjacent graves from the 2nd century B.C.E. were excavated at Mǎwángduī, near the city of Changsha in Hunan Province. Over 3,000 artifacts were discovered in those graves, including lacquerware, pottery, and silk goods; and among them were several books that had been written on silk cloth, and that included the earliest copy of the Classic of *Changes* and (at that time) the two earliest versions of the Daodejing, which is one of the key texts of Daoism and will be the subject of our lecture today. *Daoism* is sometimes spelled with a "D" and sometimes spelled with a "T." The "T" is an older Romanization; the sound has always been a "D," so it's *Daoism*. Twenty years later, in 1993, another tomb was excavated in the village of Guōdiàn in Hubei Province that was dated to about 300 B.C.E. Inside were 804 bamboo slips on which were written an even older version of the Daodejing, along with a chapter from the Records of *Rites* and content from the *Documents*; remember, those are two of the Five Confucian Classics.

If you're saying at this point, "Wait a minute, why would the same tomb have both Confucian and Daoist texts in it?" then you're asking the right sort of questions. I'll tell you the standard, commonly-repeated story of Daoism first, and then I'll explain why scholars no longer think that story really works.

The philosophy of Daoism was founded by a man referred to as Laozi, or Master Lao. His personal name was Li Dan, and he was an official in the archives of the state of Zhou and an older contemporary of Confucius. In fact, as the stories go, Confucius once travelled to consult with Laozi about the rites; and even though Laozi chastised Confucius for his arrogance and ambition, Confucius went away very impressed with his message about freedom, naturalness, and living in accordance with the Dao, or the Way. After several years of teaching his ideas, Laozi became frustrated with conditions in China at the time, and he set out for the western regions beyond its borders. A gatekeeper there stopped him at the borders and begged him to put some of his ideas into writing before he went on so that they wouldn't be entirely lost. Laozi thereupon wrote the Daodejing; and that name means "The Classic of the Way and its Power." This is a relatively brief text of some 5,000 characters. Then Laozi continued on his way into the west and was never heard from again.

Later students of Daoism, including Zhuangzi, adopted the ideas of Laozi and created a thriving philosophical school that competed fiercely with Confucianism (remember I'm telling you the traditional story still). Then after the fall of the Han Dynasty in the 3rd century C.E., when Confucianism declined, Daoism became more prominent; but in the process, it turned into a religion rather than a philosophy, complete with gods, rituals, a priesthood, and even a canon of scripture. As a native-born religion, Daoism provided a Chinese alternative to Buddhism; so educated Chinese continued to view Daoism primarily as a philosophy, but the common people were awed by its miracles, ceremonies, and spectacles of its religious practitioners.

Okay, that's the familiar story, with the biographical details about Laozi's life taken from the *Records of the Grand Historian*, one of China's earliest histories, written about 100 B.C.E. by Sima Qian. How much of that story stands up to scholarly scrutiny today? The answer is: Not much. There's no early, independent verification of a person named Laozi; in fact, the name Laozi itself simply means "the Old Master," which is a fairly generic pseudonym. The Daodejing—and the text is referred to as the Laozi also after the putative author—does indeed have about 5,000 characters, but it appears to be a collection of sayings and folk wisdom that accumulated over a couple of centuries, down to about 300 B.C.E. It's highly doubtful that it was written by just one individual, let alone by someone who was a contemporary of Confucius (though, as we continue with this lecture, I'll occasionally refer to Laozi as a convenient fiction; that just means the person or persons who were responsible for this text.)

The whole notion that there were distinct philosophical schools in pre-imperial China seems, like Laozi's biography, to be a Han Dynasty invention; where at that time, maybe in the 1st century B.C.E., they read contemporary divisions back into the past. The *Records of the Historian*, that early Chinese history, includes an outline in an essay form that gives the basic beliefs of six schools: the Yin-yang school, the Confucians, the Mohists (who taught the importance of impartial caring, which is probably a better translation than "universal love," which is sometimes given), the Logicians, the Legalists, and the Daoists. At the time of Sima Qian, these were kind of the philosophical schools that were around; and then they tended to read those back into the past. In actuality, with the exception of the Mohists, these weren't organized social groups that claimed the exclusive allegiance of various thinkers.

Instead, in the Warring States Period, before the Xing and the Han dynasties, there was an eclectic mix of ideas, with all sorts of people talking about the Way, the Dao, and the complementary forces of yin and yang; even though, in retrospect, we might classify some of those as Daoist and others as Confucian. Daoists and Confucians weren't bitter rivals in early China, which is why their texts now show up in some of the same tombs; and I'm not even sure that teachers whom we today regard as Daoist would've used that term to describe themselves. During the Han Dynasty—and remember that goes from 202 B.C.E.–220 C.E.—there emerged a sense of what "Daoists" believed, which apparently involved a whole lot of borrowing; so according to the philosophical essay in the *Records of the Grand Historian*, it describes the Daoists as follows:

> The Taoists teach men to live a life of spiritual concentration and to act in harmony with the Unseen. Their teaching is all-sufficient and embraces all things. Its method consists in following the seasonal order of the Yin-yang School, selecting what is good from the Confucian and Mohist teachings, and adopting the important points of the Logical and Legalist schools. It modifies its position with the times and responds to the changes which come about in the world. In establishing customs and practices and administering affairs, it does nothing that is not appropriate to the time and place. Its principles are simple and easy to practice; it undertakes few things but achieves many successes.

You can see that the idea there, at least from the author of that essay, is the Daoists managed to bring in all the good things from the other schools and put them into one, and then put that in harmony with the changes of the seasons or the cosmos.

With the canonization of the Five Classics in the Han Dynasty, there came a need to establish, preserve, and transmit authoritative versions of texts exactly. When I used the word *canonization*, that's just an approximate term here; the selection of texts came not from a church council, but by government fiat when the Five Classics were made the core of official state curriculum in 136 B.C.E. But as we saw with Confucianism, our modern Western categories of philosophy versus religion don't quite apply in ancient China. Thinkers with Daoist tendencies addressed political problems, ethical matters, and speculated about the nature of reality; yet at the same time, they offered a path to transcendence and an escape from worldly concerns through meditation and spiritual disciplines. As for the relationship between Laozi and Zhuangzi—remember Zhuangzi's supposed to be the second most prominent early Daoist—or the supposed distinction between popular, religious Daoism and the philosophical Daoism of the educated elite, I'll be critiquing those assumptions as well in this and in the next lecture. But the place to begin is with the Daodejing.

As I mentioned earlier, the Daodejing was originally known as the Laozi. Though its origins are much older, the standard text was established in the 3rd century C.E. in a commentary by Wang Bi, who also wrote a very important commentary on the Classic of *Changes*, and then he died at the age of 23; imagine writing two classic commentaries while still a fairly young man. The Laozi consists of two parts of roughly equal length known as the Daojing (that's the "Classic of the Way"), and that's chapters 1–37; and then the Dejing (that's the "Classic of Power" or the "Classic of Virtue"), and that's chapters 38–81; hence when you put those two parts together then it becomes the Daodejing. The Daodejing is relatively short, with each of its 81 chapters taking up only a page or two; so you can easily read it in an afternoon. It's written in a terse, almost cryptic style. Some of it rhymes, there are striking images, and the whole thing is wonderfully suggestive. It seems like it means so much, even when it's difficult to put one's finger on exactly what's going on.

The combination of brevity and profundity has made it irresistible to commentators and translators. There are over 350 Chinese commentaries that are extant—although at least twice that many are thought to have been written at some point—and there are now over 300 translations into English. In fact, the Daodejing is probably the best-known work of Chinese culture. It's been translated more times, into more languages, than any other book in history, aside from the Bible; and those translations have often been markedly different from each other. Fortunately, as Angus Graham, a prominent scholar of early Chinese thought, has observed, "[The Laozi] is a rare case of a poem which for readers in tune with it seems to work even through the feeblest translations, and no one who has glimpsed a coherence in its imagery has altogether failed to understand it."

The overriding concern of the Daodejing is the Dao or the Way, which is a transcendent order underlying all phenomena. It's somehow connected with nature as opposed to human artifice, but ultimately it's beyond words, since language is, after all, a human artifact. The paradox of describing the indescribable shows up in the very first lines; so the Daodejing begins by saying: "A Way that can be followed is not a constant Way. A name that can be named is not a constant name. Nameless, it is the beginning of Heaven and earth; Named, it is the mother of the myriad creatures." But a translation doesn't quite capture the entire meaning, since in Chinese words can function both as nouns and as verbs, at least in Classical Chinese. The word *Dao* means "a way or a teaching," but it can also be used as a verb to mean "to follow" or "to talk about." So the first line is "dao ke dao," "the Dao that can be Dao," "fei chang dao," "is not the constant Dao." Another translation has "The Dao that can be told is not the invariant Dao."

What else might be said about the Way or the Dao? According to the Daodejing, it's eternal, it's inexhaustible; it's also the origin of all things. Chapter 25 says: "A thing was formed murkily; she was generated before heaven and earth. Silent and vast, unique she stands and does not change; She turns full circle and is not used up. She can be the mother of the world. I do not know her name; I entitle her the Way." This particular translator has chosen to use feminine pronouns, which makes some sense—the Dao was often compared to a mother or had some feminine characteristics— yet that isn't quite right either, since the Dao encompasses oppositions such as male and female, or weak and strong, empty and full, beautiful and ugly; everything finds a place within the Dao, which doesn't value things according to human standards or discriminate between things according to human ways of thought.

Chapter Two of the Daodejing says this:

> The whole word recognizes the beautiful as the beautiful, yet this is only the ugly; the whole world recognizes the good as the good, yet this is only the bad. Thus Something and Nothing produce each other; the difficult and easy complement each other; the long and short offset each other; the high and the low incline toward each other; before and after follow each other. Therefore, the sage keeps to the deed that consists in taking no action and practices the teaching that uses no words.

Did you catch those last lines there? A deed that takes no action and a teaching that doesn't use words. The Daodejing is a book of wisdom, and Laozi's advice is, if you want to live peacefully and fully, you need to bring your thoughts and deeds into harmony with the Dao; or rather, you should avoid overthinking and practice *wu wei*; and *wu wei* is a term that means non-action, or perhaps a better translation would be effortless action. The goal is to act spontaneously—they use the word *zi ran*, doing what comes naturally—without trying to force a situation one way or the other. In Chapter 10 we read: "Attain utmost emptiness. Maintain steadfast tranquility. ... Be like heaven and merge with the Tao, One with the Tao, you will last long. You may die but will never perish."

Along the way, the Daodejing upends common assumptions: It might be beneficial, or even preferable, to adopt more stereotypically feminine characteristics—things like deference, quietude, and passiveness—even in circumstances where traditionally masculine virtues hold sway, like politics. Laozi, or the book of the Laozi, says be wary of ambition, desires, and possessions. Much of the Daodejing is directed toward rulers; and Laozi informs them that rather than forceful leadership and conquest, a small state with an unobtrusive government might in the end yield better results and may indeed last longer. At a time of incessant conflict—this was during the Warring States Period, which is an apt name for that time in Chinese history—a ruler who kept out of the limelight and avoided direct confrontation might fare better than one who was eager to lead his people into battle. Chapter 17: "The best of ancient kings were in their kingdoms hardly known; Next the patriarchs, loved and widely praised. Next again those the people feared. Last come those whose abuses they endured." Think about what that means: The best kings are the ones the people are hardly even aware of.

Chapter 57:

> The more taboos and prohibitions there are in the world, the poorer the people will be. The more sharp weapons the people have, the more troubled the state will be. The more cunning and skill man possesses, the more vicious things will appear. The more laws and orders are made prominent, the more thieves and robbers there will be. Therefore the sage says: I take no action and the people of themselves are transformed. I love tranquility and the people of themselves become correct. I engage in no activity and the people of themselves become prosperous. I have no desires and the people of themselves become simple.

Again, you see that notion of *wu wei* or non-action in practice (as if you could practice non-action).

The Daodejing is a rich, fascinating text that frequently employs paradoxes to make its points; which means that it can't really be skimmed. It has to be read slowly, many times, as one starts to intuit its deeper meanings. A couple more favorite passages; from Chapter 38: "The person of superior integrity does not insist upon his integrity; for this reason, he has integrity. The person of inferior integrity never loses sight of his integrity; for this reason he lacks integrity."

Or from Chapter Nine:

> Stretch a bow to the very full, and you will wish you had stopped in time; temper a sword-edge to its very sharpest, and you will find

it soon grows dull. When bronze and jade fill your hall it can no longer be guarded. Wealth and place breed insolence that brings ruin in its train. When your work is done, then withdraw! Such is Heaven's Way.

Finally, one more passage that combines cosmology, self-cultivation, government, and the key concepts of the feminine, effortless action, and insight while paradoxically advocating weakness and disparaging learning, and I think learning in this case probably means book learning, the kind of things that Confucians are good at. Do you have all that together? Chapter 10:

> In preserving the soul and embracing the One, can you avoid departing from them? In concentrating your qi [remember *qi* is vital energy; as in Neo-Confucian philosophy] and arriving at utmost weakness, can you be like an infant? In cleansing and purifying your profound insight, can you be without fault? In loving the people and governing the state, can you be without knowledge? In the opening and closing of the gates of Heaven, can you play the role of the female? In understanding all within the four reaches, can you do nothing [and that's that *wu wei*]?

If you find this way of speaking and thinking intriguing, then you really should read the entire Daodejing; it's fun, it's engaging. But don't force yourself; that would defeat the whole purpose. Do what comes naturally. Follow the Dao.

For nearly two millennia, the Chinese have read and savored the Daodejing, and they've wanted to attribute its wisdom to a historical sage named Laozi, much like Jews credited Moses as the author of the Pentateuch or Hindus imagined Vyasa to be the creator of the Mahabharata, that very long epic poem. Yet modern scholars have had serious doubts. The Daodejing seems to be a jumble of proverbs, paradoxes, observations, and advice, with frequent repetitions and disjunctions. It appears to have started as an oral compilation of aphorisms that were added to and rearranged over time—something like the biblical book of Proverbs maybe—and then eventually were attributed to the Old Master, to Laozi; or since that Chinese term could be plural as well as singular, it might be the Old Masters or the Elders.

Eventually, a version of this memorized wisdom tradition was written down in the late 4th century. The oldest extant copy, as I noted earlier, was found in a tomb at Guodian in 1993 and dated to about 300 B.C.E. It's recognizably the Daodejing that we know today, but it's only about 40 percent of the current text, with material from just 31 of the 81 current chapters, and the individual sayings aren't in the same order. So then we have a puzzle: Is the Guodian text a selection of someone's favorite lines from a more complete work, or is it an earlier version that was added to later, or is it an alternative version? Perhaps there were several similar compilations that were circulating at the time. It's hard to say; but it certainly doesn't look like something that was written, in close to its final form, by a contemporary of Confucius. That old traditional story doesn't really hold up to the evidence that we've been uncovering in China in the 20th century.

Two somewhat later copies were found at Mawangdui in 1973 dated to about 200 B.C.E. and 170 B.C.E. Those versions are quite close to the standard 3rd century C.E. text of Wang Bi, although they have some variant characters and a few more grammatical particles, which clarify some of the ambiguous passages. They also have different chapter divisions, and most curiously, the order of the two major sections is reversed. So in those two versions, they start with what today we have as chapters 38–81, that's the Dejing, which tend to be a little more politically oriented; and then they conclude with our current chapters of 1–37, the Daojing; so one might refer to them as the Dedaojing. I don't know that this makes a huge difference in interpretation, but it might: Think of how concluding the Hebrew Bible with the book of Chronicles gives it a different feel from the Christian Old Testament, which ends with the prophet Malachi.

But as interesting as such archaeological finds are to textual scholars, historians have been anxious to understand the role of the Daodejing in Chinese culture. For his two volumes of Daoist classics in the 19th-century Sacred Books of the East series, James Legge—remember he's the Victorian translator, the missionary—translated both the Daodejing and the Zhuangzi, a longer prose work supposedly written by a 4th-century B.C.E. philosopher by that name. Ever since, Westerners have read the works of Laozi and Zhuangzi together as the foundational texts of Daoism; and the Chinese themselves have considered Zhuangzi to have been an early follower of Laozi at least since the Han Dynasty. But then again, that assumption hasn't held up under close scrutiny.

The Zhuangzi is definitely worth reading. It's a spectacular work of literature and philosophy, with dazzling rhetoric, funny stories, wild flights of fancy, and arresting insights that challenge our ordinary ways of thinking. It's actually one of my favorite books ever. There's certainly some overlap between the ideas in the Zhuangzi and the ideas in the Daodejing: Zhuangzi writes about the Dao and about spontaneous action; he praises "perfected persons," as he calls them, who've transcended the physical and social constraints of ordinary life; and he's skeptical of human judgments and limited perspectives. He asks, for example: "How do I know that loving life is not a delusion? How do I know that in hating death I am not like a man who, having left home in his youth, has forgotten the way back?" Zhuangzi is perhaps most famous for dreaming that he was a butterfly, and then waking up and being unsure as to whether he wasn't now a butterfly dreaming that he was Zhuangzi.

Yet there are also stark differences between Zhuangzi and Laozi: Zhuangzi rejects political activity outright, whereas Laozi often gives advice to rulers. Zhuangzi doesn't talk about non-action or *wu wei*, and he doesn't urge the adoption of stereotypically feminine qualities. Before the Han Dynasty, no one thought to categorize Zhuangzi and Laozi in the same philosophical school; and, in fact, far from seeing Zhuangzi as a disciple of Laozi, modern scholars believe that Zhuangzi probably came first. His core writings preceded the compilation of the Daodejing.

The phrase "core writings" should've caught your attention. The text of the Zhuangzi, as it exists today, was put together by a scholar named Guo Xiang, who died in 312 C.E. It consists of 33 chapters, which seem to have accumulated over several centuries. Scholars have identified five different philosophical perspectives: that of the Zhuangzi, so this is the core text, chapters 1–7; and then his followers later on, chapters 16–27 and 32; the primitivists, who were opposed to government, luxury, and technology in ways that are perhaps reminiscent of the Daodejing, always looking for simplicity, those are chapters 8–10; and then a group that we call the syncretists, who were responsible for 11–15 and then 33, which also is a survey of all of the philosophical schools of the time; and then the hedonists, who were just interested in selfish pleasure and doing the best for themselves, not so interested in society, and those chapters are 28–31 of the Zhuangzi; so the Zhuangzi is a very complicated text with all of these different strands in it. I realize that this starts to sound like the documentary hypothesis and the Torah—remember those four strands of "J," "E," "P," and "D" that got put together and edited over time—but things are hardly ever simple when you're dealing with sacred texts.

My basic point is that you should read the Zhuangzi—it's been influential in Asian culture, particularly in Zen Buddhism, and it's been justly celebrated in the West—but be wary of claims that Zhuangzi is the second most important Daoist philosopher. I'm not sure that he would've considered himself a Daoist, and the distinction between philosophy and religion isn't all that clear in ancient China; and although some Daoists have enjoyed the Zhuangzi, others have regarded other texts as much more important within the Daoist tradition.

Maybe one more story from the Zhuangzi. It's said that Zhuangzi was once fishing somewhere—which is a good Daoist thing to do—and officials came from the state of Chou, and they invited him to come and serve there as a prime minister (it's a great honor to be invited to do so); and Zhuangzi thought for just a minute and he said, "I've heard in the state of Chou that there's a sacred tortoise, which is kept in a lacquer box," and the tortoise is 3,000 years old, it's sort of mummified there. He asked these messengers that came, "Do you think that tortoise would rather be honored and taken care of that way in the court of Chou or would it rather be alive and wagging its tail in the mud?" The messenger said, "Probably alive," and Zhuangzi said, "Ok, out with you, you're done. I would rather stay here than wag my tail in the mud."

In any case, the Zhuangzi doesn't have nearly the stature of the Daodejing; and the Daodejing really did become sacred scripture for many. During the late Han Dynasty—so this is from the second to the 3rd centuries C.E.—

Laozi came to be regarded as an immortal, a cosmic deity, and a savior of humankind. It was even said that after he left China and headed west he went to India, where he taught a simplified version of Daoism that was more appropriate for the Indians, and that become known as Buddhism later on; so some Daoists have claimed that Laozi himself was the Buddha in India. Not true, but something that made them feel better about Buddhism coming in from the west and being a foreign religion or a foreign philosophy; they said, "No, it actually has Chinese origins." Similarly, reciting the Daodejing became a devotional exercise, after the fall of the Han Dynasty, with magical possibilities.

Around 500 C.E., the Zhen'gao—and those are *Declarations of the Perfected*; we'll talk more about this text in the next time—reported the story of a father and his two sons who were instructed by a certain Old Lord to recite the Daodejing (as sort of a religious practice). The father and elder brother made it to 10,000 times—as I said, it's not a very long text; so they recited it 10,000 times—and then they flew off as immortals. The younger son, however, only made it to 9,733 repetitions, and so died a regular death.

The Daodejing is a text that, even if it won't guarantee you immortality for reciting it 10,000 times, will nevertheless enrich your life and show you new ways of thinking about the Dao, about nature, and about our existence here.

The Three Caverns of Daoist Scriptures
Lecture 23

Westerners have been reading the Daodejing and the Zhuangzi for more than 100 years, but scholars have also been aware of a much larger canon of Daoist scriptures, the Daozang. It's a complex and sometimes confusing collection of nearly 1,500 texts, whose contents were, until recently, mostly unknown in the West. In this lecture, we'll discuss the development of that collection and the rise of various Daoist movements. Note, however, that Daoism is not a cohesive religion along the lines of Buddhism or Christianity; it's more of a loose family of religions, similar to Hinduism, with different groups claiming their own revelations and scriptures. In recent decades, many of these texts have been translated into English for the first time.

Early Daoists
- In the last lecture, we saw how some thinkers in pre-imperial China who taught about the Way, simplicity, and spiritual transformation were grouped together under the label "Daoist" in the early Han dynasty. Since the 1980s, Western scholars have come to view another early text as nearly as critically important in proto-Daoism as Laozi and Zhuangzi.
    - This is the *Neiye* ("*Inward Training*"), dated to between 350 and 300 B.C.E. and preserved as a chapter in a long book attributed to the philosopher Guanzi.

    - The *Inward Training* is a relatively short work of rhymed prose that urges readers to live in harmony with the Dao by purifying their *xin* ("heart-mind") and *qi* ("vital energy") through breathing exercises, dietary regulation, and meditation. By so doing, one can become a sage.

- Since the late 20th century, our knowledge of another strand of proto-Daoism has been greatly enriched by the discovery of previously unknown texts from tombs. In particular, a tomb at Mawangdui, dating to 168 B.C.E., yielded four texts that have been categorized by scholars as Huang-Lao writings. *Huang* is the Chinese word for "yellow," referring to the mythical Yellow Emperor, and *Lao* refers to Laozi. This school combines Daoist concepts with ideas about government and cosmology.

- The most important example of Huang-Lao thought is the lengthy, eclectic *Huainanzi*, written by scholars in about 139 B.C.E. This work draws heavily on the Daodejing and Zhuangzi, but it combines Daoists perspectives with Confucianism, Legalism, yinyang thought, and Five Phases cosmology.

Celestial Masters and Ge Hong
- The first organized groups of Daoists appeared in the late Han dynasty (2nd century C.E.), though they were not educated elites but rebels. In 142, Zhang Daoling, in central China, claimed that Lord Lao (the deified Laozi, the personification of the Dao) appeared to him in a vision and told him that the end of the world was near. Zhang thereby became the first of the Celestial Masters.
  - Zhang gathered followers who would be part of a new theocratic state and asked all recruits to donate grain to the cause. He taught that one could preserve one's *qi* by limiting food and sex and that illness was the result of sin, which required confession and repentance.

  - Zhang also had his followers memorize and chant the Daodejing, and Zhang's grandson, the third Celestial Master, wrote a commentary on the Daodejing called the *Xiang'er* that was also recited. The *Xiang'er* includes explanations of cryptic lines in the Daodejing, as well as 27 precepts, such as "Do not do evil" and "Do not study false texts."

- Also in the 2nd century C.E., in east China, another group of Daoist rebels arose, who became known as the Yellow Turbans; they eventually merged with the Celestial Masters. The Yellow Turbans were inspired by a text called the *Taipingjing* ("*Scripture on Great Peace*").

- This is a lengthy transcript of conversations between a Celestial Master and six of his disciples. In his answers to their questions, the Celestial Master teaches about meditation and healing through medicinal plants, talismans, acupuncture, and music.

- He also indicates that an era of great peace will ensue when rulers follow the Dao. Unfortunately, that could happen only after the destruction of the current corrupt government; thus, the Yellow Turbans launched a rebellion in 184 C.E.

• The political situation was confused for the next 30 years, but religious rebels managed to set up a theocratic state in Sichuan for a while before surrendering to General Cao Cao in 215 and being dispersed throughout China. The lineage of Celestial Masters continues to this day in Taiwan.

• The Way of the Celestial Masters and the Yellow Turbans were popular mass movements. In the aftermath of the Han dynasty, Daoism also appealed to scholars, including Ge Hong (283–343). Ge was an official who had been trained in the Confucian classics, but he was also interested in Daoist immortals, texts, and practices, as well as the possibility of achieving longevity through alchemy.

- Ge Hong wrote the *Baopuzi* ("*Master of Embracing Simplicity*"), which is divided into 20 Inner and 50 Outer Chapters. The Inner Chapters are devoted to esoteric techniques of attaining transcendence or immortality through alchemy, meditation, visualizations, gymnastics, and so on. The Outer Chapters are devoted to the mainstream political thought and moral principles of Confucianism and Legalism.

- *The Master of Embracing Simplicity* is not Daoist scripture, though it was included in the Daozang in the 15th century, but Ge Hong's work is a key text in helping us understand early Daoism. Indeed, he is one of those figures who make it difficult to draw a distinction between a refined philosophical Daoism and a superstitious religious Daoism devoted to magic and immortality; in Ge's writings, the two strands go together.

Shangqing and Lingbao

- After the fall of the Han dynasty in the 3rd century, educated northerners fled south, taking some of these Daoists texts and traditions with them and asserting their right to rule. Displaced southern aristocrats responded by discovering their own superior versions of teachings about the Dao, from higher sources than those claimed by the Celestial Masters.

- Some 20 years after Ge Hong's death, from 364 to 370, a spirit medium named Yang Xi, living near Nanjing, began to receive midnight visitations from a group of deities descended from the Heaven of Highest Clarity (Shangqing). From these visitations, he learned about the organization of the heavens, met several celestial beings, and received scriptures, which he recorded.

- About a century later, a scholar named Tao Hongjing (456–536) collected all the Shangqing revelations he could find and compiled them into a text called the *Declarations of the Perfected*. Because this was an aristocratic, elite form of Daoism that put a great deal of emphasis on literary achievement, the revelations that came through Yang Xi were often in the form of exquisite poetry.

- A few decades after Yang Xi, another branch of Daoism was established, the Numinous Treasure School (Lingbao). Around 399, a grand-nephew of Ge Hong named Ge Chaofu compiled some of his inherited family mystical traditions into a text known as the *Five Talismans*.
    - Ge Chaofu claimed that these abstract, magical designs were instrumental in creation and had been hidden in a sacred mountain by the mythical emperor Yu. Eventually, they were revealed to a 2nd-century ancestor of Ge Chaofu, making these texts older than those of the Highest Clarity School.
    - Many Numinous Treasure texts followed. They offered a plethora of sacred diagrams and charts, drew upon Buddhist ideas, established public rituals for talisman activation, introduced new gods and heavens, and offered salvation to all.

The Daozang

- In the 5th century, a few people sensed that these various regional religious movements and lineages had enough in common that they could be brought together into something called "Daoism." At a time when Buddhism was gaining in popularity, some scholars felt that it was important to meet the challenge of that foreign religion with a system of beliefs, practices, rituals, and scriptures that were indigenous to China. Lu Xiujing (406–477), a Daoist priest, was one such scholar.

- He gathered as many sacred texts as he could find and organized them into three groups, which he called the Three Caverns. This became the basis of the Daozang or Daoist canon. There was the Cavern of Perfection, consisting of Supreme Clarity scriptures; the Cavern of Mystery, containing the Numinous Treasure scriptures; and the Cavern of Spirit, made up of the writings of yet another school of Daoism, that of the Three Sovereigns.

- About a century after the work of Lu Xiujing, four supplements were added—one for each of the Caverns, plus a general category. The Cavern of Perfection was supplemented by texts based on the Daodejing; the Cavern of Mystery was supplemented by texts based on the *Scripture on the Great Peace*; and the Cavern of Spirit was supplemented by Taiqing texts (having to do with alchemy and physical exercises). The fourth, unattached supplement consisted of Celestial Master scriptures.

- The Daoist canon kept getting larger, and in the 7th century, the texts in each of the Three Caverns were arranged into 12 subsections. From the 8th to the 13th centuries, perhaps half a dozen projects were undertaken to compile a complete Daoist canon, but all of those early versions were lost in the wars and rebellions of medieval Chinese history.

- Finally, a Ming dynasty edition of the complete canon was published in 1445, which included some 1,400 texts. Additional texts were added in 1607, bringing the total to about 1,500. Printing this collection was a tremendous project, requiring imperial sponsorship. This edition is the origin of all current copies of the Daoist canon.

- It is an eclectic collection, which includes not only Daoist scriptures but also the works of non-Daoist philosophers. There are works of alchemy; descriptions of heavens, spirits, and gods; liturgical texts; and more.

- The Daoist scriptures were never intended to be widely distributed or studied. Even after the publication of the canon in 1445, it was available in only a few Daoist monasteries.
    o A modern edition of the canon (60 volumes) was finally published in Shanghai in the 1920s, with help from the republican government. The 500 sets that were printed were sold to libraries around the world. For most of the 20th century, however, the contents of the Daoist canon were still difficult for scholars to access, much less ordinary readers.

    o In 2004, the University of Chicago published a three-volume catalogue of the Daoist canon, giving brief descriptions for every text it contains. In 2008, Rutledge came out with a two-volume *Encyclopedia of Taoism*, which offers clear explanations of major works. These scholarly sources are available in university libraries; for self-study of Daoist texts, Livia Kohn's anthology *The Taoist Experience* is highly recommended.

Suggested Reading

Bokenkamp, *Early Daoist Scriptures*.

Despeux and Kohn, *Women in Daoism*.

Hendrischke, *The Scripture on Great Peace*.

Kohn, *Daoism and Chinese Culture*.

———, ed., *The Taoist Experience*.

Major, Queen, Meyer, and Roth, trans., *The Huainanzi*.

Pregadio, ed., *The Encyclopedia of Taoism*.

Robinet, *Taoism: Growth of a Religion*.

Roth, *Original Tao and the Foundations of Taoist Mysticism*.

Sailey, *The Master Who Embraces Simplicity*.

Schipper and Verellen, eds., *The Taoist Canon*.

Thompson, "Taoism: Classic and Canon."

Ware, *Medicine and Religion in the China of A.D. 320*.

Yates, trans., *Five Lost Classics*.

Questions to Consider

1. How have scholars in the last few decades modified their views about the origins and development of Daoism?

2. Why is the massive canon of Daoist sacred texts so little known in the West?

The Three Caverns of Daoist Scriptures
Lecture 23—Transcript

I often think how exciting it would've been to have been studying world religions when Max Müller's monumental 50-volume Sacred Books of the East was first published; that is, from 1879–1910. There had been earlier English translations of a few texts—like the Qur'an, the Bhagavad Gita, some of the Upanishads, and the Confucian *Analects*—but Müller's project offered the first systematic, scholarly renditions of dozens of sacred texts from the world's major religions. For the first time, Westerners had access to books that were enormously influential and even revered within their respective cultures, but which outsiders had heretofore only heard about.

Yet the excitement of that gradual revelation or unfolding of world scripture has been matched in the last few decades in the study of Daoism. In the West, we've been reading the Daodejing and the Zhuangzi for over a hundred years; though as we saw in the last lecture, Zhuangzi may not have started out as a Daoist, even if Daoists later adopted him. But scholars have also been aware of a much larger canon of Daoist scriptures called the Daozang. It's a large, complex, and sometimes confusing collection of nearly 1,500 texts, whose contents were until recently mostly unknown in the West.

In this lecture, I'll talk about the development of that canonical collection and the rise of various Daoist movements, but it's important to recognize that Daoism isn't a cohesive religion along the lines of Buddhism or Christianity; it's more of a loose family of religions, sort of like Hinduism, with different groups claiming their own revelations and their own scriptures. In recent decades, many of these texts have been translated into English for the first time.

In the previous lecture, we saw how some thinkers from pre-imperial China who taught about the Way, and about simplicity, and spiritual transformation were grouped together under the label Daoist in the early Han dynasty, about 100 B.C.E., with the legendary Laozi given a particularly prominent place. Since the 1980s, Western scholars have come to view another early text as nearly as critically important in proto-Daoism as Laozi and Zhuangzi. This is a text called the *Neiye*, or the *Inward Training*, and it's dated to between

350 and 300 B.C.E.; and it's preserved as a chapter in a long book attributed to the philosopher Guanzi. The *Inward Training* is a relatively short work of rhymed prose, about a third the length of the Daodejing, and it urges its readers to live in harmony with the Dao by purifying their *xin* (remember that's that heart/mind combination; a word that means both "heart" and "mind") and then also purifying their *qi* ("vital energy"); and you do that through breathing exercises, through dietary regulations, and meditation, and by so doing, one can become a sage. In the *Inward Training*, it says: "In eating, it is best not to fill up; in thinking, it is best not to overdo. Limit these to the appropriate degree and you will naturally reach it [meaning vitality]." There are physical benefits to this sort of spiritual discipline; again, the *Neiye*, the *Inward Training* says: "If people can be aligned and tranquil, their skin will be ample and smooth, their ears and eyes will be acute and clear, their muscles will be supple and their bones will be strong. They will then be able to hold up the Great Circle [meaning the heavens] and tread firmly over the Great Square [which is how they refer to the Earth]." That notion of clear skin, eyes, and muscles sounds pretty good to those of us who are getting a little bit older; this is a text you may want to pay attention to.

Since the late 20th century, our knowledge of another strand of proto-Daoism has been greatly enriched by the discovery of previously unknown texts from tombs. You'll recall that in the last lecture I mentioned two versions of the Daodejing that were written on silk and found in a grave at Mawangdui, a grave that had been sealed up since 168 B.C.E., for more than 2,000 years. In that same tomb were four texts that have been categorized by scholars as Huang-Lao writings. *Huang* is the Chinese word for "yellow," and in this context it refers to the mythical Yellow Emperor who was the legendary founder of Chinese civilization and the ancestor of the Chinese people, and then the *Lao* in the term "Huang-Lao" refers to Laozi of the Daojing. This Huang-Lao school combines Daoist concepts with ideas about government and cosmology. These four brief texts from the Huang-Lao school that were found at Mawangdui were translated into English in 1997.

The most important example of Huang-Lao thought, however, is the lengthy, eclectic *Huainanzi*, which was written by scholars at the court of Liu An, the king of Huainan—he's a regional king—about 139 B.C.E. during the Han Dynasty. This work, the *Huainanzi*, draws heavily on the Daodejing and

Zhuangzi, but it combines Daoist perspectives with Confucianism, Legalism, yinyang thought, and the Five Phases cosmology in a very eclectic mix. Isabelle Robinet, a modern scholar, has described its contents as including "cosmology, philosophy, the art of government, mysticism, mythology, hagiography, ethics, education, military affairs, music, and inner nature and vital force." It brings a little bit of everything into that. I remember being very curious about the *Huainanzi* in graduate school, but it was hard to figure out since the first full English translation appeared only in 2010, long after I'd graduated. Both the *Inward Training* and the *Huainanzi* eventually made it into the Daozang, or the Daoist, canon.

The first organized groups of Daoists appeared in the late Han Dynasty; so these are people who take on that label as "Daoists" themselves. They weren't educated elites that were associated with the court as with the writers of the *Huainanzi*; in fact, they were rebels. In 142, Zhang Daoling, in central China, claimed that Lord Lao—and that's the deified Laozi; the personification of the Dao—had appeared to him in a vision and told him that the end of the world was near. Zhang thereby became the first of the Celestial Masters. He gathered followers who'd be part of a new, theocratic state and he asked all the recruits to donate grain to the cause; and then this movement eventually became known as the Way of the Five Pecks of Rice because that's how much rice he asked people to donate.

Zhang Daoling taught that one could preserve one's *qi*, that vital energy, by limiting food and sex, and that illness was the result of sin, which required confession and repentance. He also had his followers memorize and chant the Daodejing—so this is when it starts to become more of a religious text— and Zhang's grandson, the third Celestial Master, wrote a commentary on the Daodejing that was called the Xiang'er, and that commentary was similarly recited. The word *Xiang'er* means "thinking of you"; the idea seems to be that the Dao is constantly thinking of you. There are explanations of cryptic lines in the Daodejing in this commentary, but also 27 precepts including things like: "Do not do evil," "Do not study false texts," "Do not waste your essence or qi." The *Xiang'er* commentary was lost for a couple thousand years, but a copy of the first half of the commentary—so it's a commentary on Daodejing chapters 3–37—was discovered at the Silk Road oasis of

Dunhuang in the early 20th century and then finally translated into English in 1997.

About the same time as the First Celestial Masters, that Five Pecks of Rice school—so 2nd century C.E.—in East China, another group of Daoist rebels arose, and they became known as the Yellow Turbans, after their distinctive headgear. They eventually merged with the Celestial Masters. The Yellow Turbans were inspired by a text called the *Taipingjing* or *Scripture on Great Peace*. This is a lengthy transcript of conversations between a Celestial Master and six of his disciples. In answer to their questions, the Celestial Master teaches about meditation and healing through medicinal plants, talismans, acupuncture, and music. He also indicates that an era of Great Peace will ensue when rulers follow the Dao. Unfortunately, that Great Peace could only come about after the destruction of the current corrupt government, so the Yellow Turbans launched a rebellion in 184 C.E.

The political situation was pretty confused for the next 30 years—it was, after all, the end of the Han Dynasty—but religious rebels managed to set up a theocratic state in Sichuan (the province) for a while before surrendering to General Cao Cao in 215 and then being dispersed throughout China. The lineage of Celestial Masters continues to this day in Taiwan; and after being banned from Communist China for about 50 years, the Way of the Celestial Masters is now making a comeback in mainland China as well. Lengthy excerpts from the Scripture on Great Peace were translated into English in 2006; and two versions of the Scripture on Great Peace made it into the Daozang, that sort of big collection of Daoist scriptures.

The Way of the Celestial Masters and the Yellow Turbans were popular, mass movements. In the aftermath of the Han Dynasty, Daoism also appealed to scholars, including one of the most famous scholars of the time, a man named Ge Hong, who lived from 283–343. Ge was an official who'd been trained in the Confucian Classics; but he was also interested in Daoist immortals and Daoist texts and practices, as well as the possibility of achieving longevity through alchemy. He wrote a book called the *Baopuzi*, or the *Master of Embracing Simplicity*—that title is derived from a line in the Daodejing—and the *Baopuzi*, the *Master of Embracing Simplicity*, is divided 20 inner chapters and then 50 outer chapters. The inner chapters are devoted to esoteric techniques of attaining transcendence or immortality through alchemy, meditation, visualizations, gymnastics, breathing and sexual techniques, exorcisms, and talismans. The outer chapters are devoted to the mainstream political thought and moral principles of Confucianism and Legalism.

The *Master of Embracing Simplicity*, that text, isn't exactly a Daoist scripture, though it was included in the Daozang in the 15th century. That was actually the first time that the inner and the outer chapters were published together; previously they'd circulated as separate books. Nevertheless, Ge Hong's work, even if it's not scriptural, is a key text in helping us to understand early Daoism. Indeed, Ge Hong is one of those figures who make it difficult to make a distinction between a refined philosophical Daoism and a superstitious religious Daoism devoted to magic and immortality; in Ge's writings, both of those sides go together. The inner chapters were translated into English in 1966—though it's sort of an odd translation; the translator often uses the word *God* to translate the Chinese term *Dao*, which is a little problematic—and the outer chapters, about half of them were translated into English in 1978.

Ok, if you're still with me, things get even more complicated from here. After the fall of the Han Dynasty in the 3rd century, educated northerners fled down to the south—remember that most of Chinese civilization occurred in the north before the end of the Han Dynasty; so they're fleeing down to the south—and they take with them some of these Daoist texts and Daoist traditions, and then they assert their right to rule; they claim that they have the Mandate of Heaven. Displaced southern aristocrats responded by discovering their own superior versions of the teachings about the Dao, from higher sources than those claimed by the Celestial Masters.

Some 20 years after Ge Hong's death, from 364–370, during those years there was a spirit medium named Yang Xi, a man who lived near Nanjing, who began to receive midnight visitations from a group of deities who descended from the Heaven of Highest Clarity, called the Shangqing. Yang Xi had been hired by two brothers in an aristocratic family by the name of Xu to make contact with the younger brother's deceased wife. Through Yang Xi, this deceased woman told them about her status in the afterworld and the organization of the heavens; and then she introduced them to several other celestial beings, who revealed scriptures in poetry and prose, along with meditative techniques for spiritual transformation. Yang Xi wrote everything down, and then the Xu brothers shared these handwritten revelations with their friends and their relatives.

About a century later, a scholar named Tao Hongjing—so he lived from 456–536—collected all the Highest Clarity revelations, the Shangqing revelations, which he could find and then he compiled them into a text called the Declarations of the Perfected. One of the problems was by that time there already started to be some forgeries that were written; and Tao managed to discern which were the true texts from the forgeries by recognizing Yang Xi's inspired calligraphy; that was the sign that this was the real deal, the genuine item. Because this form of Daoism was aristocratic and elite, it put a great deal of emphasis on literary achievement; and the revelations that came through Yang Xi were often in the form of exquisite poetry. For instance, here are a few lines from one of the Perfected beings known as the Lady of Purple Tenuity. She says:

> With winged steps, I pace the Ultimate Void, Meandering traces, wanton as waves, The sounds of the bells carried away on the wind. You who practice inward meditation in the Belvedere of the Seven Ways, You will be able to obtain total oblivion. Why force ourselves to continue exchanging poems, Relying on these messages in the writing of the world? Free of the passions of the heart, awakening will come spontaneously, In silence, you will surely attain the highest level!

That probably loses something in translation; but you get an idea of this sort of very ethereal, sophisticated language that's used in these texts.

Yang Xi asked his celestial visitors where these texts came from, and the modern scholar Isabelle Robinet, who I just quoted a few minutes ago, has summarized the answer that they gave in the following, rather breathtaking account. She says that Yang Xi was told that the Highest Clarity scriptures were:

> The condensed form of the Primordial Breath. Born spontaneously from the Void, they existed before the start of the world.
>
> They appeared first in the form of invisible light rays and "solidified" as they descended, taking on an ever more solid form. Beginning as light, they became "cloud seals," still nebulous but as if congealing into a more permanent form. Then they were written down by the gods in non-human characters, in jade on tablets of gold and stored in the Celestial Palaces or in the sacred mountains.
>
> Their transcription into human writing happened only later, when Heaven "sent down the tokens." The sacred texts that men possess are the manifestation of Heaven's grace, but they are only a "token," a solid imprint, the impression of a celestial prototype that remains in the heavens.

That's the description, and that's kind of astonishing. Sometimes Jews and Muslims claim that the Torah or the Qur'an existed before the creation of the world, but not always quite this poetically.

A few decades after Yang Xi, another branch of Daoism was established, the Numinous Treasure school, or the Lingbao school. The story is, about 399, a grandnephew of Ge Hong named Ge Chaofu compiled some of his inherited family mystical traditions into a text known as the *Five Talismans*; they'd apparently passed these handwritten manuscripts down within the family. He claimed that these abstract, magical designs were instrumental in creation and had been hidden in a sacred mountain by the mythical emperor Yu. Yu, you may know, is the one who brought the great flood under control; but not by building an ark like Noah in the Bible. Yu instead dug canals and managed to get the waters to recede so that people could live; in fact, the Chinese say, "If it weren't for Yu, we'd all be fish."

Eventually, those texts were revealed to Ge Chaofu's 2nd-century ancestor Ge Xuan; so he claims that these texts go all the way back to the 2nd century, which makes these writings conveniently older than those of the Highest Clarity School. There were many, many of these Numinous Treasure texts that followed. They offered a plethora of sacred diagrams and charts, they drew on Buddhist ideas and established public rituals for talisman activation, they introduced new gods and heavens, and they offered salvation to all.

In the 5th century, a few people sensed that these various regional religious movements and lineages had enough in common that they could be brought together into something called Daoism. At a time when Buddhism was gaining in popularity, some Chinese scholars felt that it was important to meet the challenge of that foreign religion with a system of beliefs, practices, rituals, and scriptures that were indigenous to China. Lu Xiujing, who lived from 406–477, was a Daoist priest, and he was one of those scholars who thought it was important to give some form to these indigenous religious traditions. Lu gathered as many sacred texts as he could find, and he organized them into three groups, which he called the Three Caverns, and this became the basis of the Daozang or the Daoist canon: There was the Cavern of Perfection, which consisted of the Highest Clarity scriptures (there were 34 of those); then second was the Cavern of Mystery, containing the Numinous Treasure scriptures (27 works); and then finally the Cavern of Spirit, made up of the writings of yet another school of Daoism, that of the Three Sovereigns (just 4 works from that school).

The Three Caverns of Daoism might sound a bit like the Three Baskets of Buddhism; and there's surely some influence there. When Buddhists showed up in China with a well-organized, impressive canon, many Daoists thought that they ought to have one, too; the written word was always held in very high esteem in China. But the Three Baskets (the Tripitaka) are divided by genre; you remember that there's the Vinaya, the regulations for monks and nuns; the Sutra, the words of the Buddha; and the Abhidharma, which are philosophical treatises. The Three Caverns, by contrast, are organized by three major schools. So the relevant parallel in Buddhism isn't the Three Baskets as much as the Three Vehicles. In the parable of the burning house in the Lotus Sutra, these are people who become enlightened by listening to the Buddhas—roughly the Theravada monks and nuns; that's the first group—and then the second vehicle are those who are enlightened by self-enlightenment (so those are individuals who've received the Four Noble Truths on their own; it's a fairly rare category); and then the third vehicle is those who focus on serving others (those are the bodhisattvas of Mahayana

Buddhism). So three vehicles in the Buddhist tradition, and those are going to be more equivalent to the three canons in the Daoist scriptures.

You may have noticed that several of the sacred texts that we've talked about so far in this lecture wouldn't have made it into Lu Xiujing's collection. About a century later, four supplements were added, one for each of the Caverns, plus a general category. The Cavern of Perfection got supplemental texts based on the Daodejing (we're going to get the Daodejing and commentaries on it into this wider canon); the Cavern of Mystery was supplemented by texts based on the Scripture of the Great Peace; then the Cavern of Spirit was supplemented by Taiqing texts, having to do with alchemy and physical exercises; and then the fourth, unattached supplement consisted of Celestial Master scriptures. Now we've gone back to those first self-labeling Daoist schools, the Celestial Masters, and finally their scriptures get into this collection; remember that they started out as common, popular Buddhism so it took them a little longer for them to get into this more aristocratic, elite form of book collecting and editing.

The Daoist canon kept getting larger; and in the 7th century, the texts in each of the Three Caverns were arranged into 12 subsections. To give you an example of how these might look today, the subsections include: "Fundamental Texts," "Divine Talismans," "Secret Instructions," "Numinous Charts," "Genealogies and Registers," "Precepts and Regulations," "Rituals and Observances," "Techniques and Methods," "Various Arts" such as alchemy, geomancy, and numerology, "Records and Biographies," "Eulogies and Encomia," and finally "Lists and Memoranda"; there's just a huge, eclectic, sprawling collection that they try to bring into some kind of order.

The compilation of the complete Daoist canon was a huge undertaking, which required imperial sponsorship. There were perhaps half a dozen such projects from the 8th to the 13th centuries, with the earlier collections being handwritten texts, brought together and copied, and then woodblock printed versions of the Daoist canon starting in the 12th century. But all of those early versions of the canon were lost in the wars and rebellions of medieval Chinese history. Finally, a Ming Dynasty edition of the complete Daoist canon, the Daodejing, was published in 1445, which included some 1,400 texts. Some additional texts were added in 1607, bringing the total to about

1,500. Printing this collection was a tremendous project, again requiring imperial sponsorship; for this publication, over 121,000 hand-carved woodblocks were used. This edition is the origin of all current copies of the Daoist canon.

It's a very eclectic collection, which includes not only Daoist scriptures, but also the works of non-Daoist philosophers such as Han Feizi, who was a Legalist, and Mozi, the guy who preached universal love or impartial caring. There are works of outer alchemy, which actually involved cooking up drugs and elixirs for long life in a lab, and works of inner alchemy, meditations and visualizations, which became more popular in later dynasties Perhaps the inner alchemy became more popular than the outer alchemy because many of those alchemical recipes involved cinnabar, a mercury ore that's highly toxic; and sometimes (ironically) in trying to gain longer life, Daoist adepts actually ended up shortening their lives by injecting some of these toxic substances. In the Daoist canon there are secret talismans, charms, and registers; descriptions of heavens, spirits, and gods, including gods that dwell within one's body, inner deities; and there are also techniques for tending life, medicine and dietary guidelines, as well as breathing exercises, gymnastics, and sexual techniques. A great many of the texts are liturgical in nature; they're scriptures to be recited, hymns to be chanted, and memorials to be read during various ceremonies and services.

The Daoist scriptures, however—unlike, say, the Talmud—were never intended to be widely distributed or studied. They were esoteric texts, full of technical language and cryptic talismans, and they were intended for the use of ordained Daoist priests or initiated Daoist believers, laypersons. One of the wonderful things about the most popular of the sacred books in China—so that would be the Confucian *Analects* and the Daodejing—is that they're still quite readable by ordinary Chinese people today. The grammar's a little bit different, but the characters are still the same ones that are used today; so Chinese people today can pick up the *Analects* or the Daodejing and pretty much make sense of it. It's not at all like the disconnect between modern Hindus and the Sanskrit scriptures, or between most modern Christians and the Greek New Testament. But most of the Daoist canon is a little bit different; those texts weren't designed to be easily read by outsiders. As I said, there's a lot of technical language and metaphorical descriptions, and it's pretty hard to understand what's going on without having training or having a Daoist master who can explain the significance or the meaning of these passages.

Even after the publication of the canon in 1445, it wasn't widely available; it was only in a few Daoist monasteries. A smaller selection of about 173 texts circulated more broadly; but the Qing Dynasty—that lasted from 1644–1912—wasn't particularly supportive of Daoism. Finally, a modern edition of the Daoist canon was published in Shanghai in the 1920s, with help from the Republican government that was in power at the time; and that canon, that printed version, takes up about 60 volumes, maybe 49,000 pages, and each of those pages reproduces two pages from the Ming edition side by side. It was printed in 500 sets, and those were sold to libraries around the world. For most of the 20th century, however, the contents of that Daoist canon were still pretty difficult for scholars to get a handle on, much less ordinary readers.

But things have changed; remember, this is an exciting time to be studying Daoism. In 2004, the University of Chicago published a three-volume catalogue of the Daoist canon that gives brief descriptions of every text that it contains. In 2008, Rutledge came out with a two-volume *Encyclopedia of Taoism* that offers clear explanations of the major works. These are scholarly sources available in university libraries; but if you're interested in the wide range of Daoist texts, my first recommendation, number one recommendation, is Livia Kohn's anthology *The Taoist Experience*, which contains dozens of excerpts from miscellaneous writings in the Daoist canon and tries to capture some of that variety and eclecticism of texts that we see there.

I'll conclude with the most famous example of a female Daoist master. This Sun Bu'er, and she lived from 1119–1182. Sun Bu'er was the only woman among the Seven Perfected, which was a circle of disciples of Wang Chongyang, the founder of the Quanzhen School of Daoism, which came about in about the 12th century. Sun was a bright, educated young woman; she was married and had three sons. Over her objections, her husband left home to study with Wang—he wanted to study Daoism full time—and the next year, Sun Bu'er herself arrived to study with Wang Chongyang as well, as she was about the age of 50 or so. She and her husband, now living separately, progressed in their understanding of Daoist principles, though she far surpassed him in her knowledge of meditation and talismans; and as a nun, she gained many disciples. Sun Bu'er's story is recorded in five places in the Daozang, and she composed texts that were eventually incorporated into supplements to the canon. The legends recount that at noon on December 29, 1182, the very hour that she'd predicted, Sun Bu'er was transformed into an immortal. Her husband, though he was living at the time far away in another part of China, reported that at that moment he looked up and saw her rise up into heaven on a five-colored cloud. She looked down at him, smiled, and said, "I'm the first, after all to return to Penglai [the realm of immortals]."

The next time that someone wants to talk to you about Daoism and mentions Laozi and Zhuangzi, you can ask them if they've ever heard of the Daozang or the Three Caverns. There's a whole lot more to the Daoist tradition—hundreds and hundreds of sacred texts—and in the last few decades they're available and accessible for the first time in English, for people like you and me.

Related Traditions—Shinto and Tenrikyo
Lecture 24

Shinto is a rather unusual faith. It is very much concerned with divinities, purification, and the unseen world, yet it has no official scriptures. Shinto is a native Japanese religion concerned with harmonizing the human and natural worlds and regulating relationships with kami—local divinities that are powerful but not necessarily perfect or even immortal. *Kami* is also a term that describes the numinous power found in natural phenomena, such as mountains and seas, earthquakes and storms, and even extraordinary animals and humans. Rather than a set of doctrines, Shinto is more a collection of rituals by which people pay homage to the kami, purify themselves from ritual pollution, celebrate life stages, or express solidarity with their neighbors.

Introduction to Shinto

- Shinto is an unusual faith, with no official scriptures. It is closely tied to the Japanese landscape, with thousands of local shines; it's connected to Japanese history, especially to the origins of the imperial family; and it's a part of many Japanese customs—from annual festivals to mundane events, such as the opening of a business.

- Many Japanese don't consider themselves religious but still participate in Shinto ceremonies. Shinto doesn't require any particular beliefs; it is often thought simply to be an aspect of Japanese life. And because it's rather amorphous in its beliefs, it has long coexisted with Buddhism and Confucianism. People can draw from all three traditions without fear of contradiction or heresy.

- Although Shinto does not have scriptures in the way that we usually think of them, there are nevertheless respected ancient texts that are closely associated with Shinto myths, rituals, and sensibilities. The two most important are early histories of Japan known as the *Kojiki* and *Nihon shoki*. These texts don't provide a foundation for a prescribed set of doctrines or a moral code, but the narratives they recount can tell us something about the values and concerns of the religion, particularly in their first chapters, which include myths of origins.

The *Kojiki*

- In the 7th and 8th centuries C.E., Japan received an influx of cultural innovations from China, initially coming via Korea. The Japanese were exposed to Chinese statecraft, literature, and philosophy; Buddhism came from China to Japan; and the first writing system for the Japanese language was developed, based on Chinese characters. Of course, the Japanese had myths and legends that had been transmitted orally for many generations, but in the 8th century, these were first written down by government officials in two books.

Shinto is an unusual religion in that it focuses on divinities, purification, and the unseen world, yet it has no official scriptures or teachings.

- The *Kojiki* ("*Records of Ancient Matters*") dates to 712 C.E. It was composed orally in Japanese and then transcribed into an idiosyncratic writing system that uses Chinese characters both phonetically and semantically. The *Nihon shoki* ("*Chronicles of Japan*"), sometimes known in the West as the *Nihon-gi*, appeared eight years later, in 720. It's longer, more systematic, and written in the Classical Chinese language.

- The *Kojiki* is divided into three parts; the first tells of divinities and mythical origins, and the next two record genealogical details and anecdotes of emperors from legendary times to the death of Empress Suiko in 628 C.E.

- o The text begins with a number of deities coming into existence, including the male Izanagi ("He Who Invites") and the female Izanami ("She Who Invites"), who were married to each other.

- o The god and goddess agree to produce children through sexual intercourse after they walk around a heavenly pillar. Izanami speaks first, but they both realize that this is improper, and their first child is born malformed.

- o They then walk around the pillar again, with Izanagi speaking first, and their subsequent children, the 14 islands of Japan, are all lovely. They continue having children—some 35 kami of oceans and rivers, mountains, winds, trees, and so on—until Izanami dies in childbirth trying to deliver the fire god.

- The stories of the human emperors are rather tame in comparison to those of the gods, though it is significant that the grandson of Amaterasu, the sun goddess, presented the first emperor of Japan (also her descendant) with three sacred objects: a curved jewel, a mirror, and a sword. These ancient sacred objects are still used in the enthronement ceremonies of Japanese emperors.

- The tales in the *Kojiki* are somewhat strange, but in them, we can see some of the characteristic concerns of Shinto: kami and the natural world; life, death, and reproduction; proper order, gender relations, and purification rituals; and the divine origins of both Japan and the Japanese royal family.

Nihon shoki and *Norito*
- Because the odd writing system of the *Kojiki* is so difficult to decipher, it was not read much until the 18th century; further, the *Nihon shoki*, written in relatively clear Classical Chinese, related many of the same stories, often in more detail and with variant versions.
    - o The *Nihon shoki* has 30 chapters, the first 2 of which recount mythical stories similar to those of the *Kojiki*.

- o The next 28 chapters offer stories of the Japanese emperors, from the legendary Jimmu (said to have lived in the 7th century B.C.E.), to more historical times (starting in about the 6th century C.E.), to the reign of Empress Jito, which ended in 697.

- The *Kojiki* and the *Nihon-gi* were never particularly popular, but because they are the oldest Japanese books, they are often mentioned with regard to Shinto. A better candidate for Shinto "scripture," according to the scholar Joseph Kitagawa, is the *norito*, preserved in the *Engi-shiki* ("*Institutes of the Engi Era*") of 927 C.E. This text is a collection of government regulations in 50 chapters.
  - o Most of the book deals with various offices and ministries charged with taxation, military affairs, justice, and so forth. But the first 10 chapters cover Shinto matters, from festivals and rituals to rules for priests and shrines. The 9th and 10th chapters provide a list of 3,132 kami and the names and locations of their shrines throughout Japan.

  - o The *norito* is found in chapter 8, and it consists of 27 ritual prayers, including praises of the kami, liturgies for various shrines and festivals, petitions for good harvests and the protection of the royal palace, and much more. Unlike the *Kojiki* and the *Nihon-gi*, the ritual prayers of the *norito* were memorized by priests and used regularly in worship, in ways that are similar to the sacred texts of other religious traditions.

Later Shinto

- As you recall, Buddhism played a large role in Japanese history, and for the most part, Buddhism and Shinto coexisted fairly easily. Buddhist monks and Shinto priests worked closely together, and today, most Japanese who participate in Shinto ceremonies also take part in Buddhist rituals on occasion, as well.

- One of the most interesting figures in the history of Shinto was Motoori Norinaga (1730–1801), one of Japan's greatest scholars. Over the course of nearly 35 years of study, he painstakingly deciphered the writing system and grammar of the *Kojiki*, believing it

to be truer to an original Japanese version of religion than the *Nihon shoki*, which had been substantially influenced by Chinese thought.
- Motoori's multivolume, heavily annotated translation was one of the triumphs of the National Studies movement, which sought to understand Japan's native culture.

- Motoori combined a brilliant, critical scholarly analysis of the text with an absolute faith in the kami and their powers. At a time when Westerners were struggling with the implications of academic approaches to the Bible (roughly the era of the American Revolution), Motoori was trying to reconcile his strong commitment to rationality with his belief in the literal reality of the myths in the *Kojiki*.

- Motoori was never quite successful in establishing the *Kojiki* as the sacred scriptural foundation for a Shinto, but during the Meiji Restoration, there was an attempt to make Shinto, purged of Buddhist elements, the official religion of Japan.
  - The Meiji Restoration began in 1868 in the aftermath of foreign incursions into a Japan that had sealed itself off from the outside world for two centuries. Some mid-level samurai wrested control of the nation from the shogun in Tokyo and, claiming to act on behalf of the emperor, embarked on one of the most rapid and successful programs of modernization in world history.

  - In the hope that Shinto might offer a focus for a new national identity, it was declared the sole basis of the government. (Keep in mind that Shinto provided legitimacy for rule by the imperial family, given that there has been only a single dynasty in Japanese history.) Over the next few years, the government took control of all Shinto shrines, and Shinto priests became state employees.

  - There was a backlash from Japanese Buddhists and Christian missionaries, who wanted a more secular government with guarantees of religious freedom, and eventually, the government gave in.

- In 1882, a law was enacted dividing the religion into Shrine Shinto and Sect Shinto. Shrine Shinto, encompassing tens of thousands of local shrines, could continue to be promoted and regulated by the state because it was declared to be a nonreligious expression of Japanese morality and patriotism. Sect Shinto recognized some 13 new religious movements, including Tenrikyo.

- In the early 20th century, Shrine Shinto became entangled with ultranationalism and absolute loyalty to the emperor at a time of increasing militarism, and it was eventually seen as a factor in the lead-up to Japanese aggression in World War II. During the occupation, ties between the government and local shrines were severed. Since that time, Shinto has been regarded as a benign, if unusual, religion.

Tenrikyo
- Over the last two centuries, Japan has been the site of several impressive new religions, including Tenrikyo, which was one of the 13 prewar denominations labeled as Sect Shinto. But Tenrikyo is quite different from Shinto; it is monotheistic, and it has a strong tradition of canonized sacred texts.

- Tenrikyo was founded by a peasant woman named Nakayama Miki (1798–1887). On October 26, 1838, she went into a trance and was possessed by Tenri O no Mikoto, a deity who claimed to be the creator, the true and real kami, God the Parent. He requested Nakayama as his living shrine and spokesperson. For the next 50 years, Miki continued to receive revelations from this divinity and taught them to her followers.

- Tenrikyo recognizes three books of scripture: the Ofudesaki ("Tip of the Writing Brush"), comprising 1,711 short poems written by Miki, primarily from 1874 to 1882; the Mikagura-uta ("Songs for the Service"), which is 14 songs written by Miki and used in regular worship ceremonies; and the Osashizu ("Divine Directions"), seven volumes of nearly 20,000 revelations given by Miki's successor, Izo Iburi, from 1887 to 1907.

Suggested Reading

Aston, trans., *Nihongi*.

Breen and Teeuwen, *A New History of Shinto*.

Bock, trans., *Engi-Shiki*.

Earhart, *Japanese Religion*.

Nakayama, *Ofudesaki*.

Philippi, trans., *Kojiki*.

———, trans., *Norito*.

Thomsen, *The New Religions of Japan*.

Questions to Consider

1. How did two early histories of Japan end up playing a scripture-like role in Shinto?

2. Why has Tenrikyo been one of the few 19th-century religions to continue growing into the 21st century?

Related Traditions—Shinto and Tenrikyo
Lecture 24—Transcript

Hello, again. This lecture is about Shinto, one of the major religions in Japan; but Shinto is a rather unusual faith. Just as Confucianism has many of the characteristics of religion—such as ceremonies, a moral code, textual experts, ideas of self-cultivation and transcendence—without a great deal of emphasis on the gods or an afterlife, Shinto offers nearly the opposite. It's very much concerned with divinities, purification, and the unseen world; yet, as one mid-20th century source put it: "Shinto, 'the way of the gods,' has no official scriptures, no founder, and no organized teachings; yet it is a powerful religious influence." The source that I've just quoted was a 1948 report prepared by the General Headquarters for the Supreme Commander for the Allied Powers; that is, the Occupation forces in Japan after World War II. We'll talk later about the why the Allies took such an interest in Shinto—I'll give you a hint now: It had something to do with emperor worship—but here, I'll simply note that it wasn't the first time that Japanese governing authorities had stepped in to define a religion.

If Shinto has no official scriptures, then what's it doing in a course on sacred texts? We'll once again need to adjust our definitions and expectations a little; but it's actually fairly common for anthologies of world scripture to include selections from early Shinto writings. Shinto is a native Japanese religion concerned with harmonizing the human and the natural worlds, and regulating relationships with kami. Kami are local divinities that are powerful but not necessarily perfect or even immortal. Although generally unseen, the kami inhabit this world and can send blessings or cause misfortunes. Kami is also a term that describes the numinous power found in natural phenomena such as mountains and seas, rocks and trees, earthquakes and storms, and even in extraordinary animals and humans; it's said that a particularly old tree may have a lot of kami. Rather than a set of doctrines, Shinto is more of a collection of rituals by which people pay homage to the kami or they purify themselves from ritual pollution, often having to do with contact with the dead; or they might celebrate life stages or express solidarity with their neighbors.

Shinto is closely tied to the Japanese landscape, with thousands of local shrines; it's connected to Japanese history, and especially to the origins of the imperial family; and it's a part of many Japanese customs, from annual festivals to mundane events such as opening a business or breaking ground for a building. Many Japanese don't consider themselves religious but still participate regularly in Shinto ceremonies. You don't have to believe anything in particular; Shinto is often thought to be simply an aspect of Japanese life; and because it's rather amorphous in its beliefs, it's long coexisted with Buddhism and Confucianism. You can draw from all three traditions without any fear of contradiction or heresy.

Although Shinto doesn't have scriptures in the way that we usually think of them, there are nevertheless respected ancient texts that are closely associated with Shinto myths, rituals, and sensibilities. The two most important are early histories of Japan known as the *Kojiki* and the *Nihon shoki*. These two books are the oldest books in Japan, and they have been continuously studied by people who we might call Shinto or even other Japanese. They're not used in worship, and they don't provide a foundation for a prescribed set of doctrines or a moral code; Shinto doesn't really operate along those lines. But the narratives that those two books contain can tell us something about the values and concerns of Shinto, particularly in their first chapters, which include myths of origins.

In the 7th and the 8th centuries C.E., Japan received an influx of cultural innovations from China, coming initially via Korea. Educated Japanese learned Chinese and were exposed to Chinese statecraft, literature, and philosophy; Buddhism came from China to Japan at about the same time (it also came through Korea); and the first writing system for the Japanese language was also developed in that period based on Chinese characters. That actually wasn't a particularly natural fit. Chinese and Japanese belong to two entirely different language families; so it would make about as much sense to use Chinese characters to write English, with some characters being borrowed for their sounds perhaps and others for their meanings.

As with many peoples, the Japanese had myths and legends that had been transmitted orally for many generations, but in the 8th century C.E. these were first written down by government officials into two books that we've mentioned so far, and the first that we'll talk about is the *Kojiki*. The *Kojiki* (it means "Records of Ancient Matters") dates to 712 C.E. It was composed orally in Japanese and then was transcribed into an idiosyncratic writing system that uses Chinese characters both phonetically and semantically; so the system of writing was actually kind of made up for this text, so it's a pretty unique system of writing. The second text, the *Nihon Shoki* or "Chronicles of Japan," is sometimes known in the West as the *Nihon-gi*, and it appeared eight years later in 720. It's longer, more systematic, and it was written in the Classical Chinese language.

The *Kojiki* seems to record a more distinctly Japanese version of events; but even so, it clearly shows the influence of Chinese thought and models of historical writing. Chinese concepts such as yin and yang show up throughout, as well as a focus on the court and its officials. It's very difficult to know what Japanese religion might've looked like before the arrival of Chinese culture to the Japanese islands. The *Kojiki* is divided into three parts: The first tells of divinities and mythical origins, and then the next two record genealogical details and anecdotes of emperors from legendary times until the death of Empress Suiko in 628 C.E. The text of the *Kojiki* begins with a number of deities coming into existence, including the male Izanagi ("He Who Invites") and the female Izanami ("She Who Invites"), and those two, Izanagi and Izanami, were married to each other. Then the story goes like this:

> All the Heavenly deities commanded the two deities [Izanagi] and [Izanami], ordering them to "make, consolidate, and give birth to this drifting land." Granting to them a heavenly jeweled spear, they thus deigned to charge them. So the two deities, standing upon the Floating Bridge of Heaven, pushed down the jeweled spear and stirred with it, whereupon, when they had stirred the brine till it went curdle-curdle, and drew the spear up, the brine that dripped down from the end of the spear was piled up and became an island.

This was the first island of Japan according to the *Kojiki*, in this traditional legend.

Izanagi and Izanami agreed to produce children through sexual intercourse, but first they walked around a heavenly pillar, in opposite directions, after which Izanami said, "What a fine young man," and Izanagi, coming around the other side, said, "What a fine young woman." Then they realized that it wasn't proper for the woman to speak first, but they went ahead and their first child was born malformed. Then they went around the pillar again, with Izanagi speaking first (the male speaking first), and their subsequent children, the 14 islands of Japan, were all lovely. They kept having children, some 35 deities in all—so these are kami, deities of oceans and rivers, mountains, winds, trees, etc.—until Izanami died in childbirth trying to deliver the fire god (you can imagine how dangerous that delivery might've been).

Izanagi, the husband, went to the underworld looking for his wife, Izanami. He found her in the dark, but she'd already eaten some of the food there and couldn't return with him (it sounds a little bit like the Greek myth of Persephone). Going to consult with the lords of the underworld, she told her husband not to look at her; but when he couldn't resist and produced some light, he saw her corpse wriggling with maggots. Terrified at the sight, he ran away and then cleansed himself at a river. When he washed his left eye, the sun goddess Amaterasu was born; the moon god appeared when he washed his right eye; and then cleaning his nose, there came Susanoo, a valiant male kami. Amaterasu, the sun goddess, eventually became the ancestor of the Yamato clan, the ruling house of Japan.

The stories go on from the Kojiki: Susanoo was a wild and mischievous child; and when Amaterasu was disgusted by her brother's actions, she hid herself in a cave, after which the world was darkened (since she was the sun goddess). The other kami, trying to lure her out, gathered outside the cave and hung a mirror and a curved jewel from a tree. One of the goddesses did a spirit-possessed dance, exposing her breasts and genitals. The other deities laughed, and when Amaterasu heard that laughing and then peeked out to see what was happening, she caught a glimpse of herself in a mirror, which they'd hung up in the tree, and then that drew her out even further until she was caught by the gods and light again filled the earth.

The stories of the human emperors that follow are rather tame in comparison, though it's significant that the grandson of Amaterasu presented the first emperor of Japan—who's also her descendant—with three sacred objects: the curved jewel and mirror that were in the tree, along with a sword that Susanoo had given to his sister as a token of his apology. Susanoo had found that sword in the body of a giant eight-headed serpent he'd killed. Although they're not open to public view, the ancient sacred regalia of a jewel, a mirror, and a sword are still used in the enthronement ceremonies of Japanese emperors today.

These are perhaps strange tales; but in them we can see some of the characteristic concerns of Shinto: They're concerned with kami and the natural world; with life, death, and reproduction; with proper order, gender relations, and purification rituals; and the divine origins of both the Japanese islands and the Japanese royal family.

Because the odd, unique writing system of the *Kojiki* is so difficult to decipher, it wasn't read much until the 18th century; especially since the *Nihon shoki*—that's the second of those early histories—was written in relatively clear Classical Chinese; so lots of people could read that fairly easily, and that text related many of these same stories as in the *Kojiki*, often in more detail and with some variants as well.

The *Nihon shoki*, completed in 720 C.E., has 30 chapters, the first two of which recount the "Age of the Gods"; that is, the sort of mythical stories that I've just been telling. The next 28 chapters offer stories of the Japanese emperors, from the legendary Jimmu, said to have lived in the 7th century B.C.E., to more historical times, starting in about the 6th century C.E. when Japanese civilization as we know it gets started, to the reign of Empress Jito, which ended in 697. It covers a somewhat longer time period than the *Kojiki*, and it shows a great deal more Chinese influence.

The *Kojiki* and the *Nihon-gi* were never particularly popular or well known among the masses; but they're the oldest Japanese books, so they're often mentioned with regard to Shinto. A better candidate for Shinto scripture, however, at least according to the scholar Joseph Kitagawa, is the *norito*, preserved in a book called the *Engi-shiki* of 927. The *Engi-shiki* (it means the "Institutes of the Engi Era") is a collection of government regulations in 50 chapters. Most of the book deals with various offices and ministries charged with taxation, military affairs, justice, the treasury, the imperial household, and so forth; but the first 10 chapters cover Shinto matters, from festivals and rituals to rules for priests and shrines, with particular attention being given to the Grand Shrine at Ise, dedicated to Amaterasu, protected by the imperial family, and one of the holiest sites in Japan. The Ise Shrine, with its unique wooden architecture, has been rebuilt every 20 years according to the very precise directions of the *Engi-shiki* since the 7th century. The last rebuilding of this grand shrine was completed in 2013; and if you go online, you can see videos on YouTube or elsewhere. It's actually a long process that takes place over many years, but it finally has its culmination in 2013; and you have to go look at some of this grand ritual and ceremony.

The 9th and 10th chapters of the *Engi-shiki* provide a list of 3,132 kami and the names and locations of their shrines throughout Japan. You see, the government has been involved in regulating the religious affairs of Japan for a very long time; it specifies, "Here's the gods that are worshiped, here are the places, the shrines, etc." in basically a government document. The *norito*, which is the part of this text that seems the most like scripture, is found in chapter 8, and it consists of 27 ritual prayers. These include praises of the various kami, liturgies for various shrines and festivals, petitions for good harvests and the protection of the royal palace, exorcisms, and purification from the effects of such offenses as tampering with irrigation systems, emptying excrement in improper places, leprosy, incest, attacks of insects or birds, calamities from kami, etc. Notice that some of these are sins, but others are simply misfortunes or natural disasters. But in Shinto, sometimes the lines are sort of blurred; you need to do purification rituals for both sins and natural disasters.

Unlike the *Kojiki* and the *Nihon-gi*, the ritual prayers of the Norito were memorized by priests and they were used regularly in worship in ways that are similar to the sacred texts of other religious traditions. To give just one example, here's the prayer that should be said on rebuilding the Grand Shrine at Ise:

> By the solemn command of the Sovereign Grandchild, I humbly speak in the solemn presence of the Great Sovereign Deity. In accordance with ancient custom, the great shrine is built anew once

> in twenty years. The various articles of clothing of fifty-four types, and the sacred treasures of twenty-one types are provided, and exorcism, purification, and cleansing are performed.

These words would be said in conjunction with that once-every-20-years ceremony.

As you'll recall from earlier lectures, Buddhism played a large role in Japanese history; and for the most part, Buddhism and Shinto coexisted fairly easily. For instance, Shinto shrines and Buddhist temples were often built side by side, with the idea that kami would protect the Buddhist deities in the temples next door. At times, the kami were even considered to be manifestations of Buddhas; remember that bodhisattvas could take various forms. Buddhist monks and Shinto priests work closely together; and today, most Japanese who participate in Shinto ceremonies also take part in Buddhist rituals on occasion as well.

One of the most interesting figures in the history of Shinto was a scholar named Motoori Norinaga. He lived from 1730–1801, and he was one of Japan's greatest scholars. He's well known for his historical, literary, and linguistic analysis of the 11th-century novel, *The Tale of Genji*, which is a marvelous novel; but the project that was closest to his heart was the investigation of the *Kojiki*, which had been neglected and disregarded for nearly a thousand years. Motoori painstakingly deciphered the writing system and the grammar over the course of nearly 35 years of study, believing that the *Kojiki* was truer to an original Japanese version of religion than the *Nihon shoki*, which had been substantially influenced by Chinese thought. Motoori's multivolume, heavily annotated translation of the *Kojiki* was one of the triumphs of the National Studies movement, which sought to understand Japan's native culture, as opposed to the Confucianism and the Buddhism that had been imported from China and had long been dominant in Japanese intellectual life.

Even more strikingly, Motoori combined a brilliant, critical scholarly analysis of the text with an absolute faith in the kami and their powers. At a time when Westerners were struggling with the implications of academic approaches to the Bible—so this is roughly the era of the American

Revolution when there start to be skeptics and deists and such—Motoori in Japan was himself trying to reconcile his strong commitment to rationality with his belief in the literal reality of the myths in the *Kojiki*. Well aware of the limitations of human reason, he argued that the *Kojiki* must contain revealed, eternal truths because, he says, "who would fabricate such shallow sounding, incredible things?" (Remember those stories about Izanagi and Izanami.) You might imagine the difficulty of believing, in the early modern period, that the Sun actually is a goddess, namely Amaterasu; you can see the kind of dilemma that he's in. In later lectures, we'll see similar tensions between faith and reason in the scholarly analysis of the Bible.

Motoori was never quite successful in establishing the *Kojiki* as the sacred scriptural foundation for a Shinto, but during the Meiji Restoration there was an attempt to make Shinto, purged of Buddhist elements, the official religion of Japan. The Meiji Restoration began in 1868, in the aftermath of foreign incursions into a Japan that had sealed itself off from the outside world for two centuries. This opening up, which was pretty traumatic, began when a formidable contingent of the U.S. Navy sailed into the bay at Yokohama in 1853 under Commodore Matthew Perry, and he told the Japanese to open up to international trade or face dire consequences. Some of the midlevel samurai at the time wrested control of the nation from the Shogun who was ruling in Tokyo and, claiming to act on behalf of the emperor down in Kyoto, they embarked on one of the most rapid and successful programs of modernization in world history. In just a few years, they went from being basically a medieval culture fighting with swords and spears to being able to defeat a modern European navy; actually they defeated Russia in 1905. It was an astonishing move towards industrialization and modernization.

These samurai were hoping that Shinto might offer the focus for a new national identity; so in 1868, Shinto was declared the sole basis of the government, and a powerful Department of Shinto was established. Keep in mind that Shinto provided legitimacy for rule by the imperial family since there's only been a single dynasty in all of Japanese history. The current emperor of Japan still traces his lineage back to Amaterasu. The contrast with China is pretty striking, where there are a couple of dozen dynasties in China. What happens in Japan is there's always an imperial line, and they live in the court at Kyoto. They reign, but they don't always rule; so the most powerful person (in Japanese history) will make himself the shogun up in Tokyo and will run things, but there's still an imperial family. So in Japan, when the opportunity or the need for modernization comes, those samurai say, "We're going to support the emperor and rebel against the shogun," which offers them a locus, a place to put their loyalties and to claim nationalism; and Shintoism becomes part of that process.

A few years after this Meiji Restoration in 1868—they're restoring the emperor to power is the idea of this—the government took control of all Shinto shrines, and Shinto priests became state employees. There was a backlash, however, from Japanese Buddhists and from Christian missionaries who wanted a more secular government with guarantees of religious freedom for all; and eventually the government gave in, they backed off a bit. In 1882, there was a law that divided the religion into Shrine Shinto and Sect Shinto. Shrine Shinto encompassed tens of thousands of local shrines and could continue to be promoted and regulated by the state because it was declared to be a nonreligious expression of Japanese morality and patriotism. So this kind of local Shinto was the sort of thing you might see in, say, Mount Fuji, which is thought to be a mountain with a lot of kami there; and it's just part of what it means to be Japanese, to show respect and reverence for that mountain. That's Shrine Shinto; Sect Shinto, on the other hand, recognized some 13 new religious movements, including Tenrikyo, which we'll talk about in a moment.

In the early 20th century, Shrine Shinto became entangled with ultranationalism and absolute loyalty the emperor at a time of increasing militarism, and it was eventually seen as a factor in the lead up to Japanese aggression in World War II. During the Occupation after the war, ties between the government and local shrines were severed; and on January 1, 1946, Emperor Hirohito issued a proclamation declaring that despite his auspicious lineage that went back to the sun goddess Amaterasu, he wasn't, in fact, a living god. Since then, Shinto has been regarded as a benign, if somewhat unusual, religion, and is no longer a focus for ultranationalism in Japan.

Over the last two centuries, Japan has been the site of several impressive new religions. One of those, Soka Gakkai, is a lay Buddhist movement based on the Lotus Sutra and the teaching of the 13th-century Japanese priest Nichiren, and it claims some 12 million followers around the world. A similar, more distinctive faith is Tenrikyo, which was one of the 13 prewar denominations labeled as Sect Shinto. But the label actually doesn't work that well; Tenrikyo is quite different from Shinto. For one thing, Tenrikyo is monotheistic, and it has a strong tradition of canonized sacred texts. There are about 2 million adherents of Tenrikyo today. The religion was founded by a peasant woman named Nakayama Miki, who lived from 1798–1887. On October 26, 1838, she summoned an exorcist to heal her husband and her son, who were ailing. The procedure required the services of a female spirit medium, and when that medium could not be found, Miki offered to take her place. Followers of Tenrikyo usually refer to Nakayama Miki by her given name, Miki, so I'll do that as well in this lecture. Remember in Japan, as well as in China, the family name (Nakayama) comes before the given name (Miki).

As Miki went into a trance, she was possessed by Tenri O no Mikoto, a deity who claimed to be the creator, the true and real kami, God the Parent; and he requested that Miki be his living shrine and his spokesperson. For the next 50 years, Miki—and she's known to her followers as Oyasama, the "Beloved Parent"—continued to receive revelations from this divinity and she taught them to her followers, many of whom had come to her for healing and for easy childbirth. She taught that we're all the children of the God the Parent, who wants us to live a Joyous Life—and that's a technical term in Tenrikyo, so it's often capitalized—free from pain, illness, and conflict. This can be done by purifying our minds of the Eight Mental Dusts that should be swept away; so those Eight Mental Dusts are: miserliness, covetousness, hatred, selfish love, enmity, anger, greed, and arrogance; so we should just sweep those away. According to Miki, our bodies are only "borrowed things" and are thus not entirely under our control. Our minds, however, are our own; and they can find the Joyous Life through spontaneous acts of service, as well as performing the rituals that were revealed to Miki, including sacred music, dances, and songs.

Tenrikyo recognizes three books of scripture, the first of which is the Ofudesaki, it means the "Tip of the Writing Brush"; and that's comprised of 1,711 very short poems written by Miki from 1869–1882, with most written after 1874 when Miki was in her late 70s and early 80s. Because of persecution from the government, the collection of these sacred texts, of these hymns and poems, was held secretly by Tenrikyo leaders until 1928 when it was first published, though it was banned again during the war years. The second sacred text is the Mikagura-uta, "Songs for the Service," which is 14 songs written by Miki from 1866–1882. These are used in regular worship ceremonies, along with prescribed hand motions; and it's actually quite graceful to watch, you should look at this on YouTube and watch people recite these or sing these songs and then do the motions that go with them. Finally, the third book of Tenrikyo scripture is called the Osashizu, the "Divine Directions," which is made up of seven volumes of nearly 20,000 revelations given by Miki's successor Izo Iburi from 1887–1907, and the answers to questions, and the answers come through sort of divine revelation. The first two texts of these Tenrikyo scriptures, along with a few selections from the third, have been available in English since the 1970s.

Just a couple of quotations: The Songs for the Service begins like this:

> "Sweep away all evils [the dust that you sweep away] and save us, oh God our Parent." And he answers, "Listen, for I never tell you anything wrong. In the manner of Earth and Heaven I created man and wife, the dawn of human life.... I, God the Parent, reveal myself unto you and explain everything, and the whole world shall bloom. I hasten to save you all, Therefore, all souls of the world, rejoice and be happy."

In the Tip of the Writing Brush, God the Parent speaks through Nakayama Miki and he claims priority over the Shinto gods, declaring "I drew forth Izanagi and Izanami and taught them the providence of how to begin human beings"—remember those stories from the *Kojiki*—and the God in Tenrikyo urges proper worship and kindness. But most of what comes through these texts is a message of love and joyful existence; so it says:

> Looking all over the world and through all ages, I find no one who is evil. Among all humankind, there is no one who is evil. It is only a bit of dust stuck on. [Remember the Eight Mental Dusts that were mentioned earlier: miserliness, covetousness, hatred, selfish love, enmity, anger, greed, and arrogance; but those are just stuck on to

beings who were originally pure and not evil.] [The text continues] Hereafter, calm your minds and ponder. Make sure you will not be remorseful later. Long have you wandered on your path until now. You must be very tired of it. Finally this time, a trustworthy place of worship has begun to appear. Be convinced of it!

What a lovely message of hope and comfort! It's no wonder that Tenrikyo is one of the few of the so-called New Religions in Japan that has continued to flourish and even begun to spread abroad.

Christian Testaments Old and New
Lecture 25

Despite the fact that all Christians view the Bible as authoritative, there is a tremendous variety of doctrine and practice among different denominations in Christianity. In the next few lectures, we'll look at the origins and different voices within the Christian portion of the Bible, the New Testament. Today, the Christian Bible is nearly everywhere; it is the most published book in history, with more translations into more languages than any other text, sacred or otherwise. Yet the Bible's path from the ancient world to contemporary bookshelves and pulpits has been rather complicated. There's a fascinating story behind the book that is familiar to so many.

Hebrew Scriptures in Greek
- Christianity began in 1st-century Palestine as a Jewish reform movement. Jesus and his earliest followers were Jews who spoke Aramaic and could read the Hebrew scriptures. Jesus was apparently a charismatic teacher and miracle worker, but he didn't write anything himself, and no firsthand accounts of him have survived in Aramaic or Hebrew. The only records we have are in Greek; thus, everything we know about Jesus has been edited and translated at least once.

- According to Christian sources from the late 1st century (especially Acts 2–3, 8), in Greek, Jesus's followers saw him as the fulfillment of Hebrew prophecies. They claimed that his life had been foretold in some of the Psalms, that he was the future prophet that Moses had spoken of in Deuteronomy 18, and that Isaiah's description of God's suffering servant in Isaiah 53 was about Jesus. There were some creative reinterpretations in these readings.
    - For instance, although there had been a long tradition in Judaism of a coming Messiah, the term *messiah* ("anointed one") is always used in the Tanakh to refer to a human figure.

- ○ The notion that the Messiah would be a spiritual rather than a political leader and that he would suffer for the sins of others was a Christian reinterpretation.

- The larger point here is that the first Christians did not have any sacred texts of their own; they accepted the Jewish scriptures as authoritative. But Christianity's rise to prominence didn't begin until it was taken out of its original Jewish context and put into the larger Greco-Roman world by missionaries. Gentile Christians and even Jewish converts outside of Palestine adopted the Septuagint—the Greek translation of the Hebrew Bible—as their first scripture.

  The first generations of Christians did not have their own sacred text, and the one that eventually came together is removed from the historical Jesus who stands at the center of the faith.

  - ○ But translations can be tricky. For example, the Septuagint translated the Hebrew word *almah* ("young woman") in Isaiah 7:14 as *parthenos*, or "virgin"; thus, the verse reads, "The virgin will conceive and give birth to a son, and will call him Immanuel."

  - ○ Early Christians, reading the Greek version, seized upon this as a prophecy of Jesus's virgin birth, even though the Hebrew doesn't exactly say that.

The First Christian Writings
- The first Christian writings were not the Gospels but the letters of Paul, the earliest of which, 1 Thessalonians, was written about 49–51 C.E., about 20 years after the death of Jesus. Paul began as an opponent of Christianity, but after a visionary experience, he

joined the Christian movement and became one of its most successful missionaries.

- Paul went on three missionary journeys though Palestine, Turkey, and Greece, preaching the Christian gospel, establishing local congregations, then moving on. Every so often, Paul wrote letters, in Greek, back to the Christian communities he had founded or, in the case of Romans, to a Christian community he hoped to visit.

- In these letters, Paul clarifies doctrine, answers questions, calls people to repentance, and inspires new Christians to greater faith and commitment. He gives no indication that he thought his compositions should stand side-by-side with Hebrew scriptures. His letters were to specific people in response to specific needs. When we read them today, we're overhearing written conversations from long ago, which are sometimes difficult to interpret.

- Somewhat strikingly, Paul doesn't have much to say about the life of Jesus; he mainly talks about his death and resurrection. Perhaps this is because Paul didn't know the Jesus who existed before the Crucifixion, or perhaps Paul was adapting the Christian message to fit his audience.
    - Yet Paul also drew heavily on Hebrew concepts. In one of the rare instances where Paul reports Jesus's words, he says that at the Last Supper, Jesus blessed the bread and wine and said, "This cup is the new covenant in my blood" (1 Cor. 11:25); in a later letter, he refers to himself as a "minister of a new covenant" (2 Cor. 3:6). These seem to be allusions to the new covenant promised by the prophet Jeremiah many centuries earlier (Jer. 31:31–33).

    - Later Christians would speak of their scriptures as a "new covenant," a phrase that was translated into English as "New Testament," but in Paul's lifetime, we still don't have a Christian Bible.

The Gospels and Other Books

- Just before 70 C.E., when the Romans destroyed the Jewish temple, an anonymous Christian wrote a biographical sketch of Jesus's life. This would later be called the Gospel of Mark.

    o Within the next couple of decades, two more Christians produced revised, expanded versions of Mark's gospel, apparently drawing on a short collection of Jesus's sayings now called Q (Matthew and Luke).

    o In about 90 C.E.—some 60 years after Jesus's death—yet another gospel was written, based on a different set of sources that seem to have been connected with the apostle John.

- Over the next century, Christians continued writing new documents, including letters, sermons, histories, apocalyptic discourses, and more gospels. These all circulated separately and were accepted as authoritative by some local congregations and not others.

- By the end of the 2nd century, most Christians accepted the four standard gospels and some set of Paul's letters, but other books were disputed, including Hebrews, Revelation, 2–3 John, Jude, and 2 Peter, along with writings that never made it into the New Testament: the Didache, Shepherd of Hermas, Epistle of Barnabas, Apocalypse of Peter, and 1 Clement.

- These writings were sometimes read in church services, along with selections from the Septuagint, and were consulted when doctrinal questions arose. To promote a unity of belief and practice, it eventually became necessary to sort out which writings were to be considered reliable and authoritative.

    o In the 2nd century, a bishop named Marcion (d. c. 160) proposed a radical suggestion. In reading the Septuagint, Marcion came to the conclusion that the Jewish god of the Old Testament was an angry, vengeful deity who was entirely separate from, and inferior to, the God preached by Jesus.

- o He argued that the Christians should declare themselves a new religion, drop the Jewish scriptures altogether, and adopt a small canon consisting of just 11 books: a shortened version of the Gospel of Luke and 10 letters of Paul. His ideas didn't go far; Marcion was excommunicated and the church reaffirmed its belief in the Septuagint as sacred scripture.

- But if Marcion's Bible would have been too small, others worried that the list of sacred texts might grow too large and encompass all sorts of contradictory writings. It appears that Christian leaders came to evaluate texts on three criteria: Did they claim to be written by apostles or their associates? Were they accepted by numerous communities of Christians? Did they teach doctrine in harmony with the four gospels and the major letters of Paul?

- In the 4th century, we begin to get lists of commonly accepted texts, and finally, in an Easter letter of 367, Athanasius, the bishop of Alexandria, provides the first list that exactly matches the 27 books of the New Testament today. These consist of the four gospels; the book of Acts; 21 letters, mostly written by Paul; and the book of Revelation.

- Athanasius's letter didn't entirely settle the matter. The earliest surviving manuscript copies of the complete Christian Bible are from the late 4th and early 5th centuries, and they still include some noncanonical writings, but for the most part, there came to be a sharp division between the sacred texts on Athanasius's list—that is, the New Testament—and other early Christian writings that might be considered useful and inspiring but not scripture.

Later Developments and Translations
- In the early 16th century, the issue of the Christian canon was reopened by Martin Luther. Luther had published a German translation of the New Testament in 1522, but when his translation of the complete Bible appeared in 1534, he placed the books of the Apocrypha in a separate section between the Old and New Testaments.

- Luther also had grave doubts about the doctrinal reliability of Hebrews, James, Jude, and Revelation. He kept them in the New Testament but moved them all to the end to signal his wariness about them.

- The Catholic Church responded in 1546 with a decree from the Council of Trent reaffirming its position that the Deuterocanonical books (the Apocrypha) are of equal authority with the rest of the Bible.

* Luther's German Bible was enormously influential, in part because of the invention of the printing press about a century earlier. For the first time, ordinary Christians could acquire personal copies of the Bible and study them on their own. Indeed, one of the rallying cries of the Reformation was *sola scriptura* ("by scripture alone"), the idea being that the final authority in Christianity ought to be the Bible rather than tradition or church authorities.

* This sort of independent-minded attitude toward scripture worried many in the Catholic hierarchy. After Luther's German Bible, the floodgates of vernacular translations opened, culminating in 1611 with the King James Bible.

* When Reformers decided to base their faith on the Bible, it became crucially important to have the most accurate version possible. This meant going back to the original Greek, but unlike the Jewish Tanakh, for which there was a standard text produced by the Masoretic scribes, there was no standard Greek New Testament. Instead, there were dozens of hand-copied manuscripts, no two of which were exactly the same.

* The turn back to Greek sources occurred just about the time that the Greek-speaking Byzantine Empire fell to Muslim invaders in 1453. Eastern Orthodox scholars fled to Europe with their precious Greek manuscripts, multiplying the number of manuscripts available. The discovery of additional manuscripts has continued; today, there are more than 5,700, most of which are mere fragments.

- By the late 19th century, it had become obvious that the celebrated King James Bible was not as accurate as it could be. A Revised Version of the King James appeared in 1885, followed by the Revised Standard Version in 1952. Entirely new translations, based on modern scholarly reconstructions of the Greek New Testament soon followed. Today, the standard academic Bible is the New Revised Standard Version (NRSV).

Suggested Reading

American Bible Society, "The State of the Bible, 2013."

Armstrong, *The Bible: A Biography*.

Coogan, ed. *The New Oxford Annotated Bible*.

Harris, *The New Testament: A Student's Introduction*.

Johnson, *The New Testament: A Very Short Introduction*.

Peters, *The Voice, the Word, the Books*.

Questions to Consider

1. In what ways does the Christian Old Testament differ from the Jewish Tanakh, or Hebrew Bible?

2. Why did it take more than 300 years for the Christian New Testament to be canonized in its current form?

Christian Testaments Old and New
Lecture 25—Transcript

With this lecture, we'll turn our attention to Christian scripture; but there's a complication right out of the gate: Many of the sacred texts of Christianity aren't unique to that religion. Three-quarters of the Christian Bible is shared with Jews; so the 27 relatively short books of the New Testament have been grafted onto the Hebrew Bible, which Christians renamed the Old Testament. As we saw in previous lectures, the Old Testament isn't exactly the Hebrew Bible, also known as the Tanakh. The order of the internal books is different; and for some Christians, the Old Testament is longer than the Tanakh. Remember that the Catholic and Eastern Orthodox Bibles include the Apocrypha; those were books that were in the 3rd-century B.C.E. Greek translation of the Hebrew scriptures known as the Septuagint, but that weren't part of the Hebrew Tanakh.

The most important difference, however, is in interpretation. For Jews, the Torah, with its covenants and it laws, is paramount; while Christians have traditionally given more attention to the Prophets, searching their words for predictions and foreshadowing of Jesus Christ, the 1st-century Jew at the center of their religion. The Christian message is that Jesus was God incarnate; that is to say, Jesus was a divine being who came to earth in mortal form. After his birth sometime around 4 B.C.E., he had a three-year ministry while in his early 30s, and then he was executed by the Roman authorities. Somewhat astonishingly, he came back to life three days later—not just being resuscitated but coming back as an eternal being—and he appeared to his disciples and then ascended to heaven. In some nearly unfathomable way, Jesus's death and resurrection made it possible for others to be forgiven of their sins; to be restored to a right relationship with God, and to live forever. Though Jesus himself has ascended to heaven, he's sent the Holy Spirit to guide and to comfort believers.

In that quick summary, I tried to come up with a synopsis of Christianity that I thought most believers might agree with; but despite the fact that all Christians view the Bible as authoritative, there's still a tremendous variety of doctrine and practice among different denominations. Over the next few lectures, we'll look at the origins and different voices in the Christian portion of the Bible, the New Testament, which took several centuries to reach its final form. The first generations of Christians had no such book, and the sacred text that eventually came together—that is, from Matthew to Revelation—is at least a couple of steps removed from the historical Jesus of Nazareth who stands at the center of the faith.

The Christian Bible today is nearly everywhere. It's the most published book in history, with more translations into more languages than any other text, sacred or otherwise. For example, a recent survey reported that 88 percent of American households own a Bible, with an average of four Bibles each. Yet the Bible's path from the ancient world to contemporary bookshelves, book bags, and pulpits has been rather complicated; or perhaps I should say, there's a fascinating story behind the book that's so familiar to so many.

Christianity began in 1st-century Palestine as a Jewish reform movement. Jesus and his earliest followers were Jews who spoke Aramaic as their everyday language and who could read the Hebrew scriptures, which at that time were coalescing into the Torah, the Prophets, and the Writings; into the Tanakh. But the Torah and the Prophets were pretty established at the time of Jesus; they were still deciding what should be in the Writings portion. Jesus was apparently a charismatic teacher and miracle worker, but he didn't write anything himself, and there are no firsthand accounts that have survived in Aramaic or in Hebrew. The only records we have are in Greek, so everything that we know about Jesus has been edited and translated at least once.

According to Christian sources in Greek from the late 1st century—and especially from the book Acts 2–3, and then 8—Jesus's followers saw him as the fulfillment of Hebrew prophecies. They claimed that Jesus's life had been foretold in some of the Psalms; that he was the future prophet that Moses had spoken of in Deuteronomy 18; and that Isaiah's description of God's suffering servant in Isaiah 53 was all about Jesus. There were some creative reinterpretations in these readings. For instance, although there had been a long tradition in Judaism of a coming Messiah, a descendant of David who would restore the monarchy ever since the Exile—the term *messiah*, which means "the Anointed One," is always used in the Tanakh to refer to a human figure—the notion that the Messiah would be a spiritual rather than a political leader, and that he would suffer for the sins of others, was a Christian reinterpretation. The word *Christ* comes from the Greek word Χριστός, which literally means "the anointed one"; it's the Greek translation of the Hebrew word *messiah*. So for Christians, the passage in Isaiah 53 that says, "He was wounded for our transgressions, crushed for our iniquities; upon him was the punishment that made us whole, and by his bruises we are healed" obviously refers to Jesus. Jews read the same passage and, noting that most of it was in the past tense, said, "That must be about Moses, or it must be a metaphor for Israel as a people."

My larger point in all of this is that the first Christians didn't have any sacred texts of their own; they accepted the Jewish scriptures as authoritative. But Christianity didn't amount to much as a Jewish reform movement in Judea. Its rise to prominence began when it was taken out of its original Jewish context and then put into the larger Greco-Roman world by missionaries like Paul.

When Christians began to accept Gentile converts and spread their message in Greek—which was the widely-spoken language of commerce, thought, and culture, sort of like English today—that's when Christianity really took off. Gentile Christians and even Jewish converts outside of Palestine adopted the Septuagint, the Greek version of the Hebrew Bible, as their first scripture.

But translations are tricky, some might even say treacherous. So, for example, the Septuagint translated the Hebrew word *almah*, "young woman," in Isaiah 7:14 as *parthenos*, or "virgin" so that the verse in the Septuagint reads, "The virgin will conceive and give birth to a son, and will call him Immanuel." Early Christians, reading that Greek version, seized upon that verse as a prophecy of Jesus's virgin birth, even though the Hebrew doesn't exactly say that. Instead, it talks about a young woman, *almah*. Even today, some conservatives denounce modern Bible translations that more accurately render Isaiah 7:14 as "the young woman shall conceive," and they denounce those as anti-Christian, even though those same translations explicitly report that Jesus was born to virgin in the first chapters of Matthew and Luke.

But it's important to many Christians to see the Bible as teaching of Jesus from beginning to end—from Genesis to Revelation—with one unitary voice. Remember, though, that the Bible we have today, which combines

Jewish and Christian sources, was a later construct. As an aside, the word *Bible* comes from the Greek term βιβλία, or "books." It should be a reminder that even though we generally encounter it as a single volume, the Bible is actually a library, composed of documents that were written and rewritten over many centuries from many different perspectives. It wasn't until the 4th century that anyone used the Greek word *biblia* to refer to the Old and the New Testaments together.

As you open up the New Testament, it's not surprising that it begins with four accounts of the life of Jesus; after all, Jesus is at the center of the religion. But the first Christian writings, the earliest Christian writings, weren't the Gospels, they were the letters of Paul; the earliest of which, 1 Thessalonians, was written about 49–51 CE, maybe about 20 years after the death of Jesus. Paul began as an opponent of Christianity, a Jew who was persecuting converts to the teachings of Jesus; but after a visionary experience in which he saw the resurrected Jesus telling him to change his ways, Paul joined the Christian movement and became one of its most successful missionaries. Paul was particularly effective in presenting Jesus's message to non-Jews, and he went on three long missionary journeys though Palestine, Turkey, and Greece, preaching the Christian gospel, establishing local congregations, and then moving on. Every so often, he'd write letters, in Greek, back to the Christian communities that he'd founded; or, in the case of Epistle to the Romans, to a Christian community that he hoped to visit for the first time.

In these letters, Paul clarifies doctrine, he answers questions, he calls people to repentance, he inspires new Christians to greater faith and commitment, he attacks his rivals, he offers advice, and he greets old friends. What he doesn't do is write scripture. There are hints that he intended his letters to be circulated, but there's no indication that he thought that his compositions should stand side by side with the Hebrew scriptures, or that they would be universally applicable. Paul's letters were to specific people in response to specific circumstances and needs. When we read them today, we're overhearing written conversations from long ago; we're eavesdropping. Because we're not the original intended audience, sometimes it's a little hard to figure out just what Paul meant in this or that passage. Some of his letters, like Corinthians, are a response to a letter that came to him and we don't have; so it's like we're listening to a telephone conversation, but only on one end.

Somewhat strikingly, Paul doesn't have much to say about the life of Jesus. He mainly talks about his death and resurrection. Indeed, there are only a couple of places where Paul refers to anything that Jesus said or did during his mortal lifetime. Perhaps this is because Paul didn't know Jesus before the crucifixion; but there were other Christian leaders, like Peter, who'd been with Jesus for years and could speak more authoritatively about his words and his deeds. Or perhaps Paul was adapting the Christian message to fit his audience. There were other religious movements in the Greco-Roman world that looked to divine savior figures who'd died and then come back to life again; these are often categorized as Hellenistic mystery religions. Paul presented Jesus in a way that people would understand; whatever the reason, Paul wrote about Jesus in ways that were understandable and compelling to his Greek-speaking peers.

Yet Paul also drew heavily on Hebrew concepts. In one of those rare instances where Paul reports Jesus's words, he says that at the Last Supper, Jesus blessed the bread and wine and then said, "This cup is the new covenant in my blood" (this is from 1 Cor. 11:25); and in a later letter he refers to himself as a "minister of a new covenant" (that's in 2 Corinthians 3). These seem to be allusions to the new covenant promised by the prophet Jeremiah many centuries earlier; a covenant that would be written on the people's hearts (you can read about that in Jeremiah 31). Later Christians would speak of their scriptures as a new covenant, a phrase that was translated into English as the New Testament; but in Paul's lifetime, we still don't have a Christian Bible. Paul never told his new converts to turn to such and such a book or a chapter in their Christian bible and read from it; it was still coming into being.

Just before 70 C.E., when the Romans destroyed the Jewish Temple in Jerusalem; at a time when stories about Jesus were circulating among believers and when eyewitnesses like Peter were passing away, an anonymous Christian wrote a biographical sketch of Jesus's life. This would later be called the Gospel of Mark; and the word *Gospel* there means the "good news." Within the next couple of decades, two more Christians would produce revised, expanded versions of Mark's gospel; apparently drawing on Mark's gospel and a short collection of Jesus's sayings that scholars now call *Q*; it's a hypothetic saying. Those two Christians are Matthew and Luke. Then about 90 C.E.—some 60 years after Jesus's death—yet another gospel was written based on a different set of sources that seem to have been connected with the apostle John, the Gospel of John.

Over the next century, Christians continued writing new documents, including letters (sometimes ascribed to early leaders), sermons, histories, apocalyptic discourses, and more gospels, some of which were wildly different from the four earliest gospels. These all circulated separately as individual scrolls, and were accepted as authoritative by some local congregations and then not by others. Each congregation of Christians had their own group of scrolls that they thought were authoritative, and that they read aloud in church. By the end of the 2nd century, most Christians accepted the four standard gospels and some set of Paul's letters; but other books were disputed, including Hebrews, Revelation, 2–3 John, Jude, and 2 Peter, along with writings that never made it into the New Testament, such as the Didache, the Shepherd of Hermas, the Epistle of Barnabas, the Apocalypse of Peter, and 1 Clement, which was a letter from an early bishop of Rome.

These writings were sometimes read in church services along with selections from the Septuagint, and were consulted when doctrinal questions arose, as they inevitably did. In order to promote a unity of belief and practice, it eventually became necessary to sort out which writings were to be considered reliable and authoritative among all of the scattered Christian communities. In the 2nd century., a bishop named Marcion—and he died about 160—proposed a radical suggestion. In reading the Septuagint, Marcion came to the conclusion that the Jewish god of the Old Testament was an angry, vengeful deity who was entirely separate from and inferior to the God preached by Jesus. In other words, he's saying that the God of the Jews and the God of the Christians, the Heavenly Father, are different gods. Marcion argued that Christians should declare themselves a new religion, drop the Jewish scriptures altogether, and adopt a very small canon consisting of just 11 books: a shortened version of the Gospel of Luke and then 10 letters of Paul (Marcion really liked Paul). Marcion's ideas didn't go too far: He was excommunicated, and the Church reaffirmed its belief in the Septuagint as sacred scripture.

But if Marcion's Bible would've been too small, others worried that the list of sacred texts might grow too large and encompass all sorts of contradictory writings, especially those coming from gnostic communities; and we'll be looking at some of those texts in Lecture 28. We don't have records of specific discussions; but in hindsight, it appears that the Christian leaders evaluated sacred texts on three criteria: First, did they claim to be written by apostles or their associates? Second, were they widely accepted by numerous communities of Christians, not just by isolated congregations here or there? The third criteria: Did they teach doctrine in harmony with the four gospels and the major letters of Paul; were they orthodox in their teachings?

Based on those criteria, we start to get lists of commonly-accepted texts in the 4th century; and finally, in an Easter Letter of 367, Athanasius, the bishop of Alexandria in Egypt, provides the very first list that exactly matches the 27 books of the New Testament today. These consist of the four gospels: the books of Acts, which is a continuation of the Gospel of Luke recounting the early history of the Christian community (so Luke and Acts seem to have been written by the same person); then there are 21 letters, mostly written by Paul; and finally, the New Testament concludes with the book of Revelation, which is an apocalyptic vision of the end-times. Athanasius's letter didn't entirely settle the matter. The earliest surviving manuscript copies of the complete Christian Bible—that is the Old and New Testaments in Greek, bound together in a codex, like modern books—are from the late fourth and the early 5th centuries, and they still include some non-canonical writings; so in those collections, those codices, are things such as the Shepherd of Hermas, the Epistles of Barnabas, and 1 Clement. This was also the case with Jerome's monumental late-4th century translation of the Greek Old and New Testaments into Latin. Jerome included a non-canonical letter of Paul to the Laodiceans, which is also in the Vulgate.

But for the most part, there came to be a sharp division between the sacred texts on Athanasius's list—that is, the New Testament—and other early Christian writings that might be considered useful and inspiring, but not scripture; and, of course, there were other texts that were considered not useful and not inspiring, definitely not scripture. Note that in the centuries in which Christians were working to establish their canon, Jewish rabbis were also reformulating their religion in the aftermath of the destruction of the Temple at Jerusalem. In the Mishnah, as you recall, there was a decisive turn away from the political ambitions of the story of the Davidic monarchy or expectations of the end-times, and the Mishnah turns Jewish attentions and devotions towards legal interpretations of the Law of Moses. It's not really fair to look at Judaism today and see it as a precursor to Christianity. Rabbinical Judaism, the kind that exists today, and Christianity are actually sister religions; they both sprang from the same root and took different directions at the same time after the political and religious crises of 1st-century Judea.

The journey of ancient Jewish and Christian documents to modern Bibles isn't quite complete yet. In the early 16th century, the issue of the Christian canon was reopened by the Reformer Martin Luther. Luther had published a German translation of the New Testament in 1522; but when his translation of the complete Bible appeared in 1534, he placed the books of the Apocrypha in a separate section between the Old and New Testaments. Again, the Apocrypha are those Old Testament books that were included in the Greek Septuagint but not in the Hebrew Masoretic text; so books like Tobit, Judith, Sirach, and 1–2 Maccabees. Luther also had grave doubts about the doctrinal reliability of Hebrews, James, Jude, and Revelation. He kept them in the New Testament, but he moved them all to the end to signal his wariness about them. The Catholic Church responded in 1546 with a decree from the Council of Trent reaffirming the position of those Deuterocanonical books, the Apocrypha, saying they're of equal authority with the rest of the Bible.

Luther's German Bible was enormously influential, in part because of the invention of the printing press about a century earlier. The famous Gutenberg Bible, published in 1455, was a printed edition of the Latin Vulgate, with some copies on calfskin parchment, on vellum, and others on paper; the paper, of course, was much less expensive. For the first time, ordinary Christians could acquire personal copies of the Bible and study them on their own. Indeed, one of the rallying cries of the Reformation was *sola scriptura* ("by scripture alone"); the idea being that the final authority in Christianity ought to be the Bible rather than tradition or Church authorities. Sometimes there's some confusion: The Reformers didn't mean to get rid of all tradition. They accepted a lot of tradition; they just wanted that tradition to be based on the scripture somehow, or scripture to be the highest way of judging the truth of tradition. This sort of independent-minded attitude towards scripture—that's the kind where people have their own copies of the scripture and they study it, and read it themselves, and come to their own interpretation—worried many in the Catholic hierarchy. In fact, as early as 1408—so nearly a half a century before Gutenberg's Bible—the English translation of the Latin Vulgate done by John Wycliffe had been condemned by the Church. After Luther's German Bible came out—which incidentally was the first in a major European language to be done from Hebrew and Greek manuscripts rather than from the Latin Vulgate—the floodgates of vernacular translations opened up in all sorts of European languages.

Of course, we're mostly concerned with English translations in this course, since we're speaking in English, and the key name here is William Tyndale. He'd published his English translation of the New Testament in 1526 and was working on the Old Testament when he was tried for heresy and burned at the stake in 1536. Nevertheless, later English Bibles drew heavily from Tyndale's work, including the Geneva Bible of 1560—which was the first English Bible to be divided into chapters and verses according to the system worked out by the Frenchman Robert Stephanus in the 1550s; of course, having chapters and verses makes it much easier to argue about the Bible and to flip back and forth, and that's an important part of Protestantism (the Geneva Bible was the Bible of Shakespeare—and finally, in 1611 came the King James Bible, a masterpiece of English literature that reigned supreme among English-speaking Protestants for three centuries.

Yet, once again, our story isn't quite complete. When the Reformers decided to base their faith on the Bible, it then became crucially important to have the most accurate version possible; remember, the Bible is going to be the highest religious authority. That meant going back to the original Greek. But unlike the Jewish Tanakh, for which there was a standard text produced by the Masoretic scribes in the 7th to 11th centuries, there was no standard Greek New Testament. Instead there were dozens of hand-copied manuscripts, no two of which were exactly the same, since copying always introduces errors, and then copies of those copies then are going to perpetuate those mistakes. The turn back toward Greek sources occurred just about the time that the Greek-speaking Byzantine Empire fell to Muslim invaders in 1453. Eastern Orthodox scholars with their precious Greek manuscripts and their intimate knowledge of the Greek language fled to Europe, multiplying the number of manuscripts available into the hundreds. The discovery of additional manuscripts has continued, until today there are over 5,700 manuscripts; most of those, however, are just fragments. The earliest are bits of the New Testament written on papyrus, some of which date to the 3rd or the 4th centuries. Other valuable sources include several complete copies of the New Testament from the 4th and the early 5th centuries, such as the Codex Vaticanus, the Codex Alexandrinus (which Richard Bentley rescued from the burning British Library, if you remember from the first lecture), and the Codex Sinaiticus, found at a Greek Orthodox Monastery at Sinai in the 1840s.

Scholars can spend their whole lives sorting through these manuscripts, cataloguing differences, and trying to determine which readings are the earliest. Because mistakes in one manuscript get carried on when other copies are made from that, you can put these manuscripts into families; sort of make pedigrees and figure out where they come from and the different divisions of manuscripts or different families. Most of the variants between all of these manuscripts of the Greek New Testament are rather minor; but remember, with sacred texts—and particularly when those texts are seen as the final authority in a religion—every word matters. I suppose that this emphasis on careful analysis of the earliest sources is part of the Protestant Bias that I spoke of in an earlier lecture, but this reconstruction of the earliest Greek New Testament is truly a glorious scholarly achievement.

By the late 19th century, it had become obvious that the celebrated King James Bible wasn't as accurate as it could be. There were translation errors; its New Testament was based on late, faulty Greek manuscripts (most of the differences don't matter a lot, but there are a few that are going to make a difference in doctrine or how we interpret the religion); and the elevated, eloquent phrasing of the King James Bible didn't really match up with the rather ordinary everyday Greek style of the original, called koine; indeed, the 15th-century diction and obsolete vocabulary of the King James Bible made it increasingly difficult to understand. A Revised Version of the King

James appeared in 1885, followed by the Revised Standard Version in 1952. Entirely new translations, based on that modern scholarly reconstruction of the Greek New Testament, soon followed. Catholics produced the Jerusalem Bible in 1966 and the New American Bible in 1970. 1970 was also the year that British Christians published the New English Bible, and then American Evangelicals got the New International Version in 1978. All of these translations have since been updated, and today the standard academic Bible is the New Revised Standard Version, which I'd highly recommend. It's probably the most broadly-accepted translation today, and it's used by both Catholics and Protestants.

Okay, that's a quick overview of where the sacred texts of Christianity come from. Of course, there are many more details; in fact, there's a whole Great Courses lecture series on *The Story of the Bible*; but this at least will give you the basic idea. In the next couple of lectures, we'll take a closer look at the contents of the New Testament.

I want to end with a thought question, though; and in keeping with the themes of this course, it'll be comparative. Successful religions often take advantage of technological innovations. We saw in a previous lecture how Buddhists in Japan and China were the first people to adopt woodblock printing on a large scale in order to mass produce and disseminate their sacred texts. Early Christians were behind a similar communications revolution in the West: They were the first people to adopt the codex format for their written materials; so these are pages that are written on both sides, and then bound in a book-like form with a spine, a codex. Before Christians came along, notebooks in that form were sometimes used for unimportant or temporary jottings, but serious literature was always written in scrolls. These were pieces of papyrus or animal skins that were glued or sewn together in lengths of 20–26 feet and then rolled up. Christians, however, adopted the codex format for their writings, perhaps because it was less expensive or because at first they didn't consider their texts to be on the same level as the Jewish scriptures that they read in scrolls. But whatever the reason, they soon discovered that codices are much more convenient to work with; you can put more material into a codex—which is why we still use that form today—than in a scroll. The idea that the Old and New Testaments might be a single book is really a function of writing in codices. A similar Christian adoption of new technology happened with the invention of the moveable type printing press in the 15th century, which allowed ordinary believers to own their own codex of the complete scriptures at an affordable price; and, of course, that's crucial to the development of Protestantism.

Now my question: With the advent of the technological revolution known as the Internet, is there some religion that might be able to harness its power for their own spiritual ends? Are there certain kinds of religious practices that might be better suited to the Web than to codices? In some cases, for example in Sikhism, it's easier to find their sacred texts online than in printed form; and for traditions such as Hinduism, in which the chanting or singing of scriptures in ritual performances might take precedence over solitary study, YouTube is a marvelous resource. I'm sure that the Internet will transform religion in future generations. It'll be interesting to see how it plays out and how that affects different religious traditions; because one of the secrets to having a tradition that continues and expands is being able to take advantage of technological and also scholarly resources that come along.

Gospels and Acts
Lecture 26

At a time when the New Testament canon was still being sorted out, a Persian prophet named Mani (c. 216–276) began to preach a dualistic religion. Interestingly, Mani wrote down his revelations personally, and subsequent generations came to believe that every religion needed to have its own sacred book, preferably composed by its founder. The New Testament, however, is still an old-style sacred text. It's not a revelation to Jesus but writings about Jesus. Surprisingly, it gives us not one but four authoritative accounts of Jesus's life, and they do not always agree with one another. In this lecture, we'll see how this situation came into being and what these four accounts say.

Matthew and Mark

- The four gospels have traditionally been ordered Matthew Mark, Luke, and John. Matthew has the most connection to Jewish scripture, including about a dozen "fulfillment citations," that is, passages in which something that Jesus did is said to fulfill something that had been said by one of the Hebrew prophets. There are also discussions of how Jesus, far from being a radical critic of Judaism, actually fulfilled the Law of Moses.

- Matthew begins with Jesus's genealogy and birth, then skips nearly three decades to his baptism by John the Baptist. This is followed by a series of narratives of healings, exorcisms, confrontations with religious authorities, and miracles. There are also teaching episodes, such as the Sermon on the Mount in chapters 5–7 with the Beatitudes, the Lord's Prayer, and famous sayings, such as "Love your enemies." Jesus tells a number of parables, or didactic stories, and he preaches of the coming of the Kingdom of Heaven.
    - These narrative bits, called pericopes, are mostly independent of one another. That is, they are anecdotes without many chronological connections. It would be difficult to construct a

tight biography from them because it's not exactly clear what happened when.

- In fact, the four gospels are not really like modern biographies because they don't try to recount Jesus's life in detail from beginning to end. Rather, they offer a few characteristic acts or sayings of Jesus to give readers a sense of the man.

- Yet on closer inspection, the narratives are not exactly in random order. The stories of Jesus's preaching, as opposed to his actions, are grouped into five sections, the first of which is the Sermon on the Mount.

- Many scholars have suggested that this is not coincidental. Matthew may have organized Jesus's major sayings into five discourses that are reminiscent of the five books of Moses. In other words, the basic structure of the book of Matthew presents Jesus as the new lawgiver.

- The gospel ends with an account of the Last Supper, Jesus's arrest, Crucifixion, burial, and resurrection.

• With the opening of the Gospel of Mark, it's clear that something new is happening. Mark, using political and theological terms of the time, proclaims: "The beginning of the gospel of Jesus Christ, the son of God" (New International Version: "The beginning of the good news about Jesus the Messiah, the son of God").
  - Even though Jesus's identity is made clear to readers from the beginning, those who are around Jesus during his lifetime don't seem to realize who he is, in part because he tells those who figure out that he is the Messiah not to tell anyone.

  - Mark uses many of the same stories and sayings that are in Matthew, but he constructs a portrait of Jesus as a suffering Messiah, which is not exactly what people of the time expected.

- The Gospel of Mark seems truncated compared to Matthew. It begins with Jesus's baptism instead of his birth, and it ends rather abruptly. There is an account of the Last Supper, followed by Jesus's arrest, Crucifixion, and burial. It then tells the story of Mary Magdalene; Mary, the mother of James; and Salome finding the tomb empty three days later.
  - A man in white appeared, telling the women that Jesus had been resurrected and instructing them to tell Peter and the other disciples. The earliest and most reliable manuscripts end with this: "So they went out and fled from the tomb, for terror and amazement had seized them; and they said nothing to anyone, for they were afraid" (NRSV).

  - This is an unsatisfying ending. A longer ending of 10 additional verses was added to the text later, but scholars are unsure whether there was an original conclusion that was somehow lost earlier or whether Mark had intended to leave his readers wondering about what had happened to Jesus.

  - There's a good chance that the short ending was deliberate. Like Matthew, the Gospel of Mark is not a biography of Jesus; it's an invitation to readers to believe. The question is: Now that you know about Jesus's identity as the Messiah, are you going to be like his disciples who abandoned him to the Roman authorities and the women who fled in terror, or are you going to join Mark in proclaiming the good news?

Luke and John
- The Gospel of Luke is much smoother and more refined than Matthew and Mark. The author says that he has put together his account from earlier sources. He addresses someone named Theophilus ("lover of God") and never specifically identifies himself as Luke. In fact, none of the earliest manuscripts of any of the four gospels indicates who wrote them; the names Matthew, Mark, Luke, and John were attached to the gospels in the 2nd century.

- Luke starts with the birth of John the Baptist, followed by the angel's annunciation to Mary that she would be a virgin mother. We learn of Jesus's birth, and then there is one story from his late childhood before the gospel moves on to his ministry when he turned 30, beginning with his baptism by John.
  - Again, we get stories of healings, exorcisms, parables, moral teachings, and debates with religious authorities—many of which we have already seen in Matthew and Mark, though in a different order and with subtle variations.
  - Luke gives more attention to women, prayer, the Holy Spirit, and some of the disreputable elements of society, such as tax collectors, the poor, and Samaritans. Like the other gospels, Luke concludes with the Passion narrative of Jesus's death and resurrection.

- The first three gospels are often called the Synoptic Gospels, from a Greek word meaning "seen together." The Gospel of John, however, is different. Rather than short, independent episodes, it features lengthy discourses in which Jesus, far from trying to hide his identity, openly proclaims his divine status.

- There are only a few stories in John, apart from the Passion narrative, that appear in the other gospels. John has no exorcisms, no parables, and no proclamations of the coming Kingdom of Heaven. Jesus's ministry in John's gospel spans several

John is often considered the most spiritual or mystical of the four New Testament gospels.

years, with multiple trips to Jerusalem, and the Last Supper is not the Passover meal.

- The Gospel of John is organized into two parts: Chapters 1–12 make up the "book of signs," that is, miracles demonstrating that Jesus is the Messiah or even God himself in human form, and chapters 13–20 are the "book of glory," in which Jesus fulfills his divine destiny through his death and resurrection. John ends with an epilogue containing stories about Peter and the risen Lord.

Source Criticism and Redaction Criticism
- Since the 2nd century, Christians have wanted to weave these four accounts together into a single harmonious record of Jesus's words and deeds. Unfortunately, there are just too many differences and contradictions.

- The last two centuries have seen the rise of the historical-critical method in biblical studies. Scholars try to read the text as carefully as possible, then come to their own reasoned conclusions, without relying on tradition or theology. The goal in such an approach is to make observations and provide explanations that people from different religious perspectives, or even no religion, could agree on.

- One of the major puzzles in New Testament source criticism is the relationship among the three Synoptic Gospels. The wording is often so similar that it is obvious that some of the gospel writers were copying from each other, yet there are significant differences among the three gospels, as well.
  - Based on detailed analysis, the most widely accepted solution to the so-called "Synoptic problem" is the two-source hypothesis. Most scholars believe that Mark was written first; then, Matthew and Luke independently produced revised versions of Mark, omitting some details and stories and adding others.

  - The second source is a hypothetical collection of Jesus's sayings called Q (from German *quelle*, or "source"). This would explain why the material that Matthew and Luke have in common that is not in Mark nearly always consists of sayings rather than stories.

- After a consensus was reached about sources, scholars began to analyze exactly what changes Matthew and Luke had made to the Gospel of Mark and to speculate on the theological motivations behind those editorial choices. This approach to the New Testament is called redaction criticism.

The Book of Acts

- After the four gospels, the next book in the New Testament is Acts. It's basically an account of the early Christian community after Jesus's resurrection and tells of missionary efforts and the founding of the church. But it's not exactly an independent work. It's addressed to Theophilus, and it appears to be a sequel to Luke's gospel, written by the same originally anonymous Christian writer.

- Acts begins with the resurrected Jesus being taken up to heaven, followed by the descent of the Holy Spirit upon his disciples at the Jewish festival of Pentecost. Then follows stories of miraculous healings, proclamations of the Christian gospel, and persecutions, mostly focused on the apostle Peter.

- Peter has a revelation directing him to take Christianity to both Jews and non-Jews; then, the second half of Acts focuses on Paul, who does just that. Finally, Paul is arrested in Jerusalem, and when he appeals the charges, he is sent to Rome for trial. The book ends with Paul in the capital city of the empire, under house arrest but preaching the gospel freely.

- One of the major themes in the book of Acts is relations between Christians and Jews. A crucial question is whether Christianity is a sect of Judaism or whether it's more of a new, independent religion. Acts 15 speaks of a gathering of apostles and elders who debated the issue of whether Gentile converts could worship Jesus without first becoming Jews.

- The rest of Acts follows Paul in his missionary endeavors, and indeed, Paul was the most successful of the early Christian missionaries. In the next lecture, we will look more closely at Paul and the Gentile mission, as well as the remaining writings in the New Testament.

Suggested Reading

American Bible Society, *Synopsis of the Four Gospels, Revised Standard Version.*

Attridge, ed., *Harper Collins Study Bible.*

Barton, ed., *Cambridge Companion to the Gospels.*

Collins, *Introduction to the New Testament.*

Ehrman, *The New Testament.*

Puskas and Crump, *An Introduction to the Gospels and Acts.*

Throckmorton, Jr., *Gospel Parallels.*

Questions to Consider

1. What does it mean for Christianity that the New Testament has four equally authoritative yet different accounts of the life of Jesus?

2. What are the Synoptic Gospels, and why are they called that?

3. What interpretive tools have scholars developed to make sense of the origins and meaning of variations among the gospels?

Gospels and Acts
Lecture 26—Transcript

Hello, welcome back. There seems to have been a shift in the world's sacred texts that took place a couple centuries after the arrival of Christianity. At a time when the New Testament canon was still being sorted out, a Persian prophet named Mani—and he lived from about 216–276 C.E.—proclaimed that he'd been called to complete the partial revelations that God had entrusted to Zoroaster, to Buddha, and to Jesus. The religion of Manichaeism offered a dualistic vision in which the spiritual forces of light were in conflict with the evils of the material world, and salvation could come through knowledge of one's true self and knowledge of the divine. Although the Manichaeism has since died out, the faith flourished between the 3rd and the 8th centuries, spreading west to the Roman Empire and east to China. At one point, Manichaeism looked like a serious rival to Christianity, and Saint Augustine, the great theologian of the 4th century, was a follower of Mani for nine years before his conversion to the Christian faith.

What's interesting in the context of this course is Mani's claim that his religion was superior to those of previous eras because, unlike Zoroaster, Buddha, or Jesus, Mani had written down and collected his revelations personally rather than leaving that task to his disciples. The seven scriptures of Manichaeism have since been lost and are now known only through fragments or quotations in other sources, but in subsequent centuries there was a feeling that every religion needed to have its own sacred book, preferably composed by its founder. Thus Muhammad's revelations were put into book form within 20 years of his death, unlike the three centuries that it took Christianity to finalize the New Testament (Muhammad is coming after Manichaeism). The move from revelation to canon has been even faster in more recent religions. For instance, Joseph Smith started his preaching career with the publication of the Book of Mormon in 1830; Nakayama Miki, the founder of Tenrikyo, put together a collection of her revelations in 1882 that circulated among her followers while she was still alive: and Baha'u'llah dictated the Baha'i scriptures to scribes, and then he edited them personally and began to publish them during his lifetime in the late 19th century.

But the New Testament is still an old-style sacred text. It's not a revelation to Jesus; it consists of writings about Jesus, composed by his followers many years after his death; and although the religion is centered on a person who was thought to be the savior of the world, all that we know of that person's life comes through other people's reports, written in a language that he didn't speak. Perhaps even more surprisingly, we don't have a single, authoritative account of Jesus' life. Instead, we have four accounts of equal authority that don't always agree with each other. How did that happen and what do they say? We'll start with a quick overview.

The four gospels have traditionally been ordered Matthew Mark, Luke, and John, which is the way one encounters them in the New Testament. Matthew was the most popular gospel in the early church, and it also has the most connection to Jewish scriptures, including about a dozen "fulfillment citations"; that is, passages in which something that Jesus did, such as being born in Bethlehem to a virgin or teaching in parables, is said to fulfill something that had been said by one of the Hebrew prophets many centuries earlier. There are also discussions of how Jesus, far from being a radical critic of Judaism, actually fulfilled the Law of Moses. Matthew begins with Jesus's genealogy and birth, and then he skips nearly three decades to his baptism by John the Baptist. This is followed by a series of short narratives of healings, exorcisms, confrontations with religious authorities, and miracles like the feeding of 5,000 people with just a few loaves of bread and fishes, or the story of Jesus walking on the water. There are also teaching episodes, such as the Sermon on the Mount in Matthew 5–7 that include the beatitudes (like "blessed are the peacemakers," and so forth), the Lord's Prayer, and famous sayings like "love your enemies" and "do unto others as you would have them do unto you." Jesus tells a number of parables, or didactic stories, and he preaches about the coming of the Kingdom of Heaven.

These narrative bits or units, called pericopes, are mostly independent of each other. Actually, the word pericope is one of the most fun words in the English language; you should say it a couple of times. In these pericopes, there are anecdotes without a lot of chronological connections, so they could easily be rearranged and no one would notice the different. It's hard to construct a tight biography from them because it's not exactly clear what happened when; what the exact sequence was. In fact, the four gospels aren't really like modern biographies, since they don't try to recount Jesus's life in exact detail from the beginning to the end. Rather, they offer a few characteristic acts or sayings of Jesus to give readers a sense of the man. Yet on closer inspection, the narratives in the Gospel of Matthew aren't exactly in random order. The stories of Jesus preaching, as opposed to his actions, are grouped into five sections, the first of which is the Sermon on the Mount. Many scholars have suggested that this isn't coincidental; so Matthew may have organized Jesus's major sayings into five separate discourses that are reminiscent of the five books of Moses. In other words, the basic structure of the Gospel of Matthew presents Jesus as a new lawgiver; as one who's going to replace or supplement what was given to Moses. The Gospel of Matthew ends with an account of the Last Supper, with Jesus's arrest, crucifixion, burial, and then his resurrection.

Turning now to Mark: With the opening of the Gospel of Mark, it's clear that something new is happening. Mark, using political and theological terms of the time, proclaims: "The beginning of the gospel of Jesus Christ, the son of God." The word *gospel* means "good news," and Jesus Christ isn't exactly a name: The word *Christ* is the Greek equivalent of the Hebrew term *Messiah*, or "the anointed one"; so the latest edition of the New International Version has, "The beginning of the good news about Jesus the Messiah, the son of God." But even though Jesus's identity is made clear to readers from the beginning of Mark's gospel, those who are around Jesus during his lifetime don't seem to realize who he is, in part because Jesus keeps telling those who figure out that he's the promised Messiah not to tell anyone else. Mark uses many of the same stories and sayings that we saw in Matthew, but he constructs a portrait of Jesus as a suffering Messiah, which isn't exactly what people of the time had expected.

The Gospel of Mark seems truncated compared to Matthew. It's shorter, and it begins with Jesus's baptism instead of his birth. It also ends rather abruptly. There's an account of the Last Supper; followed by Jesus's arrest, crucifixion, and burial; and then it tells how Mary Magdalene—Mary, the mother of James—and Salome went to the tomb after three days and saw that it was empty. A man in white appeared (this is according to the Gospel of Mark), telling them that Jesus had been resurrected and instructing them to go tell Peter and the other disciples. Then the earliest and most reliable manuscripts, including the 4th-century codices Sinaiticus and Vaticanus, end with these words: "So they [this is the women] went out and fled from the tomb, for terror and amazement had seized them; and they said nothing to anyone, for they were afraid." The end.

Okay, that's a very unsatisfying ending. There are no resurrection appearances; and the women must've said something to someone, otherwise we wouldn't have the story of the man in white at the tomb, right? A longer ending of 10 additional verses was added to the text later, but scholars are unsure whether there was an original conclusion that somehow was lost very early on, or whether Mark had intended to leave his readers hanging there at the empty tomb, wondering themselves what had happened to Jesus. There's a good chance that the short ending was deliberate. Like Matthew, the Gospel of Mark isn't a biography that simply tells about Jesus; it's an invitation to readers to believe. The question is: Now that you know about Jesus's identity as the Messiah, as the son of God, are you going to be like his disciples who abandoned him to the Roman authorities and the women who fled in terror saying nothing, or are you going to join Mark in proclaiming the good news? The Gospels ask, what do you think about Jesus? Or they're designed to provoke that question: What do you think about Jesus?

Turning to the gospel of Luke, the Greek style is much smoother and more refined. Here's how the gospel begins:

> Many have undertaken to draw up an account of the things that have been fulfilled among us, just as they were handed down to us by those who from the first were eyewitnesses and servants of the word. With this in mind, since I myself have carefully investigated everything from the beginning, I too decided to write an orderly account for you, most excellent Theophilus, so that you may know the certainty of the things you have been taught.

This is all one sentence in Greek, which shows a rather sophisticated command of the language; one of the characteristics of Greek is you can make these long, long sentences called the periodic style.

Note that Luke doesn't claim to be an eyewitness himself; he's putting together this account from earlier sources. Although he's addressing someone named Theophilus, who may have been a specific individual, or perhaps any Christian reader—the name *Theophilus* means the "lover of God"—even though he addresses someone specifically, the author never specifically identifies himself as Luke. In fact, none of the earliest manuscripts of any of the four gospels indicate who wrote them. We today refer to Matthew, Mark, Luke, and John for convenience, but these names were attached to those four gospels in the 2nd century, along with very specific biographies: It's said that Matthew was an early disciple who was a tax collector; Mark was an associate of the apostle Peter; Luke was supposed to have been a physician and a travelling companion of Paul; while John was one of the apostles. But in their original form, the gospels were anonymous.

Luke starts with the birth of John the Baptist, followed by the angel's annunciation to Mary that she would be a virgin mother. We learn of Jesus's birth, and then there's just one story from his growing up years—about the time when he was lost in Jerusalem at the age of 12 and ended up in the temple, where his parents eventually found him; so just that one story—and then the gospel moves on to his ministry when he turned 30, beginning with his baptism by John. Luke provides Jesus's genealogy after his baptism, rather than before his birth, and it actually doesn't match up with the one in Matthew. Once again, in Luke, we get stories of healings, exorcisms, parables, moral teachings, and debates with religious authorities; many of which we've already seen in Matthew and Mark, though in a different order and with some subtle variations.

Luke gives more attention to women, prayer, the Holy Spirit, and some of the disreputable elements of society: people like tax collectors, the poor, and Samaritans. Samaritans were a marginalized group of Jews tracing their ancestry back to people who had remained in the land after the conquest of Israel by the Assyrians in 722 B.C.E. For instance, Luke is the only gospel that tells the parable of the Good Samaritan, who aided a traveler in distress when a priest and a Levite wouldn't, even though those people would be expected to be moral examples or good examples of religious living. The juxtaposition between "good" and "Samaritan" would've come as a shock to those who first heard Jesus tell this story; there was a lot of prejudice against

Samaritans. It would be like hearing an account today in a very conservative church in which the hero of a story, who showed true Christian kindness, turned out to be a drug addict, or a lesbian couple, or an atheist professor. Like the other gospels, Luke concludes with the Passion narrative of Jesus's death and his resurrection.

The first three gospels are often called the "synoptic gospels," from a Greek word that means "seen together." The idea is that those three gospels have so much in common that you could line them up into three parallel columns and read them with a single glance. The Gospel of John, however, is very different. Rather than short, independent episodes—those pericopes—it features lengthy discourses in which Jesus, far from trying to hide his identity, openly proclaims his divine status. His words are often cryptic to outsiders, as when he speaks about being born again, or when he declares "I am the bread of life … come down from heaven," but those in the know understand the significance of his words. There are only few stories in John, apart from the Passion narrative, that appear in the other gospels. John has no exorcisms, no parables, and no proclamations of the coming kingdom of heaven. Jesus's ministry in the fourth gospel spans several years, with multiple trips to Jerusalem, and the Last Supper isn't the Passover meal, all of which are quite different from the synoptic gospels.

John is often considered the most spiritual, or even mystical, of the four gospels; and you can see why from its very first words, which begin not with Jesus's birth or baptism, but with his primordial existence as God in heaven. The Gospel of John starts:

> In the beginning was the Word, and the Word was with God, and the Word was God. He was with God in the beginning. Through him all things came into being, not one thing came into being except through him. What has come into being in him was life, life that was the light of men; and light shines in darkness, and darkness could not overpower it.

It's that "Word" in the beginning that will eventually become Jesus Christ.

The Gospel of John is organized into two parts: Chapters 1–12 make up the "book of signs"; that is, miracles demonstrating that Jesus is the Messiah or even God himself in human form. The second part of the Gospel of John are chapters 13–20, which are the "book of glory," in which Jesus fulfills his divine destiny through his death and resurrection. Strikingly, chapters 13–19 all take place within a single 24-hour period. John ends with an epilogue, chapter 21, that contains stories about Peter and the risen Lord, with a note that this gospel was written by the "beloved disciple," who goes unnamed; remember that it's only later on that we're going to identify that disciple as John.

So there you have it: Three gospels that are rather similar, and then John; altogether four accounts of the life of Jesus. Since the 2nd century, Christians have wanted to weave these together into a single, harmonious record of Jesus's words and deeds that smoothed over or omitted some of the discrepancies. The first attempt was by an early Christian named Tatian in about 170 C.E., and his book was called the Diatessaron; it means "made from four." But it can't really be done, there are just too many differences and out-and-out contradictions between those four Gospels; so the Church ended up sticking with four distinct Gospels, though even today, Christmas pageants have to blend together details from different gospels: The three wise men and the star appear only in Matthew; the shepherds, the angels, and the manger are only in Luke.

The last two centuries or so have seen the rise of the historical-critical method in biblical studies. The term *critical* here doesn't mean criticizing or finding fault; rather, it's derived from the Greek word *kritikós*, "able to discern" or "skilled in making judgments." The idea is that scholars try to read the text as carefully as possible, and then come to their own reasoned conclusions without relying on tradition or theology. The goal in such an approach is to make observations and provide explanations that people from different religious perspectives, or even no religion, might agree upon. In an earlier lecture, we saw an example of source criticism when scholars analyzed the Pentateuch, the Five Books of Moses, to identify the different traditions behind it and how they were put together. One of the major puzzles in New Testament source criticism is the relationship between the three synoptic gospels. The wording is often so similar that it's obvious that some of the gospel writers were copying from each other; yet there are significant differences between the three gospels. This can most easily be seen in a synopsis of the gospels; that is, an edition of the gospels that lines up the three accounts side by side, in parallel.

Scholars, of course, study the Greek originals; and based on a detailed analysis of their wording, sequence, and characteristic changes that are made from one to the other, the most widely-accepted solution to the so-called "Synoptic problem" is the Two Source Hypothesis. (The Synoptic problem is that issue of how exactly are these gospels related to each other?") Most scholars now believe that Mark was written first, and then Matthew and Luke independently produced revised versions of Mark, omitting some details and stories and adding others. That's the first source in the Two Source Solution; the second source is a hypothetical collection of Jesus's sayings called *Q*, and that's short for the German word *quelle*, or "source.") This would explain why the material that Matthew and Luke have in common that's not in Mark nearly always consists of sayings rather than stories; they're just quotations mostly, not events that Jesus took part in. Somewhat confusingly, some scholars identify the material unique to Matthew and the material unique to Luke as two additional sources, called *M* and *L*; so they also talk about the Four Source Hypothesis, but it's virtually the same as the Two Source Hypothesis. So Matthew and Luke use Mark and *Q* to put together their gospels.

After a consensus was reached about sources, scholars began to analyze exactly what changes Matthew and Luke had made to the Gospel of Mark, and to speculate on the theological motivations behind those editorial choices. This approach to the New Testament is called "redaction criticism." We can get a sense of it by looking at a story that's included in all three synoptic gospels: Jesus's baptism. This episode would've been a little troubling to early Christians since it seems to indicate that Jesus was a follower of John's, when Christian doctrine insisted that Jesus was actually the superior figure. Mark begins with John the Baptist baptizing those who come to him and confess their sins. Jesus is baptized by John, and then the gospel reports that "a voice came from heaven" saying: "You are my Son, my Beloved; with you I am well pleased." When Matthew retells the story, he adds a conversation in which John at first refuses to baptize Jesus, saying,

"I need to be baptized by you!" Eventually, John is going to consent; but after he does so, a voice come from heaven saying, "This is my Son, the Beloved, with whom I am well pleased." Did you catch that in Mark, the heavenly voice speaks to Jesus as a sort of personal affirmation, while in Matthew the voice addresses the crowd and talks about Jesus? Remember that in Mark, Jesus's true identity is hidden from the crowds, so that difference sort of makes sense.

When it comes to Luke's gospel, he keeps Mark's version of the voice from heaven speaking to Jesus; but he reports that this happened after Jesus had been baptized, while he was praying. Remember that prayer is one of Luke's characteristic themes; he tries to work that into stories regularly. Even more strikingly, Luke first tells the story pf how John the Baptist was imprisoned by King Herod (and he's going to mention that imprisonment in 3:20), before he turns his attention to Jesus's baptism in verse 21; which is a little strange, because you have John in prison before Jesus is baptized. The Gospel of Luke never specifically says that John was the one who did the baptizing; but by shifting around the chronology, Luke makes it clear that John's ministry came to a decisive conclusion and then was superseded by Jesus's authority.

We'll conclude this lecture by looking at one more book in the New Testament. After the four gospels, the next book is Acts; it's basically an account of the early Christian community after Jesus's resurrection, and it tells of missionary efforts and the founding of the Church. But Acts isn't exactly an independent work. It's addressed to Theophilus, just as Luke was, and it appears to be a sequel to Luke's gospel, written by the same originally anonymous Christian writer. One mystery that remains unsolved is that although most of the book of Acts is written in the third-person voice—"he did this" or "they did that"—there are four passages, which range from 8–60 verses, where the narrator shifts to the first person plural. We see that first happening when all of a sudden the gospel will say: "When [Paul] had seen the vision, we immediately tried to cross over to Macedonia." We? Who's the "we" in "we immediately tried to cross over"?

Acts begins with the resurrected Jesus being taken up to heaven, followed by the descent of the Holy Spirit upon his disciples at the Jewish festival of Pentecost. The Spirit is manifest in their spontaneous ability to speak in tongues, or in foreign languages. Then follows stories of miraculous healings, the proclamation of the Christian gospel, and persecutions, mostly focused on the apostle Peter. During the stoning of the first Christian martyr, Stephen, we hear of a young anti-Christian zealot who held the coats of those throwing stones. This was Saul, who a few chapters later will see the resurrected Jesus in vision and convert to Christianity himself, and then is renamed Paul. Peter has a revelation directing him to take Christianity not just to Jews but also to non-Jews, to Gentiles; and then the second half of the book of Acts focuses on Paul, who does just that. Paul goes on three missionary journeys through Palestine, Asia Minor (which is present-day Turkey), and Greece, everywhere he goes preaching of Jesus, making converts, and establishing local congregations. Finally, Paul is arrested at Jerusalem, and when he appeals the charges, he's sent to Rome for trial. The book of Acts ends with Paul in the capital city of the empire, under house arrest but preaching the gospel freely.

One of the major themes in the book of Acts is relations between Christians and Jews. A crucial question is whether Christianity is sect of Judaism, or whether it's more of a new, independent religion. Remember that in the first generations, Jews and Christians shared the same scriptures (the Septuagint) and many of the same beliefs; but in this case, it's religious practices that make the crucial difference. Some early Christians felt that belief in Jesus was an add-on to Judaism; that is to say, when Gentiles were converted to the Christian gospel, they needed to keep all the requirements of the Law of Moses: kosher food, moral principles, regulations for worship, and circumcision. Others, like Paul, argued that the hundreds of rules in the Torah had been superseded by Christ, and that Gentile converts could worship Jesus without first becoming Jews and changing everything about their customs and their lifestyles. In the end, the issue was decided by a council in Jerusalem. Acts 15 speaks of a gathering of apostles and elders who were debating the matter at some length. Peter told of his revelation that the gospel should go to the Gentiles, and Paul shared stories of his success among them. Finally, James put forward a compromise position that was accepted by all: He said Gentiles could become Christian if they kept only four of the Mosaic laws, and these were to abstain from, first, food that had been offered to idols; second, abstain from blood; third, abstain from the meat of animals that had been strangled; and fourth, abstain from fornication. For listeners of this lecture who may be Christian, how many of those prohibitions have you heard in church lately? (Actually, the one about abstaining from blood I think is the desire of the Jehovah's Witnesses not to have anything to do with blood transfusions; they read Acts 15 very, very literally.)

In one of Paul's letters, he said that Peter had been made an apostle to the Jews while he, Paul, had been sent to the Gentiles; he says that in Galatians. The rest of Acts follows Paul in his missionary endeavors; and indeed, Paul was the most successful of the early Christian missionaries.

In next chapter, we'll look more closely at Paul and the Gentile mission, according to his own letters as well as the remaining writings in the New Testament; we'll take it all up there. Then, we'll as the question of how this particular collection of 27 documents, which so obviously came from the minds and pens of human beings, could nevertheless be considered as a repository of eternal truths.

Letters and Apocalypse
Lecture 27

So far, we've talked about five books in the New Testament—the four gospels and Acts. Of the next 22 books, 21 are letters, most of which are ascribed to Paul, and the final book is Revelation, an apocalyptic treatise. Letters were apparently a key mode of communication, instruction, and doctrine in the early church. In this lecture, we'll begin with a detailed analysis of one particular letter, 1 Thessalonians, which was written by Paul to a Christian community he had founded, probably around 50 C.E. If we knew nothing else about Christianity, what could we discern from this letter? We will then close the lecture with a brief survey of the other books in the New Testament.

1 Thessalonians

- In his letter to the Thessalonians, Paul expresses warm feelings for the members of this community, yet he has been a bit worried about them. The letter is his relieved response to a good report he has received about them. In various verses, he says that he is like a brother, a father, and even a mother to the community. He seems to be pulling out all the stops in his efforts to keep them on his side.

Paul's letter to the Thessalonians was probably written around 50 C.E., making it our earliest extant Christian document.

- It seems that the Thessalonians converted in response to some phenomenon that they interpreted as the Holy Spirit. The letter tells us that they are not converted Jews but former pagans or idol worshippers. This is interesting because Acts, written several decades later, tells us that Paul attended the synagogue in Thessalonica and attempted to persuade the Jews that Jesus was the promised Messiah.

- In several verses, Paul mentions that the Thessalonians faced persecution, though once again, Paul's text doesn't quite match up with Acts. From the narrative there, we might expect animosity from the local Jewish community, but Paul tells us that the opponents of the new Christians in Thessalonica are other Gentiles.

- The new Christians in Thessalonica seem to have assumed that if they converted, they would escape death. But some of those who had embraced Paul's new religion had since passed on, and it seemed as if they would not have a share in Christ's new kingdom after all. In his letter, Paul assures the Thessalonians that Christians who have died will enjoy equal blessings with believers who are still alive. When Christ comes again, deceased Christians will rise from their graves.
  o Paul explains that the righteous will be taken up from the earth and, thus, will avoid the destruction that God will pour out on the wicked.

  o This is the origin of the belief of some contemporary Christians in the rapture. But note that Paul assumes that Jesus's Second Coming will occur within the lifetime of himself and many of his original readers.

- Paul also mentions several doctrinal points: God had raised Jesus from the dead; the Holy Spirit will aid believers; prayer matters; Satan is trying to hinder the work; and Jesus will rescue believers from the "coming wrath" and will return again soon, after which Christians will be with the Lord forever.

- Note that there is nothing in the letter about atonement or forgiveness of sins, events from Jesus's life, moral instructions from the Sermon on the Mount, baptism, or the Eucharist. Paul never quotes from the Jewish scriptures, and he doesn't discuss the metaphysical nature of Christ. Instead, 1 Thessalonians seems to be a document of an apocalyptic sect that was expecting the end times to arrive at any moment.

Other Pauline Letters
- Like 1 Thessalonians, the other letters of the New Testament offer evidence of early Christian beliefs and practices, but none was composed as a comprehensive introduction to the religion. And they are not always consistent in their viewpoints.

- After the book of Acts, there are nine Pauline letters addressed to various Christian communities, arranged by length, from longest to shortest. Then follow four letters from Paul to individuals, again in order of descending length.

- Romans lays out Paul's most extensive theological arguments. All humans are sinners, he says, and are subject to God's judgment, but they can be justified, or proclaimed righteous, through their faith in Christ. This process of reconciliation with God is available to both Jews and non-Jews, apart from the Law of Moses.
  o Paul then warns Gentile converts not to think themselves superior to the Jews; God will still be faithful to his promises to Israel.

  o Paul quotes liberally from the Jewish scriptures and provides careful, sophisticated arguments. For many, Romans represents the pinnacle of Christian theology.

- Paul's response to questions he had received on practical matters from the community at Corinth is found in 1 Corinthians. Paul stresses the need for unity, explains his authority as an apostle, and gives specific advice. He condemns those who use the gifts of the Spirit as occasions to look down on others, and he reaffirms the significance of the doctrine of resurrection in Christian theology.

- The book of 2 Corinthians has several jarring shifts of tone and topic; in fact, many scholars believe that it was originally two or more separate letters that were fused together. Paul goes from what is essentially a travelogue to a defense of his ministry and a plea for reconciliation, to an appeal for donations to a fund for poor Christians in Jerusalem, to a denunciation of other missionaries.

- Galatians is Paul's angriest, most polemical letter. Apparently, the Christians at Galatia had been visited by other missionaries who told them that Gentile converts had to be circumcised, contrary to what Paul had preached and the decision of the Jerusalem Council.

- Philippians is a letter written by Paul from prison to strengthen the faith of Christians at Philippi, and Philemon is a short note written on behalf of a runaway slave, addressed to his Christian master.

- The seven letters discussed thus far are all regarded as authentic and were composed from 50 to 60 C.E., but scholars are divided about whether Colossians and 2 Thessalonians were written by Paul or a later disciple or admirer. There is broad consensus that Ephesians, 1–2 Timothy, and Titus are from a later period, perhaps 80–110 C.E., and were attributed to Paul to increase their credibility.

- Hebrews is a sermon in the guise of a letter that explains Jesus's relationship to the Israelite priesthood, proclaiming Christ as the high priest who offered himself as the final sacrifice for sin. Hebrews relies heavily on allusions to Jewish scripture and ritual, and it explores the idea that faith provides insight into heavenly realities. It doesn't sound much like Paul, and even early church fathers doubted that it had been written by him.

General Epistles and Revelation

- The remainder of the New Testament consists of short letters attributed to James, Peter, John, and Jude and the book of Revelation. These letters are often referred to as "general epistles" because they seem to have been written to Christians in general rather than to specific congregations or individuals.
  - They take up such themes as proper Christian conduct, the dangers of false teachers, the seeming delay of Jesus's Second

Coming, and the centrality of love in Christian thought and action.

- o The questions of when and by whom these documents were written are matters of debate, and indeed, there were disputes in the 2nd through 4th centuries about whether they should be included in the Christian canon, but most scholars today date them from the late 1st century to the beginning of the 2nd.

- Revelation is a work of apocalyptic literature, of which there were many examples, both Jewish and Christian, in the late Second Temple period and early centuries of the Common Era. Typically, these texts present a dualistic worldview, with sharp demarcations between the wicked majority and an oppressed minority of the righteous, who are looking for God to bring his wrathful judgment down upon their opponents.

- True to form, the book of Revelation presents itself as a series of visions and prophecies about the end times, when God will intervene directly to destroy the wicked and establish a new heaven and a new earth. There is a great deal of cryptic, sometimes violent imagery, with blood, trumpets, war, natural disasters, angels, and so on.

- The New Testament concludes with an urgent affirmation that this world is coming to an end. One might argue that a great deal of the New Testament was written as a response to what might seem to have been a failure on Jesus's part. The three Synoptic Gospels portray Jesus as the Messiah, an anointed leader or liberator, who proclaimed that God's kingdom was close at hand, yet his death left the work unfinished. Jesus must be coming back at some point to usher in the new kingdom he had promised.
  - o Paul and the Christians in Thessalonica expected his return momentarily, but when it looked as if the Second Coming might take some time, a more formal church organization developed.

- Some scholars have seen the Gospel of John as spiritualizing the concept of God's kingdom, at least to some extent, and 2 Peter, probably the last book written in the New Testament, suggests that human timetables aren't applicable to the Lord and that the delay is actually a manifestation of God's mercy; he's giving people more time to repent.

Conclusions about the New Testament

- The New Testament is an eclectic collection that Christians over the centuries have found inspiring, comforting, and motivating. In fact, perhaps part of what is means to be Christian is to continually read, interpret, apply, and argue over these texts.

- Some believers find the scholarly historical-critical method of scripture study somewhat threatening. When we look for contradictions and inconsistencies or judge sacred texts by the standards of science, archaeology, and literary scholarship, don't we diminish their authority? These are ultimately theological questions, but we can point to three observations that might be helpful in this regard.
  - Fundamentalism, like the historical-critical method, is a relatively new phenomenon. Ideas of biblical infallibility, inerrancy, and literalism themselves have a history and can be debated without overthrowing the whole religion.

  - The focal point of Christianity is a person, not a book, and although the New Testament is one of our primary means of understanding that person, there are others.

  - Finally, although it appears that there is a great deal of the human element in the sacred texts of Christianity, the New Testament never claimed to be an eternal text that had its origins in heaven. How could something human-made have ultimate significance? The religion itself offers a helpful analogy: Just as Jesus was considered in mainstream Christianity to have been both fully human and fully divine, so too, the New Testament is regarded by believers as the product of both human effort and divine inspiration.

Suggested Reading

Brettler, Enns, and Harrington, *The Bible and the Believer*.

Dunn, ed., *The Cambridge Companion to St. Paul*.

Gager, *Reinventing Paul*.

Klein, Blomberg, and Hubbard, Jr., *Introduction to Biblical Interpretation*.

Pagels, *Revelations*.

Sprong, *Re-Claiming the Bible for a Non-Religious World*.

Wright, *Paul in Fresh Perspective*.

Questions to Consider

1. Why have letters played such a crucial role in Christian doctrines and history?

2. How much of Christian teaching has been shaped by Paul, and what other strands are there in traditions and texts from the early church?

Letters and Apocalypse
Lecture 27—Transcript

So far, we've talked about five books in the New Testament: the four gospels and Acts. Of the next 22 books, 21 are letters, sometimes referred to as epistles, most of which are ascribed to Paul. The final book is Revelation, an apocalyptic treatise. Letters were apparently a key mode of communication, instruction, and doctrine in the early Christian church. Generally, I start lectures with an overview and then we focus on a few specific texts; but this time, let's switch things up. I'll begin with a detailed analysis of one particular letter, and then we can move on to a quick survey of the other books in the New Testament.

The letter that I want to examine is 1 Thessalonians, which was written by Paul to the Christian community he'd founded in the northern Greek city of Thessalonica. Paul had been away for a while, and he was probably writing from Corinth, about 50 C.E., making 1 Thessalonians the earliest extant Christian document. It's not too long, just five chapters; maybe three or four pages in printed form. When I read this letter with my students, I ask them to imagine what they'd think of the religion if this letter were the only Christian writing that had survived. That scenario isn't too far removed from the situation with other ancient religions, some of which scholars try to reconstruct on the basis of very limited sources. Or alternatively, they could guess how they might respond to this epistle if they were Jewish or a Gentile in the 1st century reading this letter. I tell them forget everything you know about Christianity and just look at the letter. This putting aside of prior understandings of tradition and theology is akin to the historical-critical method. If this one document were all we had to go by in trying to imagine those new Christians in Thessalonica, what would you say their relationship to Paul was? Why did they convert? What challenges did they face? What did they believe?

First question, about their relationship with Paul: Paul obviously has warm feelings for these people. They are his glory and his joy, he says. He thinks about them all the time, and he's eager to see them again. Yet he's also a bit worried; he says: "For this reason, when I could stand it no longer, I sent [Timothy] to find out about your faith. I was afraid that in some way the tempter might have tempted you and our efforts might have been useless." Timothy has just returned with a good report, and this letter is Paul's relieved response. At the same time, Paul is also a little bit defensive; he insists that his motives for proselytizing weren't selfish, and that he didn't use flattery or deceit with the people of Thessalonica. Why would he say that unless there were some rumors or people suspected such a thing? We also learn that the Thessalonians are people Paul mentions often in his prayers. If you yourself are a praying person, think about the people you mention regularly in your prayers and what kind of relationship you might have with them. In various verses, Paul says that he's like a brother to the Thessalonians, or like a father, and even in another place like a mother. It seems like he's pulling out all the stops, every possible relationship, in an effort to try to keep the Thessalonians on his side.

Second question: Why did they convert? We might assume that their close relationship with Paul had something to do with it; but at 1:5–6, a very specific explanation is given. It says there, and Paul is writing: "Our gospel came to you not simply with words, but also with power, with the Holy Spirit and with deep conviction … in spite of severe suffering, you welcomed the message with the joy given by the Holy Spirit." So there was some phenomenon that they interpreted as the Holy Spirit that had acted upon them; and I'm not sure whether they were speaking in tongues, or whether they'd prophesized, or what, but it had brought them joy. A few verses later there's another important clue as to their pre-conversion background. It says: "You turned to God from idols, to serve the true and living God." These new converts aren't former Jews; not long ago, they were pagans or idol worshipers.

That's interesting, because it's not the impression that we get from Acts, which was written several decades later. In Acts 17, we hear of Paul's first visit to Thessalonica. He stayed there for three weeks, attending the synagogue each Sabbath and attempting to persuade the Jews from their own scriptures that Jesus was the promised Messiah. According to Acts, several members of the congregation became Christian, along with some Gentiles who also worshipped the God of Israel, but other Jews became jealous of his success and drove Paul from the city. Yet in his epistle to the Thessalonians, Paul never mentions the synagogue, and he doesn't quote from Jewish sacred texts; so there seems to be something of a difference here. In the letter, it looks like he's talking to converted pagans, rather than converted Jews.

Third question: What challenges did these new converts face? Paul mentions persecution in several verses; though once again, it doesn't quite match up with the book of Acts. From the narrative there, we might expect animosity from the local Jewish community; but Paul writes: "You suffered from your own countrymen the same things those churches [in Judea] suffered from the Jews." In other words, the opponents of the new Christians in Thessalonica are other Gentiles; there's just sort of an analogy with Jews in Judea, not the same people. Paul cautions his readers of this letter about yielding to sexual immorality and disparaging prophecy. He urges them to show love toward each other, to live quiet, respectable lives, and to not be idle. We can assume that those were all challenges or temptations for them.

There also appears to have been some confusion over doctrine. The new Christians in Thessalonica seem to have assumed that if they converted, they'd escape death. One could imagine some sort of misunderstanding over the concept of eternal life; or perhaps they thought that the Second Coming was imminent. But that turned out not to be true: Some of those who'd embraced Paul's new religion had since passed on, and it looked like they wouldn't have a share in Christ's new kingdom after all. In his letter, Paul assures the Thessalonians that Christians who have died will enjoy equal blessings with believers who are still alive. When Christ comes again descending from heaven, deceased Christians will rise from their graves. Paul continues: "After that, we who are still alive and are left will be caught up together with them in the clouds to meet the Lord in the air." The idea is that the righteous will be taken up from the earth and so will avoid the terrible destructions that God will pour out upon the wicked. This is the origin of the belief of some contemporary Christians in the Rapture. But one of the most striking things is that Paul assumes that Jesus's second coming will occur within the lifetime of himself and many of his original readers; remember he says "we who are still alive" and then this will happen.

Finally, based on a close reading of 1 Thessalonians, what did early Christians believe? Paul mentions the following doctrinal points: God had raised Jesus from the dead; that the Holy Spirit would aid believers; that prayer matters;

that Satan is trying to hinder the work; and that Jesus will rescue believers from the "coming wrath," and that he'll return again soon (this comes up six times), after which Christians will be with the Lord forever.

Turning back to the Christian tradition as a whole, what sorts of things does Paul not talk about in this letter? You notice in this we're almost bringing a Daoist perspective to this letter; we're asking "If he says this, what brings this forth?" Or, "What is he not saying?" We're looking for opposites. What does Paul not say in this letter? There's nothing here about the atonement or forgiveness of sins; nothing about events from Jesus's life or ethical instructions like those we saw in the Sermon on the Mount. Paul never mentions baptism in the Letter to the Thessalonians, or the Eucharist; though there's a somewhat cryptic reference towards the end to a "holy kiss," which might've been a liturgical thing. Paul never quotes from the Jewish scriptures, and he doesn't talk about the metaphysical nature of Christ. Instead, 1 Thessalonians seems to be a document from an apocalyptic sect, which was expecting the end times to arrive at any moment; or at least that's the impression that we get from just reading this one letter all by itself.

By this time, you've probably already figured out the problem with this sort of close textual analysis: Perhaps when Paul was living in Thessalonica, he taught his new converts those other basic Christian beliefs and they didn't have questions or they didn't have problems with it; there may have been broad understanding and agreement about all of those things that weren't included in the letter. Nevertheless, even though this epistle was written to a particular community at a specific time in their history and thus undoubtedly presents only a limited perspective—maybe something like overhearing one side of a single telephone call—that's still the only hard data we've got for Paul, this community, and their beliefs at the time. And so it is with the other letters of the New Testament. They offer our best evidence of early Christian beliefs and practices, but none were composed as comprehensive introductions to the religion; and they're not always consistent in their viewpoints.

After the book of Acts, there are nine Pauline letters addressed to various Christian communities, arranged not chronologically but by length, from longest to shortest. Then follow four letters from Paul to individuals rather than congregations, again in order of descending length. Fortunately, most of these documents are longer and more detailed than 1 Thessalonians, so it gives us a little more to work with. Running quickly through some of the most important of these 13 letters, we can start with Romans, the longest of them, which lays out Paul's most extensive theological arguments. All humans are sinners, he says, and are thus are subject to God's judgment, but they can be justified, or pronounced righteous, through their faith in Christ. This process of reconciliation with God is available to both Jews and non-Jews, apart from the Law of Moses. For instance, Abraham was justified by faith, even though he lived long before Moses and his law. But then Paul goes on for several chapters warning Gentile converts not to think of themselves as superior to the Jews. God will still be faithful to his promises to Israel, Paul says. Then the letter closes with moral exhortations and greetings to specific individuals in Rome. Paul quotes liberally from the Jewish scriptures and he provides careful, sophisticated arguments. Indeed, for many Christians, Romans represents the pinnacle of Christian theology.

There are two letters to the Christian community at Corinth; and Corinth is in Greece today, sort of a narrow peninsula that was the site of a lot of trade, it's a very active city. 1 Corinthians is Paul's response to a letter he'd received that included questions on practical matters; so we don't have the letter that the Corinthians wrote to him, we just have Paul's response. In this lecture, Paul stresses the need for unity and he explains his authority as an apostle; and then he gives some specific advice. What should they do about a member of the community who's committed incest (that was apparently a question that they'd asked)? Or what about believers who were suing each other, or members who were visiting prostitutes? Paul answers questions about marriage and sexual relations, and about whether it's acceptable to eat food that's been offered to idols. He condemns those who use the congregational meals or gifts of the spirit as occasions to look down on others, and he reaffirms the significance of the doctrine of resurrection in Christian theology.

By the way, 1 Corinthians 13 includes one of the most famous passages in the New Testament, a poetic description of love that may sound familiar to you: "Love is patient; love is kind; love is not envious or boastful or arrogant or rude," and it goes on for several more verses. It's an inspiring tribute that's often read at weddings; but in its original context, it's not about romantic love, it's about the sort of love that members of a congregation should have for each other, which was apparently not always that easy to come by, which is why Paul wants to inspire the people in Corinth that he's writing to.

2 Corinthians has several jarring shifts of tone and topic, so much so that many scholars believe that it was originally two or more separate letters that were eventually fused together. Paul goes from what's essentially a travelogue, to a defense of his ministry and a plea for reconciliation, to an appeal for donations to a fund for poor Christians in Jerusalem, and to a denunciation of other missionaries whom Paul refers to sarcastically as "super-apostles"; we're not exactly sure who these people were.

From 2 Corinthians we can move to Galatians, which is Paul's angriest, most polemical letter. Generally Paul's epistles follow a regular pattern: They begin with salutations, a prayer or blessing, and then a section of thanksgiving to God for the congregation he's addressing. The body of the letter comes next, followed by admonitions, greetings to individuals in the congregations, and a concluding farewell. In Galatians, however, Paul is so infuriated that he skips the thanksgivings altogether—he's apparently not being very thankful at the moment he's writing this—and he launches into a diatribe. What's apparently happened is the Christians at Galatia had been visited by other missionaries who told them that Gentile converts had to be circumcised, contrary to what Paul had preached and contrary to the decision of the Jerusalem Council.

This is a big deal to Paul, not only because it throws into question the relationship of Christians to the Law of Moses, but also because it threatens what seems to be one of his standard missionary strategies. It appears—and this is mostly from the book of Acts—that when Paul arrived at a new city (and remember, Greco-Roman Christianity was primarily an urban phenomenon), he'd go to the local synagogue and preach about Jesus in terms borrowed from the Jewish scriptures, talking about how Jesus was the promised Messiah, and usually he didn't have a whole lot of success with people in the synagogue. But in addition to Jews, there were often Gentiles who were associated with the synagogue. They were people who were attracted by ethical monotheism, but they hesitated to convert to Judaism because that would require circumcision, which is a lot to ask of adult males. Paul would appeal to these people—they're sometimes called God-fearers in the New Testament; I think of them as Jewish wannabes maybe—and he'd tell them that his religion could provide everything that Judaism might offer, but they wouldn't have to undergo the knife. But all this falls apart if circumcision is considered a requirement for Christian baptism.

Philippians is a letter written by Paul from prison to strengthen the faith of Christians at Philippi; and Philemon is a short note written on behalf of runaway slave, addressed to his Christian master. The seven letters I've mentioned so far are all regarded as authentic and were composed between 50 and 60 C.E.; and by "authentic" I mean scholars generally believe that all of them were written by Paul himself. But scholars are divided as to whether Colossians and 2 Thessalonians were written by Paul or by a later disciple or an admirer; and there's broad consensus that Ephesians, 1 Timothy, 2 Timothy, and Titus are from a later period, perhaps 80–110 C.E. These letters were attributed to Paul in order to increase their credibility. Their style, vocabulary, assumptions about church organization, and even their theology differ from the seven undisputed letters, though some scholars have argued that they may contain fragments or traditions that originated with Paul.

Hebrews is another matter altogether. This is a sermon in the guise of a letter, which explains Jesus's relationship to the Israelite priesthood, proclaiming Christ the great high priest who offered himself as the final sacrifice for sin. Hebrews relies heavily on allusions to Jewish scripture and ritual, and it explores the idea that faith provides insight into heavenly realities. Given the fact that it doesn't sound much at all like Paul, even early church fathers doubted that it had been written by him; but Hebrews eventually made it into the New Testament on the basis of that claim. (Eventually people said "Ok, there's enough of a tradition for that that we'll accept that.")

The remainder of the New Testament consists of short letters attributed to James, Peter, John, and Jude, followed by the book of Revelation. These last letters are often referred to as "general epistles" or "catholic epistles" because they seem to have been written to Christians in general rather than to specific congregations or to specific individuals. They take up themes such as proper Christian conduct, the dangers of false teachers, the seeming delay of Jesus's second coming, and the centrality of love in Christian thought and action. There are lots of arguments about when these documents were written and by whom, and indeed there were disputes in the 2nd to the 4th centuries about whether they should be included in the Christian canon at all; but most scholars today date them from the late 1st century to the beginning of the 2nd.

To take just one of these general epistles, the Letter of James, it puts forward a view of salvation that's somewhat different, or at least different in its emphasis, from what Paul was preaching in Romans. Rather than justification by faith alone, James suggests that faith and works have to go together. It's not clear whether James represents the viewpoint of early Jewish-Christians as opposed to Gentile-Christians, or whether it was a later response to the Paul's letter to the Romans, but it's indicative that there was a variety of theological viewpoints within early Christianity; so much so that Martin Luther, who loved the letter to the Romans, was tempted to shift James to a secondary status within the canon.

Finally, Revelation belongs to a very different genre. It's an example of apocalyptic literature, of which there were many examples, both Jewish and Christian, in the late Second Temple Period and early centuries of the Common Era. Daniel and Revelation are the only such writings to make it into the Bible, but we see other apocalyptic writings in the Dead Sea Scrolls. Typically, these texts present a dualistic view of the world, with sharp demarcations between the wicked majority and an oppressed minority of the righteous who are looking to God to bring his wrathful judgment down upon their opponents, soon. True to form, the book of Revelation presents itself as a series of visions and prophecies about the end times, when God will intervene directly to destroy the wicked—and Revelation often refers to them as Babylon, which may have been a code name for Rome—and establish a new heaven and a new earth. Revelation also describes a new Jerusalem that will be coming as well. There's a great deal of cryptic, sometimes violent imagery, with blood, trumpets, and war; there are natural disasters, angels, a scroll with seven seals, a dragon, a beast with multiple heads, and so forth.

Whenever I read Revelation, I think, "Wow, whoever wrote this could not have been a happy person." There's a sense of besiegement and desperation underlying it all, but also a faith that ultimately God's people will be vindicated and the lovely promise that God, as it says in Revelation, "will wipe every tear from their eyes. There shall be an end to death, and to mourning and crying and pain, for the old order has passed away." Whether read metaphorically or literally, the book of Revelation has both frightened and inspired Christians through the centuries.

It's worth noting that the New Testament concludes with an urgent affirmation that this world is coming to an end; that's the message of Revelation. One might argue that a great deal of the New Testament was written as a response to what might have seemed to be a failure on Jesus's part. The three synoptic gospels portray Jesus as the Messiah, an anointed leader or liberator, who proclaimed that God's kingdom was close at hand, yet his death left the work unfinished; even though he himself was resurrected, the kingdom that he proclaimed is still nowhere to be seen, at least as of yet. There must be more to the story. Jesus must be coming back as Lord and King at some point to usher in that new kingdom that he'd promised.

We saw how Paul and the Christians in Thessalonica expected his return momentarily; but gradually, as it looked like it might take a while longer, a more formal church organization developed. Some scholars have seen the gospel of John as spiritualizing the concept of God's kingdom, at least to some extent, and 2 Peter, which was probably the last written book in the New Testament, takes on that challenge explicitly. It says: "You must understand this, that in the last days scoffers will come, scoffing and indulging their own lusts and saying, 'Where is the promise of his coming? For ever since our ancestors died, all things continue as they were from the beginning of creation.'" You can hear that skepticism, and that nervousness on the part of authors of these letters to respond to that skepticism. The author of 2 Peter goes on to suggest that human timetables aren't really applicable, since, as he says, "With the Lord one day is like a thousand years, and a thousand years are like one day." He says that the delay in Jesus's coming again is actually a manifestation of God's mercy; he's just giving people a little more time to repent. But by putting Revelation at the end of the Christian scriptures, the message is clear: God's judgment and kingdom are on their way. Get yourself ready.

Some listeners who themselves have come from a Christian background, may feel like my brief synopsis in the last two lectures hasn't really done justice to their sacred texts. I left out so much that matters, and there are many more points of view that could've been presented. That's absolutely true; and indeed, other courses are available that go into much more detail than I've been able to offer here about the New Testament. But then again, Hindus, Buddhists, or Muslims might say that same thing about the lectures in which I introduce their scriptures. There's always more to be said about writings that have been given paramount importance in cultures for hundreds of years.

The New Testament is an eclectic collection, from the Gospels, to Acts, to the Letters, to Revelation. Christians over the centuries have found it inspiring, comforting, and motivating. In fact, perhaps part of what it means to be Christian is to be continually reading, interpreting, applying, and often arguing over these texts. I've taken an approach based on the scholarly historical-critical method that's gained wide acceptance over the last couple hundred years. Some believers have found that this mode of scripture study is somewhat threatening. If the books of the New Testament weren't written by the people whose names are attached to them, or if some came from the 2nd century rather than the 1st century, doesn't that undermine their credibility? Doesn't looking for contradictions and inconsistencies, or judging sacred texts by the standards of science, archaeology, and literary scholarship diminish their authority?

These are ultimately theological questions, but I have three observations that might be helpful. The first is that fundamentalism, like the historical-critical method, is a relatively new phenomenon. Ideas of biblical infallibility, inerrancy, and literalism themselves have a history—those ideas have a history; they come from somewhere—and they can be debated without overthrowing the whole religion. For most of Christian history, believers were quite comfortable reading their scriptures from multiple angles. The most famous scheme was the four categories of interpretation in the Middle Ages: There was literal readings; allegorical readings; anagogical readings that pointed toward heaven, the afterlife, or communion with God; and finally, moral readings. Each of those readings was an appropriate way to understand the meaning of scriptures, and literal is just one of those. My second observation is that the focal point of Christianity is a person, not a book, and although the New Testament is one of our primary means of understanding that person, there are others; other ways of understanding Christ. Catholics believe that tradition and ecclesiastical authority also provide some access to Christ; and some Protestants, as well as some Catholics, look to the Holy Spirit for guidance and a more direct connection to the divine, in charismatic worship. Finally, although it appears that there's a great deal of the human element in the sacred texts of Christianity—from documents that were written by specific people in particular circumstances, to early editing and possible misattributions, to the messy processes of canonization and hand-copying manuscripts—the New Testament never claimed to be an eternal text that had its origins in heaven, like the Vedas, or the Qur'an, or even the Torah in some strands of Judaism.

Yet how could something human-made have ultimate significance? Perhaps the religion itself offers an answer, or at least a helpful analogy. Just as Jesus was considered in mainstream Christianity to have been both fully human and fully divine at the same time, so also the New Testament is regarded by believers as the product of both human effort and divine inspiration. In our next lecture, however, we'll turn to non-mainstream forms of early Christianity that had quite different ideas about the nature of Christ and which texts ought to be regarded as scripture.

Apocryphal Gospels
Lecture 28

Early Christians adopted the Jewish practice of reading selections from the Old Testament on the Sabbath, and those readings were eventually supplemented with excerpts from the Gospels and other New Testament writings, especially the letters of Paul. But in the centuries before there was an official, widely accepted New Testament, this presented a problem. There are many writings from the early centuries of Christianity that at least some believers thought of as scriptural but that were ultimately rejected by majority opinion. As we'll see in this lecture, some of these are quite different from those texts that eventually made their way into the New Testament.

The Gospel of Peter
- In 1886–1887, a French archaeological team was excavating some graves dating from the 8th to the 12th centuries in Akhmim in Upper Egypt. One grave, apparently of a Christian monk, contained a small parchment codex with excerpts from four noncanonical Christian writings, including the Gospel of Peter. The manuscript itself is probably from the 7th or 8th century, but the version of the gospel it contains appears to be one that was known in the 2nd century.

- We don't have the entire gospel, but what we have narrates Jesus's death and resurrection in much the same terms as the four canonical gospels, with some subtle variations and extra details.
  - Although it tends to put more blame on the Jews than on the Romans, it indicates that ordinary Jews began almost immediately to regret Jesus's execution (new information), and when their leaders heard this, they asked the Romans to post guards at the tomb. We even get the name of the officer in charge of the mission, Petronius.

- One of the new details that might have worried earlier Christians was this: "He held his peace, as if he felt no pain." Did Jesus only seem to suffer?

- Perhaps most significantly, we get an account of the resurrection itself. The solders on guard saw two men—perhaps angels—descend from heaven. The stone sealing the tomb rolled away on its own, and the two went inside. Shortly thereafter, three men emerged, with the third being helped along by the others and followed by a cross. The three figures became enormous. A heavenly voice asked, "Have you preached to those who sleep?" (the dead), and the cross answered, "Yes."

The Infancy Gospel of Thomas
- For a long time, Christians and historians alike believed that the church was established shortly after Jesus's resurrection, and a series of heretical movements followed that challenged both orthodoxy and the authority of church leaders. Key points of contention in the 2nd century included the relationship of Christianity and Judaism, the role of ecstatic prophecy, and whether Jesus had given secret higher teachings to his closest disciples.

- The early church fathers described some of these ideas as deviations from orthodoxy; indeed, most of what we knew about these movements came from the writings of their opponents.
  - Starting in the latter half of the 19th century, however, archeologists began uncovering some of the texts written by those who had been branded as heretics, and it seems there was considerable confusion in the early centuries of the Common Era about the tenets of the faith.

  - Rather than a simple story of orthodoxy and heresy, it now appears that there were many different strains of early Christianity, all with their own traditions and sacred texts and all vying for position.

- - o What we think of as "orthodoxy" today was simply the winner in these theological disputes, and those ideas became truly dominant only with the church councils of the 4th century.

- Alongside the four gospels that were eventually accepted into the New Testament, there were competing accounts of Jesus's life, such as the Gospel of Peter, that we now categorize as apocryphal ("hidden") gospels. These texts often told very different stories, sometimes based on quite different notions of how Jesus could be both human and divine. One of the most famous of these apocryphal writings is the Infancy Gospel of Thomas.

- This gospel originated in the 2nd century and was once a popular work. It begins with a story of the five-year-old Jesus creating 12 sparrows out of mud, then commanding them to leave. Not long afterward, Jesus was walking though the village and another child ran into him. The young Jesus angrily said, "You will go no further on your way." Because everything Jesus said came true, the other child fell down dead. The gospel contains several stories of miraculous healings or times when Jesus was smarter than his teachers or when he changed the order of nature to help out his parents.

- The Infancy Gospel of Thomas ends with the tale of Jesus being lost in Jerusalem when he was 12 and ending up in the temple (also found in Luke), but the familiar conclusion to the narrative—that "Jesus grew in wisdom and stature and grace"—feels somewhat different in the Infancy Gospel. There, Jesus is not presented as perfect from the beginning; we have seen him learn to control his supernatural powers and turn them to good ends.

The Gospel of Mary
- Some of the apocryphal gospels are today known only in a few fragments. For instance, we have only about nine manuscript pages from the Gospel of Mary, a 2nd-century text, written in Coptic, that was discovered in 1896 but not published until 1955.

- The first six pages are missing, and then we get some of Jesus's final teachings to his disciples before he ascended to heaven.

- As the disciples are mourning his departure, Mary (presumably Mary Magdalene) joins them, and Peter says, "We know that Jesus loved you more than the other women. Tell us the words of the Savior that you remember, which you know and we do not, since we did not hear them." Mary replies, "What is hidden from you I will tell you." She starts to report what the Lord had told her in a vision; then, four pages are missing.

- When the manuscript resumes, it seems that Mary is telling the disciples about how the soul ascends past seven powers or authorities: darkness, desire, ignorance, envy of death, the kingdom of the flesh, foolish wisdom of the flesh, and wrathful wisdom. One of those listening, Andrew, challenges Mary, saying he doesn't believe these are the words of the savior, but a paragraph or so later, the disciples accept Mary's words, and they begin to preach them widely.

- The Gospel of Mary wasn't accepted into the Christian canon, but it is an example of Gnostic Christianity, a form of the faith that competed with proto-orthodoxy in the early centuries.
  - Some of the general beliefs of the Gnostics included the notion that matter and spirit were opposed to each other, that this material world of evil had been created by a lesser god or demiurge, and that some people have within them a spark of the divine, imprisoned in a corruptible physical body.

  - Gnostics also believed that Jesus was a pure spiritual being who was sent by the highest God to teach them the special knowledge (*gnosis*) and ascetic practices that would lead to liberation from material existence.

- We began to understand Gnosticism much better after 1945, when a fieldworker near the Upper Egyptian town of Nag Hammadi found

a large clay jar sealed with bitumen. Inside were 13 codices bound in leather and written in the Coptic language.
- The 13 codices contained 52 separate works, mostly Gnostic texts. Although the physical books were dated to the 4th century, the writings they contained had been originally composed in Greek much earlier, then translated into Coptic.

- Among the Nag Hammadi texts were four that might be considered apocryphal gospels, including what is probably the most important example of the genre—the Gospel of Thomas.

The Gospel of Thomas and the Didache
- When the Gospel of Thomas appeared in one of the Nag Hammadi codices, scholars recognized it from three Greek fragments that had been discovered in 1896 and 1903 in Egypt.
  - In 1896, a decade after the Gospel of Peter was found, two Oxford archaeologists discovered a series of garbage dumps associated with the ancient city of Oxyrhynchus, about 100 miles south of Cairo.

  - Because Oxyrhynchus had been an administrative center, the trash included thousands of Greek and Latin papyri, discarded over the course of a nearly a millennium. Among the finds were some biblical fragments from both the Old and New Testaments and a few early noncanonical Christian writings, including some apocryphal gospels.

  - In the first year of excavation, a bit of papyrus was found containing seven sayings of Jesus; two similar fragments were discovered in 1903. The full significance of these fragments was not realized until the discovery of a complete Coptic translation of the Gospel of Thomas in the Nag Hammadi library 42 years later.

- Remarkably, the Gospel of Thomas does not include any stories about Jesus. Instead, there are 114 independent quotations, in seemingly random order, said to have been recorded by Thomas

Selections from the Gospel of Thomas

These are the secret sayings which the living Jesus spoke and which Didymos Judas Thomas wrote down.

(1) And he said, "Whoever finds the interpretation of these sayings will not experience death." (Lambdin, trans.)

(2) Jesus said: "Let him who seeks continue seeking until he finds. When he finds, he will become troubled. When he becomes troubled, he will be astonished, and he will rule over the All." (Lambdin, trans.)

(3) Jesus said: "If those who lead you say to you, 'See, the kingdom is in the sky,' then the birds of the sky will precede you. If they say to you, 'It is in the sea,' then the fish will precede you. Rather the kingdom is inside of you, and it is outside of you. When you come to know yourselves, then you will become known, and you will realize that it is you who are the sons of the living father. But if you will not know yourselves you will dwell in poverty, and it is you who are that poverty." (Lambdin, trans.)

(19) Jesus said: "Blessed is that which existed before coming into being. If you exist as my disciples and listen to my sayings, these stones will minister unto you. Indeed, you have five trees in paradise, which do not move in summer or winter, and whose leaves do not fall. Whoever is acquainted with them will not taste death." (Layton, trans.)

(75) Jesus said: "There are many standing at the door, but it is the solitaries who will enter the bridal chamber." (Layton, trans.)

(77) Jesus said: "It is I who am the light upon them all. It is I who am the all. It is from me that the all has come, and to me that the all has extended. Split a piece of wood: I am there. Lift up a stone and you will find me there." (Ehrman, trans.)

(98): Jesus said: "What the kingdom of the father resembles is a man who wanted to assassinate a member of court. At home, he drew the dagger and stabbed it into the wall in order to know whether his hand would be firm. Next, he murdered the member of court." (Layton, trans.)

(114) "Simon Peter said to them, "Mary should leave us, for females are not worthy of the life." Jesus said, "Look, I am going to guide her in order to make her male, so that she too may become a living spirit resembling you males. For every female who makes herself male will enter the kingdom of heaven." (Ehrman, trans.)

Didymus, Jesus's twin brother. The existence of a text containing nothing but quotations demonstrated the possibility that the hypothetical document called Q (the source for Matthew and Luke) might also exist, even though the Gospel of Thomas did not itself turn out to be Q.

- About half the sayings in Thomas are similar to those in the three Synoptic Gospels, but the wording is different enough that it doesn't seem as if the author was drawing from Matthew, Mark, or Luke. The Gospel of Thomas appears to be an independent compilation of oral traditions about Jesus, dating from the late 1st or early 2nd century (about the time of the New Testament gospels), though hardly anyone believes that all these statements originated with Jesus himself.

- The quotations that are not in the New Testament are perhaps even more interesting. They seem to have a Gnostic flavor to them, focusing on secret wisdom and how knowledge of one's true nature can lead to eternal life. Many of the sayings seem puzzling to us today, but some early Christians regarded the Gospel of Thomas as an authoritative sacred text.

- In 1873, a document known as the Didache ("Teachings") was discovered in a monastery library in Constantinople. It was compiled about 100 C.E. and was accepted as scripture by many Christians in the 2nd to 4th centuries. This short work includes ethical teachings, guidance for fasting and prayer, and instructions for rituals and the Eucharist. Because the Didache wasn't attributed to a specific apostle, it didn't make it onto Athanasius's list of accepted scriptural texts in 367 C.E. and was gradually lost and forgotten.

Suggested Reading

Ehrman, *Lost Christianities*.

_____, ed., *Lost Scriptures*.

Ehrman and Pleše, trans., *The Apocryphal Gospels: Texts and Translations*.

Foster, *The Apocryphal Gospels: A Very Short Introduction.*

Layton, trans., *The Gnostic Scriptures.*

Pagles, *The Gnostic Gospels.*

———, *Beyond Belief.*

Questions to Consider

1. What are the criteria by which early church fathers decided which writings should be included in the New Testament, and what were some of the texts that didn't make the cut?

2. How do apocryphal gospels differ from the canonical gospels of Matthew, Mark, Luke, and John? What makes the Gospel of Thomas special?

Apocryphal Gospels
Lecture 28—Transcript

A text isn't made sacred by what it contains, but rather by the role it plays within a religious community. There are hundreds of thousands of books about God and the divine, about myth and religious history, about salvation and enlightenment, yet only a very small subset are used in worship by specific religious groups and are regarded as especially holy and authoritative.

For Christians, there's a long tradition of solitary scripture study, especially since the Protestant Reformation, but most believers probably encountered the sacred texts of the faith when they were read aloud in church. As early as 1 Timothy, Paul (or whoever wrote 1 Timothy) urged his readers to "give attention to the public reading of scripture, to exhorting, to teaching." Early Christians adopted the Jewish practice of reading selections from the Old Testament on the Sabbath, and those readings were eventually supplemented with excerpts from the Gospels and other New Testament writings, especially the letters of Paul.

But in the centuries before there was an official, widely-accepted New Testament—which, as you'll recall, didn't take its final form until the 4th century—this is a problem; what exactly is going to be acceptable for reading in church? Other than the Septuagint, which everyone agreed upon, there were some questions about other texts. Here's a story from Eusebius's *Church History*, which was the first comprehensive account of the early centuries of Christianity, written by a bishop of Caesarea—Caesarea is near Jerusalem—about the year 325. Eusebius says there was a certain Serapion; he was a bishop in Antioch in Syria from 190–211. In one of the congregations that he oversaw, there was a bit of controversy because a Gospel of Peter was being read in church. Serapion had never heard of this text before, and at first he was inclined to accept it as apostolic; after all, Peter was an authoritative name. But later, when Serapion heard that people he considered heretics were using that Gospel of Peter as evidence that Jesus didn't really die on the cross but only appeared to do so, then he began to examine that text a little more closely. Serapion wrote a tract denouncing the falsehoods of the Gospel of Peter and forbidding its further use. There must've been many similar occasions, because there were dozens and dozens of writings from the early centuries of Christianity that at least some believers thought of as scriptural, but which were ultimately rejected by majority opinion; and some of those are quite different from those texts that eventually made their way into the New Testament.

But the story of the Gospel of Peter doesn't end there with that anecdote in church history. In the winter of 1886–1887, a French archaeological team was excavating some graves dating from the 8th to the 12th centuries in Akhmim in Upper Egypt. One grave that apparently belonged to a Christian monk contained a small parchment codex with excerpts from four non-canonical Christian writings, including the Gospel of Peter. The manuscript itself is probably from the 7th or the 8th century, but the Gospel of Peter that it contains appears to be the same one that was proscribed by Serapion so many years earlier.

We don't have the entire Gospel, just the part that narrates Jesus's death and resurrection. It tells the story in much the same terms as the four canonical gospels—it talks of a crown of thorns, of a crucifixion between two criminals, a burial in a rock tomb that was sealed by a stone—but there are also some subtle variations and some extra details that are thrown in. For example, the Gospel of Peter reports that there was an earthquake when Jesus's body was taken from the cross; in the other gospels, it says at his death was when an earthquake happened. Although it tends to put more blame on the Jews than on the Romans, it does indicate that ordinary Jews began almost immediately to regret Jesus's execution (that's sort of a new detail), and when their leaders heard this, they asked the Romans to post guards on the tomb (that's an old detail from other gospels). In the Gospel of Peter, we even get the name of the officer in charge of that mission of protecting the tomb; his name is Petronius (a new detail). Another of the new details that might've worried Serapion was a quotation, speaking of Jesus, "He held his peace, as if he felt no pain," which might imply that he only seemed to suffer. This is part of the heretical tendencies that Serapion was worried about; something called Docetism: that Jesus was divine and only appeared to be human, and thus couldn't suffer.

Perhaps most significantly, though, we get an account of the resurrection itself, not just the empty tomb that we see in the canonical gospels. It reports that the soldiers who were on guard saw two men descend from heaven (I'd assume those were angels), and then the stone that sealed the tomb rolled away on its own and the two men went inside. Shortly thereafter, three men emerged, with the third being helped along by the others and followed by a cross. The three figures became enormous, with their heads reaching up to the sky; and a heavenly voice asked, "Have you preached to those who sleep?" (meaning "have you preached to the dead"; this is a question given to the resurrected Jesus); but it's not Jesus, it's the cross that answers, "Yes."

That sounds pretty different then the gospels in the New Testament; and for a long time, Christians and historians alike believed that the Christian church was established shortly after Jesus's resurrection, and then there was a series of heretical movements that challenged both the orthodoxy and the authority of church leaders. Key points of contention in the 2nd century included the relationship of Christianity and Judaism; remember Marcion, who argued that the God of Moses was not at all the same being as the God of Jesus. Another point of dispute was the role of ecstatic prophecy; Montanus and his followers claimed to speak for God and to receive additional revelations in addition to what had been given by the apostles. A third point of disagreement was whether Jesus had given secret, higher teachings to his closest disciples, as Valentinus and the Gnostics claimed; we'll come back to the Gnostics in a few minutes.

The early Church fathers described these ideas as deviations from orthodoxy, and most of what we knew about those other Christian movements came from the writings of their opponents (these are the church fathers who are criticizing what they're hearing). Starting in the last half of the 19th century, however, archeologists began uncovering some of the texts written by those who'd been branded as heretics, and it seems there was considerable confusion in the early centuries of the Common Era about the tenets of the Christian faith. Rather than a simple story of orthodoxy and heresy, it now appears that there were many different strains of early Christianity, all with their own traditions and their own sacred texts, and all vying for position. What we think of as orthodoxy today was simply the winner of these theological disputes, and their ideas only became truly dominant with the church councils of the 4th century, such as the one that produced the Nicene Creed.

Alongside the four gospels that eventually became recognized throughout Christendom and accepted into the New Testament, there were other competing accounts of Jesus's life, like the Gospel of Peter, which we now categorize as apocryphal gospels (*apocryphal* means "hidden"). These texts often told very different stories, sometimes based on quite different notions of how Jesus could be both human and divine. For example, the New Testament gospels say very little about Jesus's life between his birth and his baptism at the age of 30; but Christians were naturally curious, and texts soon appeared that filled that gap. One of the most famous is the Infancy Gospel of Thomas, which takes up the question, What would it mean for an omnipotent being to be in the body of, say, a five-year-old?

The Infancy Gospel of Thomas, which originated in the 2nd century, was once a very popular work, as evidenced by the fact that multiple copies have survived, not only in Greek (which was probably its original language), but also in Syriac, Latin, Georgian, Ethiopic, and Slavonic. A scholarly edition was first published by the renowned biblical scholar Constantin von Tischendorf in 1853. That Gospel begins with a story of how the five-year-old Jesus was playing on the Sabbath and he made 12 sparrows out of mud. When one of the neighbors complained to Jesus's father, Joseph, that this sort of play wasn't appropriate, and then Joseph asked Jesus why he was doing things that were forbidden on the Sabbath, the text says, "But Jesus clapped his hands and cried to the sparrows saying, 'Be gone!' And the sparrows took flight and went off chirping." Everyone was amazed at this boy's power. Not long afterwards, Jesus was walking though the village and another child ran into him and bumped his shoulder. The young Jesus angrily said, "You will go no further in your way." Then, because everything that Jesus said came true, the other child fell down dead, right then and there. Needless to say, the parents were pretty upset, telling Joseph "Since you have such a child you cannot live with us in the village. Or teach him to bless and not to curse— for he is killing our children!" On another occasion—so we're still talking about stories from the Infancy Gospel of Thomas—Jesus was playing with some other children on a flat rooftop. One of the kids fell off and died, and the parents accused Jesus of having pushed him. Jesus then brought the boy back to life so that he could affirm Jesus's innocence. There are several other stories of miraculous healings, or times when Jesus was smarter than his teachers, or when he changed the order of nature to help out his parents.

The Infancy Gospel of Thomas ends with the tale of Jesus being lost in Jerusalem when he was 12 years old and ending up in the Temple—that's a story that we also read in Luke—but the familiar conclusion to the narrative, that "Jesus grew in wisdom and stature and grace," feels somewhat different in the Infancy Gospel because Jesus isn't presented as having been perfect from the beginning; we've seen him learn to control his supernatural powers and turn them to good ends.

Interestingly, one of the stories from this gospel is alluded to in the Qur'an. When an angel announces to Mary that she'll give birth to Jesus even though she's a virgin, the angel continues: "[God] will send him as a messenger to the Children of Israel: 'I have come to you with a sign from your Lord: I will make the shape of a bird for you out of clay, then breathe into it and, with God's permission, it will become a real bird." For Muslims, this may be evidence that some of Jesus's miracles were left out of the biblical accounts; for outsiders, it seems that these stories spread far enough that even Muhammad had encountered them.

Some of the apocryphal gospels are today known only in a few fragments. For instance, we have only about nine manuscript pages from the Gospel of Mary, a 2nd-century text written in Coptic, which was a late form of Egyptian written with Greek letters. This Gospel of Mary, or these fragments, were discovered in 1896, but weren't published until 1955. The first six pages are missing, and then we get some of Jesus's final teachings to his disciples before he ascended to heaven. As the disciples are mourning Jesus's departure, Mary (presumably that's Mary Magdalene) joins them, and Peter says, "We know that Jesus loved you more than the other women. Tell us the words of the Savior that you remember, which you know and we do not, since we did not hear them." Mary replies, "What is hidden from you I will tell you." Then she starts to report what the Lord had told her in a vision, and then there are four pages missing, unfortunately. When the manuscript resumes, it seems that Mary is telling the disciples about how the soul ascends past seven powers or authorities. It descends past: Darkness, Desire, Ignorance,

Envy of Death, the Kingdom of the Flesh, Foolish Wisdom of the Flesh, and finally Wrathful Wisdom. Then one of those listening, Andrew, challenges her: "Say what you will about what she has said, but I do not believe that the Savior said these things. For these teachings are strange thoughts indeed." Even Peter asks, "Did [Jesus] really speak with a woman secretly from us, not openly?" Nevertheless, a paragraph or so later, the disciples come to accept Mary's words and her understanding of this progression of the soul, and then they began to preach them widely.

It would be wonderful to know more of what was missing from this text, but the general situation may remind us of Mahayana Buddhism: the assertion that the founder of a religion taught secret doctrines to his most advanced disciples; doctrines that came to light only after his death. Yet whereas Buddhism eventually included such new writings into its canon, Christianity resisted additions to collection of sacred texts that was the New Testament, at least once an approved list was agreed upon in the 4th century. Those documents that made it in were those from the late 1st and early 2nd centuries that were orthodox, which enjoyed wide acceptance, and were ascribed to apostles and their associates. The Gospel of Mary didn't make that cut.

It is, however, an example of gnostic Christianity; a form of the faith that competed with proto-orthodoxy in the early centuries. People that we now call Gnostics weren't an organized group, and they believed in a wide variety of doctrines. Some of the general tendencies included the notion that matter and spirit were opposed to each other, and that this material world of evil had been created by a lesser god or a demiurge. Gnostics further believed that some people have within them a spark of the divine that's imprisoned in a corruptible, physical body, and that Jesus was a pure spiritual being who was sent by the highest God to teach them the special knowledge (the word *gnosis* means "knowledge") and ascetic practices that would lead to liberation from this miserable, material existence.

We began to understand ancient Gnosticism much better after 1945. In that year, a fieldworker named Muhammad Ali al-Samman was digging for fertilizer near the Upper Egyptian town of Nag Hammadi, and he found a large clay jar sealed with bitumen (the jar is very large). Inside were 13 codices bound in leather, which were written in the Coptic language. After they found this, there were some complicated tales of misunderstandings, shady business deals, and scholarly intrigues; but the Nag Hammadi library was eventually transcribed, edited, and translated, with full publications coming in the 1970s. The 13 codices contained 52 separate works, mostly gnostic texts, most of which were previously unknown. Although the physical books themselves were dated to the 4th century, the writings they contained had been originally composed in Greek much earlier, some probably as early as the 2nd century, and then they were translated into Coptic. It was a spectacular scholarly find, similar to the Dead Sea Scrolls that were discovered a year or so later. Among the Nag Hammadi texts were four that might be considered apocryphal gospels, including what's probably the most important example of the genre: the Gospel of Thomas (and this is entirely different from the Infancy Gospel of Thomas that I talked about a few minutes ago).

When the Gospel of Thomas appeared in one of the Nag Hammadi codices, scholars recognized it from three Greek fragments that had been discovered in Egypt in 1896 and 1903. In 1896, a decade after the Gospel of Peter was found, two Oxford scholars, Bernard Grenfell and Arthur Hunt, had been excavating the ancient city of Oxyrhynchus, about 100 miles south of Cairo. When they were in that archaeological dig, they came upon a series of garbage dumps, the contents of which had been well preserved in the dry desert climate. (Archaeologists love garbage; it tells so much about the everyday life of ancient societies.) Because Oxyrhynchus had been an administrative center, the trash included thousands of Greek and Latin papyri, which had been discarded over the course of a nearly a millennium. Oxyrhynchus is one of the great troves of ancient documents ever discovered. About 90 percent were scraps of fairly mundane, day-to-day business—they were court documents, sales receipts, letters, wills, inventories, tax and census records, etc.; the sorts of documents that allow archaeologists and historians to reconstruct the past—but there were also some literary texts that had been thrown out: fragments of ancient Greek poetry and plays, some lines from Homer's *Iliad*, diagrams from Euclid's *Elements*, a Latin synopsis of a few of the lost chapters from the Roman historian Livy, and some biblical fragments from both the Old and New Testaments.

There were also pieces of a few early non-canonical Christian writings, including some apocryphal gospels. In the first year of the excavation, a bit of papyrus was found that contained seven sayings of Jesus. Two similar fragments of Jesus's words were discovered in 1903, and one of those was written on the back of a land survey; papyrus was valuable and scraps were often reused. It's always exciting to find ancient writings that purport to tell us something about Jesus, but the full significance of these fragments wasn't realized until the discovery of a complete Coptic translation of the Gospel of Thomas in the Nag Hammadi library 42 years later.

Remarkably, the Gospel of Thomas doesn't include any stories about Jesus; there's nothing about his death and resurrection, which, as you recall, were at the heart of Paul's preaching. Instead, there are 114 independent quotations in seemingly random order said to have been recorded by Thomas Didymus, Jesus's twin brother; needless to say, the idea that Jesus had a twin brother isn't part of the New Testament record. The book of quotations looks a little bit like the Confucian *Analects*. The very fact that the Gospel of Thomas consists of nothing but sayings is itself important. Remember that scholars had hypothesized that there must've been a collection of quotations from Jesus that was used by Matthew and Luke—that hypothetical document called *Q*—when they revised Mark and put together their own gospels. The very existence of the Gospel of Thomas demonstrates that such a text is quite possible, even if scholars were disappointed that the Gospel of Thomas didn't turn out itself to be *Q*.

About half of the sayings in the Gospel of Thomas are similar to those in the three synoptic gospels. For instance, we read the parable of the sower and the parable of the mustard seed; we read about the difficulty of taking a speck out of someone else's eye when you've got a beam in your own; about how prophets aren't accepted by their own people, and the dangers of the blind leading the blind. If you went to Sunday School, those should all sound sort of familiar. But the wording is each of those quotations is different enough that it doesn't look like the author was drawing from Matthew, Mark, or Luke; he's not just copying down his favorite sayings from the gospels. The Gospel of Thomas appears to be an independent compilation of oral traditions about Jesus, dating from the late first or the early 2nd centuries; so it was written about the time of the New Testament gospels, although scholars don't believe that all of those sayings in the Gospel of Thomas originated with Jesus himself.

The quotations that aren't like those in the New Testament are perhaps even more interesting. They seem to have a gnostic flavor to them, focusing on secret wisdom and how a knowledge of one's true nature can lead to eternal life. Here's how the Gospel of Thomas begins:

> These are the secret sayings which the living Jesus spoke and which Didymos Judas Thomas wrote down [we'll give you three of these]. (1) And he said, "Whoever finds the interpretation of these sayings will not experience death." (2) Jesus said: Let him who seeks continue seeking until he finds. When he finds, he will become troubled. When he becomes troubled, he will be astonished, and he will rule over the all.
>
> (3) Jesus said: If those who lead you say to you, "See, the kingdom is in the sky," then the birds of the sky will precede you. If they say to you, "It is in the sea," then the fish will precede you. Rather the kingdom is inside of you, and it is outside of you. When you come to know yourselves, then you will become known, and you will realize that it is you who are the sons of the living father. But if you will not know yourselves you will dwell in poverty, and it is you who are that poverty.

As you can see, these sayings are a bit cryptic. How exactly does one escape death, and why is truth described as "troubling?" The interpretation of the kingdom of God as dependent on self-knowledge seems rather different from the more orthodox preaching of a time when Jesus will return to earth and literally rule as Lord and King.

Other sayings are even more puzzling; Number 19:

> Jesus said: Blessed is that which existed before coming into being. If you exist as my disciples and listen to my sayings, these stones will minister unto you. Indeed, you have five trees in paradise, which do not move in summer or winter, and whose leaves do not fall. Whoever is acquainted with them will not taste death.

Or saying number 75: "Jesus said: There are many standing at the door, but it is the solitaries who will enter the bridal chamber." And 98: "Jesus said: What the kingdom of the father resembles is a man who wanted to assassinate a member of court. At home, he drew the dagger and stabbed it into the wall in order to know whether his hand would be firm. Next, he murdered the member of court." What? What is that all about?

There are certainly obscure sayings in the canonical gospels; for example, Matthew 19:12 says, "There are eunuchs who have made themselves eunuchs for the sake of the kingdom of heaven"; and John 6:51 says, "I am the living bread that comes down from heaven; whoever eats of this bread will live forever." But we have nearly 2,000 years' worth of interpretations and commentaries that explain those cryptic sayings and make sense of them. Reading the Gospel of Thomas, by contrast, puts us in the position of those who heard the Christian message for the first time, when it was new and sometimes shocking or puzzling.

What could this saying possibly mean? This is 77 from the Gospel of Thomas: "Jesus said: It is I who am the light upon them all. It is I who am the all. It is from me that the all has come, and to me that the all has extended. Split a piece of wood: I am there. Lift up a stone and you will find me there." Or this saying, 114, the very last quotation: "Simon Peter said to them, 'Mary should leave us, for females are not worthy of the life.' Jesus said, 'Look, I am going to guide her in order to make her male, so that she too may become a living spirit resembling you males. For every female who makes herself male will enter the kingdom of heaven,'" which might be something that's reminiscent of something that appeared earlier in the Gospel of Thomas where it talked about: "make the male and the female be a single one, with the male no longer being male and the female no longer female ... then you will enter the kingdom" I don't know what that means; after all, these are secret teachings. But some early Christians regarded the Gospel of Thomas as an authoritative sacred text, and so it's a part of the Christian story, at least as an indication of directions that most believers chose not to go.

I'm not aware of any Christian denominations that today accept the Gospel of Thomas as canonical scripture; though individual readers might find wisdom or comfort within its 114 sayings, and some may even be interested in expanding their personal interpretations of Christianity to include more space for the mystical and the solitary, for spiritual self-knowledge and a less gendered forms of the religion.

These apocryphal gospels raise an interesting question: What if archeologists uncovered an early Christian writing that was clearly authentic and orthodox; say, a lost letter of Paul. Is it possible that the New Testament might be expanded at this late date? My guess is probably not, because of tradition and because of the canonical criteria of widespread acceptance. Actually, we have a pretty good example of such a text. In 1873, a document known as the Didache (which means "Teachings") was discovered in a monastery library at Constantinople. It was compiled about 100 C.E. (probably earlier than some of the writings that did make it into the New Testament), its teachings are quite orthodox, and it was accepted as scripture by many Christians in the second to the 4th centuries.

There are a lot of interesting things in this short work, including ethical teachings, guidance for when to fast and how to pray, and instructions for rituals such as baptism (it was supposed to be done outside, in cold running water) and there are instructions for how to perform the Eucharist (with specific prayers to be said; first the water, and then the bread). The Didache even provides tests for false prophets: If they stay with you for more than three days without paying, or if they ask for money, beware. But because the Didache wasn't attributed to a specific apostle, it didn't make it into Athanasius's list of accepted scriptural texts in 367 C.E.; and such is the power of canonization that the Didache was gradually forgotten and lost while everything on that list was diligently copied, studied, translated, and distributed as part of the New Testament.

There was, however, a 19th-century attempt to reopen the Christian canon and expand the Bible with a newly discovered ancient text—at least according to its self-proclaimed translator—a text that has attracted several million followers. That will be the subject of our next lecture, when we look at the Book of Mormon.

Related Traditions—Mormon Scriptures
Lecture 29

The story behind the transcription of the Book of Mormon is an interesting one, with Joseph Smith digging up gold plates from a hillside in upstate New York after seeing a divine messenger. In terms of number of believers and global reach, the Book of Mormon is one of the most successful scriptures of the last few centuries. It is unusual as a sacred text in that it offers a sustained, integrated narrative, rather than a collection of poems or assorted commandments and doctrines revealed to a religious founder. It is also distinctive in that it preceded a religious movement rather than resulting from one, and it was canonical from the moment it first appeared in print.

Overview of Mormon Scriptures

- Mormonism began in upstate New York in March 1830 with the publication of the Book of Mormon. Eleven days later, a church was formally organized by Joseph Smith that came to be known as the Church of Jesus Christ of Latter-day Saints (LDS). Today, this denomination, headquartered in Salt Lake City, Utah, has more than 15 million members worldwide.

- Despite the fact that Jesus Christ features prominently in the church's official name, Latter-day Saints have often been regarded as being outside the family of Christian denominations, in part because Christianity is so closely associated with a closed canon of scripture. Disagreements about which sacred texts should be authoritative are often religious boundary markers.
    - The fact that Mormonism has scriptures in addition to the Bible leads some to see it as a distinct religion rather than just a doctrinally creative sect of Christianity.

    - Mormons give full canonical authority to the Bible, yet they interpret it in terms of their unique additional scriptures: the Book of Mormon; the Doctrine and Covenants, consisting primarily of revelations given to Joseph Smith; and the Pearl of Great Price, a relatively short work that contains some of Smith's lesser-known writings, including excerpts from his inspired revision of the Bible, selections from an autobiographical essay, and a translation of Egyptian papyri from mummies that had come into his possession.

- The Doctrine and Covenants, divided into 138 chapter-like sections, is fairly typical of the sacred texts of new religious movements. It contains revelations given to the founder that were edited and revised by Smith and his successors over several decades. The contents are eclectic, including prophecies, commandments, scriptural exegesis, doctrinal exposition, and instructions for church organization, as well as advice and comfort for Mormon emigrants. Appended to the end of the book are two official declarations—one ending the practice of polygamy in 1890 and the other rescinding the priesthood ban for black members in 1978.

- Latter-day Saints assert that they have four "standard works" (their parlance for sacred texts), but actually, they have five. The fifth, rather unusually, is oral rather than written scripture; it is the text of their temple ceremony.
  o As you recall, the Hindu Brahmans resisted putting the Vedas into written form for a long time, because they believed that doing so would make the holy words common and accessible to all. It was important that the Vedas be internalized though memorization and that they were passed on directly from those who had already mastered their meanings; they needed to be spoken aloud, in specific ritual contexts, in order to actualize their sacred power.

  o This is similar to the way that Mormons feel about the temple ceremony, or endowment. This is a sort of initiation rite that portrays the creation of the world and the fall of Adam and Eve in a scripted drama, along with covenants and blessings directed toward individual believers. The text of the endowment ceremony was, for the most part, composed by Brigham Young based on an outline and key elements that had been entrusted to him by Joseph Smith.

- o Most Latter-day Saints encounter the words of the ceremony only orally, as it is performed. Although many Latter-day Saints have the script memorized, the words are considered so sacred that Mormons are forbidden from repeating them outside the temple or even discussing the details of the endowment.

Mormon chapels feature Protestant-style Sunday services that are open to all, but admittance to their temples is granted only to adult Latter-day Saints who meet strict standards of worthiness and faithfulness.

The Book of Mormon

- The primary sacred text of Mormonism is the Book of Mormon. This scripture claims to be a translation of an ancient record from the Americas, recounting the 1,000-year history of a society transplanted from Judea to the New World.

- The book begins about 600 B.C.E., when a Jewish prophet named Lehi was warned by God to take his family and flee from Jerusalem shortly before the Babylonian Conquest. Lehi and his family wandered in the desert for eight years, then were commanded by God to build a boat and sail to America.
  - o Lehi and his son Nephi continued to receive divine revelations, including the news that a Messiah, Jesus Christ, would someday be born in Israel and would atone for the sins of the world. Those who accepted this novel doctrine became known as Nephites, while their unbelieving relatives were called Lamanites.

- o The Book of Mormon tells of the interactions between these two peoples, along with another group who had also emigrated from Jerusalem with a member of the royal house of David in tow.

- o There is a long succession of wars, political intrigues, missionary efforts, sermons, and confrontations with religious dissenters, punctuated by miracles and revelations. We also read lengthy discussions of the destiny of the house of Israel, covenants, prophecy, sin, repentance, and Christian ethics, all within the context of a sweeping historical narrative.

- o About halfway through the book, escalating military conflicts lead to a breakdown of the social order. After natural disasters wreak havoc on a wicked society, the few who had remained faithful to the Nephite prophecies are vindicated by the coming of the resurrected Jesus to the Americas.

- o Jesus establishes a church, heals the sick, blesses children, teaches a version of the Sermon on the Mount, and prophesies of relations between Jews and Gentiles in the last days.

- o After a couple centuries of peace and prosperity, old antagonisms resurface, eventually leading to a war of extermination. The Nephites are destroyed by the Lamanites about 400 C.E., and the Christian traditions of the New World are lost, aside from this single record, which was buried by the last of the Nephites, the prophet Moroni, who would later appear to Joseph Smith as an angel.

- Aside from the first chapters, which take place in the vicinity of Jerusalem and for which there perhaps is some archaeological evidence, there are no artifacts from the New World that decisively support Joseph's tale of Nephites and Lamanites.
  - o Early believers regarded the Book of Mormon as the story of the origins of the American Indians, who would have been descended from the Lamanites; however, more recent LDS interpretations see the events of the Book of Mormon as taking

place in a much more limited geographical area (perhaps in Central America), with the Lamanites being absorbed into much larger Native American populations that immigrated across the Bering Strait.

- o Historicity matters to most Mormons, in part because Smith's claims of gold plates made by ancient prophets seem to require some actual historical basis, and because a work of inspired fiction or imaginative inspiration would not have the same moral authority or urgency. Yet Mormons are generally not consumed by questions of archaeological support; they assume that such evidence will someday appear.

- Whether regarded as fact or fiction, the Book of Mormon is something of an anomaly in recent world scripture in that it consists of a coherent, integrated narrative.
  - o The first quarter of the book includes first-person accounts from Nephi and his brother Jacob in the 6th century B.C.E. These pages, then, are revealed to be a document that was appended by Mormon, writing in the 4th century C.E., to a general history of Nephite civilization. The last 60 pages or so consist of additions made by Mormon's son, Moroni.

  - o The various incidents, conversations, speeches, and doctrinal expositions that make up the Book of Mormon are all presented as having been composed and edited by Nephite narrators, who are themselves characters in the story. Thus, there are several layers of possible interpretation; we can track the motives and editorial styles of the various narrators and see how they are depicted as interacting with their source materials.

  - o The stories can be rather complicated, with flashbacks, parallel narratives, embedded documents, and multiple voices, but for those with the patience to read closely, the chronologies, geographical references, and genealogical relationships are quite consistent—which is remarkable for a text that was dictated orally at one time.

Influence of the Book of Mormon

- Early Latter-day Saints tended to preach from the Bible rather than the Book of Mormon, probably because they knew the Bible better and because they thought that biblically based arguments would be more persuasive to their listeners. In the late 20th century, however, the Book of Mormon became a central component of the religion's education and worship.

- LDS liturgy has been influenced by the Book of Mormon in that the weekly Eucharist prayers are borrowed from that text and in a few hymns celebrating its coming forth, but there are no formal scripture readings in Mormon services analogous to those in other Christian or Jewish denominations, and there are no LDS holidays or churchwide commemorations based on the Book of Mormon.

- Although Mormons read the book for eternal truths and to discern God's will for them, recent scholars have seen the text as an important document in American religious history and a rich source for understanding Joseph Smith and the religious movement he founded.
    - The editor/prophets Mormon and Moroni were explicitly writing for a future audience, and their enumeration of the sins of modern America—pride, social inequality, skepticism, secret societies, rejection of prophecy and spiritual gifts, and religion as a money-making enterprise—offers insights into the religious and political tensions of Joseph Smith's day.

    - As literature, the Book of Mormon represents an interesting example of rhetoric and narrative technique in the early national period. Theologically, it responds to ambiguities and gaps in the Bible, providing an alternative to Protestant interpretations of Paul and renegotiating the boundaries between the Old and New Testaments. Nephite prophets testify to the enduring nature of God's promises to Israel, vigorously denying any hint of supersessionism.

- o Perhaps most importantly, the Book of Mormon challenges the uniqueness of the Bible. One of its main messages is that God has spoken to many peoples around the world at various times in history. In short, Mormonism does to the Christian Bible what Christianity did to the Jewish scriptures; it expands the canon and, in so doing, offers a broader perspective from which to reinterpret the familiar words.

Suggested Reading

Barlow, *Mormons and the Bible.*

Bowman, *The Mormon People.*

Bushman, *Joseph Smith.*

———, *Mormonism.*

Church of Jesus Christ of Latter-day Saints, *Book of Mormon, Doctrine and Covenants, Pearl of Great Price.*

Davies, *An Introduction to Mormonism.*

Givens, *By the Hand of Mormon.*

Gutjahr, *The Book of Mormon: A Biography.*

Hardy, ed., *The Book of Mormon: A Reader's Edition.*

———, *Understanding the Book of Mormon.*

Skousen, ed., *The Book of Mormon: The Earliest Text.*

Questions to Consider

1. What elements of the Book of Mormon make it a distinct addition to the library of recent world scriptures?

2. Does it make a difference that the Book of Mormon gave rise to a religious community, rather than the much more common pattern of a religious movement developing canonical scriptures over time?

Related Traditions—Mormon Scriptures
Lecture 29—Transcript

Welcome back. Here's a story that Mormons tell: On the evening of September 21, 1823, Joseph Smith, who was a 17-year-old farm boy in upstate New York, was lying in his bed praying for forgiveness of his sins. Suddenly, the room began to light up and an angel appeared, standing in the air. The divine messenger introduced himself as Moroni, and he told Joseph about a record of the ancient inhabitants of the Americas that was written on thin metal sheets and buried in a hill not far from his house. The angel quoted several scriptures from the Bible that he said were about to be fulfilled, and then he disappeared upward in a conduit of light. Moroni came twice more in the night to deliver the same message, and then once again the next day when Joseph was walking back to his house from the fields. Mormons usually speak of Joseph Smith as Joseph, much as followers of Tenrikyo refer to their founder, Nakayama Miki, by her given name of Miki, so I'll usually call him Joseph.

Continuing the story: That afternoon Joseph went to the hillside that he'd seen in vision and he quickly found a large rock that he'd seen in vision, and under that rock was a stone box containing the gold plates and a translating device called "the interpreters," which Joseph described as two seer stones that were set in an eyeglasses-like frame. (Seer stones were a relatively common element of folk religion in New York at the time, and Joseph later used the biblical terms Urim and Thummim to refer to the seer stones.) When he tried to remove the plates, however, from that stone box, the angel reappeared and told him that the time was not right, but to return to the hill the next year on that same date. A similar scenario was played out three more times until their fourth meeting at the hill in 1827 when Joseph was finally allowed to take the plates home and begin translating. Perhaps not coincidentally, he'd recently married Emma Hale, who accompanied him to the hill; so Joseph was a little more mature at that point.

Eyewitnesses report that Joseph would put the interpreters that came with the plates—or later a seer stone that he already had in his possession—into a hat to exclude the light, and then he placed his face in the hat and apparently read aloud the translation that he saw in the seer stone. Some modern

Mormons have started comparing this process to reading text messages on a smart phone; others believe that Joseph received spiritual impressions that he put into his own words. As Joseph dictated the text, a scribe would write down his words, repeating them back to him phrase by phrase so that he could verify their accuracy. The plates themselves lay covered on the table. Joseph's first scribe was his wife Emma, followed by Martin Harris, an older, somewhat prosperous neighbor. In this laborious fashion, a manuscript of 116 pages was written, which Harris then lost when he took it home to show his skeptical wife (it seems that the manuscript was stolen and has never been recovered.)

Several months later, a young schoolteacher named Oliver Cowdery showed up at the Smiths's home, having heard stories of angels and gold plates, and he became Joseph's principal scribe when the translation resumed, using the same procedure as before. Over the next four months, the two men produced a manuscript that was soon published as the Book of Mormon. Joseph said that the gold plates were taken back by the angel after the translation was completed, though 11 men, including Martin Harris and Oliver Cowdery, signed affidavits testifying that they'd actually seen the plates while they were in Joseph's possession.

It's a wild story, but the Book of Mormon is around for anyone to take a look at; and the original manuscript written by Joseph's scribes does show that it was written quickly from dictation, one time through from start to finish with no punctuation or paragraphing, and with immediate corrections inserted when the scribe read back a phrase and then Joseph said that he'd gotten something wrong.

In terms of number of believers and global reach, the Book of Mormon is probably the second most successful new scripture of the last few centuries, after the Sikh Adi Granth. It's rather unusual as a recent sacred text, however, in that it offers a sustained, integrated narrative rather than being a collection of poems or assorted commandments and doctrines directly revealed to a religious founder. The Book of Mormon is also distinctive in that it preceded a religious movement rather than resulting from one. Typically, as we've seen, sacred texts take shape over the course of many decades (in the case of Islam), or even over many centuries (as in Judaism, Buddhism, and

Christianity) as they gradually come to be accepted as authoritative by a religious community. By contrast, the Book of Mormon came into existence before there were any Mormons, and it was canonical from the moment it first appeared in print.

Mormonism began in upstate New York in March, 1830 with the publication of the Book of Mormon. Eleven days later, a church was formally organized by Joseph Smith, who lived from 1805–1844, and the church that he established came to be known as the Church of Jesus Christ of Latter-day Saints. Today, this denomination, headquartered in Salt Lake City, Utah, has over 15 million members worldwide. The second largest branch of Mormonism, the Independence, Missouri–based Community of Christ, has about 250,000 members.

Despite the fact that Jesus Christ features prominently in the Church's official name, Latter-day Saints, or frequently referred to as Mormons, have often been regarded as being outside the family of Christian denominations, in part because Christianity is so closely associated with a closed canon of scripture. Disagreements about which sacred texts should be authoritative are often religious boundary markers. For instance, Buddhists and Jains aren't considered branches of Hinduism, despite a number of similar beliefs and the astonishing pluralistic nature of Hinduism, because those two newer religions reject the authority of the Vedas. So also the fact that Mormons have scriptures in addition to the Bible leads some to see it as a distinct religion rather than just a doctrinally creative sect or denomination of Christianity; though perhaps the situation is more like Mahayana Buddhism or Christianity than like Islam. Remember that in Islam, Muslims regard the Qur'an as a replacement for Jewish and Christian scriptures that have been corrupted and misunderstood over time. By contrast, Mahayana Buddhists simply added new sacred texts to the canon; and Christians just adopted the Hebrew scriptures as their own, while reinterpreting them along distinctively Christian lines.

Mormons add the Book of Mormon to the Bible, and they give full canonical authority to the Bible. They carry copies of it to church with them every Sunday and they study it regularly; yet they interpret the Old and the New Testaments in terms of their unique, additional scriptures. Those scriptures consist of the Book of Mormon, which we'll come back to in a few minutes; the Doctrine and Covenants, consisting primarily of revelations given directly to Joseph Smith; and finally the Pearl of Great Price, a relatively short work that began as a British missionary pamphlet in 1851 and wasn't formally canonized until 1880.

The Pearl of Great Price gathered together some of Smith's lesser-known writings, including excepts from his inspired revision of the Bible, selections from an autobiographical essay, and a translation of Egyptian papyri from mummies that had come into his possession, which he called the Book of Abraham; though the surviving papyri turned out to be a copy of the Book of Breathing, a funerary text related to the Egyptian Book of the Dead.

We can talk for a minute about the Doctrine and Covenants, which is divided into 138 chapter-like sections. It's fairly typical of sacred texts of new religious movements. The Doctrine and Covenants contains revelations given to the founder, in this case Joseph Smith, which were edited and revised by Smith and his successors over several decades. The contents are rather eclectic; they include prophecies, commandments, scriptural exegesis, doctrinal exposition, and instructions for church organization, as well as advice and comfort for Mormons as they immigrated, sometimes under intense persecution, from New York to Ohio to Missouri and then to Illinois.

After Joseph Smith was assassinated in 1844, most Mormons trekked across the continent to Utah on foot under the leadership of Brigham Young. But unlike the Adi Granth and the Ofudesaki, there's very little poetry in the Doctrine and Covenants. Nearly a hundred of these revelations were received by Joseph Smith from 1829–1833, and then there were a few each year after that for a total of 138 sections that include 3 sections from later church leaders. After the 1830s, Smith's doctrinal innovations tended to be communicated to his followers in sermons rather than in formal revelations. Appended to the end of Doctrine and Covenants are two official declarations: one ending the practice of polygamy in 1890, and the other rescinding the priesthood ban for black members in 1978.

Latter-day Saints will tell you that they have four "standard works"—that's their parlance for sacred texts—but actually, they have five; and the fifth, rather unusually, is oral rather than written scripture: It's the text of their temple ceremony. You will recall that Hindu Brahmins resisted putting the Vedas into written form for a very long time because they believed that doing so would make those holy words common and accessible to everyone. It was important that the Vedas be internalized though memorization; that they were passed on directly from those with proper authority who'd already mastered their meanings, and they needed to be spoken aloud in very specific ritual contexts in order to actualize their sacred power. This is similar to the way that Mormons feel about the temple ceremony, or the endowment as they call it.

While Mormon chapels feature Protestant-style Sunday services that are open to everyone, their temples are particularly sacred spaces where admittance is only granted to adult Latter-day Saints who meet strict standards of worthiness and faithfulness. In those buildings, eternal marriages are performed, as well as ordinances such as baptisms, priesthood ordinations, confirmations, and the sealing of parents to children on behalf of deceased ancestors, thus ensuring that people born before Joseph Smith's restoration of the full gospel have access to all of God's blessings. This is also the reason why Mormons have been doing genealogy for a long time, to find the names of those ancestors so that each of them individually can receive these ordinances in the temple and have the opportunity to become Mormon in the next life, though it's certainly not a guarantee of that.

Mormons also participate in the endowment, which is a sort of initiation rite that portrays the creation of the world and the fall of Adam and Eve in a scripted drama, along with covenants and blessings directed toward individual believers. The wording of the ceremony is exact and invariable, though the church has made minor changes from time to time. The text of the endowment ceremony was for the most part composed by Brigham Young based on an outline and key elements that had been entrusted to him by Joseph Smith; so the endowment can be thought of as Brigham's contribution to Mormon scripture. Most Latter-day Saints only encounter these words orally as the ceremony is performed. It takes about an hour and a half; and because regular temple attendance is encouraged, many Latter-day Saints have the script memorized. But the words are considered so sacred that Mormons are forbidden from repeating them outside the temple, or even discussing the details of the endowment. Separated from their ritual context, or if they were put in written form, the words would lose their significance and become debased.

The primary sacred text of Mormonism, however, and the one that Latter-day Saints are most eager to share with the world, is the Book of Mormon. This scripture claims to be a translation of an ancient record from the Americas, which recounts the thousand-year history of a society that was transplanted from Judea in the Old World to the New World. The book begins about 600 B.C.E. when a Jewish prophet named Lehi was warned by God to take his family and flee from Jerusalem shortly before the Babylonian conquest. They wandered in the Arabian Desert for eight years, and then were commanded by God to build a boat and sail to the Americas. Lehi and his son Nephi continued to receive divine revelations, including the news that a Messiah, Jesus Christ, would someday be born in Israel and would atone for the sins of the world. Those who accepted this novel doctrine became known as Nephites, while their unbelieving relatives were called Lamanites, after one of the other brothers in the family who wasn't quite so open to these ideas.

The Book of Mormon tells of the interactions between these two peoples, the Nephites and the Lamanites, along with another group known as the Mulekites, who'd also emigrated from Jerusalem at about the same time with a member of the royal house of David in tow. There's a long succession of wars, political intrigues, missionary efforts, sermons, and confrontations with religious dissenters, punctuated by miracles and revelations. We also read lengthy discussions of the destiny of the house of Israel, of covenants, prophecy, sin, repentance, and Christian ethics, all within the context of a sweeping historical narrative that sort of pulls everything together and puts everything in a place in this grand story.

About halfway through the book, escalating military conflicts, along with a striking reversal in which the Lamanites are more righteous than the Nephites, lead to a breakdown of the social order. After terrible natural disasters wreak havoc on a wicked society, the few who'd remained faithful to the Nephite prophecies are vindicated by the coming of the resurrected Jesus to the Americas. While he's there, Jesus establishes a church, he heals the sick, he blesses children, he teaches a version of the Sermon on the Mount, and he prophesies of relations between Jews and Gentiles in the last days. After a couple centuries of peace and prosperity, old antagonisms resurface, eventually leading to a war of extermination. The Nephites are destroyed by the Lamanites about 400 C.E., and the Christian traditions of the New World were thereby lost, aside from this single record, which was buried by the last of the Nephites, the prophet Moroni, who would later appear to Joseph Smith as an angel. Mormons believe that most angels are resurrected human beings or the souls of those who are yet to be resurrected; so Moroni is a character in the Book of Mormon, and then he's the one who buries the plates, and then he's also, as an angel, the one who tells Joseph Smith where to find them and what to do with them.

It's natural to wonder how this complicated, detailed narrative fits with what was known about pre-Columbian civilizations, both in Joseph Smith's time and today. Aside from the first chapters that take place in the vicinity of Jerusalem, for which there's perhaps some archaeological evidence, there are no artifacts from the New World that decisively support Joseph's tale of Nephites and Lamanites. Early believers regarded the Book of Mormon as the story of the origins of the American Indians, who would've been descended from the Lamanites; however, more recent Latter-day Saint interpretations, based on a closer analysis of the text, see the events of the Book of Mormon as taking place in a much more limited geographical area—so not North and South America, but perhaps in Central America—with the Lamanites being absorbed into much larger Native American populations that immigrated across the Bering Straits. Apparently the peoples of the Book of Mormon didn't leave much of an imprint on material culture or even DNA.

Historicity matters to most Latter-day Saints—they believe that the events described in the Book of Mormon actually happened—in part because Joseph's claims of gold plates made by ancient prophets seems to require some actual historical basis (Joseph Smith had these plates that he came from the ancient world), and because a work of inspired fiction or imaginative inspiration wouldn't have the same moral authority or urgency. Yet Mormons are generally not consumed by questions of archaeological support or the lack thereof. They assume that such evidence will someday appear; and in the meantime, they urge readers to seek spiritual confirmation of the truth of the Book of Mormon, pointing to a passage in its last chapter that says:

> And when ye shall receive these things, I would exhort you that ye would ask God, the Eternal Father, in the name of Christ, if these things are not true; and if ye shall ask with a sincere heart, with real intent, having faith in Christ, he will manifest the truth of it unto you, by the power of the Holy Ghost.

Whether regarded as fact or fiction, however, the Book of Mormon is something of an anomaly in recent world scripture in that it consists of a coherent, integrated narrative. The language, which imitates the King James Bible, can be a bit awkward and repetitious, but there's a clear structure underlying it all. The first quarter of the book consists of first person accounts from Nephi and his younger brother Jacob in the 6th century B.C.E. Then these pages, a little bit later on, are revealed to be a document that was appended by Mormon, writing in the 4th century C.E., to a general history of Nephite civilization; so he's writing at pretty much the end, and then he's looking back and he puts those first chapters in. The bulk of the work is Mormon's abridgment of earlier records, which is why it's called the Book of Mormon. The last 60 pages or so are additions made by Mormon's son, Moroni. The various incidents, conversations, speeches, and doctrinal expositions that make up the Book of Mormon are all presented as having been composed and edited by Nephite narrators, who are themselves characters in the story. So there are always several layers of possible interpretation; we can track the motives and the editorial styles of the various narrators—they actually tell us explicitly "This is what I'm trying to do with putting this information together"—and see how those narrators are depicted as interacting with their source materials.

The stories can be rather complicated, with flashbacks, parallel narratives, embedded documents, and multiple voices; indeed, there are more than 200 named individuals and some 90 different places that are mentioned in the Book of Mormon narrative. But for those with the patience to read closely, the chronologies, the geographical references, and the genealogical relationships are quite consistent, which is remarkable for a text that was dictated orally, one-time through from beginning to end. All of these details are easier to follow in the Reader's Edition that was published by the University of Illinois rather than in the official LDS version, which puts things in an old biblical style with just double columns (though you can get the official LDS version for free). Editions of the Book of Mormon after 1830 introduced several thousand changes into the text, but these were almost entirely grammatical or stylistic in nature; the original narrative, with its twists and turns, parallel narratives and flashbacks, intertextual allusions, and thick connections, has all remained unchanged.

Early Latter-day Saints tended to preach from the Bible rather than the Book of Mormon, probably because they knew the Bible better and because they thought that biblically-based arguments would be more persuasive to their listeners. In fact, for a long time, Mormons didn't read the Book of Mormon all that closely; instead, they regarded its very existence as proof of Joseph Smith's prophetic calling, much as Muslims thought of the Qur'an and Muhammad. In the late 20th century, however, the Book of Mormon became a central component of LDS education and worship. Today, in Mormon services or in conversations among church members, you're likely to hear references to dozens of favorite verses and stories. You might hear, for example, about Lehi's dream of a tree with delicious fruit, which can be reached by following an iron handrail through the mists of darkness and ignoring the jeers of those looking out from a large and spacious building. (It's an allegory, of course.) Young Mormons can tell you about the missionary successes of the sons of Mosiah; about the faithfulness of Helaman's 2,000 stripling warriors who were inspired by the faith of their mothers and who were protected in battle. They could tell you how Alma the younger repented of his sins. They may be able to recount some of the exploits of the valiant Captain Moroni; though in this respect, the Book of Mormon is a little like the Bhagavad Gita: There are celebrations of military prowess and victories on the battlefield; but taken as a whole, the Book of Mormon strongly condemns militarism. Warfare leads the Nephites to utter destruction.

Other well-known stories include the martyrdom of Abinadi; how Samuel the Lamanite prophet was protected from the stones and arrows of his enemies while he preached from atop a city wall; King Benjamin's command to give to those in need, observing that "When ye are in the service of your fellow beings, ye are only in the service of your God"; and Alma's (Alma the elder's) invitation to baptism for those who, as it says, "are willing to bear one another's burdens, that they may be light; yea, and are willing to mourn with those that mourn; yea, and comfort those that stand in need of comfort, and to stand as witnesses of God at all times and in all things and in all places," words that are repeated at many LDS baptismal services today.

Latter-day Saint liturgy has been influenced by the Book of Mormon in that the weekly Eucharist prayers are borrowed from that text, as are a few hymns that celebrate the coming forth of the Book of Mormon; but it's perhaps surprising that there are no formal scripture readings in Mormon services analogous to those in other Christian or Jewish denominations, and there are no LDS holidays or church-wide commemorations based on the Book of Mormon, though Latter-day Saints do celebrate a Pioneer Day every July 24. In LDS popular culture, however, the Book of Mormon looms large in artwork, children's songs, dramatizations, and even toy action figures. Illustrations from the Book of Mormon are to be found in Mormon meeting houses and actually sometimes even included in missionary editions of the Book of Mormon, and they're well known by children and Mormons everywhere.

In recent years, outsiders have been paying more attention to the Mormon scripture, and not only in a Broadway musical comedy of the same name; which, by the way, is more about LDS missionaries and the power of religious imagination rather than the actual contents of the Book of Mormon. When Mormons read the book for eternal truths and to discern God's will for them, scholars have seen the text as an important document in American religious history and a rich source for understanding Joseph Smith and the religious movement that he founded. The editor/prophets Mormon and Moroni, coming at the tail end of Nephite civilization, were explicitly writing for a future audience at a time when the record would be rediscovered and translated (so they knew that their civilization was coming to an end, so they wrote this and then buried it to be recovered later on) and their enumeration of the sins of modern America that they saw, supposedly in prophesy—sins of pride, social inequality, skepticism, secret societies, rejection of prophecy and spiritual gifts, and religion as a money-making enterprise—all of those offer insights into the religious and political tensions of Joseph Smith's day.

As literature, the Book of Mormon represents an interesting example of rhetoric and narrative technique in the early national period. Theologically, it responds to ambiguities and gaps in the Bible, providing an alternative to Protestant interpretations of Paul and renegotiating the boundaries between the Old and New Testaments since it portrays Old Testament prophets as being rather familiar with the future life and mission of Jesus Christ. Nephite prophets testify of the enduring nature of God's promises to Israel, and they vigorously deny any hint of supersessionism, which, as you may remember is the idea that the Church is going to supersede or replace Israel and its covenants; the Book of Mormon completely rejects that and says that modern Gentiles who join the church will actually be brought into the house of Israel. But perhaps most importantly, the Book of Mormon challenges the uniqueness of the Bible. One of the Book of Mormon's main messages is that God has spoken to many peoples around the world at various times in history. In short, Mormonism does to the Christian Bible what Christianity did to the Jewish scriptures: It expands the canon and in so doing offers a broader perspective from which to reinterpret the familiar words.

The Book of Mormon is perhaps the quintessential American scripture, yet its appeal has reached beyond national borders, even to rather unlikely places. Somewhat embarrassingly now, there are a few verses in which Nephite narrators regard the darker skins of the Lamanites as a curse. Nevertheless, when Joseph William Billy Johnson came across a copy of the Book of Mormon in Ghana in 1964 and read it, he became convinced that it was the word of God. The LDS Church had no official presence in his country, because at that time men of African descent were barred from holding the priesthood and thus from nearly all leadership positions. Johnson, however, began preaching the Book of Mormon, and over the next 14 years he established several congregations that were entirely independent of the Utah church. He said, "The Book of Mormon is a powerful book, and I got nearer to God when I read it." Johnson told of miraculous healings that had come from placing the book on the sick and then praying for their recovery. Johnson and his converts kept in contact with the Mormon Church, and when the priesthood ban was lifted in 1978, they welcomed the opportunity to be ordained and to become affiliated with Latter-day Saints around the world.

The first official representatives from Salt Lake City to arrive in Ghana were astonished to find seven congregations waiting for them, with 500 to maybe 1,000 members in all. In Cape Coast, in the chapel there, they saw a lifesize sculpture of the angel Moroni, copied from the cover of the Book of Mormon; the very book that Johnson had seen years earlier and read, and had been converted by simply reading the words and feeling the spirit of the book.

Islam and Scriptural Recitation
Lecture 30

In 1352, Ibn Battuta, a native of Morocco, arrived in the West African empire of Mali, where he was impressed by the eagerness of his fellow Muslims to memorize the Qur'an. It's interesting to note that even in the 14th century, Islam was a universal religion that had crossed geographic and ethnic boundaries. (Today, it has some 1.6 billion adherents.) Memorizing the Qur'an has long been a celebrated act of devotion; even today, every year during the month of Ramadan, more than 100 students from 70 countries compete in a memorization contest in Cairo. In this lecture, we'll discuss Muhammad, the Qur'an, and attitudes of Muslims toward this sacred scripture.

Muhammad and the Rise of Islam

- Muhammad was born about 570 C.E. in Mecca, a trading town in Arabia that was the site of an ancient shrine called the Ka'ba, said to have been built by Abraham but at that time housing images of hundreds of gods. After being orphaned at a young age, Muhammad worked in the caravan trade and eventually married his boss, an older widow named Khadijah. This gave him a measure of prominence and security, though he still felt spiritual yearnings and would regularly retreat to a cave in the hills outside of Mecca to pray and meditate.

- On one such occasion, when he was 40 years old, Muhammad heard a voice commanding, "Recite." "Recite what?" he asked. The terrifying command was repeated twice more, and then the words came to him. With the verses etched into his memory, Muhammad came down from the hills and saw the angel Gabriel, who told Muhammad that he was the messenger of God. Afraid that he might be losing his mind, Muhammad went home to Khadijah, who told him she thought that his revelation was from God.

- The words continued to come: affirmations of the power and mercy of the one God, denunciations of idolatry and evil doing, warnings of the last judgment, commandments to live uprightly and treat others with kindness. After three years, Muhammad began to share these revelations with people outside his family, and he gradually gained a following.

- Trouble and persecution came when his preaching of monotheism threatened the livelihood of those who depended on the Ka'ba to bring religious pilgrims to Mecca; thus, when a delegation arrived in 622 from Medina, a town 250 miles to the northeast, inviting Muhammad to come and settle a dispute between clans, he jumped at the chance. His move from Mecca to Medina, now referred to as the Hijra, is the pivot of the Muslim calendar. Years are designated either B.H. or A.H.

- Muhammad became the spiritual and political leader of the community in Medina, and when conflict eventually broke into fighting with Mecca, Muhammad and his forces captured that city in 630; the Prophet lived there for the next two years until his death. His successors—not prophets but caliphs ("successors")—continued to expand the realm of Islam militarily. From 632 to 661, under the first four caliphs, Muslim armies conquered Egypt, Mesopotamia, and Persia.

- A year after Muhammad's death, a battle took place in which many of the original reciters of his words were killed. As a result, the first caliph, Abu Bakr, ordered the collection of all the revelations that had come to Muhammad in the 23 years from his first encounter with the angel Gabriel until his death. Around 650, under the third caliph, Uthman, these revelations were put into the standard form of 114 suras of the current Qur'an, and divergent copies were destroyed.

- Uthman's Qur'an was something like the Masoretic text of the Hebrew Bible; it presented the word of God in a fixed form, right down to mysterious, disconnected Arabic letters that appear at the beginning of 29 suras. Most Muslims, however, believe that the Qur'an was not the product of human editing; rather, it came through an inspired process that re-created the Qur'an that existed in heaven before it was revealed to Muhammad.

- After the assassination of the fourth caliph, 'Ali, who was Muhammad's son-in-law, the Muslim community split.
  o The majority followed the lead of the Umayyad clan, who established a powerful empire that lasted from 661 to 750 and expanded the realm of Islam to North Africa and Spain. These were the Sunni Muslims. Others, however, believed that the leadership of Islam should stay within the Prophet Muhammad's family line. These became known as Shia Muslims.

  o Today, about 85 percent of Muslims are Sunni and 15 percent are Shia. There are, however, a few countries, such as Iran and Iraq, where the Shia are in the majority.

- All Muslims, whether Sunni or Shia, hold to the Five Pillars: (1) the confession of faith ("There is no God but Allah, and Muhammad is his prophet"), (2) prayer five times a day facing Mecca, (3) fasting during daylight hours for the month of Ramadan, (4) charitable giving to the poor and needy, and (5) pilgrimage to Mecca at least once in a lifetime, if possible. In addition, the Qur'an is revered by all Muslims; thus, it serves as a sort of foundation for the Five Pillars.

Significance of the Qur'an

- The Qur'an is what we might call "postcanonical scripture." That is, Muhammad was well aware that Jews and Christians had sacred texts that had already been in circulation for centuries, which they claimed had come from the one God. What was the point of yet another book of scripture? What made the Qur'an different from, and superior to, the Bible?

- The first difference is that Muslims believe the Qur'an came by direct revelation. Jews had long accepted the Torah as revelation to

Moses, but much of the rest of the Tanakh seemed to be the work of inspired poets, historians, and editors. The Hebrew Bible is the story of a relationship—the relationship of God and Israel; it isn't a transcript of God's utterances. And the New Testament is even farther removed—the gospels are collections of stories about Jesus, and the epistles are letters, written by Paul or John, not by God.

- A second difference between the Bible and the Qur'an is that the latter is regarded by Muslims as the complete and final revelation of God. One of the major themes in the Qur'an is that God had sent earlier prophets to humankind, but their words had been ignored or distorted.
  - Four special messengers received heavenly books: the Scrolls was revealed to Abraham; Moses received the Torah; David, the Psalms; and Jesus, the Gospel (a book actually written down by Jesus himself, not the four gospels of the New Testament), but all of these were lost, corrupted, or misinterpreted.

  - God gave the Qur'an to Muhammad as a corrective, a perfect text that could resolve all confusion and teach the truth clearly. This is the last word that would ever be needed; thus, Muhammad was the "seal of the prophets"—the final prophet and authenticator of all his predecessors.

- A third unique aspect of the Qur'an, again, according to Muslims, is the perfect beauty of its language. It is written in a rhythmic form of Arabic, with a great deal of alliteration, assonance, and end rhymes. In the centuries following Muhammad, Islamic thinkers developed the concept of the "inimitability" of the Qur'an, though the seeds of the idea are within the text itself.

- At a time when many believed that God's messengers could be identified by the miracles they performed, Muslims held up the Qur'an as Muhammad's greatest miracle, especially given that he was thought to have been illiterate or, at least, unacquainted with books. The elevated style and content of the Qur'an constitute a sign of its truth.

In a religion that strictly forbids graven images, calligraphy is a prestigious form of art; mosques are often decorated with Qur'anic calligraphy.

Reverence for the Qur'an

- Because the language of the Qur'an is inseparable from its content and because both come directly from God, a translation of the Qur'an is not the real Qur'an. For that matter, the real Qur'an is not the lines written on a page but, rather, the words as they are spoken and heard. The Qur'an as a book is merely an aid to memorization or recitation.

- In Muslim countries, the sounds of the Qur'an are everywhere, particularly given that the recitation of the Qur'an is a sophisticated and esteemed art form. The sacred words can be heard not only in mosques but on radio and television, in taxicabs and concert halls, and at weddings, festivals, and funerals.

- There are two basic forms of Quranic recitation: one with strict rules for ordinary study and practice and the other more freeform, featuring a great deal of melodic modulation and technical artistry, performed by trained experts.

- Memorizing, reciting, and listening to the Qur'an are ways of communing with God in a bodily fashion, perhaps something like taking the Eucharist in the Christian faith. But it's not just a Sunday or a seasonal thing. There is no tradition of separating church and state in Islam; thus, the Qur'an infuses everyday life, even in aspects that would seem political or secular to Westerners.

- And even though the Qur'an as a physical object is just a shadow of the true aural Qur'an, it is nevertheless a sacred object. It is kept apart from other books, with nothing placed on top of it. Many Muslims wash their hands before reading the Qur'an, and it is usually referred to not just as "the Qur'an" but as "the Glorious Qur'an" or "the Noble Qur'an."
  - The respect shown for the Qur'an may not be quite like that of the Sikhs for the Adi Granth, because Muslims do not treat the Qur'an as a living guru, yet it is higher than that shown for the Bible, which is widely distributed in hundreds of languages and is, at least as a physical object, regarded as a regular book.
  - Further, the primacy of the spoken or chanted version of scripture is familiar from Hinduism, but unlike the Sanskrit of the Vedas, Arabic is still a living language, and the meaning of the Qur'an matters enormously to believers.

Suggested Reading

Cook, *The Koran: A Very Short Introduction*.

Mattson, *The Story of the Qur'an*.

Levering, ed., *Rethinking Scripture*.

Nigosian, *Islam*.

Ruthven, *Islam in the World*.

Sells, *Approaching the Qur'an*.

Questions to Consider

1. How does the relationship between Islam and the Qur'an differ from that of Christianity and the Bible?

2. Why is the recitation and memorization of the Qur'an (in its original Arabic!) so crucial to Muslim faith?

Islam and Scriptural Recitation
Lecture 30—Transcript

Hello, thanks for joining me again. In 1352, Ibn Battuta, a native of Morocco, arrived in the West African empire of Mali. He wasn't a novice traveler. In the previous quarter century, he'd seen North Africa, Arabia, East Africa, Persia, Turkey, Kazakhstan, India, Indonesia, China, and Spain. Over his lifetime, Ibn Battuta travelled some 73,000 miles, which is astonishing in the time before planes, trains, and automobiles. In Mali, Ibn Battuta was impressed by some aspects of their culture, such as their honesty and the fact that one needed to get to the mosque early on Fridays to get a seat, yet he was disappointed in some other things that he saw. He criticized their laxness in keeping some of the dietary regulations and what he considered the insufficient modesty of their women; but one thing that caught his attention was their eagerness to memorize the Qur'an. In fact, he reports that some Muslim leaders put their children in chains until they'd memorized that sacred text.

I wouldn't recommend this today as a method of dealing with kids who don't want to do their homework, but Ibn Battuta's story illustrates several important points. The first is that Islam, even in the 14th century, was a universal religion that had crossed geographical and ethnic boundaries; so even in West Africa, Islam is going to be very significant in the government and in the culture. Ibn Battuta had been trained as a judge, an expert in Muslim law, and he was able to find employment most everywhere he went, all of those places that I talked about. Islam, which began in the 7th century C.E., is one of the world's great missionary religions, along with Buddhism and Christianity, spreading far beyond the land of its origins. Today, Islam is the second largest religion on the planet, after Christianity, with some 1.6 billion adherents. By comparison, there are about 2 billion Christians, 1 billion Hindus, 500 million Buddhists, 28 million Sikhs, 14 million Jews, and 4 million Jains.

The second point from this story about Ibn Battuta looking at or observing Muslim customs in West Africa is that Ibn Battuta had a tremendous advantage as a world traveler in that he spoke Arabic. For Christians, the meaning of their scriptures is more important than the exact words, perhaps because the New Testament, written in Greek, is already one step removed from Jesus's actual words, which would've been in Aramaic. As a result of that commitment to meaning, Christians have been eager to translate their sacred text into as many languages as possible. Currently, the New Testament is available in some 1,300 languages, with at least one book of the Bible in another thousand tongues. By contrast, Muslims believe that the Qur'an was revealed by God to Muhammad in Arabic, so there's an incentive for Muslims all over the world to learn that language in order to hear God's word in its original, inimitable form. Consequently, Ibn Battuta, knowing Arabic, could communicate with other Muslims wherever he went around the world. Because Islam began in Arabia, it's a common misconception that most Muslims are Arabs. Actually, only about 18 percent of Muslims today are Arabs. The eight countries with the largest Muslim populations are, in order: Indonesia (the largest), then Pakistan, India, Bangladesh, Egypt, Nigeria, Iran, and Turkey. Of those, only one, Egypt, speaks Arabic as its native language.

But there's something about the Qur'an, in the eyes of believers, that defies translation. It's also not a text that easily sits within the covers of a book. The name Qur'an means "recitation," and the words have to be spoken aloud to be truly appreciated; and not just read aloud, it's far better if they're spoken from the heart. Which bring us to point number three: Memorizing the Qur'an has long been a celebrated act of devotion. The book is fairly substantial. It consists of 114 chapters, called Suras, divided into about 6,200 verses, totaling more than about 78,000 words; so it's over half the length of the Greek New Testament. Christians might memorize individual verses or short passages, but I don't know many (I actually don't know any) who can recite Matthew, Mark, Luke, John, and Acts from the beginning to the end from memory, especially in Greek, which is as foreign to most Christians as Arabic is to most Muslims.

There is a wonderful 2011 documentary called *Koran by Heart* about the world's oldest Qur'an memorization contest. Every year, more than 100 young students from 70 countries come to Cairo during the holy month of Ramadan to compete. Not only must they memorize the entire text of the Qur'an, they also have to be able to recite it according to traditional rules of intonation; it's almost like it's being sung. The film follows three 10-year-olds, two boys from Senegal and Tajikistan, and then a girl from the Maldive Islands in the Indian Ocean. It puts human faces on an often misunderstood religious tradition, and it focuses on the deep relationships that Muslims have with their sacred text. In addition, in this film you get to hear a lot of Qur'anic recitation, one of the most beautiful, poignant sounds on earth even if you don't understand Arabic.

In this lecture, I'll talk a little about Muhammad, the Qur'an, and attitudes of Muslims toward this scripture, especially as compared to the way that other faiths respond to their sacred texts. In the next lecture, we'll go into more detail about the contents and themes of the Qur'an.

We'll start with Muhammad, who was born about 570 C.E. in Mecca, a trading town in Arabia that was the site of an ancient shrine called the Ka'ba, said to have been built by Abraham, but at that time housing the images of hundreds of gods. After being orphaned at a young age, Muhammad worked in the caravan trade, and eventually married his boss, an older widow named Khadijah. This gave him a measure of prominence and security, though he nevertheless felt spiritual yearnings and would regularly retreat to a cave in the hills outside of Mecca to pray and to meditate. On one such occasion, when Muhammad was 40 years old, he felt a tremendous pressure on him, a squeezing, and then he heard a voice commanding, "Recite." "Recite what?" he asked, and the terrifying command was repeated twice more, and then the words came: "Recite—in the name of your Lord who created – created man from clots of blood. Recite! Your Lord is the Most Bountiful One, who by the pen taught man what he did not know." Then it continues. With the verses etched into his memory, he came down from the hills and he saw an angel, who said, "O Muhammad, you are the messenger of God and I am Gabriel."

Coming down from the cave and returning back home, he was afraid that he might be losing his mind; and he talked to his wife Khadija, who listened to his story and then told him that she thought that this was an actual revelation from God. Khadija was the first one to believe in Muhammad's message, even at a time when Muhammad himself wasn't quite sure what was going on. In the years to come, the words continued to flow: affirmations of the power and mercy of the One God, denunciations of idolatry and evildoing, warnings of the last judgment, and commandments to live uprightly and treat others with kindness. After three years, Muhammad began to share these revelations with people outside of his family, and he gradually gained a following.

Trouble and persecution followed when his preaching of monotheism threatened the livelihood of those who depended on the Ka'ba to bring religious pilgrims to Mecca; so when a delegation arrived in 622 from Medina, which was a town about 250 miles to the northeast, inviting him to come and settle a dispute between clans, he jumped at the chance. These visitors had heard of Muhammad, they'd heard of his spiritual closeness with God, and they invited him to come back with him. It was a great opportunity for Muhammad; and his move from Mecca to Medina, now referred to as the Hijra, is actually the pivot of the Muslim calendar today. Years are designated either B.H., Before the Hijra, or A.H., After the Hijra. The Muslim calendar is a lunar calendar rather than a solar calendar, so you just can't add and subtract the dates from the Western calendar to get the right year in the Muslim calendar. Muhammad became the spiritual and political leader of the community in Medina; and when conflict continued with Mecca, eventually breaking out into actual fighting, Muhammad and his forces captured Mecca in 630.

Muhammad lived for two more years—he actually returned to Medina, where he dies—and then is his successors were appointed. They, of course, can't be prophets because Muhammad was the seal of the prophets, the last of them, and instead they were referred to as caliphs, "successors," "lieutenants," and they continued to expand the realm of Islam militarily. From 632–661 under the first four caliphs—and particularly under three of the four caliphs—Muslim armies conquered Egypt, Mesopotamia, and Persia. The words *Muslim* and *Islam* are both derived from the same Arabic root, which indicates those who submit themselves to God. *Allah* is the Arabic name for "God," the same God that's worshipped by Jews and Christians.]

A year after Muhammad's death, there was a battle in which many of the original reciters of his words, those companions of his who'd memorized the revelations when they came, were killed in this battle. As a result, the first caliph, Abu Bakr, ordered the collection of all of the revelations that had come to Muhammad in the 23 years from his first encounter with the angel Gabriel until his death. As I said, these had been memorized by his companions as they'd come down from heaven, and then some of them had been written down on palm leaves, flat rocks, pieces of wood, leather, or animal bones, and those are what Abu Bakr asked to be collected. Then, around 650, under the third caliph, Uthman, these revelations were put into the standard form of 114 suras of the current Qur'an and divergent copies were destroyed.

Uthman's Qur'an was something like the Masoretic text of the Hebrew Bible. It presented the word of God in fixed form, right down to mysterious, disconnected Arabic letters that appear at the beginning of 29 suras. Those mysterious letters, there might be one or as many as five; they just appear at the beginning. We're not sure what they mean, but they're part of the text, so they're copied and they're part of every copy of the Qur'an today. Most Muslims, however, believe that the Qur'an wasn't the product of human editing; rather, it came through an inspired process that recreated on earth the Qur'an that existed in heaven before it was revealed to Muhammad. The very order of the suras that we have now isn't a random order; it's the order that was intended by God, which matches this heavenly book. Note that the fixed form of the Qur'an came just 20 years after Muhammad's death, much faster than the formation and canonization of the New Testament, which took several centuries, as we heard in a previous lecture.

After the assassination of the fourth Caliph, Ali, who was Muhammad's son-in-law, the Muslim community split. The majority followed the lead of the Umayyad clan, who established a powerful empire that lasted from 661–750 and expanded the realm of Islam to North Africa and into Spain. These were the Sunni Muslims. Others, however, believed that the leadership of Islam should've stayed within the Prophet Muhammad's family line, and these became known as Shia Muslims. Today, about 85 percent of Muslims are Sunni and maybe 15 percent Shia. There are, however, a few countries, such as Iran and Iraq, where the Shia are in the majority. *Sunni* means "the trodden path" or "habitual practice," and it refers to the example set by Muhammad. *Shia* means "partisan" or "faction"; that is, the party of Ali and his descendants.

All Muslims, whether Sunni or Shia, hold to the Five Pillars: The first is the confession of faith; "There is no God but Allah, and Muhammad is his prophet." The second is prayer five times a day facing Mecca, and the set prayers are quotations from the Qur'an, recited in Arabic. The third of the Five Pillars is fasting during the daylight hours of the month of Ramadan; so you eat a big meal right before the sunrise, and then you don't have food or water for the whole day until the sun goes down again and then you can eat once again, and they keep that going for a month. The fourth of the Five Pillars is paying a tax that's devoted to the benefit of the poor and needy. The fifth is pilgrimage to Mecca at least once in a person's life, if they're physically and financially able to do so. In addition to the Five Pillars, the Qur'an is revered by all Muslims, so it serves as a sort of foundation for the faith. There are other important texts in Islam, such as the Hadith, which are traditions about the life of Muhammad, and mystical Sufi writings, which we'll discuss in Lecture 32; but nothing comes close to the holiness or the authority of the Qur'an.

The Qur'an is what we might call "post-canonical scripture." That is to say, Muhammad was well aware that Jews and Christians had sacred texts that had already been in circulation for centuries, which they claimed had come from the One God. Indeed, the Qur'an calls those believers "people of the book" who would be rewarded for their faith and good works on the day of judgment. What was the point of yet another book of scripture? What made the Qur'an different from and superior to the Bible?

The first difference is that Muslims believe the Qur'an came by direct revelation. Jews had long accepted the Torah as revelation to Moses, but much of the rest of the Tanakh seemed to be the work of inspired poets, historians, and editors. The Hebrew Bible is the story of a relationship: the relationship of God and Israel. It isn't a transcript of God's utterances aside from some "thus says the Lord" passages in the Prophets, and the New Testament is even farther removed. The Gospels are collections of stories about Jesus, and the epistles are letters, written by Paul or John; they're not written by God. The Harvard scholar Wilfred Cantwell Smith observed that for Christians, the revelation of God is in a person, Jesus Christ, and the New Testament is simply a record of that revelation. So, he says, "The Qur'an is to Muslims what Christ is to Christians."

Calling both the New Testament and the Qur'an "sacred texts" doesn't quite capture how they function differently in the two religious traditions. The great 14th-century Muslim historian Ibn Khaldun, who was a contemporary of the traveler Ibn Battuta, wrote: "The Qur'an is alone among the divine books, in that our Prophet received it directly in the words and phrases in which it appears. In this respect, it differs from the Torah, the Gospel, and other heavenly books. The prophets received them in the form of ideas during the state of revelation." Muhammad, by contrast, didn't get impressions that he then put into his own words; he didn't just get ideas, he received exact phrases in Arabic. Aisha, Muhammad's last and most beloved wife, remembered her husband saying that revelation came upon him like the ringing of a bell or the voice of an angel, after which the words were impressed upon his memory. She herself could remember seeing his physical discomfort when inspiration came upon him or overcame him, as he'd begin to sweat, even on cold days. It was a very physical process by which he received these communications from heaven. The products of those unsettling episodes were the verbatim words of God, spoken in Arabic, and dictated to Muhammad by the angel Gabriel. In early Muslim theology, one of the major debates was whether the Qur'an was created by God or whether it was coeternal with him. Both points of view show an exalted view of the text. (Eventually the view that's going to win out is the one that says that the Qur'an is eternal and unchanged; that it existed before the beginning of the world.)

A second difference between the Bible and the Qur'an is that the latter is regarded by Muslims as the complete and final revelation of God. One of the major themes in the Qur'an is how God had sent earlier prophets to humankind, but their words then had been ignored or distorted, and ultimately rejected by many. The Qur'an names a couple dozen of these figures, many familiar from the Bible, such as Adam, Noah, Ishmael, Joseph; and then there were others who were prophets in Arabia, like Hud and Salih. Four special messengers received heavenly books: The Scrolls were revealed to Abraham, Moses received the Torah, King David received the Psalms, and Jesus the Gospel, which was regarded as a book that was actually written down by Jesus himself; they weren't talking about the four gospels of the New Testament. But all of these heavenly books were either lost, corrupted, or misinterpreted. God gave the Qur'an to Muhammad as a corrective; as a perfect text that could resolve all confusion and teach the truth clearly. This is the last book, the last revelation, which would ever be needed; and thus Muhammad was the seal of the prophets, the final prophet and authenticator of all his predecessors.

As we'll see in the next lecture, the Qur'an sometimes retells stories from the Bible, but it does so in ways that emphasizes the moral point of the story rather than the narrative. It's worth noting that Muslims believe that Jesus was a true prophet sent by God; it's just that Christians got off track when they started worshipping him as the son of God or even as God himself. That's the sort of mistake that God sent Muhammad to fix. Another difference between Muslim and Jewish and Christian traditions, in Islam, it's thought that Ishmael was the favored son of Abraham, and it was actually Ishmael who Abraham attempted to sacrifice before that was broken off by an angel and the son, Ishmael, was saved.

A third unique aspect of the Qur'an, again according to Muslims, is the perfect beauty of its language. It's written in a rhythmic form of Arabic, with lots of alliteration, assonance, and end-rhymes, although some suras are more poetic and lyrical than others. In the centuries following Muhammad, Islamic thinkers developed the concept of the "inimitability" of the Qur'an, though the seeds of that idea are within the text itself. As post-canonical scripture, the Qur'an is very self-referential and even self-conscious. God warns Muhammad that many people are going to reject his revelations, and he tells Muhammad how to respond to those objections. For example, there are half a dozen so-called "challenge verses" that each go something like Sura 52:29–34 that says, and this is God speaking:

> By the grace of your Lord, you are neither oracle nor madman. If they say, "He is only a poet: we shall await his fate," say, "Wait if you wish; I too am waiting [see how God is giving Muhammad the words that he ought to be saying]"—does their reason really tell them to do this, or are they simply insolent people? If they say, "He has made it up himself"—they certainly do not believe—let them produce one like it, if what they say is true.

That's sort of the essence of these challenge verses: If other people aren't impressed by this, if they don't believe, have them write a sura and see how it compares with what I'm giving you, is what God would say to Muhammad.

At a time when many believed that God's messengers could be identified by the miracles they performed, Muslims held up the Qur'an as Muhammad's greatest miracle, especially since he was thought to have been illiterate, or at least unacquainted with books. The elevated style and content of the Qur'an constitute a sign, as it says in Qur'an 98.1:"The unbelievers of the People of the Book and the idolaters would never leave off; till the Clear Sign came to them, a Messenger from God, reciting pages purified, therein true Books." The Book is a sign.

For an introduction to the sounds of the Qur'an, with clear explanations for non-Arabic speakers along with recordings of famous reciters, I highly recommend Michael Sells's book *Approaching the Qur'an*, which includes a CD of Qur'anic recitations. Because the language of the Qur'an is inseparable from its content, and both come directly from God, a translation of the Qur'an is not the real Qur'an. The real Qur'an has to be in Arabic; and this is why one of the most widely-used English translations of the 20th century went by the title *The Koran Interpreted*. For that matter the real Qur'an isn't the lines and squiggles written on a page, but rather the words as they're spoken and heard. The Qur'an as a book is merely an aid to memorization or recitation. There's a separate word, *Mus'haf*, or "codex," which refers to the Qur'an as a physical object, the bound pages in which the holy words are written. The Qur'an itself, as its name implies, a recitation. In Muslim countries, the sounds of the Qur'an are everywhere, particularly since the recitation of the Qur'an is a sophisticated and esteemed art form. So the sacred words can be heard not only in mosques, but also on the radio and TV; in taxicabs and concert halls; at weddings, festivals, and funerals.

There are two basic forms of Qur'anic recitation: one with strict rules for ordinary study and practice, and the other that adds musical modes to those strict rules. That second form features a great deal of melodic modulation and technical artistry; it's performed by trained experts. Memorizing, reciting, and listening to the Qur'an are ways of communing with God in a bodily fashion, in a physical way, perhaps something like taking the Eucharist in the Christian faith.

But it's not just a Sunday or a seasonal thing, though many Muslims recite the entire Qur'an in 30 sequential segments during the month of Ramadan when they're fasting. There's no tradition of separating church and state in Islam, so the Qur'an infuses everyday life, even in aspects that would might political or secular to Westerners. Public meetings often begin with the recitation of a few verses from the Qur'an. Even though the Qur'an as a physical object is just a shadow of the real, aural Qur'an, it's nevertheless a sacred object. It's kept apart from other books with nothing placed on top of it. You don't want to have too many Qur'ans around, because that would show that you weren't taking them seriously or reading them; and you'd never put the Qur'an on the floor. Many Muslims do their ablutions before reading the Qur'an since Sura 56 states, "In a book that is protected, which none touches save the purified ones. A revelation from the Lord of the worlds." It's usually referred to not just as "the Qur'an" but as "the Glorious Qur'an" or "the Noble Qur'an." A translation wouldn't require the same degree of reverence; but oftentimes translations are printed in bilingual copies, in which there's Arabic on one side of a page and then the target language or vernacular on the other side, and that sort of Qur'an has to be treated with the utmost respect as well.

In a religion that's very strict in its forbidding of "graven images," calligraphy is one of the most prestigious forms of art; and passages from the Qur'an are frequently taken as source texts for rich visual elaboration in lovely Arabic script of many different styles. Mosques in particular are decorated with Qur'anic calligraphy, usually in an elevated location where you can look up and be inspired by it.

At this point, it might be good to take a moment for few comparisons. The respect shown for the Qur'an may not be quite like that of the Sikhs for the Adi Granth, since Muslims don't treat the Qur'an as a living guru, yet still, the respect shown for the Qur'an is probably higher than that shown for the Bible, at least in its physical form, since the Bible is widely distributed in hundreds of languages and is for the most part regarded as a regular book; of great spiritual significance, of course, but the physical object is usually not given sacred status. The primacy of the spoken or chanted version of scripture is familiar from Hinduism, but unlike the Sanskrit of the Vedas, Arabic is still a living language, and the meaning of the Qur'an matters enormously to believers; it's not just the pronouncing of sacred syllables.

As an aside, it's worth noting that even in the West, the custom of private, silent reading is only a couple centuries old. For most of history, books were always read aloud, even when people were reading by themselves. This transition to a more analytical, distanced mode of interacting with texts through this personal, silent reading was aided and abetted by the invention of the printing press that made documents so much more readily available. Perhaps ready access to vocalized texts in the form of CDs and DVDs or on the Internet will allow us to recapture some of the magic of aural learning.

I'll conclude with Sura 97, in a fine English translation by Tarif Khalidi. But to really get a sense of the Qur'an, you should get online and listen to it recited in the original Arabic, as God intended it to be heard. This short, early sura describes Muhammad's first revelation through the angel Gabriel, back in 620 in that cave outside of Mecca. That experience, which is known as the "Night of Power," is commemorated every year on one of the last 10 days of the month of Ramadan. This is how Sura 97 goes, thinking of that first revelatory experience:

> We [and this is God speaking] sent it down in the Night of Power! But how can you know what is the Night of Power? The Night of Power is better than a thousand months. In it, the angels and the Spirit are sent swarming down, by their Lord's leave, attending to every command. Peace is it that Night, till the break of dawn.

Holy Qur'an
Lecture 31

Outsiders coming to new holy books often read them superficially, or they bring assumptions about what "scripture" should sound like, both of which can make it difficult to understand what believers see in their own sacred texts. Even today, many readers are tempted to approach a sacred text with the question: Is the religion portrayed here good or bad? It's possible to peruse the Qur'an looking for evidence that Islam is a violent religion, or incompatible with democracy, or discriminatory toward women. But a more thoughtful exercise is to try to identify the major themes that the Qur'an puts forward, particularly in their original context of 7th-century Arabia.

Basic Themes of the Qur'an
- As we noted in our last lecture, the Qur'an is thought by Muslims to be a direct revelation from God. God is, in fact, the main speaker throughout, referring to himself in the first person and, occasionally, in the third person. Muhammad's voice is also heard, but it's usually prefaced by the command "Say" from God.

- There is no large narrative structure in the Qur'an, as there is in the Bible or the Hindu epics. The 114 suras are individual units, and they are not arranged in the order that Muhammad received them. Instead, they are organized roughly by decreasing length. The longest, sura 2, has 286 verses, while the shortest suras (103, 108, 110) have just 3 verses apiece. Every sura except 9 begins with the invocation "In the name of God, Most Gracious, Most Merciful."

- The earlier, shorter suras from the Meccan period tend to be more focused and lyrical, while the longer suras, received at Medina, are more prosaic and can jump from topic to topic. Each sura has a traditional name derived from its main theme, its first word, or some unique topic or term. Hence, the second sura is called "The Cow," even though only 6 of its 286 verses discuss the sacrifice of a heifer by the ancient Israelites.

- The first sura in the Qur'an, called "The Opening," encapsulates the message of Islam in just seven verses. It is recited by Muslims multiple times each day as part of the five obligatory prayers and conveys the news that Muhammad brought to the world: that there is but one God, who is both just and merciful; human beings should worship him alone; and they should surrender themselves to him by following the path he has established. God will help those who call upon him, but those who reject God will incur his wrath now and at the day of judgment.
    - Muslims have long classified suras as belonging either to the Meccan period (i.e., before the Hijra in 622) or the Medinan period. It is not always obvious which suras are which, and indeed, some passages within the same sura may have been revealed in different locations.

    - The consensus is that "The Opening" was received in Mecca, and its emphasis on strict monotheism would have been revolutionary among the Bedouin tribes.

- Another startling teaching was the Qur'an's insistence on the resurrection. According to sura 45, Arabs at the time did not believe in any kind of life after death, but the angel Gabriel brought to Muhammad the sura on resurrection (75). The sura concludes with the question of whether it is harder to believe in resurrection than in creation. If God created men and women, then surely, he could reassemble them after death.

Bible Stories in the Qur'an
- The earliest suras are short and lyrical, often using formulaic oaths to praise God's majesty and mercy. But eventually, the revelations to Muhammad began to refer to past events, to earlier prophets that God had sent and what happened to those who ignored their warnings. There are also retellings of biblical stories, though the emphasis is on the meaning of events rather than narration of them. The Qur'an assumes that its hearers are already familiar with the stories, and it often adds dialogue and details that are not in the Bible.

- For instance, sura 20 tells the story of Moses in Egypt, but the parting of the Red Sea gets just two verses; what matters is not so much the deliverance of the Israelites from bondage as the confrontation between Moses and the unbelieving Egyptians at the pharaoh's court.

- In sura 71, God tells Noah to warn the people and give them a chance to repent before he sends the flood. That episode is not in the Bible, nor is the observation that when Noah preached, people stuck their fingers in their ears so they couldn't hear him.

- Mary, the mother of Jesus, is mentioned frequently in the Qur'an, with nonbiblical details about her birth and early years. In addition, the Qur'an has a story about Jesus making birds out of clay and bringing them to life that is also found in the Infancy Gospel of Thomas.

- Scholars are often interested in tracking Muhammad's sources in the Bible or in Jewish and Christian traditions that were circulating in Arabia in the 7th century. Most Muslims, though, view God himself as Muhammad's sole source, and if there are similarities with what's in the Bible, it's because God was behind that book, as well.

• The relationship between the Bible and the Qur'an is not like that of the Old and New Testaments. Christians adopted the Hebrew Bible and consider it authoritative, even if some parts have been updated or made obsolete by the revelation in Christ. In contrast, Muslims regard the Bible as corrupted with additions and interpolations, such as the idea of God as a father, the Crucifixion and resurrection of Jesus, the divinity of Christ, or the Trinity. The Qur'an is a replacement for the Bible; it's God's final and complete word.

• In general, the Qur'an warns the world about the evils of polytheism and idolatry and about the need to turn to God and keep his commandments before the coming day of judgment, but a few passages give special attention to Jews and Christians.

- It appears that early on, Muhammad viewed Jews as natural allies and potential converts; after all, they, too, were monotheists and believed in prophets sent by God. Many of the early references to Jews in the Qur'an are rather positive. Yet when Jews didn't convert as expected and after religious and even military confrontations, the Qur'an has a few strong words of condemnation.

- Nevertheless, for most of history, Muslims and Jews seemed to get along fairly well, at least by the standards of premodern societies and certainly better than Christians and Jews. Despite some tensions between the two communities, the Qur'an famously enjoins, "Let there be no compulsion in religion" (2:257).

Islamic Laws
- After Muhammad became both the political and the religious leader in Medina, he received revelations having to do with laws and regulations. These later, longer, more prosaic suras, which appear toward the beginning of the Qur'an, address such topics as gambling, marriage, inheritance, infanticide, property rights, criminal law, the rights of orphans, and so forth.

- Sura 2, "The Cow," is a good example. Indeed, it is sometimes regarded as the Qur'an in miniature because it reiterates so many of the principles found elsewhere in the scripture. In relatively short passages, it moves through the topics of faith and disbelief; the creation, Adam, and Satan; Bible stories of Moses, the Israelites, and Jesus; polemics against Jews and Christians; Islamic practices and regulations; and more.

- Non-Muslims might assume that the Qur'an is something of a jumble, but Muslims see little distinction between sacred and secular matters in a life that is entirely devoted to God, and they regard it as a sign of God's grace that the basic message of Islam is spread throughout the Qur'an. You can't read more than a few pages without encountering references to the one God, his

Selections from the Qur'an

Sura 1 ("The Opening"):

In the name of God, the Merciful, the Compassionate. Praise belongs to God, the Lord of all Being, the All-merciful, the All-compassionate, the Master of the Day of Doom. Thee only we serve; to Thee alone we pray for succour. Guide us in the straight path, the path of those whom Thou hast blessed, not of those against whom Thou art wrathful, nor of those who are astray. (Arberry, trans.)

Sura 75 ("The Resurrection"):

Yes indeed! I swear by the Day of Resurrection! Yes indeed! I swear by the soul that remonstrates! Does man imagine We shall not reassemble his bones? Indeed. We can reshape his very fingers! In truth, man wishes to persist in his debauchery; He asks when the Day of Resurrection shall come. When eyes are dazzled, and the moon is eclipsed, and sun and moon are joined together, Man that Day shall ask: "Where to escape?" No, there is no refuge! (Khalidi, trans.)

Sura 82 ("The Splitting"):

When heaven is split open, when the stars are scattered, when the seas swarm over, when the tombs are overthrown, then a soul shall know its works, the former and the latter. O Man! What deceived thee as to thy generous Lord who created thee and shaped thee and wrought thee in symmetry and composed thee after what form He would? (Arberry, trans.)

Sura 24 ("Verse of Light"):

God is the light of the heavens and the earth. The parable of his light is as if there were a niche and within it a lamp; the lamp enclosed in glass. The glass as it were a brilliant star, lit for a blessed tree, an olive, neither of the East nor of the West, whose oil is well-nigh luminous, though fire scarce touched it. Light upon light! God doth guide whom he will to his light. God doth set forth parables for men, and God doth know all things. (Ali, trans.)

outreach to humankind, the straight path that he has set, and the coming judgment.

- Much attention has been given to laws in the Qur'an regarding women. There are several that seem discriminatory by modern standards: Men are allowed to have up to four wives, and a daughter receives only half the inheritance of a son. Yet in the context of 7th-century Arabia, much of what the Qur'an teaches would have been regarded as progressive. Women had some inheritance rights, they were granted protections in divorce proceedings, and they were entitled to control of their own property, even if they were married.
    - In addition, the Qur'an strenuously condemned the pre-Islamic practice of female infanticide and made it clear that women and men are equal in their relationship with God.

    - Many of the traditions that we today associate with Islam arose after the Prophet Muhammad. For instance, the Qur'an urges both women and men to be modest, and it nowhere explicitly requires that women cover their heads or faces. The practice of veiling is more culture-specific; full veiling is rather rare, and most Muslim women live in countries where they can choose whether or not to wear a head scarf (hijab).

    - Keep in mind, too, that Muslim women have, at some point, been elected to lead the three most populous Muslim countries: Indonesia, Pakistan, and Bangladesh.

- Such laws and practices, of course, raise the question of interpretation. If all Muslims follow the Qur'an, how can they practice it differently in different countries? Who determines the rules?
    - Consider, for example, the Qur'anic allowance of polygamy. Some have pointed out that polygamy was common in ancient societies, and limiting wives to four is better than no limits at all. Others, however, have noted a subtle discouragement of polygamy in the Qur'an (sura 4:129). At any rate, polygamous unions make up only 1 to 3 percent of Muslim

marriages today, and most Muslims live in countries where such marriages are restricted.

- o In general, women are treated with respect in the Qur'an, though they are not treated equally to men. It's up to Muslims themselves to decide how best to interpret their sacred text, but the dilemma of how to implement the principles of an ancient document in the modern world is not unique to Islam.

- Most Muslims believe that reading and reciting the Qur'an has enriched their lives and made them better people—kinder, more moral, and closer to God. It is a custom among some Muslims to say this prayer after completing a recitation of the Qur'an: "O God, make the Qur'an a mercy for me, and set it for me as a model, a light, a guidance and a mercy" (Nigosian, 75). That seems like a noble sentiment.

Suggested Reading

Abdel Haleem, trans., *The Qur'an: A New Translation*.

Ali, trans., *The Holy Qur'an with English Translation and Commentary*.

Esack, *The Qur'an: A User's Guide*.

Khalidi, trans., *The Qur'an*.

Lawrence, *The Qur'an: A Biography*.

Rippin, ed., *The Blackwell Companion to the Qur'an*.

Saeed, *The Qur'an*.

Sardar, *Reading the Qur'an*.

Siddiqui, *How to Read the Qur'an*.

Questions to Consider

1. How do the earlier revelations that Muhammad received at Mecca differ from those received at Medina?

2. What are the strong religious claims that the Qur'an makes concerning its origins and significance? Why is it such a self-referential text?

Holy Qur'an
Lecture 31—Transcript

Today, over a billion-and-a-half Muslims around the world regard the Qur'an as God's last revelation. For the faithful, the Qur'an is a focal point; the central source of inspiration and guidance in all matters of life; a text whose origin is with God himself. Indeed, the Qur'an is the world's most widely-read book in its original language, and it's probably the most liturgically rehearsed and memorized of the world's sacred texts.

Yet the normative experience for Muslims isn't reading the text from the beginning to the end; rather, one's life is punctuated by recitations of verses from here or there in all sorts of social and religious contexts. As we saw in the last lecture, it's primarily considered an oral book, a recitation; that is to say, what Muhammad heard from the angel Gabriel and then recited to his followers must be heard again and again in Arabic. The text is stored in writing in the physical book, but even today among Muslims the most valued medium of storage for the Qur'an is memory. As the words are read aloud from a book, or, better yet, recited from memory, God's direct speech is once again made manifest in the world. There's a sense of nearness to God that comes from hearing the words of the Qur'an; and this is a tremendous blessing to humankind. As the writer and cultural-critic Ziauddin Sardar puts it, the Qur'an is a text that "polishes the souls of individuals so that their humanity can shine."

But what a person who learns the Qur'an in Arabic experiences as a work of consummate power and beauty can, in translation, seem difficult or confusing, and perhaps even alienating. Let's start with a few observations and quotations, and then we can talk about the strong claims that this text makes for itself, and what those claims might mean in an era of religious pluralism and secularism.

As with all sacred texts, and especially with the Qur'an, it helps to have a good translation. There have been many over the years—even Max Müller's *Sacred Books of the East* included a new translation of the Qur'an—but there are a few that I just want to give you titles for. Arthur Arberry's *The Koran Interpreted* has long been a favorite among Western scholars since it tries to reproduce the word order and the syntax of the original Arabic and it adopts the reverential diction of the King James Bible. Abdullah Yusuf Ali's *Holy Qur'an* is popular with English-speaking Muslims; and then I've particularly enjoyed two new translations: Tarif Khalidi's Penguin version, and Muhammad Abdel Haleem's rendition for the Oxford World's Classics series.

When you open the Qur'an, one of the first things you'll notice is that God is the main speaker throughout, referring to himself in the first person as "I" or "We" (kind of a majestic, royal "we"), and occasionally referring to himself in the third person "He." Muhammad's voice is heard as well, but it's usually prefaced by the command "Say," so that it's actually God telling Muhammad what he ought to say in different circumstances and to different people. You'll also quickly realize that the book doesn't have an overarching narrative structure such as we find in the Bible or in the Hindu Epics, nor is there theological development or internal divisions of genre or topic to hold it all together. The 114 suras are individual units, and they're not arranged in the order that Muhammad received them.

Instead, they're—like the letters of Paul—organized roughly by decreasing length. So after a short introductory sura, then the next sura, number 2, is the longest in the book; while the shortest suras, which are placed near the end—those are 103, 108, 110—all have just three verses apiece. Every sura except for number 9 begins with the invocation "In the name of God, Most Gracious, Most Merciful." The earlier, shorter suras from the Meccan period—so the time when Muhammad was living in Mecca—tend to be more focused and lyrical; while the longer suras, received at Medina, are more prosaic and can jump from topic to topic. Each sura has a traditional name derived from its main theme, or from its first word, or some unique topic or term. Hence the second sura is called "The Cow," even though only 6 of its 286 verses talk about the sacrifice of a heifer by the ancient Israelites.

It's often good to begin at the beginning. The very first sura in the Qur'an, called "The Opening," encapsulates the message of Islam in just seven verses. It's recited by Muslims multiple times each day as part of the five obligatory daily prayers. Rather atypically, the words are those of believers rather than God. Of course, it begins with the Basmala that says "In the name of God, the Merciful, the Compassionate," and then it continues:

> Praise belongs to God, the Lord of all Being, the All-merciful, the All-compassionate, the Master of the Day of Doom. Thee only we serve; to Thee alone we pray for succour. Guide us in the straight path, the path of those whom Thou hast blessed, not of those against whom Thou art wrathful, nor of those who are astray.

This was the news that Muhammad brought to the world: There is but one God who is both just and merciful. Human beings should worship him alone, and they should surrender themselves to him by following the path that he's established. God will reach out and help those who call upon him, but those who reject his ways will incur his wrath now and at the day of judgment.

Muslims have long classified suras as either belonging to the Meccan period—that is, before the Hijra in 622 C.E.—or in the Medinan era. It's not always obvious which are which, and, indeed, some passages within the same sura may have been revealed in different locations; but the consensus is that The Opening was received in Mecca, and its emphasis on strict monotheism would have been revolutionary among the Arab tribes with their multiple gods and idols. Another startling teaching was the Qur'an's insistence on the resurrection and judgment. Arabs at that time, according to sura 45, said to themselves: "There is nothing but our present life; we die, and we live, and nothing but Time destroys us." But the Angel Gabriel brought to Muhammad the sura on Resurrection, number 75, in which he said:

> Yes indeed! I swear by the Day of Resurrection! Yes indeed! I swear by the soul that remonstrates! Does man imagine We shall not reassemble his bones [this is God speaking]? Indeed, We can reshape his very fingers! In truth, man wishes to persist in his debauchery; He asks when the Day of Resurrection shall come. When eyes are dazzled, and the moon is eclipsed, and sun and moon are joined together, Man that Day shall ask: "Where to escape?" No, there is no refuge!

The sura continues and then asks in conclusion whether it's harder to believe in resurrection than in creation. After all, if God created men and women from scratch, surely he can reassemble them, too.

Of course, the rhythms and rhymes of the original Arabic don't come through in translation, but some of the poetic imagery does. Listen to the beginning verses from sura 82, "The Splitting":

> When heaven is split open, when the stars are scattered, when the seas swarm over, when the tombs are overthrown, then a soul shall know its works, the former and the latter. O Man! What deceived thee as to thy generous Lord who created thee and shaped thee and wrought thee in symmetry and composed thee after what form He would?

After Muhammad became both the political and the religious leader in Medina, he received revelations having to do with laws and regulations. These longer, later, more prosaic suras, which appear toward the beginning of the Qur'an, address topics such as gambling, marriage, inheritance, infanticide, property rights, criminal law, the rights of orphans, and so forth; so these are all of the regulations and revelations that come when Muhammad actually needs to govern or give guidance to a community. Sura Two, "The Cow," is a good example of all of these practical, day-to-day regulations mixed together. Indeed, it's sometimes regarded as the Qur'an in miniature because it reiterates so many of the principles found elsewhere in scripture.

In relatively short passages, it moves through the following topics: It starts by speaking about faith and disbelief; then the Creation, Adam, and Satan; then Bible stories about Moses, the Israelites, and Jesus; polemics against Jews and Christians; it speaks about Abraham and Ishmael building the Ka'ba together; and then it continues by talking about Islamic practices like the direction of prayer and pilgrimage; there are regulations about food; there's instructions about kindness to the vulnerable; rules about inheritance, fasting, and pilgrimage; and then—we're just taking these topics as they come in order in the second sura—it continues with moral exhortations; issues of holy war, marriage, divorce, and women's life stages; there are stories of Saul and Goliath; rules about charity, usury, and debt; and then finally the sura concludes with a plea for God's mercy. There's a lot that's packed into that one sura, even if it is the longest in the Qur'an.

Non-Muslims might assume that the Qur'an is something of a jumble; but Muslims see little distinction between sacred and secular matters in a life that's entirely devoted to God, and regard it as a sign of God's grace and mercy that the basic message of Islam is spread throughout the Qur'an. You can't read more than a few pages without encountering references to the one God—the phrase "There is no God but him" appears some 30 times—and then it also speaks, all throughout the Qur'an, about this God who's aware of our needs and our prayers; who's accessible to us. I like Qur'an verse 50:16 says, "We [this is God speaking] are nearer to him than his jugular vein."

God has sent down the Qur'an through Muhammad his prophet, and this text tells us all that we need to know and do in order to enter paradise; for this life is a time of testing. Death will be followed by a resurrection and then a judgment, and divine retribution awaits the disobedient and the decadent. But there's still time to turn to God—this is one of the main messages of the Qur'an—you can turn to God whose mercy and forgiving nature are mentioned about 500 times in the Qur'an. The key is to submit to God and to follow the right path, which has been defined through prophecy and revelation. The Qur'an insists that this isn't a new teaching: God has sent prophets in the past with the same messages, but the people hardened their hearts and rejected the words of the prophets and messengers, or they may have changed it from its pure form.

The Qur'an has a remarkable degree of self-awareness. It recognizes that it's coming at a time when Jews and Christians already have well-established canons, and it's keenly aware that people may question its status and validity. About a third of the suras begin with a passage that refers in some way to the process of revelation, assuring listeners of the authenticity of the voice that they hear recited in the Qur'an. Again and again, the Qur'an claims kinship with the revelations of Judaism and Christianity; though it also insists upon the independence and superiority of its witness, free from the distortions and corruptions like those that the Bible imposed on the messages that God had sent through Noah, Abraham, Moses, and Jesus.

So while the Qur'an has some of the same themes and characters that we find in the Bible, many of the stories that it tells—or rather that it refers to, because the Qur'an rarely narrates stories from beginning to end—many of those familiar Bible stories take on a somewhat different meaning in the Qur'an. For instance, in the Garden of Eden story, the emphasis is on Satan's willful arrogance and defiance rather than on Adam's succumbing to temptation or on an original sin. Sura 20 tells the story of Moses in Egypt, but the parting of the Red Sea gets just two verses. What matters in the Qur'anic retelling isn't so much the deliverance of the Israelites from bondage as much as the confrontation between Moses and the unbelieving Egyptians at Pharaoh's court. In Sura 71, God commands Noah to warn the people and give them a chance to repent before he sends the flood. That episode isn't in the Bible, but it's completely in line with the basic message of the Qur'an, which is God has sent his messengers and prophets again and again to call people to change their ways, and then they were rejected; so the story of Moses sort of takes that pattern. One thing that I really like in the Qur'an is that it says that when Noah preached, the people who were listening stuck their fingers in their ears so they couldn't hear him. It's not a detail from the Bible, but it's one that seems sort of vivid to me.

Mary, the mother of Jesus, is mentioned frequently in the Qur'an, with non-biblical details about her birth and her early years. Then there's this story about Jesus:

> Then God will say, "Jesus, son of Mary! Remember My favour to you and to your mother: how I strengthened you with the holy spirit, so that you spoke to people in your infancy and as a grown man; how I taught you the Scripture and wisdom, the Torah and the Gospel; how by My leave, you fashioned the shape of a bird out of clay, breathed into it, and it became, by My leave a bird."

The story of Jesus making birds out of clay and then bringing them to life also appears in the Infancy Gospel of Thomas, which is one of the apocryphal gospels we talked about in Lecture 28. Outside scholars are often interested in tracking Muhammad's sources in the Bible or in the Jewish and Christian traditions that were circulating in Arabia in the 7th century. Most Muslims, however, view the Qur'an as an eternal text revealed from God, with no human writing, borrowing, or editing whatsoever. Any similarities between the Qur'an and the Bible are the result of the Bible containing at least some traces of the truth.

So the relationship between the Bible and the Qur'an isn't like that of the Old and New Testaments. Christians adopted the Hebrew Bible, they read it regularly, and they consider it authoritative, even if some parts have been updated or made obsolete by the revelation in Christ, such as details of the sacrifices in the temple or other parts of the Law of Moses. By contrast, Muslims don't add the Qur'an to the Bible; they don't really read the Bible. It's regarded as too corrupted with additions and interpolations, such as the idea of God as the heavenly father of his human children. In Islam, God is not so much a heavenly father; he's an absolute monarch or a divine king who calls for submission and obedience. Muslims believe that the whole truth about Jesus can only be found in the Qur'an, where we learn that Jesus was born of a virgin, with no father, but he was still fully human; definitely not the "son of God." Jesus was a prophet, according to the Qur'an, whom God saved from death on the cross by taking him directly up into Paradise, but he'll return to earth again at the last day in the second coming. The Qur'an is a replacement for the Bible; it's God's final and complete word.

If you hear criticisms of Christian doctrine in Sura 112, you're probably on the right track; and this is an example of tensions starting to build between Muslims and Jewish, and in this case Christian communities: "Say: He is God, the One and Only; God, the Eternal, Absolute; He begetteth not, Nor is He begotten; And there is none like unto Him." Later suras are even more pointed in their condemnation of Christian teachings. They say, for example:

> Those who say: "the Messiah, son of Mary, is God," are infidels. ... Those who say "God is the third of three," are infidels, for there is no God but One ... Those who associate anything with God, God will prohibit them from entering Paradise, and their refuge shall be Hell."

In general, the Qur'an warns the whole world about the evils of polytheism and idolatry, and about the need to turn to God and keep his commandments before the coming Day of Judgment; but a few passages give special attention to Jews and Christians. It appears that early on, Muhammad viewed Jews as natural allies and potential converts; after all, they, too, were monotheists and they believed in prophets that had been sent by God, the same prophets that were celebrated in the Qur'an. Many of the earliest references to Jews in the Qur'an were rather positive. Yet when they didn't convert as expected, and after political and even military confrontations, the Qur'an has a few strong words of condemnation.

Nevertheless, for most of history, Muslims and Jews seemed to get along fairly well, at least by the standards of pre-modern societies; certainly better than Christians and Jews. For instance, Maimonides, the great 12th-century Jewish scholar, was a very successful physician in Muslim Egypt. It's worth noting that before 623, Muslims prayed as Jews did, facing Jerusalem. It was only after that date that the direction of prayers shifted to Mecca; and despite tensions between the two communities, the Qur'an famously enjoins, "Let there be no compulsion in religion."

Is the Qur'an a text that can be adapted to a secular, pluralistic, democratic world; or does an objective reading highlight its exclusive, anti-modernist tendencies? That's a difficult question, and one that doesn't touch only on Muslim scripture. It's fair to ask how any ancient or medieval texts could still be regarded as authoritative in a post-modern age.

It's important to recognize that the Qur'an makes very strong scriptural claims. If we were to place to Qur'an along with other world scriptures on the spectrum of divine or human origins, the Muslim sacred book would be all the way over on one side, toward the divine side. Muslims believe that the Qur'an in Arabic is the direct speech of God, unmediated and uninterpreted. The Qur'an is God's final revelation and Muhammad is the "seal of the prophets," meaning that he's the last one, the perfect culmination of the prophetic tradition. In fact, Muhammad was simply a conduit for the Qur'an, which existed in heaven before the world began, unchanged and eternal. Most Muslims believe that there's no human influence at all in the book; its message was too consequential to be left to fallible human design concerning a choice of language or the structuring of its themes.

They might also point out the marvelous poetic qualities of its verses, and the minimal time lapse between the revelation of the suras and their canonization in book form; it was just a few decades. They might insist that there's been no human editing or modification as evidenced by the fact that, for all practical purposes, the Qur'an exists in a single recension; that is, there aren't hundreds or even thousands of different variants, as there is for the New Testament. The Qur'an is, in its present form, perfect and inimitable. Some Christians have wanted to make similar claims for the perfection and infallibility of the Bible; but the human elements of the Old and New Testaments are much more evident in the language, the editing, the canonization process, and the transmission of manuscripts.

The claims of the Qur'an to be divine scripture are very strong, and they're undoubtedly part of the religion's appeal. Who wouldn't be interested in eternal truth that came directly from God? As Professor Shabbar Akhtar has observed, "The Qur'an ... was replete with certainty. No faith was founded in doubt, only certainty seduces." By contrast, the celebration of individual autonomy, skepticism, freedom of interpretation, and human achievement are modern values that the Qur'an pushes back against, which may make it a difficult book for modern outsiders to appreciate. We can talk about the tensions between the principles espoused by the Qur'an and those of a modern pluralistic, or even secular age; but first, let's identify some of the strengths of the religious vision put forward by the Qur'an.

Within the Muslim community, the Qur'an evokes an impressive reverence and faithfulness. The holy book, as it's constantly recited publicly and privately, points toward higher things; and it promotes an enviable degree of God-consciousness. It allows adherents to maintain a perpetual awareness of God, which is important because human beings are forgetful by nature, by habit, and by preoccupation; it's easy to get caught up in the day to day concerns of the world, which can obscure or hide the central reality of the moral imperative for generosity and justice. Reciting the Qur'an several times a day in prayer can remedy that natural tendency to forgetfulness; it's a reminder, a constant reminder, of our relationship with God and of the coming Day of Judgment. Qur'an 6:155 says: "This too is a blessed scripture which We have sent down—follow it and be conscious of your Lord, so that you may receive mercy." The Qur'an certainly makes demands on believers who choose to submit to God's will, as revealed in its suras. Yet this strict obedience, this deliberate erasure of selfhood, isn't regarded as humiliating or demeaning, but instead it's seen as a path to self-realization. With an awareness of what man is in God's eyes, humans can then recognize their true worth and potential.

Yet at the same time, these strong, inspiring, motivating claims of divine authority can also put the Qur'an at odds with the modern world; where they can almost seem like a vulnerability. The Qur'an presents something of an all or nothing religiosity; so any hint of human influence might seem, at least to some believers, as possibly undermining the whole. Again, some Christians have felt the same way about the Bible, but claims of perfection and inerrancy are generally not contained within the Old and New Testaments themselves as they are in the Qur'an. They were interpretations that were imposed on Bible by later generations of believers.

Close readings of the Qur'an, which might uncover contradictions, anachronisms, obscurities, borrowings from other religious traditions, or outdated ethical principles can produce intense anxiety in those who regard the text as revealed, and sometimes can call forth considerable creativity or ingenuity on the part of commentators. For example, it's often been noted that the contents of the Qur'an don't seem to be arranged in any particular order, and topics, even within individual suras, can appear to be jumbled together. Yet Muslims believe that the current organization is divinely mandated, it's not random; so what appears to be a weakness must actually be a strength. They might point out that a strictly chronological arrangement—so if you organize the Qur'an in the order in which Muhammad received the suras— that might give the impression of theological development over time, when there's none; it was a perfect, eternal book. Or if you arrange the Qur'an by topics, that might make it a little less useful. The translator Muhammad Abdel Haleem explains:

> In a religion that seeks to affect people's beliefs and behaviour in all aspects of life, it is never sufficient to say something once or

twice, and if the material on God, on earlier prophets, or on the Day of Judgment were each dealt with only once, the effect would not be so all pervasive. This technique compresses many aspects of the Qur'anic message into any one sura, each forming self-contained lessons. This is particularly useful as it is rare for anyone to read the whole Qur'an at once: it is mainly used in short sections in worship and preaching.

That's a very nice response to a common critique of the Qur'an's repetitiveness and lack of obvious structure; our translator finds some meaning and reason in the form that the Qur'an takes now. Note that logic and reason aren't foreign to traditional interpretations made within the context of faithful inquiry. The schools of Islamic law are wonderful testaments to the power of the human mind to find order and meaning in texts; and I suppose the same observation could be made about rabbinical readings of the Torah contained in the Talmud, or biblical exegesis of the Christian Church Fathers. Yet the criticisms made by outsiders, in the context of skepticism rather than faith, can seem much more threatening.

Outsiders might ask: What about Qur'anic teachings on holy war, or the subordinate position of women, or polygamy, or religious intolerance, or slavery? Indeed, even insiders, some Muslims, are sometimes questioning about those difficult issues. Some believers, and certainly outsiders, may be comfortable putting the revelations given to Muhammad some 14 centuries ago into their historical context; saying, for example, that in 7th-century Arabia, the teachings of the Qur'an on women were actually rather progressive, at least for the time, so the tradition is to affirm the worth and equality of women, and that's what Muslims should stand for today. Yet other believers are wary of any interpretations that take the Qur'an out of the eternal realms and tie it to historical time and circumstances.

This is a crucial issue for contemporary Muslims, and in our next lecture we'll continue our exploration of how a medieval text can still be relevant in the modern world as we talk about the Hadith and Sufism; but for now, as a reminder of the power of this sacred text, let me conclude with one of the most beautiful and beloved passages in the Qur'an, the so-called "Verse of Light," from sura 24:35, which is inscribed on many mosques in lovely calligraphy, and it's given all sorts of mystical or allegorical interpretations. It says:

> God is the light of the heavens and the earth. The parable of his light is as if there were a niche and within it a lamp; the lamp enclosed in glass. The glass as it were a brilliant star, lit for a blessed tree, an olive, neither of the East nor of the West, whose oil is well-nigh luminous, though fire scarce touched it. Light upon light! God doth guide whom he will to his light. God doth set forth parables for men, and God doth know all things.

Powerful words, and provocative sentiments.

Hadith and Sufism
Lecture 32

Two primary ways that Muslims have responded to the message of the Qur'an are through legal interpretation based on the Hadith and the mystical movement of Sufism. One interpretive path that Muslims have generally not taken is that of the historical-critical method. Thus, to address some variants in the Qur'anic texts, commentators developed the idea of abrogation—that some of the commandments from God had only temporary application, and those could be superseded by later revelations. A greater challenge than apparent contradictions was the sparseness of the Qur'an; it doesn't provide enough details for regulating a complex society. For help here, Muslims turned to the Hadith.

Hadith: Stories of the Prophet

- Unlike Jesus, Muhammad was never considered absolutely sinless, but he was nevertheless held up as a model of integrity and good conduct. Believers naturally wanted to follow his example, even in things that might seem relatively minor. There are literally thousands of anecdotes concerning the behavior of the Prophet, and they provide a lens through which to interpret the Qur'an.

- For believers who want to know about Muhammad's life, the Qur'an can be frustrating; it doesn't have much in the way of biography. God speaks to his messenger throughout, but Muhammad's name occurs only four times, and incidents in his life are referred to rather than recounted. It is only in the Hadith—some of which are rather lengthy—that we learn about his marriages, his political leadership, or his night journey.

- In the first couple of centuries after Muhammad, these stories proliferated wildly, and there was a suspicion that many of them might be fraudulent. For this reason, scholars began to collect and evaluate them in systematic ways. A Hadith came to have two parts: the *isnad*, or chain of sources, and the *matn*, or the story itself.

- One of the early collectors of Hadith, the 9th-century Persian scholar al-Bukhari, is said to have traveled all over the Middle East in search of stories about the Prophet.
    - He interviewed 1,000 experts and heard some 600,000 Hadith (many of them variants of one another). Of these, he memorized 200,000 and finally came up with just 2,700 that he thought were unquestionably authentic.

    - Bukhari published his collection in 97 sections, each devoted to a particular topic, such as faith, prayer, festivals, alms, sales, loans, gifts, war, marriage, and good manners, as well as Muhammad's comments on specific suras from the Qur'an.

    - Bukhari's collection is highly regarded by Sunni Muslims. (The word *Sunna* means "well-trodden path," and it refers to the example set by Muhammad.) Shia Muslims have different opinions about the reliability of early witnesses and have their own collections of Hadith. The term *Shia* means "faction" or

The Dome of the Rock, or perhaps the Al-Aqsa Mosque next door, is thought to be the starting point for Muhammad's ascent to heaven.

"party," and they are the 15 percent or so who believe that the leadership of Islam should have stayed within the Prophet's family line.

- The Hadith are accepted as religiously authoritative, but they are not scripture in the same sense as the Qur'an. The Hadith are accounts of Muhammad's actions and sayings, but the Qur'an is the direct revelation of God's words; thus, the Hadith are never recited or used in worship. The relationship of Hadith to Qur'an is somewhat like Talmud to Torah. Both the Hadith and the Talmud are large collections of oral traditions that are intensely studied to determine rules and regulations for believers. However, the various Talmuds are records of legal debates, while the Hadith are raw materials for legal opinions.

Sharia

- Both Judaism and Islam have relatively small, closed canons, but the second tier of sacred literature is vast. Eventually, the analysis of Qur'an and Hadith produced Sharia, or Muslim law ("a path to be followed" or "the way"), yet this is not a single law code—it's more of an ideal for a devout Muslim life—and the exact regulations are different in different countries.

- Islam has no hereditary or ordained priesthood; instead, leadership in the community comes from legal scholars who are expert in Sharia. Eventually, there arose four major schools of Islamic law. When faced with new situations or difficult cases, these scholars (*ulama*) would consult the Qur'an, the Hadith, and traditional interpretations of the Qur'an known as *tafsir*. From these sources—and applying the typical types of reasoning associated with one of the four legal schools—a correct judgment could be made.
  o For instance, the Ayatollah Khomeini, who led the 1979 revolution in Iran and governed the country until his death, first came to prominence as an Islamic legal scholar.

  o In 1984, a translation of 3,000 of his rulings on everyday life was published, called *A Clarification of Questions*. This work addressed such topics as flossing, artificial insemination, and organ donation.

Sufism

- The mystic strand of Islam, called Sufism, which developed in the 8th century, sought to experience God directly, by giving oneself entirely to him and, in return, being enveloped in his love. Early Sufis were often ascetics who gained a reputation for purity and used music, dancing, poetry, meditation, ecstatic trances, and recitation of the names of God as spiritual practices.

- In centuries when Islamic law was closely connected with the government and sometimes corrupt rulers, Sufi mystics gained popular followings and were crucial in the spread of Islam to Africa, India, and Southeast Asia. Eventually, Sufis were organized into various orders or brotherhoods.

- Because Sufis emphasized the spiritual, emotive aspects of religion rather than the letter of the law, they were sometimes regarded as suspect by conservative authorities. Nevertheless, Sufi ideas and sensibilities are widespread throughout Islam, particularly in Shia communities. Sufis themselves stressed the importance of studying with a recognized master (something like Zen Buddhists), and they often emphasized the need to keep Sharia law as the basis for more advanced spiritual practices.

- Sufism is also popular in the West among non-Muslims, in part because of its sensuous allegorical love poetry and its willingness to overlook doctrinal differences in the belief that many paths lead to God, though whether Sufism can be separated from the Islamic profession of faith is an open question. The situation is somewhat similar to the way that Tibetan Buddhism and the Dalai Lama are regarded in the West, where they have a prominence out of proportion to their actual role in the tradition.

- The Qur'an and the Hadith are foundational sacred texts for all Muslims, just as the Tanakh and the Talmud are foundational for

Jews. Yet Sufism, as an esoteric strand in the tradition, is probably more widespread in Islam than comparable forms of Jewish and Christian mysticism.

Celebrated Sufi Authors
- Even though Sufi classics are not scripture and are more highly regarded in some places than in others, Westerners studying Islam are likely to encounter some of them. Two of the most celebrated Sufi authors are Attar and Rumi, whose poetry has become an integral part of Iranian national literature.

- Farid al-Din Attar (1145–1221) was from Nishapur in northeast Iran. Attar penned a prose account of the lives and miracles of Sufi mystics called *Memorial of God's Friends*, which is somewhat reminiscent of the tales of Zen masters. His most important work is *The Conference of the Birds*, a long allegorical poem about a group of birds who journey in search of a mythic bird king. The allegory points toward the various excuses people give for not seeking God, and each bird represents a human weakness. Throughout their journey, about 100 stories or parables are told.
    o Of course, Sufis, like other Muslims, looked to the Qur'an for guidance, but they often practiced a type of allegorical interpretation called *ta'wil*, which sought for deeper, hidden meanings, in contrast to the plain sense and close readings of *tafsir* commentaries.

    o We can see an example in *The Conference of the Birds*, where Attar suggests that, like Adam leaving paradise, "The man whose mind and vision are ensnared by heaven's grace must forfeit that same grace, for only then can he direct his face to his true Lord" (40). Apparently, being too blessed, or even too religious, can sometimes hinder spiritual progress.

- Jalal al-din Rumi (1207–1273) is even more famous than Attar. Born in Afghanistan, his family migrated to Turkey, where he became a Sufi and a prolific poet, writing thousands of verses. He was also the founder of the Mevlevi order of Sufis, popularly known as "whirling dervishes" for their distinctive devotional dancing. His masterpiece is the *Mathnawi*, an anthology of didactic poetry in six books, with about 25,000 rhyming couplets in all.

- o The *Mathnawi* retells stories from the Qur'an, the Hadith, the Bible, and Persian folktales. Along the way, it teaches the principles of Sufism and interprets the Qur'an.

- o In the *Mathnawi*, Rumi explores the themes of spiritual yearning and hope for union with God, returning again and again to the images of passionate love, intoxication, the ocean, and music.

Preserving the Sacred Texts of Islam

- Islam is a large, rich, and diverse religious tradition. It's important not to judge it by the actions of a vocal, sometimes violent, antimodern, and antipluralistic minority.

- For many centuries, Timbuktu, in the West African nation of Mali, was a center of Islamic scholarship and learning. Prominent families there had preserved thousands of manuscripts of the Qur'an, commentaries, biographies of the Prophet, and prayer books, as well as works on secular subjects, such as astronomy, medicine, and poetry. Most of these manuscripts are in Arabic, with some dating back to the 13th century.

- When rebels and Islamist militias affiliated with al-Qaeda took over Timbuktu in April 2012, they instituted public floggings; banned music, dancing, and soccer; and destroyed the tombs of Sufi saints. Abdel Kader Haidara, the head of a private library, feared for the safety of the ancient manuscripts in the city's libraries and research institute. He organized his friends and associates to hide away some 300,000 manuscripts to protect them from the Islamists.

- In January 2013, Timbuktu was retaken by a coalition of government and French troops, and retreating Islamists trashed the libraries and burned whatever they could find. Although it's true that this destruction was carried out by Muslims, it's also true that it was Muslims who created the manuscripts in the first place, preserved them for centuries, and risked their lives to save them.

Suggested Reading

Attar, *Farid ad-Din 'Attar's Memorial of God's Friends.*

———, *The Conference of the Birds.*

Brown, *Hadith.*

Burton, *An Introduction to the Hadith.*

Calder, Mohaddedi, and Rippin, eds. and trans., *Classical Islam.*

Dreazen, "The Brazen Bibliophiles of Timbuktu."

Jamal, ed. and trans., *Islamic Mystical Poetry.*

Rumi, *The Masnavi, Book One.*

Ruthven, *Islam in the World.*

Questions to Consider

1. Why are the Hadith—traditions about the life of Muhammad—considered authoritative but not scriptural by Muslims?

2. How does Sufism make room for alternative forms of religiosity in Islam, and why was that important in the spread of the faith?

Hadith and Sufism
Lecture 32—Transcript

In this lecture, we'll be looking at the two primary ways that Muslims have responded to the message of the Qur'an. The first is legal interpretation based on the Hadith, and the second is the Islamic mystical movement known as Sufism. But first, I can point to one interpretive path that Muslims have generally not taken: that of the historical-critical method.

Some aspects of the Qur'an are clearly in need of interpretation. For instance, Qur'an 6:67 allows the drinking of wine, "And from the fruit of palm trees and vines you derive intoxicants as well as a goodly provision," whereas a later revelation at 2:219 states that there is both benefit and sin in intoxicants, though the bad outweighs the good. Finally, at Qur'an 5:90, there's complete condemnation: "O believers, wine and gambling, idols and divining arrows are an abhorrence, the work of Satan. So keep away from it, that you may prevail." So did God change his mind about alcohol? What's happening here?

Non-Muslims might see the Qur'an as the development of Muhammad's thought. They could look to his biography for clues—such as his concerns for the rights of orphans and women might stem from his own early loss of parents and his marriage to Khadija, an independent businesswoman—and they might also trace elements of the Qur'an to the Jewish, Christian, or pagan influences that he would've encountered in 7th-century Arabia. As a quick example of the last, the Qur'an sees the universe as inhabited by God, angels, devils, jinn, and humans. Jinn are invisible, spiritual creatures who can choose either good or evil and will be rewarded accordingly at the Judgment Day, though they often cause trouble for humans. The Qur'an says that God created humans from clay and jinn from fire. The singular noun is jinni, which is the origin of our English word *genie*, which you may recall from some stories from *1001 Nights*, Aladdin.

Orthodox Muslims don't look for human elements in the text; in fact, they oppose the idea that Muhammad had any role in the creation of the Qur'an. It all came directly from God, and the Qur'an as it exists today is an exact replica of the heavenly book that was in existence before the foundation of the world. This is one reason that the discovery of thousands of Qur'anic fragments in the Great Mosque of Sana'a in Yemen in 1972 wasn't greeted with the enthusiasm that attended the Cairo *genizah* or the Dead Sea Scrolls. Over 12,000 pieces of parchment from over 900 manuscripts of the Qur'an were found by workmen renovating an attic wall in that mosque. Some of those fragments have been dated to the 7th and 8th centuries, though they don't have as many variant readings as some scholars were expecting. But even looking for variants among the manuscripts could be disconcerting to some Muslims, since any deviations from the Qur'an established by Uthman are threatening to traditional understandings of the text. The situation is similar to how conservative Christians and Jews have been wary of historical explanations of biblical contradictions and repetitions; explanations that might undermine notions of inerrancy or the Mosaic authorship of the Torah. Sikhs as well have sometimes been hostile to the historical-critical analysis of the Adi Granth. Faith in sacred texts can be delicate, but it can also be resilient.

Back to wine: What's the story there? Muslim commentators eventually developed the idea of abrogation; that some of the commandments from God had only temporary application, and those could be superseded by later revelations that met the needs of a changing community. This was always a limited interpretive tool. Muslim jurists hold that only about 20 of the Qur'an's 6,200 verses were abrogated by later verses; so the Qur'an as it finally exists now, in its final form, there aren't going to be any more changes to it, it's reached its perfection. A greater challenge than apparent contradictions was the sparseness of the Qur'an; it doesn't provide enough details for regulating a complex society, or even for many aspects of an individual's life. For help in those areas, Muslims turned to the Hadith: Records of the words or the actions of Muhammad as recounted by the first generation of Muslims.

Muhammad is considered to be sinless; a perfect man who's held up as a model of integrity and good conduct. Believers naturally wanted to follow his example, even in things that might seem relatively minor. For instance, one of Muhammad's early followers reported that "he has seen no one more given to smiling than God's messenger." There's a message there that for those who want to follow the example of Muhammad, we ought to smile regularly. There are other traditions: "Anas used to tell of the Prophet that he would visit the sick, attend funerals, accept a slave's invitation, and ride on a donkey." Another: "Abu Hurayra told that when God's messenger was asked to invoke a curse on the polytheists he replied, 'I was not sent as one given to cursing; I was sent only as a mercy.'" The third caliph, Uthman, said that when the Prophet did his ritual washings, he poured water on his hands three times, he washed his mouth, then his face three times, right arm to the elbow three times, left arm three times, then he wiped his hand over his head, then washed his right foot three times and left foot three times; so that's the way that Muslims do their ablutions to this day, they follow that same detailed pattern. These stories about Muhammad, what he did and what he said, sound a bit like the remembrances of Confucius in the *Analects*.

There are literally thousands of these anecdotes, and they provide a lens through which to interpret the Qur'an. For instance, on women's issues, one can catalog all of the relevant verses in the Qur'an, and then add to them Hadith such as: "Anas related that the Honorable Prophet said: He who brings up two girls through their childhood will appear on the Day of Judgment attached to me like two fingers of a hand." Another Hadith: "It is related from Abdullah ibn Omar, 'The Apostle of God forbade the killing of women and children.'"

For believers wanting to know about Muhammad's life, the Qur'an can be a little bit frustrating. There isn't much in the way of biography; God speaks to his messenger throughout the text, but Muhammad's name only occurs four times, and incidents in his life are referred to rather than recounted. The Qur'an doesn't tell stories about the life of Muhammad. It's only in the Hadith—some of which are rather lengthy—that we learn about Muhammad's marriages, his political leadership, or the night journey in which he rode a winged horse to Jerusalem (which was a long ways off), and he met prophets like Abraham, Moses and Jesus, and then ascended to the seven heavens before returning to Mecca. By the way, that's why Jerusalem is the third holiest site in Islam, after Mecca and Medina. The Dome of the Rock, or perhaps the Al-Aqsa Mosque next to it, is thought to be the starting point for Muhammad's ascent into the heavens.

In the first couple of centuries after Muhammad, these stories proliferated wildly, and there was a gnawing suspicion that many of them might be fraudulent; so Muslim scholars began to collect and evaluate them in very systematic ways. A Hadith came to have two parts: the first was the *isnad*, or the chain of sources; that so-and-so reported that he heard so-and-so say that once he saw Muhammad do such-and such. These chains of witnesses can grow quite long, and scholars investigated not only the likelihood of transmission—to make sure that they all lived at appropriate times; that they could actually have had conversations—but they also investigated the character and the reliability of each person in the chain. The second part of a Hadith, the *matn*, is the story itself.

As an example, one particularly important Hadith recounts the circumstances of Muhammad's first revelation:

> Ibn Humayd has related to me on the authority of Salma [then there are four more names in this chain of sources, until we get to someone who overheard a question] Relate to us, O 'Ubayd, how it was when the Apostle of Allah - upon whom be Allah's blessing and peace - first began his prophetic career, when Gabriel – upon whom be peace – came to him ... Said the Apostle of Allah ... "He came to me while I was asleep, bringing a silken cloth on which was some writing. He said: 'Recite,' but I answered: 'What shall I recite?' Then he so grievously treated me that I thought I should die, but he pushed me off and said: 'Recite.'" [You remember this story, right? The multiple commands to recite that will lead to Sura 96, the first of the Suras to be revealed.] [Then continuing with the Prophet's explanation from this Hadith] "Thereupon I awoke from my sleep, and it was as though he had written it on my heart."

One of the early collectors of Hadith, the 9th-century Persian scholar al-Bukhari, is said to have traveled all over the Middle East in search of stories about the Prophet. He interviewed a thousand experts and heard some 600,000 Hadith; of course, many of those were repetitions or variants of each other. Of these, he memorized 200,000 and finally came up with just 2,700 that he thought were unquestionably authentic; though when it's put in book form there are actually 7,400 entries because there are some duplicates.

Bukhari published his collection in 97 sections, each devoted to a particular topic; so there are Hadith on faith, prayer, festivals, alms, sales, loans, gifts, war, marriage, and good manners, as well as Muhammad's comments on specific suras from the Qur'an. The English translation is in nine volumes. It's a huge work, and it's only one of six collections of Hadith that are highly regarded by Sunna Muslims. The word *Sunna*, remember, means "the trodden path," and it refers to the example set by Muhammad; so the Hadith are particularly important in showing believers what Muhammad did and how we can follow his actions.

Shia Muslims have different opinions about the reliability of early witnesses, so they have their own collections of Hadith, four in particular. The term *Shia*, as you'll recall, means "faction" or "party," and they're about 15 percent or so of the Muslims who believe that the leadership of Islam should've stayed within the Prophet's family. Most Shia live in Iran and Iraq, and they accept traditions about their early leaders, or imams, as authoritative.

Just to be clear, the Hadith are accepted as religiously authoritative, but they're not scripture; not in the same sense as the Qur'an. The Hadith are accounts of Muhammad's actions and sayings, but the Qur'an is the direct revelation of God's words; so the Hadith are never recited or used in worship, and it's acceptable to argue about the Hadith or to question the validity of some of them. The relationship of Hadith to the Qur'an is somewhat like the Talmud to the Torah. Both the Talmud and the Hadith are large collections of oral traditions—and remember that there are multiple Talmuds as well; there's one from Palestine and one from Babylonia—and those are intensely studied, those oral traditions, to determine rules and regulations for believers. But the Talmuds are records of legal debates, while the Hadith are raw materials for legal opinions.

Both Judaism and Islam have relatively small, closed canons, but that second tier of sacred literature is vast. Eventually, the analysis of the Qur'an and Hadith produced Islamic jurisprudence, or *fiqh*, which offers practical interpretations of Sharia, the ideal of Islamic law. The exact regulations of *fiqh* are different in different countries in the Muslim world, and leadership in the Muslim community comes from legal scholars rather than, say, priests; and these legal scholars are experts in one of the four major schools of Islamic law, at least the four major schools in the Sunni tradition. When faced with new situations or difficult cases, these scholars, called *ulama*, would consult the Qur'an, the Hadith, and traditional interpretations of the Qur'an known as *tafsir*; and those are clarifications of grammar, words, meanings, and metaphors in the text. From all of these sources, and then applying the typical types of reasoning associated with one of the four legal schools, a correct judgment could be made.

The Hadith and Islamic jurisprudence are important elements in responding to one of our questions from the previous lecture: how to preserve the authority of the Qur'an while acknowledging that the world has changed in significant ways over the past 14 centuries. Most religious traditions have at least a few passages in their sacred texts that sincere believers wish weren't there; things that may have made sense long ago, but now seem unenlightened or offensive, or clearly influenced by historical human concerns and prejudices, perhaps things regarding gender relations or slavery; discrimination based on race or physical disabilities; preference for monarchy; or divine commands to kill and destroy. Typically, religious people note the historical context of those problematic issues as they try to make sense of them and try to put them in a historical perspective; or they might look to apply general principles—the "essence of the faith"—rather than specific details; or they might posit a progressing understanding of God and his ways. Those are techniques that are used in lots of religious traditions; and Muslims have also taken some of those approaches, though, as we've seen, strong claims of the Qur'an as to its divine nature make some of that difficult.

But Muslims have another interpretive tool at their disposal. They can blame traditional practices that seem unfair or discriminatory in the modern world on the misuse of Hadith citations, while still respecting the divine nature of the Qur'an. As I said, the Hadith and *fiqh* can be questioned in ways that the Qur'an can't. For example, Mona Siddiqui, who's a British Muslim scholar, has observed that many scholars argue that "despite verses which reflect a male privilege in the Qur'an, it was not the Qur'an but the Hadith attributed to Muhammad which promoted female subservience," and then she gives an example from the Hadith where Muhammad at one time was supposed to have said: "If a man calls his woman to bed and she refuses to come, the angels will continue to curse her until the morning." Siddiqui notes that these kinds of Hadith contradict stories of conjugal love between Muhammad and his wives, and they're in conflict with the essential message of the Qur'an, which, as she says, "calls for mutual love and understanding in marriage, where husband and wife should like 'garments for each other'"

More examples of Islamic jurisprudence can be seen if we turn to the Shia traditions, where they have their own, distinctive schools of Islamic law. The Ayatollah Khomeini, who led the 1979 revolution in Iran and then governed the country until his death, first came to prominence as an Islamic legal scholar. In 1984, a translation of 3,000 of his rulings on everyday life was published, called *A Clarification of Questions*. Those 3,000 rulings included things like the following, number 2629: "It is not unlawful to swallow the food that exits from between the teeth as a result of flossing if one's nature has no aversion to it." Number 2874: "It is not unlawful to introduce a man's semen into the uterus of his wife with devices like suction cups." (Don't think too hard about that one.) Number 2882: "When the preservation of a Muslim's life rests on grafting an organ from a dead Muslim, severing that organ and grafting it are acceptable."

There are some Hadith about Muhammad cleaning his teeth and the way he did that, but obviously he wasn't thinking about modern dental floss, much less artificial insemination or organ transplants; but in the contemporary world, such questions arise and they have to be answered somehow. Nevertheless, for some people, a religion of thousands of rules and regulations isn't entirely satisfying, and that seemed to have been true even for the Ayatollah. In 1989, one of his poems appeared in an Iranian newspaper, which included these lines:

> I have become imprisoned, O beloved, by the mole on your lip! ...
> Heartache for the beloved has thrown so many sparks into my soul
>
> That I have been driven to despair and become the talk of the bazaar.
>
> Open the door of the tavern and let us go there day and night,
>
> For I am sick and tired of the mosque and seminary.

What is that all about? A man renowned for his strict asceticism has written an anguished love poem that says, in effect, "Let's skip the mosque and go get drunk?" (Remember that alcohol is strictly forbidden in Islam.) I seriously doubt that Khomeini ever drank wine, but in this case he's drawing on mystical traditions within Islam. The poem that he wrote uses striking, even shocking imagery to try to express a union with God that's ultimately beyond words; so it relies on allegory: The beloved stands in for God, wine represents God's love, and getting drunk means losing oneself in that love. The mosque and seminary refer to outward religiosity, while the tavern is the divine presence.

The mystic strand of Islam, called Sufism, which developed in the 8th century, sought to experience God directly by giving oneself entirely to him and in return being enveloped in his love. Early Sufis were often ascetics—so the term *Sufi* is derived from the word for "wool," the rough fabric that holy men wore instead of luxurious silk—and these men, these Sufis, gained a reputation for purity (and that's another possible derivation for the word *Sufi*), and they employed music, dancing, poetry, meditation, ecstatic trances, and reciting the names of God as spiritual practices. In centuries when Islamic law was closely connected to the government and sometimes corrupt rulers, Sufi mystics gained popular followings and were crucial in the spread of Islam to Africa, India, and Southeast Asia. Eventually, Sufis were organized into various orders or brotherhoods, though there have been prominent female Sufis as well. Because Sufis emphasized the spiritual, emotive aspects of religion rather than the letter of the law, they were sometimes regarded as suspect by conservative authorities, which is true to this day; some strands of Islam are pretty nervous about music and such, and dancing, and Sufis use that as spiritual practices. Nevertheless, even though there's some criticism even to this day, Sufi ideas and sensibilities are widespread throughout Islam, particularly in Shia communities.

Sufism isn't a distinct form of Islam like Sunni or Shia; rather, it's a mode of religiosity, something like charismatic Christians who are still Catholics or Protestants. Sufis themselves stress the importance of studying with a recognized master, like Zen Buddhists, and they often emphasize the importance of keeping Sharia law as the basis for more advance spiritual practices; it's not an anything goes form of religion. Sufism is also popular in the West among non-Muslims, in part because of its sensuous allegorical love poetry and its willingness to overlook doctrinal differences in the belief that many paths lead to God, though it's an open question as to whether Sufism can be separated from the Islamic profession of faith; I'm not sure if it works to be a non-Muslim Sufi, but I suppose people have different opinions about that. The situation is somewhat similar to the way that Tibetan Buddhism and the Dalai Lama are regarded in the West, where they have a prominence probably out of proportion to their actual role within the tradition. Vajrayana is certainly part of Buddhism—that's Tibetan Buddhism—but it's a minority position. The Qur'an and the Hadith are foundational sacred texts for all Muslims, with the Qur'an alone being accepted as God's word just as the Tanakh and the Talmud are foundational for Jews; yet Sufism, as an esoteric strand in the tradition, is probably more widespread in Islam than comparable forms of mysticism in Judaism and Christianity. So even though Sufi classics aren't scripture and are more highly regarded in some places than in others, Westerners studying Islam are likely to encounter some of them at some point. Consequently, it might be useful to talk for a few minutes about a couple of the most celebrated Sufi authors: Attar and Rumi.

Both were Persians from the 13th century, and their poetry has become an integral part of Iranian national literature. Farid al-Din Attar, who lived from 1145–1221, was from Nishapur in northeast Iran. Attar penned a prose account of the lives and miracles of Sufi mystics called *Memorial of God's Friends*, which is somewhat reminiscent of tales of Zen masters. It's well worth taking a look at, but Attar's most important work is *Conference of the Birds*, a long allegorical poem about a group of birds who journey in search of the mythic bird-king, Simorgh. They are led by a hoopoe bird, which begins by telling stories to talk them out of their reluctance to travel. The allegory points toward the various excuses that people give for not seeking God, and each bird represents a particular human weakness. Throughout their journey, about a hundred stories or parables are told. The birds pass through seven valleys: the valleys of Quest, Love, Insight and Mystery, Detachment, Unity, Bewilderment, and Poverty and Nothingness. Many of the birds drop out along the way, so that only 30 actually arrive at the court of the Simorgh, having lost their worldly concerns and habits on the journey. In the end, however, what they find is not a ruler but a lake, wherein they see their reflection. They've found within themselves the sovereign that they were looking for. The name of the king, Simorgh, is a pun for "thirty birds."

Of course, Sufis, like other Muslims, looked to the Qur'an for guidance; but they often practiced a type of allegorical interpretation called *ta'wil*, which sought for deeper, hidden meanings in contrast to the plain sense and close readings of *tafsir* commentaries. We can see an example of this in the *Conference of the Birds* where Attar suggests that, like Adam leaving Paradise, "The man whose mind and vision are ensnared by heaven's grace must forfeit that same grace, for only then can he direct his face to his true Lord." Apparently, being too blessed, or even too religious, can sometimes hinder spiritual progress.

Our other example of Sufism is Jalal al-Din Rumi, who lived from 1207–1273, and he's even more famous than Attar. Born in Afghanistan, Rumi's family migrated to Turkey, where he became a Sufi and a prolific poet, writing thousands of verses. He was also the founder of the Mevlevi order of Sufis, popularly known as "whirling dervishes" for their distinctive devotional dancing. His masterpiece is the *Mathnawi*, an anthology of didactic poetry in six books with about 25,000 rhyming couplets in all. The *Mathnawi* retells stories from the Qur'an, the Hadith, the Bible, and Persian folktales. Along the way, it teaches the principles of Sufism and interprets the Qur'an; so a quotation from the Qur'an shows up every 30 verses or so. Indeed, it's often said that the *Mathnawi* is "the Qur'an in Persian." In the *Mathnawi*, Rumi explores the themes of spiritual yearning and hope for union with God, returning again and again to images of passionate love, intoxication, the ocean, and music. For instance, here's the famous musical analogy of its opening lines:

> Hearken to the reed-flute, how it complains, Lamenting its banishment from its home: "Ever since they tore me from my [reed] bed, My plaintive notes have moved men and women to tears. I burst my breast, striving to give vent to sighs, And to express the pangs of my yearning for my home [this is the flute speaking]. He who abides far away from his home is ever longing for the day he shall return."

Rumi is eminently quotable; I'll share just one favorite line: "He who accepts everything as true is a fool; But he who says all is false is a knave."

As we conclude this section on Muslim sacred texts, I want you to keep in mind that Islam is a large, rich, diverse religious tradition. Don't judge it by the actions of a vocal, sometimes violent, anti-modern, anti-pluralistic minority.

Let me end with a story. For many centuries, Timbuktu, in the West African nation of Mali, was a center of Islamic scholarship and learning. Prominent families there had preserved thousands of manuscripts of the Qur'an, commentaries, biographies of the Prophet, and prayer books, as well as secular subjects such as astronomy, medicine, and poetry. Most of these manuscripts are in Arabic, with some dating back to the 13th century. When rebels and Islamist militias affiliated with al-Qaeda took over Timbuktu in April, 2012, they instituted public floggings; they banned music, dancing, and soccer; and they destroyed the tombs of Sufi saints. Abdel Kader Haidara, the head of a private library, feared for the safety of the ancient manuscripts in the city's libraries and research institute. Rightfully so: When a coalition of government and French troops retook Timbuktu in January, 2013, retreating Islamists trashed the libraries and burned whatever they could find. Everyone assumed that a priceless cultural heritage, some of which had survived nearly a thousand years, had been lost. But then it turned out that Haidara had organized his friends and associates. Over the course of two months, they'd entered libraries under the cover of night and had spirited out some 300,000 manuscripts, packed in 1,700 metal footlockers, which they hid in homes around the city. Through the fall of 2012, an unlikely group of librarians, archivists, and ordinary Malians undertook the dangerous task of smuggling these lockers out of Timbuktu and transporting them to the capital of Bamako, some 400 miles to the south, where they would be safe. There are efforts underway now to preserve and to digitize these documents.

It's true that the people who wanted to destroy the manuscripts were Muslims, but so were the people who created them in the first place, who preserved them for centuries, and who risked their lives to save them.

Related Traditions—Baha'i Scriptures
Lecture 33

In choosing which sacred texts to explore, we've looked at religions with at least 2 million or so believers, religions that have continued through several generations and expanded beyond their native borders, and scriptures that have been translated into foreign languages. The most recent additions to the library of scriptures we have considered are from 19th-century religions, including Mormonism and Tenrikyo. What might be the next faith traditions that would meet our criteria for study of their sacred texts? Candidates include Scientology, the Unification Church, Falun Gong, and Cao Dai. In this lecture, however, we'll look at the Baha'i faith, the second most widespread religion in the world after Christianity in terms of its presence in different nations.

Background to the Baha'i Faith
- The Baha'i faith began in 1863, when Baha'u'llah (1817–1892) announced in Bagdad that he was the prophetic fulfillment of Babism, a 19th-century offshoot of Shia Islam.

- Shia is one of the two major divisions of Islam, and Shia Muslims believe that the leadership of the faith should have stayed within the family of Muhammad. Most Shia came to accept a succession of 12 legitimate imams, or divinely appointed leaders, from the 7th to the 9th centuries.
    o The 12th imam was thought to have to have been hidden by God and will return someday as the Mahdi (the "Guided One"), along with Jesus, to usher in the messianic age of peace, justice, and Islamic law.

    o Iran is one of the few countries where Shia Muslims are in the majority, and in 1844, Sayyid Ali-Muhammad Shirazi, a 24-year-old Iranian merchant, announced that he was the "Bab," meaning "The Gate," an intermediary between believers and the Mahdi.

- o Later, he intimated that he was the Mahdi himself. The Bab gained tens of thousands of followers, called Babis, but he also made some powerful enemies and was executed by a government firing squad in 1850.

- Mirza Husayn Ali Nuri, who would later take the honorific title of Baha'u'llah ("Glory of God"), was an early follower of the Bab. Along with many other believers, Baha'u'llah was persecuted and imprisoned. In 1852, while he was jailed in a dungeon in Tehran (the famous "Black Pit"), he saw a vision of a maiden of heaven who told him that God had a special mission for him. After Baha'u'llah's release and exile, he became a leader of the Babis.

- In his writings, the Bab had indicated that a future messianic figure was still to come, and in 1863, in the Garden of Ridvan, near Baghdad, Baha'u'llah declared that he was the promised one whose coming was foretold by the Bab. Over the next few years, most Babis became Baha'is, that is, members of the community that regarded Baha'u'llah as the inaugurator of a new religious dispensation and the fulfillment of the messianic expectations of all the world's major religions.

- The Persian and Ottoman empires were not sympathetic to the Baha'i faith, and Baha'u'llah endured a long series of exiles, imprisonment, and house arrests. Shortly before his death in 1892, Baha'u'llah appointed his eldest son, Abdu'l-Baha (1844–1921), as his successor. The next leader of the Baha'i community was Shoghi Effendi (1897–1957), a grandson of Abdu'l-Baha. Since 1963, the highest authority in the faith has been the Universal House of Justice, an elected body of nine members headquartered in Haifa.

- Baha'is believe in the oneness of God, the oneness of religions, and the oneness of humanity. In other words, there is one all-powerful Creator who has spoken to different prophets (or manifestations of God) at various times and places. These messengers represent progressive revelations.

- o All the major religions came from the same God, but they can be unified under the teachings of Baha'i. There may be future manifestations of God, as well, but not for at least 1,000 years.

- o As the oneness of God and the oneness of religions are recognized, so also there should be a oneness of humanity, with all races and ethnicities being treated equally and seen as part of a great whole. Significantly, men and women should be equal, as well.

- o Baha'is regard humanity as progressing and look to a future of increasing peace, justice, and unity.

- The message of Baha'i has not always been well-received, particularly in Iran, the native land of its founders. Although Baha'is consider their faith a distinct world religion, it comes from an Islamic background, much as Buddhism had its origins in Hinduism or Christianity, in Judaism. The Islamic elements of the faith have convinced some that Baha'is are apostate Muslims, and they have sometimes been harshly persecuted; in some countries, they face legal restrictions.

Baha'i Scriptures

- The Baha'i faith, like Judaism, Christianity, and Islam, is very much a text-based religion, though technically, the Baha'i canon is much larger than those of the other three faiths.
  - o Baha'is believe that everything written by the Bab and Baha'u'llah should be accepted as revelations from God. In addition, the writings of Abdu'l-Baha are also regarded as scripture, along with his authenticated talks. The works of Shoghi Effendi are inspired interpretations. They are authoritative but not scriptural in the same way as the writings of the three founders. Official communications from the House of Justice are also considered authoritative but not scripture.

  - o Because the Bab, Baha'u'llah, and Abdu'l-Baha spent many years in prison or under house arrest, they wrote voluminously.

The Bab's writings would probably fill 50 volumes, while Baha'u'llah is said to have written 100 volumes worth of books, tracts, prayers, and letters (called tablets). Abdu'l-Baha wrote several books and 27,000 letters, perhaps comprising 50 volumes in total. Not all of the writings of the three founders have been edited and translated, and Baha'is today tend to focus on a few particular books.

- The Bab is regarded as the forerunner of Baha'u'llah, much like Elijah or John the Baptist. As a result, his writings are not studied to the same extent as the writings of Baha'u'llah, at least not in English-speaking countries. The Baha'i's Publishing Trust (the faith's official press) has published a single volume of selections from the Bab's writings, though some of his prayers and meditations are still in common use.

- The majority of sacred texts that Baha'is study regularly are from Baha'u'llah. Even before his 1863 announcement at the Garden of Ridvan that he was the Promised One, he was producing works that would later have the status of revelations.
  - Around 1858, he wrote The Hidden Words, a collection of 153 wisdom sayings, about half in Arabic and half in Persian. These are spoken by God in the first-person and addressed to humanity in general.

  - Sometime between 1857 and 1863, Baha'u'llah produced The Seven Valleys and The Four Valleys, two short tracts that were written in response to the questions of Sufi mystics. The Seven Valleys represent the journey of the soul toward God, passing through the Valleys of Search, Love, Knowledge, Unity, Contentment, Wonderment, and finally, the Valley of True Poverty and Absolute Nothingness.

  - The last of the major pre-Rivdan scriptures is the Kitab-i-Iqan ("The Book of Certitude"), published in 1862. In this revelation, Baha'u'llah expounds the ideas of the oneness of God, progressive revelation, and the unity of the prophets.

He interprets key passages from the Qur'an, as well as a few from the New Testament, and sets the stage for his declaration at Ridvan by reinterpreting the Qur'anic verse on Muhammad as the seal of the prophets to allow for further messengers or manifestations of God.

- After Baha'u'llah had made public his identity as the Promised One, he continued to write. Probably the most important of the scriptures after 1863 was the Kitab-i-Aqdas ("Most Holy Book"), which sets forth guidelines for the organization and practices of the Baha'i community.
    - In this text, Baha'u'llah appointed his son Abdu'l-Baha as his successor, outlined the future institutions of the guardianship (a position held by Shoghi Effendi) and the Universal House of Justice, and delineated the rules for Baha'is concerning prayer, fasting, houses of worship, pilgrimage, criminals, marriage, inheritance, and scripture.

    - Some of the distinctive customs of Baha'is come from the Most Holy Book, including the rejection of congregational prayers (aside from a prayer for the dead), the requirement that marriages have the consent of parents, the requirement to write a will, the reciting of scripture both morning and evening, and daily obligatory prayer.

- Among the large number of revealed letters (tablets) by Baha'u'llah, the Epistle to the Son of the Wolf is especially noteworthy. This long letter is Baha'u'llah's last major work, written to a fierce opponent of the Baha'is, and it offers a summary of the doctrines Baha'u'llah had been teaching for more than 30 years.

- A thematic compilation by Shoghi Effendi titled Gleanings from the Writings of Baha'u'llah, first published in 1935, is often the first scripture that Baha'is encounter.

- The scriptural writings of Abdu'l-Baha include a 1908 publication, *Some Answered Questions*, that came out of conversations with

Selections from Baha'i Writings

World Order of Baha'u'llah (pp. xi–xii):

The Baha'i Faith recognizes the unity of God and of His Prophets, upholds the principle of an unfettered search after truth, condemns all forms of superstition and prejudice, teaches that the fundamental purpose of religion is to promote concord and harmony, that it must go hand-in-hand with science, and that it constitutes the sole and ultimate basis of a peaceful, an ordered and progressive society. It inculcates the principle of equal opportunity, rights and privileges for both sexes, advocates compulsory education, abolishes extremes of poverty and wealth, exalts work performed in the spirit of service to the rank of worship, recommends the adoption of an auxiliary international language, and provides the necessary agencies for the establishment and safeguarding of a permanent and universal peace.

The Hidden Words, #34:

O Dwellers of My Paradise! With the hands of loving-kindness I have planted in the holy garden of paradise the young tree of your love and friendship, and have watered it with the goodly showers of My tender grace.

Gleanings from the Writings of Baha'u'llah:

Consider the past. How many, both high and low, have, at all times, yearningly awaited the advent of the Manifestations of God in the sanctified persons of His chosen Ones. How often have they expected His coming, how frequently have they prayed that the breeze of Divine mercy might blow, and the promised Beauty step forth from behind the veil of concealment, and be made manifest to all the world.

Short obligatory prayer:

I bear witness, O my God, that Thou hast created me to know Thee and to worship Thee. I testify, at this moment, to my powerlessness and to Thy might, to my poverty and to Thy wealth. There is no other God but Thee, the Help in Peril, the Self-Subsisting.

Epistle to the Son of the Wolf:

I was but a man like others, asleep upon My couch, when lo, the breezes of the All-Glorious were wafted over Me, and taught Me the knowledge of all that hath been.

Laura Clifford Barney. In this book, Abdu'l-Baha offers Baha'i perspectives on a number of issues in which Christians and other Westerners might be interested, including Jesus, baptism, life after death, and the Bible.

Baha'i Prayers
- One final scriptural text that is used extensively by Baha'is is a collection of prayers written by the Bab, Baha'u'llah, and Abdu'l-Baha. These lovely meditations are arranged by topic; for example, there are prayers for divine aid and for one's children, families, forgiveness, healing, marriage, praise and gratitude, protection, and unity. The volume begins with the three possible daily prayers. Believers between the ages of 15 and 70 must recite one each day, though they may choose among the short, medium, or long prayers.

- As an example of how Baha'i sacred texts might enrich and deepen one's spiritual life, we can turn to Robert Hayden, who grew up in a Detroit ghetto and, in 1976, became the first African American poet laureate of the United States. He first encountered the Baha'i faith in graduate school and converted in 1943.
    o Allusions to the revelation of Baha'i appear throughout his work, from the early poem "Baha'u'llah in the Garden of Ridwan," in which he imagines the prophet's state of mind at the time he declared that he was the manifestation of God, to "The Prisoners," based on Hayden's efforts to share Baha'i teaching with the inmates of Jackson State Prison in Michigan.

    o Hayden's "Words in the Mourning Time," written at a difficult period in American history, laments the assassinations of Martin Luther King and Robert Kennedy, as well as the horrors of the Vietnam War. In the 10th section, the poet looks forward to a future of joy and peace promised in the revelation to Baha'u'llah.

Suggested Reading

Abdu'l-Baha, *Some Answered Questions*.

Baha'i Prayers.

Baha'u'llah, *Gleanings from the Writings of Baha'u'llah*.

———, *The Kitab-i-Aqdas*.

———, *Writings of Baha'u'llah*.

Hatcher and Martin, *The Baha'i Faith: The Emerging Global Religion*.

Momen, *The Baha'i Faith: A Beginner's Guide*.

Smith, *An Introduction to the Baha'i Faith*.

Questions to Consider

1. How might a new religion bring together all religions?

2. If all the voluminous writings of the two founders of Baha'i are considered sacred texts, what determines which ones receive the most attention within the faith?

Related Traditions—Baha'i Scriptures
Lecture 33—Transcript

Hello. Thanks for joining me again.

Thirty-three lectures into this course on sacred texts, with all our discussions of canon, authority, and transmission, it may have occurred to you that I am engaged in a canonization project of my own. The essence of canon is making lists and setting boundaries, from Bishop Athanasius' list of New Testament books in 367, to Zhu Xi's advocacy of the Four Books of Confucianism in the 12th century, to Max Müller's Sacred Books of the East, to the editors of the Chinese Buddhist canon that was published in Japan in the 1920s—in each case people were making judgments about which texts were worthy of special reverence and treatment, and which were not.

In this Great Courses lecture series, I have been delineating the category of world scripture. Libraries are full of spiritual writings, many of which have been considered authoritative by at least some adherents of various religions. Which are significant enough to deserve a lecture in a course on sacred texts, and which will we pass over in silence? (That's by far the great majority.) Especially if we've only got 36 lectures to work with? A few choices were obvious; a course like this would have to include the Vedas, the Tanakh, the Buddhist Tripitaka, the Daodejing, the New Testament, and the Qur'an, and there was space for a few significant subsects of the major religious traditions, such as the Dead Sea Scrolls and the Christian apocryphal gospels, as well as some older, influential religions whose numbers have dwindled—Zoroastrianism, Jainism. Yet the question of what to include and what to omit becomes more difficult with regard to newer religions.

Why do Mormons, and Baha'is get lectures, but not Christian Scientists or Scientologists? In general, my rule was to try to include sacred texts of religions with a least a couple million believers, religions that have continued through several generations, and have expanded beyond the borders of their native land, and translated their scriptures into foreign languages. So I left out the sacred texts written by American Shakers, as well as those by Hong Xiuquan, the Chinese prophet who led millions of followers in the disastrous Taiping Rebellion of 1850 to 1864, because those religions have not continued, even though their texts are still around. Also, Mary Baker Eddy's *Science and Health* (that was first published 1875), is an interesting religious document, but it does not have enough adherents today to meet my criteria for world scripture.

The most recent additions to the library of world scripture that I have considered in this course are all from the 19th-century religions—Mormonism (with about 15 million believers); the Baha'i faith (the subject of this lecture, with 6 million), and Tenrikyo (with about 2 million believers). It's an intriguing question to ask what might be the next faith tradition to break into the world religion category (as I've defined it here). For 20th-century examples, we can look to Scientology, which had its origins in 1952 with the publication of *Scientology: A History of Man* by L. Ron Hubbard, or the Unification Church founded in South Korea in 1954 by Reverend Sun Myung Moon.

Also worth watching is Falun Gong, or Falun Dafa. It's a movement that began in China in 1992, which combines elements of Buddhism, Daoism, slow physical exercises, and the ideas of its founder Lǐ Hóngzhì. Falun Gong apparently has a couple million followers around the world—it's actually a little hard to know exactly how many there are—and its core texts have been translated into some three dozen languages, yet many believers hesitate to call it a religion, in part because that would have political repercussions in China. Already, Falun Gong has been rather brutally repressed by the Chinese government. Again, we'll see if this is a faith that can be transmitted through several generations past its founder.

My best guess as to the next likely candidate for world scripture status is Cao Dai, the third largest religion in Vietnam (after Buddhism and Catholicism). In 1920, a Vietnamese civil servant named Ngo Van Chieu began to receive revelations from Cao Dai, the one supreme god who is manifest in many forms and religions. According to Cao Dai, there have been three spiritual outpourings in world history. The first was when Hinduism, Judaism, and the Chinese Book of Changes were revealed; the second was the era of Buddhism, Daoism, Confucianism, and Christianity; and finally, the new revelations in the early 20th century in Vietnam that would unify all the world's religions. Cao Dai combines Jewish monotheism with Buddhist ideas of reincarnation and karma, Confucian ethics, and a church hierarchy based on Catholicism (there is a Cao Dai pope). Today it has somewhere between two and five million followers. It's large enough to be counted as a world religion and it has five or six books that could be considered as sacred texts, but there are not many followers outside of Vietnam and its scriptures have only recently been translated into English (and are rather hard to come by). Nevertheless, Cao Dai has survived and prospered for nearly a century and may become more well known in the next few decades.

The Baha'i faith, the subject of this lecture, is a bit older than Cao dai, and it has spread much farther. Indeed, it is the second most widespread religion in the world after Christianity, in terms of its presence in different nations. The religion began in 1863, when Baha'u'llah (1817–1892) announced in Baghdad that he was the prophetic fulfillment of Babism. Babism arose in the cultural context of Shi'a Islam, and is regarded by the Baha'is as an independent faith, the goal of which was to prepare the people for the coming of Baha'u'llah. When I say independent faith, I mean independent from Islam. The goal of Babism is it's able to break from Islam and then prepare the way for Baha'u'llah and Baha'i. So we're going to need to back up a little bit to catch the story.

Shi'a Islam is one of the two divisions of Islam—the other is Sunni—and Shi'a Muslims believe that the leadership of the faith should have stayed within the family of the Prophet Muhammad. Most Shi'a came to accept a succession of 12 legitimate Imams, or divinely-appointed leaders, from the 7th to the 9th centuries. The Twelfth Imam was thought to have to have been hidden by God, and will return someday as the Mahdi ("the Guided One"); when he returns, he'll return with Jesus as well, to usher in the Messianic Age of peace, justice, and Islamic law. Iran is one of the few countries where Shi'a Muslims are in the majority, and in 1844, Sayyid Ali-Muhammad Shirazi, a 24-year-old Iranian merchant, announced that he was the Madhi, ("the one who ariseth"). The Bab, as he's called, gained tens of thousands of followers, called Babis, and he also made some powerful enemies and was eventually executed by a government firing squad in 1850. Even though they're coming out of the cultural context of Shi'a Islam, it's a separate sort of religion.

Interestingly, the first person to proclaim a decisive break with Islam, proclaiming that Sharia Law had been superseded by Babi Law, was the fiery female missionary Tahirih, who symbolically took off her veil in front of a crowd of shocked men. In 1852, she too was executed as a martyr.

Mirza Husayn Ali Nuri, who would later take the honorific title of Baha'u'llah ("Glory of God"), was an early follower of the Bab. He, along with many other believers, was persecuted and imprisoned. In 1852, while he was jailed in a dungeon in Tehran (the famous "Black Pit"), he saw a vision of a maiden of heaven who told him that God had a special mission for him. After Baha'u'llah's release and exile, he became a leader of the Babis. The Bab, in his voluminous writings, had indicated that a future Messianic figure was still to come (he referred to him as "he whom God shall make manifest"), and in 1863, in the garden of Ridvan, near Baghdad, Baha'u'llah declared that he was the promised one whose coming was foretold by the Bab. Over the next few years, most Babis became Baha'is, that is, members of the community that regarded Baha'u'llah as the inaugurator of a new religious tradition and as the fulfillment of the messianic expectations of all of the world's major religions; in a number of religions, there's some notion that there's going to be a heavenly figure who's going to come at the end of time, and Baha'u'llah claimed that he was the fulfillment of many of those traditions. The Persian and Ottoman empires weren't sympathetic to the Baha'i faith, and Baha'u'llah endured a long series of exiles, imprisonment, and house arrests that took him from Persia, to Baghdad, to Constantinople, to Edirne in northwest Turkey, and then finally to Acre, near modern day Haifa, Israel—Acre is sometimes referred to as "Akka" in the Arabic pronunciation—and he lived there for the last 24 years of his life.

Shortly before his death in 1892, Baha'u'llah appointed his eldest son, Abdu'l-Baha, who lived from 1844–1921, as his successor. During the early years of the 20th century, Baha'i spread to Europe and North America, in part because Abdu'l-Baha took two speaking tours in the West from 1911–1913 to spread the message about Baha'u'llah. The next leader of the Baha'i community after Abdu'l-Baha was Shoghi Effendi. He lived from 1897–1957 and he was a grandson of Abdu'l-Baha; and since 1963, the highest authority in the faith has been the Universal House of Justice, an elective body of nine members headquartered in Haifa.

Baha'is believe in the oneness of god, the oneness of religions, and the oneness of humanity. In other words, there's one all-powerful creator who's spoken to different prophets or manifestations of god at various times and places including Krishna, Zoroaster, Abraham, Moses, Jesus, Muhammad, and then finally the Bab and Baha'u'llah. These messengers represent progressive revelations so that all of those major religions come from the same God, but they can all be unified in the end under the teachings of Baha'i. There may someday be future manifestations of God as well, but not for at least 1,000 years. As the oneness of God and the oneness of religions are recognized, so also there should be a oneness of humanity, with all races and ethnicities being treated equally and seen as part of a great whole. Significantly, men and women should be equal as well. Baha'is regard humanity as progressing, and they look to a future of increasing peace, justice, and unity.

Shoghi Effendi summarized the tenets of the religion as follows; he says:

> The Baha'i Faith recognizes the unity of God and of His Prophets, upholds the principle of an unfettered search after truth, condemns all forms of superstition and prejudice, teaches that the fundamental purpose of religion is to promote concord and harmony, that it must go hand-in-hand with science, and that it constitutes the sole and ultimate basis of a peaceful, an ordered and progressive society.

He continued; and keep in mind that this quotation is from 1938 when World War was looming. He said:

> It inculcates the principle of equal opportunity, rights and privileges for both sexes, advocates compulsory education, abolishes extremes of poverty and wealth, exalts work performed in the spirit of service to the rank of worship, recommends the adoption of an auxiliary international language, and provides the necessary agencies for the establishment and safeguarding of a permanent and universal peace.

There's a lot to like here; but the message of Baha'i hasn't always been well received, particularly in Iran, the native land of its founder. Although Baha'is consider their faith a distinct world religion, it comes out of an Islamic background, much as Buddhism had its origins in Hinduism or Christianity in Judaism. This can be seen, for example, in their adoption of messianic ideas from Shia Islam; from their reverences for Muhammad as a prophet; and in the way that the Qur'an is quoted and sometimes imitated in some of their scriptures. In addition, Baha'is are asked to abstain from alcohol; they pray daily, although they face Acre rather than Mecca; and they fast for an entire month, though Baha'i months are only 19 days long; and finally, because they're encouraged to make a pilgrimage at least once in their life, though the Baha'i pilgrimage isn't to Mecca, it's to the Acre/Haifa area. These Islamic elements of the faith have convinced some that the Baha'is are actually apostate Muslims, and they've sometimes been harshly prosecuted. Some 200 were executed in Iran between 1978 and 1998; and in recent years, Baha'i leaders have been arrested and imprisoned in Iran, Afghanistan, and Egypt. Baha'is also face legal restrictions in Indonesia and Morocco.

The Baha'i faith—like Christianity, Judaism, and Islam—is very much a text-based religion, though technically the Baha'i canon is a lot larger than the other three faiths. The Baha'is believe that everything written by the Bab and by Baha'u'llah should be accepted as revelations from God. In addition, the works of Abdu'l-Baha are also regarded as sacred writings or scriptures, along with his authenticated talks. I should point out that the station of Abdu'l-Baha is different from that of the Bab and Baha'u'llah. The former two are considered messengers from God, while Abdu'l-Baha is regarded as the perfect example of the way Baha'i should act. The works of Shoghi Effendi are inspired interpretations, including his English translations of Baha'u'llah's Arabic and Persian writings that were done in a formal, somewhat archaic style reminiscent of the King James Bible. Effendi's writings are authoritative, but they aren't regarded as scripture. Official communications now from the international House of Justice are also considered authoritative but not scripture and they usually deal with matters that weren't addressed in the sacred writings.

Because the Bab, Baha'u'llah, and Abdu'l-Baha spent many years in prison or under house arrest, they wrote voluminously; they had a lot of time to write letters and other sorts of texts. The Bab's writings would probably fill 50 volumes, while Baha'u'llah is said to have written 100 volumes worth of books, tracts, prayers, and letters, which are often called "tablets." All told,

Baha'u'llah composed or received some 15,000 texts—remember, these are regarded as revelation—and the pages of those texts probably add up to 70 times the length of the Qur'an, or 15 times longer than the Old and New Testaments combined. Abdu'l-Baha wrote several books and 27,000 letters, perhaps comprising 50 volumes in total. Not all of the sacred writings of these three men have been edited and translated, and Baha'is today tend to focus on a few particular books. I should note, however, that all the sacred texts that I'm about to talk about are available online in official translations at reference.bahai.org. The Baha'i faith is very missionary-minded; and they, along with the Mormons, have remarkably attractive websites that are attuned to Western sensibilities and technological advances. You can check out more about Baha'i at bahai.org and bahai.us.

The Bab is regarded as the forerunner of Baha'u'llah, much like Elijah or John the Baptist in Jewish and Christian traditions. As a result, the Bab's writings—which include a commentary on the sura of joseph from the Qur'an and doctrinal expositions—aren't studied to the same extent as the writings of Baha'u'llah, at least not in English-speaking countries. The Baha'i Publishing Trust—and that's the faith's official press—has published a single volume of selections from the Bab's writings, though some of his prayers and meditations are still in common use. The majority of the sacred texts that the Baha'i study regularly are from Baha'u'llah. Even before his 1863 announcement at the Garden of Ridwan that he was the promised one, he was already producing works that would later have the status of revelations. Around 1858, he wrote the *Hidden Words*, a collection of 103 wisdom sayings, about half in Arabic and the other half in Persian. These are spoken by God in the first person and are addressed to humanity in general.

For example, Number Seven in the Arabic side says: "O Son of Man! If thou lovest Me, turn away from thyself; and if thou seekest My pleasure, regard not thine own; that thou mayest die in Me and I may eternally live in thee." You can hear the archaic grammar of the King James Bible in Shoghi Effendi's English translation here. The Persian verses draw on the imagery of Bat poetic tradition. For instance: "O DWELLERS OF MY PARADISE! With the hands of loving-kindness I have planted in the holy garden of paradise the young tree of your love and friendship, and have watered it with the goodly showers of My tender grace."

Sometime between 1857 and 1863, Baha'u'llah produced *The Seven Valleys* and *The Four Valleys*, two short tracts that were written in response to the questions of Sufi mystics. They outline a path of spiritual progress somewhat similar to Attar's *Conference of the Birds* that I mentioned in the last lecture. These texts are written in eloquent Persian, and they quote liberally from the Qur'an and Rumi's *Mathnawi*. *The Seven Valleys* represent the journey of the soul towards God, passing through the valleys of search, love, knowledge, unity, contentment, wonderment, and finally the valley of true poverty and absolute nothingness.

The last of the major pre-Ridwan scriptures is the Kitab-i-Iqan, "The Book of Certitude," published in 1862. This was the first book of Baha'i scripture to actually be published, and it provides a basic overview of Baha'i beliefs. In this revelation, Baha'u'llah expounds on the ideas of the oneness of God, progressive revelation, and the unity of the prophets, who were sent to different people at different times and were invariably misunderstood. He interprets key passages from the Qur'an, as well as a few from the New Testament, and he sets the stage for his declaration at Ridwan by reinterpreting the Qur'anic verse on Muhammad—the verse that mentions Muhammad as the seal of the prophets—in order to allow for some future messengers of manifestations from God.

For just a flavor of his writing, consider this quotation:

> Consider the past. How many, both high and low, have, at all times, yearningly awaited the advent of the Manifestations of God in the sanctified persons of His chosen Ones. How often have they expected His coming, how frequently have they prayed that the breeze of divine mercy might blow, and the promised Beauty step forth from behind the veil of concealment, and be made manifest to all the world.

Tradition has it that Baha'u'llah wrote the 200 manuscript pages of the *Book of Certitude* in just two days and two nights in a frenzy of inspiration. Witnesses report that when Baha'u'llah was writing or when he was dictating scripture, he was transformed with an aura of great power and energy such that the words flowed out of him at great speed, sometimes with 1,000 verses being revealed in the space of an hour. His primary scribe had to develop a special sort of speedwriting to keep up and get it all down on paper.

After Baha'u'llah had made public his identity as the promised one, he continued to write and write. Probably the most important of the scriptures after 1863 was the Kitab-i-Aqdas, the "Most Holy Book," which sets forth guidelines for the organization and practices of the Baha'i community. In this text, Baha'u'llah outlined the future institutions of guardianship—and that's a position that was held by Shoghi Effendi—and then later the Universal House of Justice; and he delineated the rules for Baha'is concerning prayer, fasting, houses of worship, pilgrimage, criminal law, marriage, inheritance, and scripture. Some of the distinctive customs of the Baha'is come from the Most Holy Book, including their rejection of congregational prayers aside from a prayer for the dead that's said together; the requirement that marriages have the consent of parents; the requirement to write a will; and the reciting of scripture both morning and evening; and daily obligatory prayer in either a long, a medium, or a short form. When the Most Holy Book was finally published in an authoritative English edition in 1992, it was a welcome event for British, Australian, and North American Baha'is.

Two further books are particularly worth mentioning. Among the large number of revealed letters (called tablets) by Baha'u'llah, the Epistle to the Son of the Wolf is especially noteworthy. This long letter is Baha'u'llah's last major work, written to a fierce opponent of the Baha'is, and it offers a summary of the doctrines Baha'u'llah had been teaching for over 30 years. Finally, Gleanings from the Writings of Baha'u'llah, a compilation edited by Shoghi Effendi published in 1935, is often the first scripture that Baha'is have encountered. The quotations in that book are organized into five sections: "The Day of God," "The Manifestation of God," "The Soul and Its Immortality," "The World Order and Most Great Peace," and "The Duties of the Individual and the Spiritual Meaning of Life."

As I mentioned earlier, Abdu'l-Baha wasn't a messenger of God, but he was the authorized interpreter of the writings of the Bab and Baha'u'llah, and his works are given scriptural status. A good place to start is with his 1908 publication *Some Answered Questions*, which came out of conversations with Laura Clifford Barney. In this book, Abdu'l-Baha offers Baha'i perspectives on a number of issues that Christians and other Westerners might be interested in, including Jesus, baptism, life after death, and the Bible.

Given the thousands and thousands of documents written by the founds of Baha'i—particularly the letters or tablets—the work of collecting, authenticating, transcribing, editing, and translating the sacred texts of this religion is ongoing; indeed, it constitutes one of the major concerns of the Universal House of Justice. It's similar to the current efforts of the Mormon Church in the Joseph Smith Papers Project to produce a complete, scholarly collection of all the documents written or dictated by its founder. But in the LDS case, there are many fewer writings to deal with—only 20 volumes are projected—and the results won't be considered canonical scripture.

One final scriptural text that's used extensively by Baha'is is a collection of prayers written by the Bab, Baha'u'llah, and Abdu'l-Baha. These lovely meditations are arranged by topic. For example, there are prayers for divine aid, for one's children, for families, forgiveness, healing, marriage, praise and gratitude, protection, and unity. The volume begins with the three possible daily prayers; so believers between the ages of 15 and 70 have to recite one each day, though they can choose between the short, medium, or the long prayers. The short obligatory prayer is as follows:

> I bear witness, O my God [remember that opening, because we'll hear it again in just a few minutes], that Thou hast created me to know Thee and to worship Thee. I testify, at this moment, to my powerlessness and to Thy might, to my poverty and to Thy wealth. There is none other God but Thee, the Help in Peril, the Self-Subsisting.

As an example of how Baha'i sacred texts might enrich and deepen one's spiritual life, we can turn to Robert Hayden, who grew up in a Detroit ghetto and in 1976 became the first African American poet laureate of the United States. He first encountered the Baha'i faith in graduate school and converted in 1943, saying, "I believe in the essential oneness of all people, and I believe in the basic unity of all religions. I don't believe races are important, I think that people are important." Allusions to the revelation of Baha'i appear throughout his work, from an early work, "Baha'u'llah in the Garden of Ridwan," in which he imagines the prophet's state of mind at the time he declared that he was the manifestation of God ("Energies like angels dance / Glorias of recognition") to a later poem, "The Prisoners," based on Hayden's efforts to share Baha'i teaching with the inmates of Jackson State Prison in Michigan. Hayden wrote: "We shared reprieving Hidden Words [remember that's the name of one of the Baha'i scriptures] / revealed by the Godlike imprisoned / One, whose crime was truth," recalling that Baha'u'llah also spent years behind bars or under house arrest.

Finally, Robert Hayden's poem "Words in the Mourning Time," written at a difficult period in American history. That poem laments the recent assassinations of Martin Luther King and Robert Kennedy, as well as the horrors of the Vietnam War. In the 10th section, he looks forward to a future of joy and peace promised in the revelation to Baha'u'llah. Three times, Hayden repeats the words "I bear him witness now," words that would've been very familiar to him from those daily short obligatory prayers. Towards the end of the poem, he repeats Baha'u'llah's own description of his first visionary experience in the black pit of Tehran as recounted in the Epistle to the Son of the Wolf. "I was but a man like others, asleep upon My couch, when lo, the breezes of the All-Glorious were wafted over Me, and taught Me the knowledge of all that hath been."

At a time when dungeon-like hopelessness was hanging over our nation, it still seemed possible that the breezes of God might arrive to awaken our souls and teach us the meaning of all.

Abandoned Scriptures—Egyptian and Mayan
Lecture 34

We've now completed our basic tour of the sacred texts of the world's major living religions, but this by no means exhausts the category of sacred texts. A vast number of scriptures have been left behind in the development of religious traditions—sacred texts that still exist today but are no longer connected to any contemporary faith communities. It's interesting to consider how we interpret the stories from these texts with no commentaries, no records of social practices, and no one living who still holds to the values of these faiths. In this lecture, we'll look at two such scriptures: the Egyptian Book of the Dead and the Mayan Popol Vuh.

Is the Book of the Dead Scripture?

- When Napoleon's army invaded Egypt in 1798, no one could read ancient Egyptian; indeed, all knowledge of the language had been lost since the 5th century C.E. One of the French soldiers discovered the Rosetta Stone in 1799, which had the same text written in Egyptian hieroglyphs, demotic (a simplified Egyptian script), and Classical Greek. This triple text was the key that ultimately enabled scholars to read ancient Egyptian.

- The decipherment of hieroglyphs was an astonishing scholarly triumph, and archaeologists started reading whatever they could find. Many of the texts they discovered had to do with religion, including funerary texts, hymns, ritual texts, and magical texts. One text that was commonly buried with mummies was what we today call the Book of the Dead, though for Egyptians it was the "Book of Coming Forth by Day."

- The text is clearly religious in nature, consisting of spells that would bring about the resurrection of the deceased and guide his or her journey through the underworld to a happy afterlife. But does it count as a sacred text?

- o Not all religious writings are scripture. Think, for example, of Dante's *Divine Comedy*, Bunyan's *Pilgrim's Progress*, or the *Book of Common Prayer*. These books are seriously religious, well-respected, and loved by many, but they are not scripture. Was the Egyptian Book of the Dead more like Dante or more like the Bible?

- o One of the insights of modern religious studies is that the concept of "scripture" is relational. As the religion scholar William Graham has noted: "No text, written, oral or both, is sacred or authoritative in isolation from a community. A text is only 'scripture' insofar as a group of persons perceives it to be sacred or holy, powerful and meaningful, possessed of an exalted authority, and in some fashion transcendent of, and hence distinct from, other speech and writing."

- o We often think of scriptures as containing revelations, sacred narratives, commandments, and doctrines, but in this course, we have seen examples of sacred texts that consist mostly of poetry or are primarily collections of sayings. Could a book of magical spells be considered scripture? It depends on how it is regarded or used by believers. But again, there is no contemporary community that still mummifies its dead or believes in the Egyptian gods; thus, we must piece together the evidence from archaeology.

- The Book of the Dead was obviously a popular work, given that several thousand copies have survived from the 15th through the 1st centuries B.C.E. Around 600 B.C.E., a standard edition emerged, with 192 spells in a set order. Clearly, people wanted to be buried with the Book of the Dead because repeating its words gave them power over gods and protection from specific dangers in their journey through the Other World.

- Western awareness of the Book of the Dead came about the same time as Max Müller's Sacred Books of the East series. A German translation of one particular copy was done in 1842, and in 1886, the Swiss scholar Édouard Naville published his three-volume Egyptian edition that compared several manuscripts. In 1895, E. A. Wallis Budge published his famous version, which featured a transcription of the Egyptian hieroglyphs with an interlinear English translation running beneath.

Contents of the Book of the Dead

- The Book of the Dead contains magical formulas for preserving the body from snakes or decay, for not having one's heart or head taken away in the realm of the dead, and for reviving one's mummy, thereby enabling it to eat, drink, and breathe.

- Throughout the text, there is an emphasis on knowing the names of various divinities in order to have power over them; traveling with Re, the sun god, over the expanse of the sky; and transforming oneself into animals and even into gods. Some of the spells are as short as a few sentences, while others extend to several pages.

- One of the lengthier spells that has received a great deal of attention is 125, which describes the judgment of the dead. The primary

Before about 600 B.C.E., copies of the Book of the Dead seem to have been individualized, with variations in the spells and illustrations selected.

illustration shows the weighing of the deceased person's heart in a balance against *maat*, the principle of truth, morality, and justice, represented by an ostrich feather.

- o The lists of sins and crimes in the spell ("I have not stolen," "I have not slain sacred cattle") provide a synopsis of commonly accepted moral principles in ancient Egypt. But did Egyptians really strive to live by these principles?

- o On the one hand, the text is a spell, implying that by saying the right words at the right time, one can escape the consequences of sin.

- o On the other hand, spell 17 promises protection and blessings for anyone who reads at least part of the Book of the Dead daily, long before they are face to face with the gods. Perhaps the Book of the Dead was meant to constrain behavior in this life after all.

- For living religious traditions, reading sacred texts can help us better understand the actions and thinking of believers around the world, and there's always the possibility of conversion. But that's not the case with lost traditions. Why, then, might we care about abandoned sacred texts?
  - o First, the Book of the Dead has great historical value. Ancient Egypt was a fascinating culture, and the Book of the Dead reveals much about religious beliefs and practices of the time.

  - o Second, the text may tell us not just about Egyptians but about humanity in general. Other people in different lands and eras have had similar hopes and fears about death and have wondered about the influence of gods and morality. A faith in the magical power of words, especially if pronounced at the right time and place, is something that we have seen in many of the world's sacred texts.

  - o Third, reading the Book of the Dead gives us a chance to reflect on our own religiosity. Are my prayers ever attempts to get God to do my bidding? Do I think that I can somehow escape the consequences of my mistakes by saying the right words? How much of my good behavior is done for the sake of a pleasant afterlife?

The Popol Vuh

- We have all seen images of magnificent ruins in Mesoamerica that were constructed by the Maya people in the period from 250 to 900 C.E. For unknown reasons, the civilization went into serious decline in the 9th century. Cities were abandoned, political structures collapsed, and the writing system was neglected, although Mayans still existed when the Spanish arrived in the 16th century.

- The Maya produced books, now called codices, that were made of bark paper folded accordion-style, with hieroglyphs and detailed illustrations on both sides. Unfortunately, zealous Catholic priests burned as many codices as they could find, and only a few have survived, which means that we know much less about ancient Mesoamerican civilization than ancient Egypt.

- One codex, now lost, contained sacred stories of the Maya. Sometime between 1554 and 1558, an unnamed Indian rewrote that text into Quiché, a late form of the Mayan language, which he transcribed into the Roman alphabet. Sometime around 1701 to 1703, a Dominican friar, Father Francisco Ximénez, found that Quiché text and translated it into Spanish.
    - Ximénez's manuscript was discovered in 1854 by two European scholars visiting Guatemala City. Upon their return home, one published Ximénez's translation, and the other published the Quiché version with a French translation.

    - The French scholar had also stolen the manuscript itself, which eventually made its way to the Newberry Library in Chicago, where it was rediscovered once again in 1928 and finally published in English in 1950.

- The Popol Vuh ("Council Book") recounts the origins of the world, the creation of animals and humans, the adventures of two sets of twins, the discovery of corn and fire, and a history of the Quiché branch of the Maya. It also includes guidelines for religious ritual and divination. The episodes are not related in strictly chronological order, and there is a great deal of doubling of characters, events, and phrasing.
    - The most famous stories are of the hero-twins Hunahpu and Xbalanque. Their father and uncle, One Hunahpu and Seven Hunahpu (also twins), were celebrated players of the Mesoamerican ballgame.
    - The twins are clever tricksters, who manage to defeat the gods of the underworld; afterward, they ascended into the sky to become the sun and the moon.
    - The Popol Vuh continues with a lengthy account of the creation of humans and the history of the Quiché Maya, then concludes: "Everything has been completed here concerning Quiché."

- We don't know whether the Popol Vuh was ever an authoritative text or how believers used it. However, the strange narratives in the text are clearly connected to the world of the Yucatan Peninsula; they mention calabash trees, chili peppers, and monkeys, as well as such customs as the ballgame and human sacrifice. And there may be more here than meets the eye. Some scholars have suggested that astronomical information is encoded in the progress of the hero-twins through the underworld and in other episodes.

- As with the Book of the Dead, the Popol Vuh may contain some wise insights or universal truths, and it certainly offers a chance to reflect on the religious assumptions of our own culture. But the Mesoamerican text also has stories that can be analyzed in terms of plot, character, and theme and may have interesting things to say about human relationships, life and death, or the connection between the human and natural worlds.

- All sacred texts, even abandoned ones, deserve an extra measure of respect simply because so many people have held them in high esteem. They have often been primary elements in how individuals viewed themselves and the world, yet they can be puzzling. This leads us to one last reason to read them today: as a reminder of the incredible variety of human religious experience and a warning about how much we still don't know.

Suggested Reading

Christenson, trans., *Popol Vu: Literal Poetic Version*.

Faulkner, trans., *The Ancient Egyptian Book of the Dead*.

Graham, "Scripture."

Johnston, ed., *Religions of the Ancient World*.

Kemp, *How to Read the Egyptian Book of the Dead*.

Taylor, ed., *Journey through the Afterlife*.

Tedlock, trans., *Popol Vuh: The Definitive Edition of the Mayan Book of the Dawn of Life and the Glories of Gods and Kings*.

Questions to Consider

1. How might we approach sacred texts for which there is no longer a living faith community?

2. Why is there such variety in sacred texts, with some primarily telling stories and explaining things and others providing liturgy by which the world or individuals are transformed?

Abandoned Scriptures—Egyptian and Mayan
Lecture 34—Transcript

We've now completed our basic tour of the sacred texts of the world's major living religions, but this by no means exhausts the category of sacred texts. I thought it might be useful to talk about two examples from the vast number of scriptures that have been left behind or abandoned in the development of religious traditions; that is, sacred texts that still exist today, but are no longer connected to any contemporary faith communities.

But first, let me start with a strange story that may be a little hard to figure out. It's from the *Zuo Commentary* on the *Spring and Autumn Annals*, which, as you'll recall, was one of the Five Confucian Classics; the *Zuo Commentary* itself was very early and was eventually canonized as one of the Thirteen Confucian Classics in the 12th century. The *Spring and Autumn Annals* has an entry from 594 B.C.E. that says, "A body of men from Qin invaded Jin," and then that's all there is; you remember there are just these very short notices of things that happened. Then the *Zuo Commentary* adds a little more detail and it says that Wei Ke, a commander of Jin forces, captured Du Hui, a soldier of Qin known for his extraordinary strength, which would've been an unexpected turn of events. Then the *Zuo Commentary* tells a backstory:

> Earlier, Wei Ke's father Wei Wuzi had a favorite concubine who had borne him no children. Falling ill, he gave orders to his son, saying, "See that she is provided with a husband." When his illness became more severe, however, he said, "See that she is put to death and buried with me [so that he could have her companionship in the next life]!"
>
> At length, when he died, his son Wei Ke arranged for the concubine to be married, saying, "When the illness was severe, my father's mind became deranged. I abide by the orders he gave when his mind was clear."

If you've never heard this tale before, and you probably haven't, its meaning may not be obvious. Who are we supposed to identify with; with Wei Kei, the disobedient son, or Du Hui, the captured soldier? Is it better to be captured rather than killed? Is returning with a captive a good thing for Wei Ke? What about the concubine? Does she want to be remarried, or would she prefer to be buried with her deceased husband? What's happening here? Fortunately, the *Zuo Commentary* continues and says:

> When Wei Ke engaged the Qin forces in battle at Fushi, he saw an old man tying grasses together in such a manner as to block Du Hui's way. Du Hui stumbled over the grasses and fell to the ground, making it possible for Wei Ke to capture him. That night, the old man appeared to Wei Ke in a dream and said, "I am the father of the woman you gave away in marriage. You followed the orders that your late father gave when he was still in his right mind. I have done this to repay you."

This is an example of the kind of supernatural stories that undermine assumptions about Confucianism being exclusively secular or this-worldly; and within the context of Confucianism, we actually have a pretty good idea of why this story matters. The story supports the important principle of filial piety—that is, respect for parents—but it adds an escape clause for at least some cases when obedience to parents would conflict with other moral principles; remember that key line: "I abide by the orders he gave when his mind was clear," and then there's this supernatural event that's going to affirm that this was the right thing to do. In the end, this novel interpretation that says "I can decide whether my father was in his right mind or not in his right mind," it comes to its culmination when he captures an enemy. That capturing of an enemy is connected to a deceased ancestor helping out a living descendant; though in this case, it was that old man, the deceased father, who was helping his daughter. That's a little bit more unusual; in a society where sons are supposed to matter more than daughters, where daughters marry away into other families, this story is evidence that parents could still care deeply about the happiness and wellbeing of their girls in ways that reach beyond the bounds of death.

We can figure out the key elements that make this story both intelligible and also challenging in the culture—that idea of filial piety and when is it right or not appropriate to obey your parents; relations between fathers and daughters; helpful ancestors; supernatural rewards—we know all of this or how to interpret this story because this sacred text has been part of continuous tradition. We know what sorts of issues were important in Confucianism through the centuries and even today. But what if all we had were just a few stories, with no commentaries, no records of social practices, and no one living who still held to Confucian values? In this lecture, we'll take a look at two left-behind scriptures: the Egyptian Book of the Dead and the Mayan Popol Vuh. Both of those are going to be much harder to understand because we don't have the kind of continuous tradition that we have with Confucianism.

When Napoleon's army invaded Egypt in 1798, no one could read the ancient Egyptian hieroglyphs; in fact, all knowledge of the language had been lost since the 5th century C.E., though there were plenty of inscriptions around. One of the French soldiers with Napoleon discovered the Rosetta Stone in 1799, which had the same text written in Egyptian hieroglyphics, and then again in demotic, which is a simplified Egyptian script, and then in Classical Greek. This triple-text was the key that, after much painstaking philological reconstruction, enabled scholars to actually read ancient Egyptian, because they knew how to read Greek and then they could sort of figure out the correspondence between those three languages. Simply being able to read a sacred text in its original language can be the first challenge when there are no longer any living believers that you can just ask.

The decipherment of hieroglyphs was an astonishing scholarly triumph, and newly-literate archaeologists (I mean literate in the language of ancient Egypt) started reading whatever they could find. Not surprisingly for a script whose name in Greek, *hieroglyphs*, means "sacred inscription"—in Egyptian, the script is called "god's speech"—many of these texts had to do with religion. There were funerary texts, hymns, ritual texts, and magical texts; but unlike other ancient writings that might be recovered from Confucianism—like the kind of writings that we find in graves sometimes—or Buddhism, or Judaism, scholars had to reconstruct Egyptian religion from scratch—they didn't know much at all about it. Fortunately, there were thousands of inscriptions and documents from which they could piece together a basic knowledge of the ancient Egyptian gods, myths, rituals, and beliefs about the soul and the afterlife.

One text that was commonly buried with mummies was what we today call the Book of the Dead, though for Egyptians it was the "Book of Coming Forth by Day." This text is clearly religious in nature, consisting of spells that would bring about the resurrection of the deceased and guide his or her journey through the underworld to a happy afterlife. Does it count as a sacred text? Remember, not all religious writings are scripture. Think, for example, of Dante's *Divine Comedy* or Bunyan's *Pilgrim's Progress*, or the *Book of Common Prayer*; these books are seriously religious, they're well-respected, and even loved by many, but they're not scripture. Was the Egyptian Book of Dead more like Dante or more like the Bible?

One of the insights of modern religious studies is that the concept of scripture is relational. As William Graham has noted:

> Neither form nor content can serve to identify or to distinguish scripture as a general phenomenon ... the sacrality or holiness of a book is not an a priori attribute but one that is realized historically in the life of communities who respond to it as something sacred or holy.... No text, written, oral or both, is sacred or authoritative in isolation from a community. A text is only "scripture" insofar as a group of persons perceives it to be sacred or holy, powerful and meaningful, possessed of an exalted authority, and in some fashion transcendent of, and hence distinct from, other speech and writing.

We often think of scriptures as containing revelations, sacred narratives, commandments, and doctrines; but in this course, we've seen examples of sacred texts that consist mostly of poetry (like the Zoroastrian Gathas or the Sikh Adi Granth), or texts that are primarily collections of sayings (the Confucian *Analects* fit into that category, as does the Christian Gospel of Thomas). Could a book of magical spells be considered scripture? That depends on how it's regarded or used by believers; but again, there's no contemporary community that still mummifies its dead or believes in the Egyptian gods, so we have to piece together the evidence from archaeology.

We can tell that the Book of the Dead was obviously a popular work since several thousand copies have survived from the 15th–1st centuries B.C.E. It was highly valued; indeed, some of the copies were lavishly illustrated and would've been very expensive to produce. Although it didn't have a regular form for the first thousand years, around 600 B.C.E. a standard edition emerged with 192 spells in a set order. Before that time, copies seemed to have been individualized, with some scrolls being quite long (even over 100 feet long) and others being short, depending upon the particular spells and illustrations that were selected; those illustrations are an important part of the book and they're often referred to as "vignettes." Even when the standard text of the Book of the dead was mass-produced—and I mean by hand, of course; this is before printing—it was common to write out the text and then leave blank spots so that the purchasers could insert the name of the scroll's deceased owner at appropriate places in the various spells. So you have a parent or someone that you want to bury this text with; you buy a copy of the text that's already been made, and there are blank spots in the text where you put in your mother or father's name and then bury that scroll with the coffin. Clearly this was a book that was supposed to do something. People wanted to be buried with the Book of Dead because repeating its words would give them power over gods and protection from specific dangers in their journey to the Otherworld.

What do these spells look like? Western awareness of the Egyptian Book of the Dead came about the same time as Max Müller's Sacred Books of the East series. A German translation of one particular copy was done in 1842, and in 1886 the Swiss scholar Édouard Naville published his three-volume Egyptian edition that compared several manuscripts; so it's something like Müller's critical edition of the Sanskrit Rig Veda that appeared 10 years earlier. Then, in 1895, E. A. Wallis Budge published his famous version, which featured a transcription of the Egyptian hieroglyphs with an interlinear English translation running beneath all those little pictures of birds, hands, feet, eyes, beetles, human figures, and feathers. That edition, that translation, captured the imagination of schoolchildren everywhere and is still in print today, even though its scholarship is more than a hundred years out of date. Just to make this really clear: The Egyptian Book of the Dead isn't part of Müller's Sacred Books of the East series, but it happened about at the same time, when European and American scholars were rediscovering or discovering sacred texts of the world for the first time, at least in that comprehensive sort of view.

More accurate translations are available now, and as one thumbs through them, there are magical formulas for preserving the body from snakes or decay, for not having one's head or heart taken away in the realm of the dead, and for reviving one's mummy; that is, "going out into the day," thereby enabling it to eat, drink, and breathe, so it enables its resurrection. For instance, here is spell number 55, the "Spell for Giving Breath in the Realm of the Dead": "I am the jackal of jackals, I am Shu [Shu was a primordial deity] who draws the air into the presence of the sunshine to the limits of the sky, to the limits of the earth, to the limits of the plume of the nebeh-bird, and air is given to those youth who open my mouth so that I may see with my eyes." When you pronounce this text, it's supposed to do something; it's supposed to bring the corpse—or yourself in this case—back to life.

Throughout the text, there's an emphasis on knowing the names of various divinities so as to have power over them. It also talks about traveling with Re, the sun god, over the expanse of the sky; and then transforming oneself into animals and even into gods. Some of the spells are as short as a few sentences, while others extend to a several pages. One of the lengthier spells that's gotten a lot of attention is number 125, which describes the judgment of the dead. The primary illustration or vignette shows the weighing of the deceased person's heart in a balance against *maat*, the principle of truth, morality, and justice, which is represented by an ostrich feather. The idea is that if the heart is too heavy it's thrown to the crocodile down there and you lose your chance at eternal life.

The title of this particular spell—and these are written in red, as opposed to black ink for the rest of the text—says, "To be said on reaching the Hall of the Two Truths so as to purge N [that "N" is what scholars use to represent one of those blank spots; and so it might have lots of different names depending on who owns the scroll] of any sins committed and to see the face of every god." The Hall of Two Truths may encourage you to ask, "So what are the Two Truths?" Actually, they're referring to two figures of Truth, or *maat*, which are represented as goddesses. Then the spell proper begins this way: "Hail to you, great God, Lord of the Two Truths! I have come to you, my Lord, I was brought to see your beauty. I know you, I know the names of the forty-two gods, who are with you in the Hall of the Two Truths."

The text then goes on to name each of the 42 gods, some of whom have rather frightening designations like Flame-grasper, Bone-smasher, and Blood-eater; and then to specify what exactly you have to say to each one of those gods. It's usually some declaration of innocence; so you might say to one, "I have not stolen," and then to another, "I have not slain sacred cattle," or "I have not committed adultery," or "I have not wanted more than I had" (which sounds pretty conservative), or "I have not winked" (and I'm not sure what the problem is with winking or what that means). Similarly, in the Hall of Two Truths, the deceased person proclaims to Osiris that he or she hasn't committed 35 sins or crimes, some of which are specifically religious like "I have not stolen the cakes of the dead," "I have not stopped a god in his procession," while others probably represent more universal ethical principles: "I have not robbed the poor," "I have not added to the weight of the balance," and "I have not taken milk from the mouth of children." Still others seem impossible to honestly proclaim; so when you get to this point, you're supposed to say in this Hall of Two Truths: "I have not caused pain. I have not caused tears." How many of you right now could honesty say that you've never caused tears? Then the insistence at the end: "I am pure, I am pure, I am pure."

These are interesting lists since they provide a synopsis of commonly accepted moral principles in ancient Egypt. If you were to make up a list for modern America or Britain, what sins would put on there and which would you be eager to declare your innocence of? But did Egyptians really strive to live by these principles in the Book of the Dead? On the one hand, the title states that this series of pronouncements is to "purge N [that person, that name] of any sins committed," so it's a spell; you've committed sins, but by saying the right words at the right time, you can escape the consequences of those mistakes or errors. Indeed, Spell Number 30 can be recited to make sure that your heart, when it's sitting there in the balance, doesn't speak up to denounce you for your wrongdoings; it's a spell to keep your heart quiet during this court proceeding. On the other hand, Spell Number 17 promises protection and blessings for anyone who reads at least part of the Book of the Dead daily; so they'd be reading this while they're alive, long before they're face-to-face with those terrifying gods. Perhaps the Book of the Dead was indeed intended to constrain behavior in this life after all since people were encouraged—at least some people were encouraged—to think about it regularly, and to think about its principles and precepts and the ethical injunctions that it contains.

What are we to make of all this? For living religious traditions, reading sacred texts can help us better understand the actions and the thinking of believers around the world; and there's always the possibility of conversion. Even if the chances are remote, contemporary religions are live options. But I don't think that anyone today expects that after they die, their heart will be weighed by the jackal-headed god Anubis, with Osiris looking on. The afterworld described in the Book of the Dead seems impossibly remote and fanciful today; so why might we care about abandoned sacred texts like this? I can think of three or four reasons: First, a text like the Egyptian Book of the Dead has a great deal of historical value. It reveals a lot about religious beliefs and practices of the time. Second, the text may tell us not just about Egyptians, but about humanity in general. Other people in different lands and eras have had similar hopes and fears about death and have wondered about the influence of gods and morality. A faith in the magical power of words, especially if pronounced at the right time and the right place, is something that we've seen in many of the world's sacred texts. Third, reading the Book of the Dead gives us a chance to reflect on our own religiosity, such as it is: Are my prayers ever attempts to get God to do my bidding? Do I think that I can somehow escape the consequences of my mistakes by saying the right words at the right time? How much of my good behavior is done for the sake of a pleasant afterlife or the hope of heaven? A fourth reason to read abandoned scriptures is for their value as literature. This doesn't really work for the Book of the Dead, which has no narratives; but it might apply to the Mayan Popol Vuh, which is one of the most mysterious sacred texts to have appeared in the last couple of centuries.

We've all seen images of magnificent ruins in Mesoamerica that were constructed by the Maya people in the Classic Period, from 250–900 C.E. For unknown reasons, the civilization went into serious decline in the 9th century: Cities were abandoned, political structures collapsed, and the writing system was neglected, although there were still Mayans around when the Spanish arrived in the 16th century. There were ancient books, which we now call codices, which were made of bark paper and folded accordion-style, and then they were written on both sides in Mayan hieroglyphs with detailed illustrations. So the physical format is going to be different; they're not scrolls, they're codices, but they looked a little bit like the scrolls of the ancient Egyptian Book of the Dead in the way that they combined text hieroglyphs with pictures, with illustrations. Alas, zealous Catholic priests burned as many of those as they could find and only three Mayan codices have survived, which means than we know much less about ancient Mesoamerican civilization than that of ancient Egypt. The three codices today are in Madrid, Dresden, and Paris, and they're primarily records of astronomical data.

But there was once another codex, now lost, which contained sacred stories of the Maya. Sometime between 1554 and 1558, an unnamed Indian rewrote that text—either as he heard it recited, or as he heard someone else read it, or he might've read it himself—and he translated, he rewrote that text, into Quiché, a late form of the Mayan language, which he transcribed into the Roman alphabet. This was a sacred text written after the virtual disappearance of the belief system, so these Mayan myths were sort of on their way out; they were hard to recover. The situation is a little bit like the Jewish Mishnah that was written after the destruction of the Temple in Jerusalem, even though it has lots of details about how temple worship should take place.

One hundred fifty years after this text was written in Quiché by an unknown Indian, a Dominican friar, Father Francisco Ximénez, found that Quiché text, which he copied and translated into Spanish; so this would be about 1701–1703. Ximénez's manuscript was discovered in 1854 by two different European scholars (actually independently) visiting Guatemala City. Upon their return home, one of them published Ximénez's translation, and the other published the Quiché version (remember in the Roman alphabet) along with a French translation. It appears that the French scholar also took the manuscript, too, which eventually made its way from Paris to the Newberry Library in Chicago in 1912, where it was rediscovered once again in 1928 and then finally published in English in 1950.

The Popol Vuh (and the name means the "Council Book") is a fascinating text that recounts the origins of the world, the creation of animals and humans (it actually takes four attempts to get things right until the humans as we know them today are in the world); it also retells the adventures of two sets of twins, the discovery of corn and fire, and a history of the Quiché branch of the Maya. It also includes guidelines for religious ritual and divination. The episodes aren't related in strictly chronological order, and there's a great deal of doubling of characters, events, and phrasing. The most famous stories are those of the hero-twins Hunahpu and Xbalanque. These are deities; humans beings haven't been created according to this text. Their father and uncle—so their names are One Hunahpu and Seven Hunahpu, and they're also twins—were celebrated players of the Mesoamerican ballgame in which a hard rubber ball had to be put through a high vertical ring attached to the walls on either side of the ball court, but without using one's hands; so you use your elbow or your hips, or you kick it, it's sort of a combination of soccer and basketball.

These two twins played so noisily that the gods of the underworld were upset, and they summoned the brothers to the Dark House in the underworld, where they were tricked and then sacrificed. One Hunahpu's severed head was put in a fork in a tree, which then bore fruit. One of the daughters of the lords of the underworld came to pick that fruit, and when she did so the skull of One Hunahpu spit into her hand and she became pregnant with the hero-twins. The girl's father, who's unhappy about this pregnancy, orders his warriors to sacrifice her and bring back her heart; however, they let her go and returned with a fake heart. She then flees to live with One Hunahpu's family—so this is the family of these twins that she's pregnant with—and at length she gives birth to Hunahpu and Xbalanque.

The twins are clever tricksters who turn their menacing half-brothers into monkeys and defeat the arrogant Seven Macaw. Seven Macaw was a bird who when shot by a blowgun then tore off Hunahpu's arm; and they managed to get their revenge on this bird and actually get back the arm as well by posing as itinerant dentists and pulling out all of his teeth and then replacing them with corn. As far as I know, this may be the only sacred text in the world in which dentists figure as heroic protagonists.

The twins learn from a rat that their father's ballgame equipment is hidden under the eaves of the roof. With the help of this rat, they retrieve the gear and then they start playing this ballgame. The lords of the underworld invite them for a match and they go, despite their grandmother's foreboding. The twins are required to pass through a series of deadly tests in six houses: the Dark House (that was the one that did in their father and uncle), the Razor House, the Cold House, the Jaguar House, the Fire House, and the Bat House; and there are all kinds of deadly contraptions and devices that are in these houses. The twins manage survive through cleverness—for example, they send a mosquito to learn the names of the gods; when the gods are bitten by the mosquito they slap at it and call each other by name, and that's where the mosquito overhears this and reports this to them; remember, names matter, they give power over beings, in ancient Egypt and apparently they did in Mesoamerica as well—so they get through these houses, but when Hunahpu pokes his head out of the Bat House, he's decapitated. Xbalanque, however, manages to retrieve the head by swapping the head for a ball in the next round of the ballgame, and then he revives his brother Hunahpu. Sometime later, the twins get their revenge by going in disguise among the gods of the underworld and performing a trick in which one brother sacrificed the other and then brought him back to life. The gods are delighted by this and they insisted that it be done to them; but after the two rulers of the underworld, One Death and Seven Death, are sacrificed, the twins refuse to bring them back and the lords of the underworld admit defeat. The hero-twins then ascend into the sky where they become the sun and the moon

The Popol Vuh continues with a lengthy account of the creation of humans and the history of the Quiché Maya; and then it concludes: "This is enough about the being of Quiché, given that there is no longer a place to see it. There is the original book and ancient writing owned by the lords, now lost, but even so, everything has been completed here concerning Quiché, which is now named Santa Cruz."

Again, what are we to make of all this? Was the Popol Vuh ever an authoritative text? Did believers pattern their lives by its precepts, or did they use it in religious rituals and ceremonies? We don't know, aside from the fact that illustrations from some of those stories that I've told you appear as decorations on ceramics or other art objects. As I said before, we know much less about ancient Mesoamerica than ancient Egypt and the Book of the Dead. Nevertheless, the Popol Vuh has value as a historical record. Clearly, these strange narratives are connected to the world of the Yucatan Peninsula, since they mention calabash trees, chili peppers, monkeys, macaws, and jaguars, as well as customs like the ballgame and human sacrifice.

Yet there may be more here than meets the eye. Some scholars have suggested that there's astronomical information encoded in the progress of the hero-twins through the testing houses in the underworld and in other episodes; that is to say, "the characters' movements and fates set the pattern for the rising and setting of Mars, Venus, and other heavenly bodies." But who's to say? There are no religious authorities today who can definitively pronounce, "Oh yeah, you have that right" or "That's nonsense; that's not what we meant at all." By the way, Dennis Tedlock, in preparing his translation of the Popol Vuh, consulted with a modern Quiché diviner or "daykeeper." This man had never heard of the Popol Vuh before—it truly was an abandoned scripture or lost scripture—yet he recognized within it certain ritual practices that he carried on himself.

As with the Book of the Dead, the Popol Vuh may contain some wise insights or universal truths, and it certainly offers a chance to reflect upon the religious assumptions of our own culture. But the Mesoamerican text has stories as well, which can be analyzed in terms of plot, character, and theme, and that may have interesting things to say about human relationships, families, about life and death, or the connection between the human and the natural worlds. It's literature; and for that reason, it's probably more fun to read than the spells of the Book of the Dead.

It seems to me that sacred texts, even abandoned ones, deserve an extra measure of respect, simply because so many people held them in high esteem for so long. They've often been primary elements in how individuals view themselves and the world; yet they're sometimes so strange and puzzling, a fact that lends itself to one last reason to read them today: that is, as a reminder of the incredible variety of human religious experience and, particularly in the case of abandoned scriptures like the Book of the Dead and the Popol Vuh, a warning about how much we still don't know, and the difficulties of interpreting documents that have fallen out of a continuing tradition.

Secular Scripture—U.S. Constitution
Lecture 35

In the last two lectures, we've speculated about which new religious writings are most likely to become part of the library of world scriptures in the future, and we've discussed sacred texts that are no longer supported by a faith community. In this lecture, we'll continue to test our assumptions about sacred texts by turning the topic on its head: If it is really true that sacred texts are defined less by their specific contents than by the role they play in the lives of believers, is it possible to have writings that are basically secular in nature yet are treated as if they were scripture? Our test case will be the Constitution of the United States.

Informative Uses of Sacred Texts

- For a volume titled *Rethinking Scripture*, Miriam Levering used her fieldwork with Chinese Buddhist nuns to categorize different ways that scripture is received and used by believers, and she did so with an eye to comparative studies that might take into account different notions of the origins or contents of sacred texts. Levering outlined four "modes of reception": informative, transactive, transformative, and symbolic.

- In the informative mode, it's the ideas within the text that matter most. You will recall that the Mahayana canon is very large, and it is possible to devote one's entire life to mastering just a portion of its contents. Some Buddhist nuns feel called to this work.

- In contrast, the Constitution is not long, yet thousands of people have also spent their lives analyzing, debating, and writing about every phrase it contains. Such efforts are justified because the words matter; they can spell the difference between retaining or losing property, exercising or being denied political rights, and more. The Constitution is a binding document that regulates not only the government but also the day-to-day lives of American citizens.

- There is obviously much more law than just the Constitution, but the Constitution holds a fundamental, paramount position. Other significant legal and historical sources may have second- or third-tier status. For example, we might consider the 85 Federalist papers as something akin to the Muslim Hadith—not exactly scripture in the same way as the Qur'an but still a respected, authoritative source for its interpretation.

- Unlike most diverse religious traditions, there is a final authority to determine the meaning of the Constitution: the Supreme Court. Since 1790, the court has issued more than 30,000 opinions, and these, in turn, have been studied, cited, and argued about as binding documents. In another parallel with sacred texts discussed earlier in this course, the Supreme Court, like the Jewish Talmud, records and preserves its dissenting opinions.

Transactive Uses of Sacred Texts

- The second of the four modes sketched out by Levering is the transactive, which uses a text to make something happen. Levering describes how Buddhist nuns use the sutras in rituals intended for specific purposes, such as "to create merit" or "to offer devotion and praise." With regard to the Constitution, legal professionals depend on it to make law, of course, but it is also used by the rest of us, particularly in ritual or ceremonial situations.

- The Declaration of Independence is more likely to be recited than the Constitution, particularly on the Fourth of July, a holiday created to honor its signing. On that day, students, politicians, and ordinary citizens often read the Declaration aloud at ceremonies or other gatherings. Our dispute with Britain has long since been resolved, but is it true that the words of the Declaration no longer matter?
  - One sentence from the second paragraph may be the most important statement in American political culture: "We hold these truths to be self-evident, that all men are created equal, that they are endowed by their Creator with certain unalienable rights, that among these are life, liberty and the pursuit of happiness."

- From one perspective, the notion that all men are created equal is manifestly false, yet there is also a sense that these lines represent our highest values and aspirations: Everyone should be equal in dignity and worth and equal before the law. Intoning these words aloud, in public, has the effect of reinforcing our commitment to making our nation such a place.

- The Constitution is also used in ceremonial contexts. Every year, about half a million people from around the world fulfill the qualifications to become U.S. citizens. As part of the naturalization ceremony, they take an oath that they will "support and defend the Constitution," similar to oaths taken by the president on inauguration day and members of the armed forces when they enlist.

- Many people can recite the preamble to the Constitution; they may know the wording of the First or Second Amendments by heart; and September 17—the day the Constitution was signed in 1787—is a national holiday. The Constitution is something that keeps Americans together and binds us to our past, even if we are not intimately familiar with all of its articles and sections.

Constitution Day, September 17, is commemorated by public schools with speeches, trivia contests, and other activities focused on the U.S. Constitution.

Transformative and Symbolic Uses of Sacred Texts

- Sometimes scriptures are used not to influence one's relationships with others or to change the world but to transform oneself. Levering reports, "As Chinese Buddhists read, listen to, study and comment on sutras in order to become informed by their account of reality, they also seek ... to be transformed in their personal capacity to experience wisdom and compassion." Are there times when people look to the founding documents of America as a source of private insight or inspiration or see them as manifestations of larger truths?

- One of the most religious-like facts about the Constitution and the Declaration of Independence is that we treat them as if they were icons or holy relics. Visitors can go to the National Archives in Washington, DC, and see original copies in a large bronze display case under bulletproof glass—similar to a shrine.

- Many famous lines from significant American documents and speeches are carved into monuments and buildings on the National Mall in Washington, including quotations from the Declaration of Independence on the Jefferson Memorial.
    - Those who commissioned the monuments probably had transactive functions in mind, but those of us who walk through to read and reflect may find the experience transformative.

    - Transactive, transformative, and symbolic aspects are combined when we display copies of the Declaration of Independence or the Constitution on our walls.

Additional Religious Parallels
- We can point to additional parallels between the founding documents of America and the sacred texts of the world. For example, like the letters of Saint Paul, the Declaration and the Constitution were not written with the idea that they would someday be canonized, yet over time, their stature has grown.
    - In 1816, Jefferson complained, "Some men look at constitutions with sanctimonious reverence and deem them like the ark of the covenant, too sacred to be touched." He well knew the arguments, horse-trading, and compromises that went into the creation of the Constitution. Jefferson went on to suggest that constitutions ought to change with the times.

    - However, as early as 1796, George Washington included in his Farewell Address a plea that "the Constitution ... be sacredly maintained." Although the human origins of the Constitution are well documented, it is the latter impulse that has generally prevailed.

- Like the sacred texts of Confucianism, which were always regarded as the products of human effort, though done by sages, there has long been a temptation in the United States to regard the Founders as men blessed with preternatural wisdom and moral courage. A close look at their biographies and the transcripts of their deliberations quickly dispels assumptions of their near-divinity. Respect is due the oldest written national constitution still in force in the world, along with the men who crafted it, but it didn't arrive immaculately from heaven.

- Another aspect of the Constitution that seems at least quasi-religious is that there are different schools of interpretation, just as there are for the Vedas, the Bible, and the Qur'an. For the Constitution, these interpretive modes include textualism, which analyzes the exact meaning of the words; originalism, which looks to the intentions of those who drafted and ratified its provisions; and living constitutionalism, which prefers to read the document as having a dynamic meaning that can and should change to accommodate social and technological innovations.

- Sanford Levinson has written a fascinating book, *Constitutional Faith*, in which he identifies what he calls Protestant and Catholic strains in constitutional interpretation. This distinction may remind us of arguments over Protestant bias that we noted earlier. Some legal scholars and judges are more interested in origins than in developments, in the critical-historical analysis of the text rather than in later traditions, or in the legitimacy of individual as opposed to institutional determinations of meaning.

- Perhaps one reason that America has a text-based government is that it was largely settled by Protestants. Just as it seemed natural to them to look to a single volume of holy writ as the basis for religion, so also a government might have as its foundation a revered, authoritative political document. Further, America has always been something of an experiment—a nation created by a set of documents rather than a shared ethnicity, religion, or longstanding ties to the land. It's not surprising that we regard our secular writings with almost religious-like devotion.

- Scholars have long debated the idea of "civil religion," but some have now begun to talk about "constitutional idolatry," wondering if we have gone too far in our deference to an 18th-century document that is in some ways undemocratic, giving disproportionate political power to small states, rural districts, and the wealthy, and that sets up a divided form of government that has generally failed elsewhere in the world. "Idolatry" is a strong word, but it's hard to imagine other political documents around the world being treated in the same way that Americans revere the Declaration and the Constitution.

- The Constitution, unlike most sacred texts, does not regard itself as having final authority but includes provisions for updating and amendments.
    - Consequently, we end up with a document that resembles the Qur'an, in which some verses are thought to have been abrogated by later revelations, or the Bible, in which the New Testament explicitly rejects the requirements of the Law of Moses. Thus, the Constitution is not a closed canon.

    - Indeed, it's worth thinking about an even larger secular canon that might include Lincoln's Gettysburg Address, Patrick Henry's "Give me liberty or give me death" speech, the Seneca Falls "Declaration of Sentiments," and others.

- A final piece of evidence about the equivalence of secular and religious sacred texts can be found in Martin Luther King's "I have a dream" speech. One of the characteristics of sacred texts is that they often draw on earlier scriptures, and it is telling that King quotes from the Bible and the Declaration of Independence in much the same way: He treats both as unfulfilled promises of better days to come.

Suggested Reading

Kammen, ed., *The Origins of the American Constitution.*

Levering, "Scripture and Its Reception."

Levinson, *Constitutional Faith.*

Meier, *American Scripture.*

Rakov, ed., *The Annotated U.S. Constitution and Declaration of Independence.*

Ravitch, and Thernstrom, eds., *The Democracy Reader.*

Questions to Consider

1. If texts are made sacred in relationship to a community, is it possible for basically secular texts to have scripture-like functions within a nation? Is there such a thing as "civic religion"?

2. What American political texts are most likely to be memorized, recited on holidays, or even carved in stone?

Secular Scripture—U.S. Constitution
Lecture 35—Transcript

In the last couple of lectures, we've started to wrap up our survey of sacred texts by looking more closely at the margins; at those difficult cases that can help us better define the topic. We've speculated about which new religious writings are most likely to become part of the library of world scriptures in the future, and we've discussed a couple of sacred texts that are no longer supported by a faith community. In this lecture, we'll continue to test our assumptions and findings by turning the topic on its head. If it's really true that sacred texts are defined less by their specific contents than by the role that they play in the lives of believers, is it possible to have writings that are basically secular in nature, and yet are treated as if they were scripture? As you can tell from the title of this lecture, I've got a test case in mind: the Constitution of the United States, written in 1787.

It's certainly true that some works of literature have inspired passionate followers. There are people who devotedly read and reread the works of Jane Austen, or Harry Potter novels, or Sherlock Holmes stories. They may organize themselves into clubs, attend conventions, purchase all sorts of paraphernalia, or even dress up like favorite characters on occasion; but the respect and even reverence that many Americans have for the Constitution goes far beyond fandom. For citizens of the United States, the Constitution is very literally binding and authoritative in their lives; in many ways, it defines who we are as a nation. Although God isn't mentioned once within its pages, much less the afterlife or revelation, it nevertheless invokes a religious-like fervor among many Americans, with shrines, holidays, pilgrimages, icons, etc. But to investigate this phenomenon in a systematic, comprehensive way, let's begin with an important article about the uses of scripture in a Buddhist convent in Taiwan. In our discussion, we can expand our focus to include that close companion of the Constitution, the Declaration of Independence, and we'll also have opportunities to review some of what we've learned in this course so far.

By the way, I'm going to regard the Declaration as a secular, political document since it's basically an enumeration of the reasons that the American colonists gave for their rejection of British sovereignty, though I admit that

that text mentions God in four places. You can probably recite at least a couple of them, which is significant in and of itself. In the first paragraph, the Declaration of Independence alludes to "the laws of Nature and of Nature's God," and it subsequently asserts that men are "endowed by their Creator with certain unalienable rights." Then, in its concluding paragraph, the signers appeal to "the Supreme Judge of the world" and confess their "firm reliance on the protection of Divine Providence." But truth be told, these are rather vague, generic expressions of religiosity. There's no mention, for instance, of Jesus Christ, or Moses, or the Bible; nothing about revelation, or heaven and hell.

But back to the article on Buddhist scripture: For a volume titled *Rethinking Scripture*, Miriam Levering used her field work with Chinese Buddhist nuns in Taiwan to categorize different ways that scripture is received and employed by believers, and she did so with an eye to comparative studies that might take into account very different notions of the origins or contents of sacred texts. She outlined four "modes of reception," as she calls them: informative, transactive, transformative, and symbolic. I know that those may sound a bit abstract, and there will be some overlap among those four categories, but these sorts of scholarly distinctions are nevertheless useful tools for getting us to think harder and more perceptively about sacred texts.

In the informative mode, it's the ideas within the text that matter most. You'll recall that the Mahayana canon is very large, and it's possible to devote one's entire life to mastering just a portion of its contents; so some of the Buddhist nuns feel called to this work of understanding these texts—someone has to know these documents, these scriptures, well enough to pass them on to the next generation—so they devote their time to the private, solitary study of the sutras, and then they also deliver and listen to dharma talks that explicate their meaning. In this mode, it's the meaning that matters.

Turning to the Constitution, the Constitution isn't long at all; you can read it pretty carefully, including the amendments, in an hour or so. Yet thousands and thousands of people have spent their lives analyzing, debating, and writing about every phrase. Think about all those politicians, law professors, historians, judges, and lawyers. Think about the tens of thousands of books and learned articles. Such efforts are justified because the words matter;

they can spell the difference between retaining or losing property, between exercising or being denied political rights, between liberty or incarceration, war and peace, even life and death. The Constitution is a binding document that regulates not only the government, but also the day-to-day lives of American citizens.

There's obviously a lot more law than just the Constitution, but the Constitution holds a fundamental, paramount position. Yet other significant legal and historical sources may have second- or third-tier status. So perhaps in our thought experiment about secular scripture, we might consider the 85 Federalist papers that were written in 1787 and 1788 as something like the Muslim Hadith; not exactly scripture in the same way as the Qur'an, but nevertheless a respected, authoritative source for its interpretation. So the Federalist papers: not exactly scripture like the Constitution, but nevertheless an authoritative source. Unlike most diverse religious traditions, there's a final authority to determine the meaning of the Constitution: It's whatever the Supreme Court says it is. Since 1790, the Court has issued over 30,000 opinions, and those in turn have been studied, cited, and argued about as binding documents.

In one more parallel with sacred texts that we've discussed earlier in this course, the Supreme Court, like the Jewish Talmud, records and preserves dissenting opinions. Jewish law was established by majority opinion, but the interpretations of dissenting rabbis might be used in later arguments or even provide a basis for reevaluating judgments at a later time, much as Justice Harlan's famous dissent in *Plessy v. Ferguson* in 1896 paved the way for later, more colorblind interpretations of the Constitution that rejected the notion of "separate but equal."

Continuing our discussion of the informative mode, the exact words of the Declaration of Independence probably matter less than those of the Constitution. The objections to British imperial overreach in the mid-18th century seem rather remote from our current concerns, and I doubt that there are many Americans who could come up with more than 2 or 3 of the 27 grievances enumerated by the Continental Congress in 1776. For instance, "He [this is the British king] has called together legislative bodies at places unusual, uncomfortable, and distant from the depository of their public records." It's hard to get too excited about that in the 21st century. The continuing appeal of the Declaration isn't so much in the meaning of the words as in other modes of reception that we're going to talk about next.

The second of the four modes sketched out by Levering is the transactive mode, which uses a text to make something happen; other scholars use the term *performative*. Levering describes how Buddhist nuns employ the sutras in rituals intended to, as she says, "obtain protection or powers; to create merit, to bring benefits to others; to enact confession or repentance; to make vows; to offer devotion and praise; and to express and bring into effect relationships between members of the community living and dead." Usually, these results come from chanting or reciting the sutras. With regard to the Constitution, legal professionals depend on it to make law—that's an important result, of course—but think about when it's used by the rest of us, particularly in ritual or ceremonial situations.

Actually, it's the Declaration of Independence that's more likely to be recited than the Constitution, particularly on the Fourth of July, a holiday created to honor its signing. On that day, students, politicians, and ordinary citizens often read the Declaration aloud in its entirety in ceremonies, gatherings, and on the radio; for instance, the staff at National Public Radio's *Morning Edition* have been reading the Declaration on air every July 4th for more than 20 years. Why exactly do we do this? Why do we recite this or read this text aloud? Is it to commemorate our founders and our national heritage? To demonstrate our loyalty to the country and to its traditions? To gain merit of some sort? Note that the words don't really matter that much, given the fact that our dispute with Britain has long ago been resolved.

But perhaps that's not exactly right. There's one sentence from the second paragraph of the Declaration that may be the most important statement in American political culture: "We hold these truths to be self-evident, that all men are created equal, that they are endowed by their Creator with certain unalienable rights, that among these are life, liberty and the pursuit of happiness." From one perspective, the notion that all men are created equal is manifestly false. Men and women come into this world with astonishing disparities in talents, capabilities, intelligence, and all sorts of socioeconomic advantages and disadvantages. Even in 1776, plenty of people understood that the institution of slavery made a mockery of that assertion. Yet there's also a sense that those famous lines represent our highest values and aspirations: Everyone should be equal in dignity and worth, and equal before the law; and intoning these words aloud, in public, has the effect of reinforcing our commitment to making our nation such a place.

The Constitution is also used in ceremonial contexts. Like a religion, Americanism is something that you can convert to. Every year, about half a million people from around the world fulfill the qualifications to become U.S. citizens, and those qualifications include a brief test that may include questions about the Constitution and the Declaration. As part of the naturalization ceremony, they take an oath that they'll "support and defend the Constitution," similar to oaths taken by the President at his or her inauguration, and members of the Armed Forces upon their enlistment. Many people can and occasionally do recite the preamble to the Constitution; perhaps you can say this with me:

> We the People of the United States, in Order to form a more perfect Union, establish Justice, insure domestic Tranquility, provide for the common defence, promote the general Welfare, and secure the Blessings of Liberty to ourselves and our Posterity, do ordain and establish this Constitution for the United States of America.

Or people may know and be able to recite the first or the second amendments by heart. As of 2004, September 17—the day the Constitution was signed in 1787—has become a national holiday. Federal workers don't get the day off, but every school that receives federal funds is required to commemorate that day in some fashion. I suppose that at least part of the transactive function of school-sponsored speeches, lessons, activities, poster making, and Constitution trivia contests that occur on September 17 on Constitution Day is to get federal dollars. The Constitution is something that keeps Americans together and binds us to our past, even if we're not intimately familiar with all of its articles and sections.

Levering's third and fourth modes of scriptural reception are the transformative and the symbolic. Sometimes scriptures are used not to influence one's relationship with others or to change the world, but rather to transform one's self. Levering reports that "as Chinese Buddhists read, listen to, study and comment on sutras in order to become informed by their account of reality, they also seek at the same time to be transformed in their personal capacity to experience wisdom and compassion."

One of the most religious-like facts about the Constitution and the Declaration of Independence is that we treat them as if they were icons or holy relics. You can go to the National Archives in Washington, D.C., and there in the rotunda you can see original copies, along with the Bill of Rights, in a large bronze display case under bulletproof glass. Since 1952, they've been encased in airtight containers filled with inert helium to preserve them, and every night, as I understand it, they're mechanically lowered into a vault of reinforced concrete and steel with heavy doors that come over in order to preserve them in case of some sort of attack or destruction. Under the watchful eye of guards, you can get in line in the rotunda there and you can file past these sacred texts; and that really does seem like the right sort of term in that setting. File past to pay your respects; it's very much like a shrine.

By the way, there isn't really an original copy of the Bill of Rights. What they have on display in the National Archives is a 1789 document that was sent to the states for ratification. On that document, if you look closely, it has the 12 amendments that were proposed by Congress, not just the 10 that actually became law in 1791 and are now known as the Bill of Rights. If you go to the National Archives' website and you look at what they have there, they have a transcription of what they have under glass, but they fudge the discrepancy; you'll only see the 10 Bill of Rights, not those extra 2 proposed amendments that are on the document that's under glass. But remember, in this case it's not the exact words that matter so much as the symbolism. By the way, the two unratified amendments concern the apportionment of representatives and the forbidding of any particular congress from voting to change its own salary; that last amendment was finally adopted in 1992 as the 27th Amendment.

I confess that I've made this pilgrimage to the National Archives myself. I wasn't trying to impress anyone or make a point; it was simply an opportunity for me to reflect on my own relationship to these documents and the principles I feel they stand for: freedom, equality, the rule of law. It was a personal, transformative experience. Well, I had my children in tow at the time, so I suppose that I was also trying to pass a little of this on to them as well, which is also quite religion-like.

Think of what it means to go to the Jefferson Memorial and read these words inscribed: "We hold these truths to be self-evident"; they're carved in stone, along with the concluding lines:

> We ... solemnly publish and declare, That these United Colonies are and of Right ought to be Free and Independent States. ... And for the support of this Declaration, with a firm reliance on the protection of divine Providence, we mutually pledge to each other our Lives, our Fortunes and our sacred Honor.

You can go see those lines, those words, carved into the Jefferson Memorial; though it's a little ironic that those are there because Jefferson didn't write most of them. They were added to his original draft by other members of the Continental Congress. But, then again, sacred texts, in all of their revised and edited glory, often belong more to the community than to the original authors. Indeed, think about going down to the National Mall and all of the famous lines from significant American documents and speeches that are carved into granite or marble there in Washington, D.C. Why do we do that? Why do we inscribe some lines into stone and others not? Surely those who commissioned those monuments had transactive functions in mind—they wanted to make something happen; they wanted to send a message—but for those of us who walk through, to read and to reflect, we may find it more of a transformative experience, something that matters to us personally. Transactive, transformative, and symbolic aspects are all thrown together when we display copies of the Declaration of Independence or the Constitution in maybe framed copies on our walls, perhaps copies that we bought at gift shops at the National Mall or at Williamsburg; or when we carry around pocket-size copies of the Constitution, which are often handed out in bulk on Constitution Day.

There are still more parallels between the founding documents of America and the sacred texts of the world. Like the letters of Saint Paul, the

Declaration and the Constitution weren't written with the idea that they'd someday be canonized; yet over time, their stature has grown. In 1816, Jefferson complained that:

> Some men look at constitutions with sanctimonious reverence and deem them like the ark of the covenant, too sacred to be touched. They ascribe to the men of the preceding age a wisdom more than human, and suppose what they did to be beyond amendment.

Jefferson well knew the arguments, the horse-trading, and the compromises that went into the creation of that document (the Constitution), including the embarrassing determination that some inhabitants of the new nation would count for three-fifths of a person. Jefferson went on to suggest that constitutions ought to change with the times. On the other hand, as early as 1796, George Washington included in his Farewell Address a plea that "the Constitution...be sacredly maintained." Although the human origins of the Constitution are well-documented, it's the latter impulse that's generally prevailed; the impulse to treat it as something sacred. In 1987, on the 200th anniversary of the Constitution, former Chief Justice Warren Burger said, "Teach the [Constitution's] principles, teach them to your children, speak of them when sitting in your home, speak of them when walking by the way, when lying down and when rising up, write them upon the doorplate of your home and upon your gates" in a very explicit allusion to how Jews were instructed in Deuteronomy 6:7-9 to treat the Torah.

Like the sacred texts of Confucianism, which were always regarded as the products of human effort, though done by sages, there's long been a temptation in the U.S. to regard the founders of our nation as sages; that is, as men blessed with preternatural wisdom and moral courage. A close look at their biographies and the transcripts of their deliberations quickly dispels assumptions of their near divinity, although one popular history of the Constitutional Convention was titled *Miracle at Philadelphia*. Respect is certainly due for the world's oldest written national constitution still in force, along with the men who crafted it, but it didn't arrive immaculately from heaven.

Another aspect of the Constitution that seems at least quasi-religious is that there are different schools of interpretation, just as there are for the Vedas, or the Bible, or the Qur'an. For the Constitution, these interpretive modes include Textualism, which analyzes the exact meaning of the words; Originalism, which looks to the intentions of those who drafted and ratified its provisions; and Living Constitutionalism, which prefers to read the document as having a dynamic meaning, which can and should change to accommodate social and technological innovations.

The scholar Sanford Levinson has written a fascinating book titled *Constitutional Faith* in which he identifies what he calls Protestant and Catholic strains in constitutional interpretation. This distinction may remind us of arguments over "Protestant bias," which I noted in earlier lectures. Some legal scholars and judges are more interested in origins rather than in developments; in critical-historical analysis of the text rather than in later traditions; or in the legitimacy of individual as opposed to institutional determinations of meanings. You can hear those Protestant biases; sometimes they're on one side. Perhaps one reason that America has a text-based government is that it was largely settled by Protestants. Just as it seemed natural to them to look to a single volume of holy writ as the basis for religion, so also a government might have as its foundation a revered, written, authoritative political document. Of course, Jews and Catholics also came to accept this notion of a text-based government; and as I'm delivering this lecture, the U.S. Supreme Court today currently has no Protestant judges sitting on the bench, they're all either Jewish or Roman Catholic.

America has always been something of an experiment, a nation created by a set of documents rather than a shared ethnicity, or a shared religion, or longstanding ties to the land; we are, as it were, a people of the booklet (these aren't long documents). It's not surprising that we regard those secular writings with almost religious-like devotion. Scholars have long debated the idea of "civil religion," but some have now begun to talk about "Constitutional Idolatry," wondering if we've gone too far in our deference to an 18th-century document that's in some ways undemocratic, giving disproportionate political power to small states, to rural districts, and the wealthy, and that set up a divided form of government that's working for more than 200 years here in the United States, but has generally failed elsewhere in the world where it's been implemented and tried. Perhaps *idolatry* is too a strong word. That word might better fit if we're talking about the way that Chairman Mao's *Little Red Book* was utilized during the Chinese Cultural Revolution; that surely might count as a secular scripture, or it's treated as scripture. But at the same time, it's hard to imagine other important political documents around the world being treated in the same way that Americans revere the Declaration and the Construction, even roughly comparable writings like the French "Rights of Man" or the United Nation's "Universal Declaration of Human Rights."

So far, I've been arguing that the Constitution is like a sacred text; but for at least one faith community, it's considered to have come from God, even if through human intermediaries. The Mormons, America's quintessential homegrown religion, have a passage in their Doctrine and Covenants in which God extolls the importance of moral agency and individual responsibility, and then concludes: "[F]or this purpose have I established the Constitution of this land, by the hands of wise men whom I raised up unto this very purpose…"

Yet the Constitution, unlike most sacred texts, doesn't regard itself as having final authority. It includes provisions for updating and amendments, assuming that future generations may have to undo or add to some of its stipulations, even if the process was deliberately designed to be difficult. Consequently, we end up with a document that resembles the Qur'an, where some verses are thought to have been abrogated by later revelations if you remember that discussion; or the Bible, in which the New Testament explicitly rejects the requirements of the Law of Moses, even though Christians still carry Leviticus and Deuteronomy with them to church every week. To our credit, we didn't just erase those portions of the Constitution that were invalidated by the 13th amendment on slavery, or the 15th and 19th amendments on voting rights of racial minorities and women. We've kept the original wording as a testament to how far we've come as a nation; and I suppose that the 18th and the 21st amendments, which establish and then repeal Prohibition, are a constant reminder not to revise our national charter too hastily.

So the Constitution isn't a closed canon; it wasn't designed to be a closed canon. There may be future changes and amendments to come. Indeed, it's worth thinking about an even larger secular canon. Besides the Declaration of Independence and the Constitution, what other documents in American history and politics might attain a similar, elevated status over time? What else gets carved into stone, or memorized, or recited at public events? Surely Lincoln's Gettysburg Address; but there are probably others. What about Patrick Henry's "Give me liberty or give me death" speech of 1775; or the Seneca Falls "Declaration of Sentiments" in 1848; Lincoln's Second Inaugural Address of 1865; FDR's the "Four Freedoms" speech in 1941; and Martin Luther's "Letter from Birmingham Jail" in 1963? It would be interesting exercise to come up with a canon of secular American scripture, but I'll leave that up to you; it's actually a fun game to play.

Let me conclude with one more piece of evidence about the equivalence, at least in some situations, of secular and religious sacred texts. After the Declaration, the Constitution, and probably the Gettysburg Address, I'd guess that the next most prominent, celebrated text in U.S. history is Martin Luther King's "I Have a Dream" speech, delivered in front of the Lincoln Memorial on August 28, 1963, as part of the March on Washington. One of the characteristics of sacred texts is that they often draw upon earlier scriptures; and it's telling that King quotes from the Bible and the Declaration of Independence in much the same way: He treats both of those as unfulfilled promises of better days to come. He cites, for example, Amos 5:24 when he says: "No, we are not satisfied and we will not be satisfied until justice rolls down like waters and righteousness like a mighty stream." Then later in his talk he says, "I have a dream that one day this nation will rise up and live out the true meaning of its creed: 'We hold these truths to be self-evident, that all men are created equal.'" Powerful words that were symbolic, transactive, and deeply transformative.

Heavenly Books, Earthly Connections
Lecture 36

As we come to the end of this course, it might be useful to spend some time answering two questions: Where do we go from here, and what difference might the comparative study of scripture make in our lives? The first half of this lecture answers the first question by offering recommended readings for each of the major religious traditions we've studied. The second part of the lecture attempts to answer the second question by returning to the reasons we listed in Lecture 1 for studying other people's scriptures. In particular, we'll discuss how reading world scripture can help us better understand the lives of others and perhaps even provide greater insight into our own intellectual and spiritual commitments.

Readings from Early Religions

- If you read only one text from Hinduism, it should be the Bhagavad Gita. You might also try the Isha and Katha Upanishads, which provide a good introduction to Vedic literature.

- For Judaism, you might try something from each of the three sections of the Tanakh. From the Torah, you might sample Genesis, which includes some of the most famous stories in the Hebrew Bible. From the Prophets, read 2 Isaiah (chapters 40–55), which most scholars date to the 6th century B.C.E., during the Babylonian Exile. From the Writings, try the brief book of Ruth, a simple yet moving tale of ordinary people and extraordinary kindness.
    - For those from a Christian background, it's worth looking at the Jewish Publication Society translation of the Tanakh to see how Jews read their own sacred texts. As you recall, the entire Tanakh is regarded as holy, but the Torah is especially sacred and is read aloud in synagogues over the course of a year.

    - Conservative Jews believe that the Torah was revealed by God to Moses, and some assert that it predated the world and was used as a blueprint for creation. Other Jews accept the results of the historical-critical method and view the Torah, like the Prophets and the Writings, as the product of many sources edited and revised over centuries.

- o Jewish tradition claims that Moses received not only the written Torah at Mount Sinai but also the oral Torah, which was eventually written down in the 3rd century C.E. as the Mishnah, then later expanded into the two Talmuds. If you're interested in exploring this literature, a good place to start is the tractate Aboth ("The Fathers") in the fourth division of the Mishnah. The Aboth is a brief collection of wise sayings and moral maxims from famous rabbis.

- One of the most beloved texts from the Theravada tradition of Buddhism is the Dhammapada, which sets forth the basic principles of Buddhist doctrine and morality. The canon of Mahayana Buddhism is vast, but one book considered by many to be the fullest expression of the Buddha's teachings is the Lotus Sutra. Read the first four chapters, which include the parables of the burning house and the prodigal son. From Zen Buddhism, read the *Mumonkan* ("*Gateless Gate*"), which is a 13th-century collection of 48 koans in the form of brief anecdotes about Zen masters and their students.

- For East Asian religion and philosophy, read the *Analects of Confucius* and the Daodejing. The *Analects* are brief, fairly straightforward sayings of Confucius. The Daodejing was originally an anonymous collection of wisdom sayings that was later attributed to Laozi and eventually elevated to the status of a divine text.

Readings from Common Era Religions
- Recommended readings for Christianity include one of the gospels, perhaps Luke; the book of Acts, which offers a history of the early Christian movement; and something from Paul, either Romans or 1 Corinthians. If you're curious about Christian sacred texts outside the Bible, you might start with the Coptic Gospel of Thomas, which offers 114 short sayings attributed to Jesus.

- As we saw, Muslims view their scripture, the Qur'an, as a miraculous transcript of a heavenly book. It is God's primary revelation to humankind, given to Muhammad with the angel Gabriel as a mediator, and most Muslims believe that the Qur'an is co-eternal with God, uncreated. Thus, for Islam, the choice of which sacred text to read is obvious. But the Qur'an, with its 114 suras, is a bit long.
  - Newcomers might want to start with some of the shorter, earlier, more lyrical revelations toward the end of the volume, then read a few of the longer suras that appear at the beginning (2, "The Cow"; 4, "Women"; and 5, "The Table").

  - If you're coming from a Jewish or Christian background, it might also be interesting to read some of the middle suras that are named after biblical characters: 10, "Jonah"; 12, "Joseph"; 19. "Mary"; or 71, "Noah." And some Muslims feel that sura 112 contains the essence of Islam: "Say: He is God the One, God the eternal. He begot no one nor was He begotten. No one is comparable to Him."

  - If you're interested in the Hadith, or traditions about the Prophet, the best place to begin is with Al-Nawawi's 13th-century collection *Forty Hadith*, which has long been the most popular introductory anthology of Hadith.

- The Adi Granth is the paramount scripture of Sikhism. As you recall, it's a collection of poetry by the Sikh gurus and some of their Hindu and Muslim predecessors that was designated by the Tenth Guru as the perpetual Guru of the community. Two recommended readings in this tradition are *The Name of My Beloved: Verses of the Sikh Gurus*, translated by Nikky-Guninder Kaur Singh, and *Songs of the Saints from the Adi Granth*, translated by Nirmal Dass.

- The best avenue into the scriptures of the Latter-day Saints is, of course, the Book of Mormon, which was thought to have been miraculously translated from ancient gold plates that were given to Joseph Smith by the angel Moroni. Two recommendations here are

3 Nephi, which tells the story of the resurrected Jesus appearing to people in the Americas, and 1 Nephi, which gives a good sense of the narrative and characteristic themes of the book.

- Finally, if you're curious about Baha'i, start with The Hidden Words—a collection of mystical sayings by Baha'u'llah. In addition, many have found the book *Some Answered Questions* to be a clear introduction to Baha'i teachings.

- In addition to reading some of the scriptures from this course, go on the Internet and look for examples of sacred texts in use, perhaps Vedic ceremonies, Buddhist sutra chanting, Qur'anic recitations, or the singing of the Adi Granth in a Sikh temple. Even better, try to attend a worship service of a religion that is not your own.

Concluding Our Study

- In our first lecture, we noted several good reasons to read other people's scriptures: they're easily accessible; they're usually central to the faith tradition; they lend themselves to comparative study; they can be sources of wisdom, beauty, and awe; and they help us better understand the lives of others and perhaps even provide greater insight into our own intellectual and spiritual commitments.

- People often argue about religion, and scripture can sometimes be used as a weapon or a wedge, particularly because many sacred texts make strong, mutually exclusive claims about God, reality, and salvation. Yet reading scripture can also be a bridge between people with different ideas about God and reality. A sacred text may or may not contain the truth about unseen forces or other realms of existence, but it most certainly contains truths about millions of believers who have accepted the text as authoritative.

- If you want to understand what's going on in the Middle East or in much of Africa, you need to read the Qur'an; many of the basic values of China and Japan will not make sense until you've considered the Confucian *Analects* and the Daodejing; and it's impossible to grasp American politics and culture without a basic knowledge of the Bible. Reading sacred texts provides in-depth knowledge and takes you into the heart of various traditions.

- If you come from the background of a particular faith, it can be disconcerting or even threatening to realize that other people believe different things with just as much sincerity as you do and that from a certain perspective, all religions seem rather implausible. But it's possible to remain true to one's own faith tradition while acknowledging the good in others.

- Many people nowadays say that they are spiritual but not religious, perhaps because they are wary of the track record of religious institutions. This might lead some to pick and choose passages from the sacred texts of the world to create a unique, personalized faith. However, as personally satisfying as a few random verses might be, it is still important to read sacred texts in the context of their own traditions. Taking sacred texts seriously means appreciating their

The Scriptural Reasoning movement recognizes that Christians, Jews, and Muslims may become aware of deep differences as they study one another's texts.

role in communities that provide support and solace but also make demands on believers.

- In the 1990s, Peter Ochs of the University of Virginia and David Ford at Cambridge began the Scriptural Reasoning movement, which encourages small groups of believers from Judaism, Christianity, and Islam to get together and read passages from their sacred texts. The point isn't to disparage or convert but to understand and learn from one another. The model for interactions is hospitality—to be a gracious host when inviting outsiders to comment upon one's own scriptures and an attentive guest when listening to insiders share their sacred texts.

- Scriptural Reasoning brings together adherents of the three Abrahamic religions, but an even broader vision of religious dialogue has been presented by the Dalai Lama, the spiritual leader of Tibetan Buddhists. In his book *Toward a True Kinship of Faiths*, he explores similarities and differences among Buddhism, Hinduism, Jainism, Sikhism, Christianity, Islam, and Judaism, with constant attention to sacred texts.
    - The Dalai Lama observes that an acceptance of religious pluralism does not necessarily undermine claims of exclusive truth. Even if all the major religions can't be equally true, they can nevertheless be equally legitimate; they are worthy of respect because we can imagine why intelligent, moral people might choose to believe, even if we ourselves don't share that belief.

    - It seems true that reading other people's sacred texts with empathy and understanding can make the world a better place. There will always be differences between religions that matter a great deal, but as we come to better understand and perhaps even admire those of different faith traditions, we can marvel at the religious diversity in the world and what those many traditions and scriptures mean in the human experience.

Suggested Reading

Gyatso, *Toward a True Kinship of Faiths.*

Ford, "An Interfaith Wisdom."

Smith, *What Is Scripture?*

Questions to Consider

1. Which sacred texts are most likely to reward reading by outsiders?

2. How can reading other people's scriptures lead to greater harmony and understanding in the world?

3. What difference might the comparative study of sacred texts make in our lives?

Heavenly Books, Earthly Connections
Lecture 36—Transcript

Hello, thanks for spending so many hours with me. As we come to the end of these lectures on sacred texts of the world, it might be useful to spend some time answering two questions: First, where do we go from here; and second, what difference might the comparative study of scripture make in our lives?

One of the pleasures of putting together this course has been the taking the opportunity myself to reread so many sacred texts. As I was writing lectures, I reread the entire Bible, including the Apocrypha; the Qur'an; the Bhagavad Gita; the Lotus Sutra; and much more. For good measure, I even read a couple of the gospels in Greek and the Daodejing in Classical Chinese. As I did so, I was constantly reminded what an odd thing it is to learn about written texts in an oral presentation like this one. I'll feel like a failure as your professor if after listening to all these lectures you don't actually read some of the scriptures that we've been talking about; so I'm going to make some specific recommendations, which will also give us a chance for a quick review of where we've come in these 36 lectures. For each of the major religious traditions, I'll give two or three texts, maybe 30–100 pages each, which would be a good place to start if you're coming to them for the first time. There are many translations available, but for a quick rule of thumb, the Penguin Classics and the Oxford World's Classics series consistently offer fine translations of many of the world's most significant sacred texts.

We'll start with Hinduism. If you're interested in Hinduism and you read only one thing from this religion, it ought to be the Bhagavad Gita. Although it's Smriti (remember that's "what's remembered") rather than Shruti ("what's heard"), it's nevertheless the most well-known and beloved scripture in Hinduism, and it's not too long. If you've already read the Gita and are feeling a little more adventurous, you might try a couple of the Upanishads, which are part of the Vedas and thus do count as Shruti. Remember that Smriti are authoritative writings that are attributed to human beings, while Shruti are considered to be divine in their origins; revelations of sacred syllables reverberating through the cosmos as perceived and transmitted orally by ancient sages. The Isha and Katha Upanishads are easy to read and they provide a good introduction to this literature.

For Judaism, it would be nice to try something from each of the three sections of the Tanakh. From the Torah, you might sample Genesis, which includes some of the most famous stories in the Hebrew Bible—stories of Adam and Eve, Noah and the Flood, and Abraham sacrificing Isaac—along with themes of covenant and strong female characters, and a marvelous story, it's almost a novella, of Joseph in Egypt. From the Prophets section, I'd recommend 2 Isaiah—that is, Isaiah 40–55—which most scholars date to the 6th century B.C.E., during the Babylonian exile. There, in magnificent poetry, you can read about the one God, his relationship with Israel, and his love for all humankind, with promises of deliverance, restoration, and renewal. From the Writings, you can't go wrong with the brief book of Ruth, a simple yet moving tale of ordinary people and extraordinary kindness.

By the way, if you've come from a Christian background, you should definitely take a look at the Jewish Publication Society translation of the Tanakh to see how Jews read their own sacred texts. As you'll recall, the entire Tanakh is regarded as holy, but the Torah, the first five books, is especially sacred and is read aloud in synagogues over the course of a year. Conservative Jews believe that the Torah was revealed by God to Moses, and some go so far as to assert that it predated the world and was used as a blueprint for creation. Other Jews accept the results of the historical-critical method, and view the Torah, the Prophets, and the Writings as the product of many sources edited, revised, and put together over centuries. Jewish tradition claims that Moses not only received the written Torah at Mount Sinai but also the oral Torah, which was eventually written down in the 3rd century C.E. as the Mishnah, and then later expanded into the two Talmuds. If you're interested in exploring that literature, a good place to start is the tractate Aboth (it means "The Fathers") in the fourth division of the Mishnah. The Aboth is a brief collection of wise sayings and moral maxims from famous rabbis; it's an easy document to sort of dip in and read around a little bit and get the feel of what's going on, and sometimes be inspired by what you might find there.

Moving on to Buddhism, one of the most beloved texts from the Theravada tradition is the Dhammapada, which sets forth the basic principles of Buddhist doctrine and morality in 423 verses. It's engaging; it's easy to read. The canon of Mahayana Buddhism is huge, but there's one book that's considered by many to be the fullest expression of the Buddha's teachings, and that's the Lotus Sutra. The book is a bit on the long side, maybe 300 pages, but if you were to read the first four chapters, 80 pages or so, you'll have a good idea of what it was all about. Those chapters include the famous parables of the Burning House and the Prodigal Son (not the prodigal son from the gospels; it's sort of this Buddhist version of a story that's similar in some ways). The Buddhist sutras were considered the words of Buddha, recalled and transmitted by his disciple Ananda, who'd heard them firsthand, memorized them, and passed them on; though the miraculous nature of transmission is much more pronounced in the Mahayana sutras, where there were bodhisattvas and celestial beings that were listening in to these sermons of the Buddha. For those of you who might like to try something from Zen Buddhism, which is a branch of Mahayana, you could read the *Mumonkan* (*The Gateless Gate*, it's called), which isn't the word of the Buddha but rather a 13th-century collection of 48 koans in the form of brief anecdotes about Zen masters and their students.

For East Asian religion and philosophy—and the boundaries between those two disciplines aren't very sharp in China and Japan—there are two texts that you should definitely start with: the *Analects* of Confucius and the Daodejing. The *Analects* are brief, fairly straightforward sayings of Confucius. The Daodejing, as you'll recall, was originally an anonymous collection of wisdom sayings that was later attributed to Laozi (the legendary Laozi) and then eventually elevated to the status of a divine text. You'll probably need to read this provocative but cryptic book more than once; and that's okay, because the Daodejing reads pretty quickly.

Two more major traditions to go: For Christianity, you should read one of the gospels. Mark is the earliest and the shortest; Matthew has the most connections to Judaism and includes the Sermon on the Mount; while the gospel of John is often regarded as the most spiritual. But I might recommend Luke, perhaps the most literary of the four; and then you could continue with the book of Acts, which was also written by Luke and offers a history of early Christianity. So for Christianity, read one of the gospels, maybe Acts, and then something from Paul. My Protestant friends would urge me to recommend the *Letter to the Romans*, since it offers the fullest account of Paul's theology; but in a post-theological world, I might say, if you're new to Christianity go with 1 Corinthians, which takes up a variety of issues that were of pressing, practical importance to the first generations of believers. Perhaps I should explain: By "post-theological world," I mean that today, even many Christians aren't that concerned about the nuanced differences of theology between different denominations and such. If you just want a sort of basic idea, go with 1 Corinthians.

If you're curious about Christian sacred texts that are outside the Bible, you might start with the Coptic Gospel of Thomas from the Nag Hammadi Library, which offers 114 short sayings attributed to Jesus. Many, as you remember, are similar to what we find in the four canonical gospels, but there are others that are puzzling and a bit strange; but they might provide insight into what it could've been like to hear the Christian message for the first time. The Gospel of Thomas can also serve as an example of an abandoned or a left-behind scripture.

The New Testament writings don't present themselves as direct revelation, but rather as reflective accounts of God's revelation in Jesus and the consequences of that divine intervention. Yet in some mysterious fashion, these human compositions are thought to have been inspired to such an extent that they're without substantive error and they contain all necessary spiritual truths, at least from a conservative Protestant perspective. Muslims, by contrast, view their scripture, the Qur'an, as a miraculous transcript of a heavenly book, the original of which is in Arabic. It's God's primary revelation to humankind, given to Muhammad with the angel Gabriel as an intermediary; and most Muslims believe that the Qur'an is coeternal with God, uncreated. So for Islam, the choice of which sacred text to read is obvious; but the Qur'an, with its 114 suras, is a bit on the long side, some 400–500 pages in translation. For newcomers, I recommend starting with some of the shorter, earlier, more lyrical revelations toward the end of the volume and then reading a few of the longer suras that appear at beginning—these were later revelations dating from the Medina period—maybe Sura 2, "The Cow"; 4, "Women"; and Sura 5, "The Table." If you're coming from a Jewish or Christian background, it might also be interesting to read some of the middle suras that are named after biblical characters: Sura 10 is named "Jonah"; 12, "Joseph"; 19, "Mary"; maybe 71, "Noah." Some Muslims feel that Sura 112 contains the essence of Islam; indeed, Muhammad himself declared that this short sura was equal to a third of the Qur'an. In its entirety, 112 says: "Say: He is God the One, God the eternal. He begot no one nor was He begotten. No one is comparable to Him." Muhammad says that sura is worth a third of the Qur'an.

Speaking of the words of Muhammad, if you're interested in the Hadith, or traditions about the Prophet, the best place to begin is with Al-Nawawi's 13th-century collection of *Forty Hadith*, which has long been the most popular introductory anthology of Hadith; that's the one that children begin to read right after the Qur'an. Each of the Hadith (there are actually 42) is about a paragraph long, so you can zip through this pretty quickly. It's well worth the effort.

Then a few suggestions for the newer, smaller religious traditions: The Adi Granth, also known as the Guru Granth Sahib, is the paramount scripture of Sikhism. As you'll recall, it's a collection of poetry by the Sikh gurus and some of their Hindu and Muslim predecessors, which was designated by the Tenth Guru as the perpetual guru of the community, and it's been treated accordingly ever since as a living guru in book form. The Adi Granth is rather large; and although translations are available online, it's somewhat difficult to find selections that would make for a good introduction. I'd recommend a 1995 anthology by Nikky-Guninder Kaur Singh, which is unfortunately now out of print, though a reprint was done by Penguin India a few years ago; and the other recommendation is Nirmal Dass's lovely translations of the writings of non-Sikh holy men that were incorporated into the Adi Granth.

The best avenue into the scriptures of the Latter-day Saints is, of course, the Book of Mormon, which was thought to have been miraculously translated from ancient gold plates that were given to Joseph Smith by the Angel Moroni. My Mormon friends might recommend that you jump right to the book of 3 Nephi, which tells the story of the resurrected Jesus appearing to the people in the Americas; but I'm going to suggest that you start with 1 Nephi instead, which makes up the first 50 or so pages of the Book of Mormon. It's one of the more action-packed segments, and it will give you a good sense of the narrative and its characteristic themes, including revelation, deliverance, prophecy, and the importance of scripture, as well as the allegory of the tree of life. I think you'll find it easier to follow the story, the narrative, if you read it in the Reader's Edition that was published by the University of Illinois Press (though I would say that, since I was the editor for that particular volume).

Finally, if you're curious about Baha'i, I'd recommend that you start with the Hidden Words, a collection of mystical sayings by Baha'u'llah, which he described as the essence of (and this is from the preamble) "that which hath descended from the realm of glory, uttered by the tongue of power and might, and revealed unto the prophets of old" In addition to the Hidden Words, many have found the book *Some Answered Questions* to be a clear introduction to Baha'i teachings. This volume, which originated from a series of conversational talks given by Baha'u'llah's son Abdu'l-Baha from 1904–1906, is also considered to be one of the sacred writings of the faith.

My goodness, we've covered a tremendous number of sacred texts in this course if those are only a few of the highlights; yet we've also learned that there's more to scripture than just words on a page. There's a great deal of variety in how these writings have been regarded and utilized in study, worship, and ritual. Remember that in some traditions, worship requires the exact words, like readings of the Hebrew Torah in conservative synagogues or memorizing the Qur'an in Arabic, while other faiths emphasize making the contents as comprehensible as possible; so the meaning is what particularly matters, and in this way Buddhists and Christians nearly always use their scriptures in translation. In Hinduism and Zoroastrianism, the sounds have sometimes been much more important than the meaning; and in many traditions, sacred books have been treated as holy artifacts. As an aside, the Sanskrit and the Avestan scripts—so those are the language of the Vedas and the Zoroastrian scriptures—each have 53 letters, making them two of the largest alphabets in the world, in part because priests in both of those traditions needed to pronounce their sacred texts as precisely as they could; they want the sacred texts to mirror as closely as possible the sounds, the sacred syllables, which they need to pronounce.

So in addition to actually reading some of the scriptures from this course, I have another assignment for you: I want you to get on YouTube and look for examples of sacred texts in use; perhaps Vedic ceremonies, or Buddhist sutra chanting, or Qur'anic recitations, or the singing of the Adi Granth in a Sikh temple or *gurdwara*. Watch some videos of religious weddings and see how sacred texts are employed there; or even better, you could attend a worship service of a religion that's not your own, and maybe even find someone to talk to. You'll discover that most places of worship welcome visitors, and if you already know a little about their beliefs and scriptures—that is, if you show some genuine curiosity and respect—you're sure to find believers who are more than happy to converse with you.

Now for the second big question: What difference might the comparative study of sacred texts make in our lives? Way back in the first lecture, I suggested that there were several good reasons to read other people's scriptures: They're easily accessible; they're usually central to the faith tradition; sacred texts can be compared with one another; they can be sources of wisdom, beauty, and awe; and finally, reading world scripture can help us better understand the lives of others and perhaps even provide greater insight into our own intellectual and spiritual commitments. As we close out this course, I want to talk a little more about that last reason: greater understanding.

People argue about religion all the time, and scripture can sometimes be used as a weapon or a wedge, particularly since many sacred texts make very strong, mutually exclusive claims about God, reality, and salvation. Yet reading scripture can also be a bridge between people with very different ideas about God, reality, and salvation. When you hold a particular sacred text in your hands, it may or may not contain the truth about unseen forces or other realms of existence, but it most certainly contains truths about millions upon millions of believers who have accepted that text as authoritative; people who have structured their lives around its precepts, or found meaning and satisfaction in its words, and comfort. These are texts that people have made a part of themselves through study and memorization; that have shaped the mental worlds that they live in, and that are often intrinsic to their identity.

If you want to understand what's going on in the Middle East or in much of Africa, you need to read the Qur'an. Many of the basic values of China and Japan aren't going to make sense until you've thought hard about the Confucian *Analects* and the Daodejing. It's impossible to grasp American politics and culture without a basic knowledge of the Bible. When you turn on the news or you travel as a tourist, you often see the results of religiosity, you see religion in practice; but reading sacred texts will provide a more in-depth knowledge and take you into the heart of the tradition where things get complicated. People submit to the authority of these texts, but they also struggle with them and they're inspired by them. To live religiously, for many believers, is to be in a perpetual conversation with the texts that one holds sacred.

Wilfred Cantwell Smith, speaking of Islam, has observed that:

> The attempt to understand the Qur'an is to understand how it has fired the imagination, and inspired the poetry, and formulated the inhibitions, and guided the ecstasies, and teased the intellects, and ordered the family relations and the legal chicaneries, and nurtured the piety, of hundreds of millions of people in widely diverse climes and over a series of radically divergent centuries.

But, of course, that's as true of Hinduism, Judaism, Buddhism, and Christianity as it is of Islam; and that may lead to a conundrum. It's useful, and often appropriate, to take an academic, religiously-neutral approach to world religions. We can study them, and we can study their sacred texts carefully and empathetically, while still remaining basically agnostic about their truth claims. But if we read world scripture as an expression of deeply human needs and aspirations, where does that leave those who might care personally about spiritual matters of transcendence or ultimate truth? As I was writing these lectures, I checked out hundreds of books from my university library, carrying big stacks of volumes back and forth from my office. Eventually the librarians noticed this pattern, and one asked me, "Doesn't reading about all these religions diminish your own belief, your own faith? That's what happened to me." That's not an unreasonable response. If you come from the background of a particular faith, it can be disconcerting or even threatening to realize that other people believe very different things with just as much sincerity as you do. Their ideas make as much sense to them; they have their own set of proofs and confirmations that aren't all that different from yours; and from a certain perspective, all religions seem rather implausible. With so many texts from so many faiths, who's to say, "I'm right, and all the rest of you are all wrong"?

Perhaps that's the case—I suppose we'll all find out in the end one way or the other—but the situation doesn't have to be quite so polarizing. It's possible to remain true to one's own faith tradition while realizing that it falls short of perfection and at the same time acknowledging the good in others; perhaps even admiring qualities that their religion has that are less pronounced in your own. The term "holy envy" has been used in such situations, and I've often felt it. The world's great religions have survived and flourished because they have by and large inspired their adherents to be better people, to care for others, and to work towards a higher vision of what life can be. There's no question that religion has also been a cause of conflict—of wars, oppression, and even atrocities—but if violent, extreme strands of devotion are not tempered over time, they tend to burn themselves out. That's not what most people are looking for.

Notice that I'm talking about religious traditions. Remember that texts become scripture when they're accepted as authoritative by faith communities, which may present a second conundrum. Many people nowadays say that they're spiritual but not religious, perhaps because they're wary of the track record of religious institutions (often with good reason). You could regard the sacred texts of the world as all equally true more or less, and pick out passages from here or there that make sense to you and inspire you, in effect creating a unique, personalized faith. Actually, I worry that I may have encouraged such an approach by recommending so many scriptures that are collections of quotations, like the Aboth, the Dhammapada, the *Analects*, the Gospel of Thomas, and the Hidden Words. But as personally satisfying as a few random verses might be, it's still important to read scriptures within the context of their own traditions, as I've tried to do in this course. Taking sacred texts seriously means appreciating their role within communities that provide support and solace, but also make demands on believers.

Let me conclude with two approaches to sacred texts that I think tend toward building bridges rather than erecting barriers or leveling differences. In the 1990s, Peter Ochs of the University of Virginia and David Ford at Cambridge University began the Scriptural Reasoning movement, which encourages small groups of believers from Judaism, Christianity, and Islam—from the three Abrahamic religions—to get together and read passages from their sacred texts. The point isn't to disparage or to convert, but rather to understand and learn from each other. The model for interactions is hospitality: to be a gracious host when inviting outsiders to comment upon one's own scriptures, and an attentive guest when listening to insiders share their sacred texts. David Ford, another founder of Scriptural Reasoning, has offered a series of guidelines, including the following; he says:

> The aim is not consensus—that may happen, but it is more likely that the conclusion will be a recognition of deep differences. Do not be afraid of argument, as one intellectually honest way of responding to differences—part of mutual hospitality is learning to argue in courtesy and truth ...Be open to mutual hospitality turning into friendship.

Scriptural Reasoning, although it originated in academia, offers a model of sacred reading, as opposed to secular reading. Again, David Ford: "Acknowledge the sacredness of others' scriptures to them (without having to acknowledge its authority for oneself)—each believes in different ways (which can be discussed) that their scripture is in some sense from God and that the group is interpreting it before God, in God's presence." There are both academic and nonacademic groups practicing Scriptural Reasoning today, though the movement is probably more prominent in Britain than in the United States. You can see some examples of Scriptural Reasoning in action, some discussions, at www.scripturalreasoning.org.

Scriptural Reasoning brings together adherents of the three Abrahamic religions—Judaism, Christianity, and Islam—but an even broader vision of religious dialogue has been put forward by the Dalai Lama, the spiritual leader of Tibetan Buddhists. In his book *Toward a True Kinship of Faiths*, he explores similarities and differences between Buddhism, Hinduism, Jainism, Sikhism, Christianity, Islam, and Judaism, with constant attention to sacred texts. Perhaps not surprisingly, he identifies the ethics of compassion as a common ground for all. But I'm also impressed by his observation that an acceptance of religious pluralism doesn't necessarily undermine claims of exclusive truth. Even if all the major religions can't equally be true, they can nevertheless be equally legitimate; meaning that they're worthy of respect, since we can imagine why intelligent, moral people might choose to believe, even if we ourselves don't share that belief. The Dalai Lama writes:

> The establishment of genuine inter-religious harmony, based on understanding, is not dependent upon accepting that all religions are fundamentally the same or that they lead to the same place ... I have no doubt that a sincere believer can, with integrity, be a pluralist in relation to religions other than his own, without compromising commitment to the essence of the doctrinal teachings of his own faith.

I certainly can't speak with the authority of the Dalai Lama, but I believe that reading other people's sacred texts with empathy and understanding can make the world a better place. There will always be differences between religions and those differences matter a great deal; but as we come to better understand and perhaps even admire those of different faith traditions, we can marvel at the religious diversity in the world and what those many traditions and scriptures might mean in the human experience.

Recommended Texts and Translations

Hinduism

Flood, Gavin, and Charles Martin, trans. *The Bhagavad Gita: A New Translation*. New York: W.W. Norton, 2012.

Miller, Barbara Stoler, trans. *The Bhagavad-Gita: Krishna's Counsel in Time of War*. New York: Bantam, 1986.

Olivelle, Patrick, trans. *Upanisads*. Oxford World's Classics. Oxford: Oxford University Press, 1996.

Patton, Laurie L., trans. *The Bhagavad Gita*. London: Penguin, 2008.

Roebuck, Valerie J., trans. *The Upanishads*. London: Penguin, 2003.

Judaism

Danby, Herbert, trans. *The Mishnah*. London: Oxford University Press, 1933.

Neusner, Jacob, trans. *The Mishnah: A New Translation*. New Haven: Yale University Press, 1988.

Note on the Bible: The New American Bible (Catholic), the New International Version (evangelical), the New Jerusalem Bible (Catholic), and the Revised English Bible (ecumenical) are all good translations, though the New Revised Standard Version (NRSV) is the most ecumenical and also the widely used version in academia. If you're new to the Bible, the NRSV is recommended. For the Hebrew Bible, be sure to take a look at the Jewish Publication Society Tanakh.

Buddhism

Carter, John Ross, and Mahinda Palihawadana, trans. *The Dhammapada: The Sayings of the Buddha*. Oxford World's Classics. Oxford: Oxford University Press, 2008.

Hurvitz, Leon, trans. *Scripture of the Lotus Blossom of the Fine Dharma (The Lotus Sutra)*. Rev. ed. New York: Columbia University Press, 2009.

Roebuck, Valerie J., trans. *The Dhammapada*. London: Penguin, 2010.

Sekida, Katsuki, trans. and commentator, and A. V. Grimstone, ed. *Two Zen Classics: Mumonkan and Hekiganroku*. New York and Tokyo: Weatherhill, 1977.

Shibayama, Zenkei. *Zen Comments on the Mumonkan*. Translated by Sumiko Kudo. New York: Harper & Row, 1974.

Watson, Burton, trans. *The Lotus Sutra*. New York: Columbia University Press, 1993.

East Asian Religions
Dawson, Raymond. *Confucius: The Analects*. Oxford World's Classics. Oxford: Oxford University Press, 2008.

Ivanhoe, Philip J., trans. *The Daodejing of Laozi*. Indianapolis, IN: Hackett, 2002.

Lau, D. C., trans. *Confucius: The Analects*. London: Penguin, 1979.

———, trans. *Lao Tzu: Tao Te Ching*. London: Penguin, 1963.

Leys, Simon, trans. *The Analects of Confucius*. New York: Norton, 1997.

Mair, Victor H., trans. *Tao Te Ching: The Classic Book of Integrity and the Way*. New York: Bantam, 1990.

Christianity
"The Gospel of Thomas." In *Lost Scriptures: Books That Did Not Make It into the New Testament*, edited by Bart D. Ehrman, pp. 19–28. New York: Oxford University Press, 2003.

Note on the Bible: The New American Bible (Catholic), the New International Version (evangelical), the New Jerusalem Bible (Catholic), and the Revised English Bible (ecumenical) are all good translations, though the New Revised Standard Version (NRSV) is the most ecumenical and also the widely used version in academia. If you're new to the Bible, the NRSV is recommended.

Islam

Abdel Haleem, M. A. S., trans. *The Qur'an: A New Translation*. Oxford: Oxford University Press, 2004.

Ali, Maulana Muhammad, trans. *The Holy Qur'an with English Translation and Commentary*. 7th rev. ed. Lahore: Ahamadiyya Anjuman Ishaat Islam, 2002.

——, trans. *A Manual of Hadith*. 2nd ed. Lahore: Ahamadiyya Anjuman Ishaat Islam, 1990.

Ibrahim, Ezzeddin, and Denys Johnson-Davies, trans. *An-Nawawi's Forty Hadith*. Cambridge: Islamic Texts Society, 1997.

Khalidi, Tarif, trans. *The Qur'an*. New York: Penguin, 2008.

Newer Religions

Abdu'l-Baha. *Some Answered Questions*. Translated by Laura Clifford Barney. Wilmette, IL: Baha'i Publishing Trust, 1990.

Baha'u'llah. *The Hidden Words of Baha'u'llah*. Translated by Shoghi Effendi. Wilmette, IL: Baha'i Publishing Trust, 2003.

Dass, Nirmal, trans. *Songs of the Saints from the Adi Granth*. Albany: State University of New York Press, 2000.

Hardy, Grant, ed. *The Book of Mormon: A Reader's Edition*. Urbana, IL: University of Illinois Press, 2003.

Singh, Nikky-Guninder Kaur, trans. *The Name of My Beloved: Verses of the Sikh Gurus*. San Francisco: Harper San Francisco, 1995.

Bibliography

Abdel Haleem, M. A. S., trans. *The Qur'an: A New Translation*. Oxford: Oxford University Press, 2004.

Abdu'l-Baha. *Some Answered Questions*. Translated by Laura Clifford Barney. Wilmette, IL: Baha'i Publishing Trust, 1990 (1908).

Alexander, Philip S., ed. and trans. *Textual Sources for the Study of Judaism*. Chicago: University of Chicago Press, 1990.

Ali, Maulana Muhammad, trans. *The Holy Qur'an with English Translation and Commentary*. 7th rev. ed. Lahore: Ahamadiyya Anjuman Ishaat Islam, 2002.

Alter, Robert, trans. *The Five Books of Moses*. New York: Norton, 2004.

Alter, Robert, and Frank Kermode, eds. *The Literary Guide to the Bible*. Cambridge, MA: Harvard University Press, 1987.

American Bible Society, "The State of the Bible, 2013." http://www.americanbible.org/state-bible.

———. *Synopsis of the Four Gospels, Revised Standard Version*. Rev. ed. New York: American Bible Society, 2010.

Armstrong, Karen. *The Bible: A Biography*. New York: Grove Press, 2007.

Aston, William George, trans. *Nihongi: Chronicles of Japan from the Earliest Times to A.D. 697*. 2 vols. London: Kegan Paul and Japan Society of London, 1896.

Attar, Farid Ud-Din. *Conference of the Birds*. Translated by Afkham Darbandi and Dick Davis. London: Penguin, 1984.

———. *Farid ad-Din 'Atar's Memorial of God's Friends: Lives and Sayings of Sufis*. Translated by Paul Losensky. New York: Paulist Press, 2009.

Attridge, Harold W. ed. *Harper Collins Study Bible*. Rev. ed. New York: HarperCollins, 2006. (Includes the New Revised Standard Version, with the Apocrypha.)

Baha'i Prayers: A Selection of Prayers Revealed by Baha'u'llah, the Bab, and Abdu'l-Baha. Wilmette, IL: Baha'i Publishing Trust, 1991.

Baha'u'llah. *Gleanings from the Writings of Baha'u'llah*. Wilmette, IL: Baha'i Publishing Trust, 1976.

———. *The Kitab-i-Aqdas: The Most Holy Book*. Wilmette, IL: Baha'i Publishing Trust, 1992.

———. *Writings of Baha'u'llah: A Compilation*. Rev. ed. New Delhi: Baha'i Publishing Trust, 1994.

Barlow, Philip. *Mormons and the Bible: The Place of the Latter-day Saints in American Religion*. New York: Oxford University Press, 1991.

Barton, Stephen C., ed. *Cambridge Companion to the Gospels*. Cambridge: Cambridge University Press, 2006.

Berlin, Adele, and Marc Zvi Brettler, eds. *The Jewish Study Bible*. Oxford: Oxford University Press, 2004. (Includes the JPS Tanakh translation.)

Blenkinsopp, Joseph. *The Pentateuch: An Introduction to the First Five Books of the Bible*. New York: Doubleday, 1992.

Bock, Felicia Gressitt, trans. *Engi-Shiki: Procedures of the Engi Era*. Books I–X. 2 vols. Tokyo: Sophia University, 1970–1972.

Bokenkamp, Stephen R. *Early Daoist Scriptures*. Berkeley: University of California Press, 1997.

Bokser, Ben Zion, ed. and trans. *The Talmud: Selected Writings*. New York: Paulist Press, 1989.

Bowman, Matthew. *The Mormon People: The Making of an American Faith*. New York: Random House, 2012.

Boyce, Mary, ed. and trans. *Textual Sources for the Study of Zoroastrianism*. Chicago: University of Chicago Press, 1990.

———. *Zoroastrians: Their Religious Beliefs and Practices*. London: Routledge, 2001.

Breen, John, and Mark Teeuwen. *A New History of Shinto*. Malden, MA: Wiley-Blackwell, 2010.

Brettler, Marc Zvi. *How to Read the Bible*. Philadelphia: Jewish Publication Society, 2005.

Brettler, Marc Zvi, Peter Enns, and Daniel J. Harrington. *The Bible and the Believer: How to Read the Bible Critically and Religiously*. New York: Oxford University Press, 2012.

Brockington, John, and Mary Brockington, trans. *Rama the Steadfast: An Early Form of the Ramayana*. London: Penguin, 2007.

Brown, Jonathan A. C. *Hadith: Muhammad's Legacy in the Medieval and Modern World*. Oxford: Oneworld, 2009.

Burton, John. *An Introduction to the Hadith*. Edinburgh: Edinburgh University Press, 1994.

Burtt, E. A., ed. *The Teachings of the Compassionate Buddha: Early Discourses, the Dhammapada, and Later Basic Writings*. New York: Penguin, 1982.

Bushman, Richard L. *Joseph Smith: Rough Stone Rolling*. New York: Knopf, 2005.

———. *Mormonism: A Very Short Introduction*. New York: Oxford University Press, 2008.

Calder, Norman, Jawid Mohaddedi, and Andrew Rippin, eds. and trans. *Classical Islam: A Sourcebook of Religious Literature*. London: Routledge, 2003.

Chan, Wing-tsit, trans. *A Source Book in Chinese Philosophy*. Princeton: Princeton University Press, 1963.

Chang, Chung-Yuan, trans. *Original Teachings of Ch'an Buddhism, Selected from the Transmission of the Lamp*. New York: Pantheon, 1969.

Charlesworth, James H., ed. *The Old Testament Pseudepigrapha*. 2 vols. Garden City, NY: Doubleday, 1983.

Chien-hsing Ho. "The Finger Pointing toward the Moon: A Philosophical Analysis of the Chinese Buddhist Thought of Reference." *Journal of Chinese Philosophy* 35(1): 159–177.

Christenson, Allen J., trans. *Popol Vu: Literal Poetic Version: Translation and Transcription*. Norman, OK: University of Oklahoma Press, 2004.

Church of Jesus Christ of Latter-day Saints, *Book of Mormon, Doctrine and Covenants, Pearl of Great Price*. Rev. ed. Salt Lake City, UT: Church of Jesus Christ of Latter-day Saints, 2013.

Cohen, Abraham. *Everyman's Talmud*. New York: Schocken, 1995.

Collins, John J. *The Dead Sea Scrolls: A Biography*. Princeton: Princeton University Press, 2013.

Collins, Raymond F. *Introduction to the New Testament*. Garden City, NY: Doubleday, 1983.

Conze, Edward, trans. *The Large Sutra of the Perfect Wisdom*. Berkeley, CA: University of California Press, 1975.

Conze, Edward, I. B. Horner, D. Snellgrove, and A. Waley, eds. *Buddhist Texts through the Ages*. Boston: Shambala, 1990.

Coogan, Michael D. *The Old Testament: A Historical and Literary Introduction to the Hebrew Scriptures*. Oxford: Oxford University Press, 2006.

———, ed. *The New Oxford Annotated Bible*. 4th ed. Oxford: Oxford University Press, 2010. (Includes the New Revised Standard Edition, with the Apocrypha.)

———. *The Old Testament: A Very Short Introduction*. Oxford: Oxford University Press, 2008.

Cook, Michael. *The Koran: A Very Short Introduction*. Oxford: Oxford University Press, 2000.

Cowell, E. B., ed. *The Jataka*, 6 vols. Cambridge: Cambridge University Press, 1895–1907.

Darmsteter, James, trans. *The Zend-Avesta*. 3 vols. Oxford: Oxford University Press, 1880–1887.

Dass, Gucharan. *The Difficulty of Being Good: On the Subtle Art of Dharma*. Oxford: Oxford University Press, 2009.

Dass, Nirmal, trans. *Songs of Kabir from the Adi Granth*. Albany: State University of New York Press, 1991.

———, trans. *Songs of the Saints from the Adi Granth*. Albany: State University of New York Press, 2000.

Davidson, Ronald, M. "Atisa's *A Lamp for the Path to Awakening*." In *Buddhism in Practice*, edited by Donald S. Lopez, Jr., pp. 290–301. Princeton: Princeton University Press, 1995.

Davies, Douglas J. *An Introduction to Mormonism*. Cambridge: Cambridge University Press, 2003.

Denny, Frederick M., and Rodney L. Taylor, eds. *The Holy Book in Comparative Perspective*. Columbia, SC: South Carolina University Press, 1985.

Despeux, Catherine, and Livia Kohn. *Women in Daoism*. Cambridge, MA: Three Pines, 2003.

Dimmitt, Cornelia, and J. A. B. van Buitenen, eds. and trans. *Classical Hindu Mythology: A Reader in the Sanskrit Puranas*. Philadelphia: Temple University Press, 1978.

Doniger, Wendy, trans. *The Rig Veda*. London: Penguin, 1981.

———. *The Hindus: An Alternative History*. New York: Penguin, 2009.

Dreazen, Yochi. "The Brazen Bibliophiles of Timbuktu: How a Team of Sneaky Librarians Duped Al Qaeda." *New Republic*. April 29, 2013, 34–37.

Duchesne-Guillemin, Jacques, trans. *The Hymns of Zarathustra*. Translated by M. Henning, Boston: Beacon Hill, 1952.

Dundas, Paul. *The Jains*. 2nd ed. London: Routledge, 2002.

Dunn, James D. G. *Cambridge Companion to St. Paul*. Cambridge: Cambridge University Press, 2003.

Earhart, H. Byron. *Japanese Religion: Unity and Diversity*. 5th ed. Boston: Wadsworth, 2013.

Edgerton, Franklin, trans. *The Beginnings of Indian Philosophy: Selections from the Rig Veda, Atharva Veda, Upanisads, and Mahabharata*. Cambridge, MA: Harvard University Press, 1865.

Ehrman, Bart D. *Lost Christianities: The Battles for Scripture and the Faiths We Never Knew*. New York: Oxford University Press, 2003.

———. *The New Testament: A Historical Introduction to the Early Christian Writings*. 5th ed. New York: Oxford University Press, 2011.

———, ed. *Lost Scriptures: Books That Did Not Make It into the New Testament*. New York: Oxford University Press, 2003.

Ehrman, Bart D., and Zlatko Pleše, trans. *The Apocryphal Gospels: Texts and Translations*. New York: Oxford University Press, 2011.

Esack, Farid. *The Qur'an: A User's Guide*. Oxford: Oneworld, 2005.

Faulkner, Raymond O., trans. *The Ancient Egyptian Book of the Dead*. Rev. ed. Edited by Carol Andrews. New York: Macmillan, 1985.

Feiser, James, and John Powers, eds. *Scriptures of the World's Religions*. 4th ed. New York: McGraw-Hill, 2012.

Flood, Gavin, ed. *The Blackwell Companion to Hinduism*. Oxford: Blackwell, 2003.

———. *An Introduction to Hinduism*. Cambridge: Cambridge University Press, 1997.

Flood, Gavin, and Charles Martin, trans. *The Bhagavad Gita: A New Translation*. New York: W.W. Norton, 2012.

Ford, David F. "An Interfaith Wisdom: Scriptural Reasoning between Jews, Christians and Muslims." In *The Promise of Scriptural Reasoning*, edited by David F. Ford and C. C. Pecknold, pp. 1–22. Malden, MA: Blackwell, 2006.

Foster, Paul. *The Apocryphal Gospels: A Very Short Introduction*. Oxford: Oxford University Press, 2009.

Friedman, Matti. *The Aleppo Codex: A True Story of Obsession, Faith, and the Pursuit of an Ancient Bible*. Chapel Hill, NC: Algonquin Books of Chapel Hill, 2012.

Friedman, Richard Elliot. *Who Wrote the Bible?* New York: Summit Books, 1987.

Gager, John G. *Reinventing Paul*. New York: Oxford University Press, 2000.

Gardner, Daniel K., trans. *The Four Books: The Basic Teachings of the Later Confucian Tradition*. Indianapolis, IN: Hackett, 2007.

Gernet, Jacques. "Christian and Chinese Visions of the World in the Seventeenth Century." *Chinese Science* 4 (1980): 17.

Gethin, Rupert. *Sayings of the Buddha: A Selection of Suttas from the Pali Nikayas*. Oxford: Oxford University Press, 2008.

———. *The Foundations of Buddhism*. Oxford: Oxford University Press, 1998.

Giller, Pinchas. *Reading the Zohar: The Sacred Text of the Kabbalah*. Oxford: Oxford University Press, 2001.

Givens, Terryl L. *By the Hand of Mormon: The American Scripture That Launched a New World Religion*. New York: Oxford University Press, 2002.

Goldman, Robert P., Sally Goldman, and Barend A. van Nooten, trans. *The Ramayana of Valmiki: An Epic of Ancient India*. Princeton: Princeton University Press, 1984.

Goodall, Dominic, ed. and trans. *Hindu Scriptures*. Berkeley: University of California Press, 1996.

Graham, William A. "Scripture." In *The Encyclopedia of Religion*, 2nd ed., edited by Lindsay Jones, pp. 8194–8205. Detroit: Thompson Gale, 2005.

Griffith, Ralph T. H., trans. *The Hymns of the Rig Veda*. London: 1889.

Guru Granth Sahib, Khalsa Consensus Translation, http://www.sikhs.org/english/eg_index.htm.

Gutjahr, Paul. *The Book of Mormon: A Biography*. Princeton: Princeton University Press, 2012.

Gyatso, Tenzin (Dalai Lama XIV). *Essence of the Heart Sutra: The Dalai Lama's Heart of Wisdom Teachings*. Translated by Geshe Thupten Jinpa. Boston: Wisdom Publications, 2002.

———. *Toward a True Kinship of Faiths: How the World's Religions Can Come Together*. New York: Doubleday Religion, 2010.

———. *The World of Tibetan Buddhism: An Overview of Its Philosophy and Practice*. Boston: Wisdom Publications, 1995.

Halbertal, Moshe. *People of the Book: Canon, Meaning and Authority*. Cambridge, MA: Harvard University Press, 1997.

Hardy, Grant, ed. *The Book of Mormon: A Reader's Edition*. Urbana, IL: University of Illinois Press, 2003.

———. *Understanding the Book of Mormon*. New York: Oxford University Press, 2010.

Harris, Stephen L. *The New Testament: A Student's Introduction*. 7th ed. New York: McGraw-Hill, 2012.

Harris, Stephen L., and Robert L. Platzner. *The Old Testament: An Introduction to the Hebrew Bible*. 2nd ed. Boston: McGraw-Hill, 2008.

Harvey, Peter. *An Introduction to Buddhism: Teachings, History and Practices*. Cambridge: Cambridge University Press, 1990.

Hatcher, William S., and J. Douglas Martin. *The Baha'i Faith: The Emerging Global Religion*. San Francisco: Harper & Row, 1984.

Hendricks, Robert G., trans. *Lao-Tzu: Te-Tao Ching*. New York: Ballantine, 1989.

Hendrischke, Barbara. *The Scripture on Great Peace: The Taiping jing and the Beginnings of Daoism*. Berkeley: University of California Press, 2006.

Hoffman, Adina, and Peter Cole. *Sacred Trash: The Lost and Found World of the Cairo Geniza*. New York: Schocken, 2011.

Holder, John J., trans. *Early Buddhist Discourses*. Indianapolis, IN: Hackett, 2006.

Holm, Jean, ed. *Sacred Writings*. London: Pinter, 1994.

Holtz, Barry W. *Back to the Sources: Reading the Classic Jewish Texts*. New York: Summit Books, 1984.

Inagaki, Hisao, and Harold Steward, trans. *The Three Pure Land Sutras: A Study and Translation from Chinese*. 3rd ed. Kyoto: Nagata Bunshodo, 2000.

The Israel Museum, *The Digital Dead Sea Scrolls*. http://dss.collections/imj.org.il/.

Ivanhoe, Philip J., trans. *The Daodejing of Laozi*. Indianapolis, IN: Hackett, 2002.

Jacob, Louis. *The Talmudic Argument: A Study in Talmudic Reasoning and Methodology*. Cambridge: Cambridge University Press, 1984.

Jacobi, Hermann, trans. *Jaina Sutras*. 2 vols. Oxford: Oxford University Press, 1884, 1895.

Jaini, Padmanabh S. *The Jaina Path of Purification*. Berkeley: University of California Press, 1979.

Jamal, Mahmood, ed. and trans. *Islamic Mystical Poetry: Sufi Verse from the Early Mystics to Rumi*. London: Penguin, 2009.

Jewish Publication Society. *JPS Torah Commentary*. 5 vols. New York: Jewish Publication Society, 1989–1996.

Johnson, Luke Timothy. *The New Testament: A Very Short Introduction*. Oxford: Oxford University Press, 2010.

Johnston, Sarah Iles, ed. *Religions of the Ancient World: A Guide*. s.v. "Sacred Texts and Canonicity." Cambridge, MA: Harvard University Press, 2004.

Kammen, Michael, ed. *The Origins of the American Constitution: A Documentary History*. New York: Penguin, 1986.

Kemp, Barry. *How to Read the Egyptian Book of the Dead*. New York: Norton, 2007.

Khalidi, Tarif, trans. *The Qur'an*. New York: Penguin, 2008.

Khoroche, Peter, trans. *Once the Buddha Was a Monkey: Arya Sura's Jatakamala*. Chicago: University of Chicago Press, 1989.

Kirkland, Russell. *Taoism: The Enduring Tradition*. New York: Routledge, 2004.

Klein, William W., Craig L. Blomberg, and Robert I. Hubbard, Jr. *Introduction to Biblical Interpretation*. Rev. ed. Nashville, TN: Thomas Nelson, 2004.

Kohn, Livia, ed. *The Taoist Experience: An Anthology*. Albany: State University of New York Press, 1993.

———. *Daoism and Chinese Culture*. Cambridge, MA: Three Pines Press, 2001.

———. *Introducing Daoism*. London: Routledge, 2009.

Kohn, Livia, and Michael LaFargue, eds. *Lao-tzu and the Tao-te-ching*. Albany, NY: State University of New York Press, 1998.

Kugel, James. L. *How to Read the Bible: A Guide to Scripture, Then and Now*. New York: Free Press, 2007.

Lao, D. C., trans. *Lao Tzu: Tao Te Ching*. London: Penguin, 1963.

Lau, D. C., trans. *Confucius: The Analects*. London: Penguin, 1979.

———, trans. *Mencius*. Rev. ed. London: Penguin, 2003.

Lawrence, Bruce. *The Qur'an: A Biography*. New York: Atlantic Monthly Press, 2006.

Layton, Bentley, trans. *The Gnostic Scriptures*. Garden City, NY: Doubleday, 1987.

Legge, James, trans. *The Chinese Classics*. 5 vols., 2nd rev. ed. (Four Books, *Documents*, *Odes*, *Spring and Autumn Annals*, with *Zuo Commentary*.) Oxford and London: Clarendon Press and Oxford University Press, 1893–1895.

———, trans. *The Chinese Classics*. 2 vols., 2nd rev. ed. (Four Books.) Oxford: Clarendon Press, 1893–1895.

———, trans. *The Li Ki* (*Records of Rites*). 2 vols. Oxford: Oxford University Press, 1885.

Levering, Miriam, ed. *Rethinking Scripture: Essays from a Comparative Perspective*. Albany, NY: State University of New York Press, 1989.

———. "Scripture and Its Reception: A Buddhist Case." In *Rethinking Scripture: Essays from a Comparative Perspective*, edited by Miriam Levering. Albany, NY: State University of New York Press, 1989.

Levinson, Sanford. *Constitutional Faith*. Princeton: Princeton University Press, 1988.

Leys, Simon, trans. *The Analects of Confucius*. New York: Norton, 1997.

Littlejohn, Ronnie L. *Confucianism: An Introduction*. London: I. B. Tauris, 2011.

Lopez, Donald S., Jr. *The Story of Buddhism: A Concise Guide to Its History and Teachings*. New York: HarperCollins, 2001.

———. *The Tibetan Book of the Dead: A Biography*. Princeton: Princeton University Press, 2011.

Mair, Victor H., trans. *Tao Te Ching: The Classic Book of Integrity and the Way*. New York: Bantam, 1990.

Major, John S., Sarah Queen, Andrew Meyer, and Harold Roth, trans. *The Huainanzi: A Guide to the Theory and Practice of Government in Early Han China, by Liu An, King of Huainan*. New York: Columbia University Press, 2010.

Mann, Gurinder Singh. *The Making of Sikh Scripture*. Oxford: Oxford University Press, 2001.

Matt, Daniel Chanan, trans. *Zohar: The Book of Enlightenment*. New York: Paulist Press, 1983.

Mattson, Ingrid. *The Story of the Qur'an: Its History and Place in Muslim Life*. 2nd ed. Malden, MA: Blackwell, 2008.

McLeod, W. H., trans. *Textual Sources for the Study of Sikhism*. Chicago: University of Chicago Press, 1990.

Meier, Pauline. *American Scripture: Making the Declaration of Independence*. New York: Knopf, 1997.

Miller, Barbara Stoler, trans. *The Bhagavad-Gita: Krishna's Counsel in Time of War*. New York: Bantam, 1986.

Mitchell, Donald W. *Buddhism: Introducing the Buddhist Experience*. New York: Oxford University Press, 2002.

Mittal, Sushil and Gene Thursby, eds. *The Hindu World*. New York and London: Routledge, 2007.

Moerman, D. Max. "The Death of the Dharma: Buddhist Sutra Burials in Early Medieval Japan." In *The Death of Sacred Texts*, edited by Kristina Myrvold. Burlington, VT: Ashgate, 2010.

Momen, Moojan. *The Baha'i Faith: A Beginner's Guide*. London: Oneworld, 2007.

Murcott, Susan, trans. *The First Buddhist Women: Translations and Commentaries on the Therigatha*. Berkeley: Parallax Press, 1991.

Nakayama, Miki. *Ofudesaki: The Tip of the Writing Brush*. 6th ed. Tenri, Japan: Tenrikyo Church Headquarters, 1993.

Narasimhan, Chakravarthi V., trans. *The Mahabharata*. Rev. ed. New York: Columbia University Press, 1998.

Nesbitt, Eleanor. *Sikhism: A Very Short Introduction*. New York: Oxford University Press, 2005.

Neuser, Jacob, trans. *The Mishnah: A New Translation*. New Haven: Yale University Press, 1988.

———. *Making God's Word Work: A Guide to the Mishnah*. New York: Continuum, 2004.

Nickelsburg, George W. E. *Jewish Literature between the Bible and the Mishnah: A Historical and Literary Introduction*. Philadelphia: Fortress Press, 1981.

Nigosian, S. A. *Islam: Its History, Teaching, and Practices*. Bloomington, IN: Indiana University Press, 2004.

Novak, Philip, ed. *The World's Wisdom: Sacred Texts of the World's Religions*. New York: HarperCollins, 1994.

Nylan, Michael. *The Five "Confucian" Classics*. New Haven: Yale University Press, 2001.

Nylan, Michael, and Thomas Wilson. *Lives of Confucius*. New York: Doubleday, 2010.

O'Flaherty, Wendy Doniger, ed. and trans. *Textual Sources for the Study of Hinduism*. Chicago: University of Chicago Press, 1990.

Olivelle, Patrick, trans. *The Law Code of Manu*. Oxford: Oxford University Press, 2004.

———, trans. *Upanisads*. Oxford World Classics. Oxford: Oxford University Press, 1996.

Olson, Carl, ed. *Original Buddhist Sources: A Reader*. New Brunswick, NJ: Rutgers University Press, 2005.

Pagels, Elaine. *Revelations: Visions, Prophecy, and Politics in the Book of Revelation*. New York: Viking, 2012.

———. *Beyond Belief: The Secret Gospel of Thomas*. New York: Random House, 2003.

———. *The Gnostic Gospels*. New York: Random House, 1979.

Palmer, Martin, trans. *The Book of Chuang Tzu*. London: Penguin, 1996.

Patton, Laurie L., trans. *The Bhagavad Gita*. London: Penguin, 2008.

Peters, F. E. *The Voice, the Word, the Books: The Sacred Scripture of the Jews, Christians, and Muslims.* Princeton: Princeton University Press, 2007.

Philippi, Donald L., trans. *Kojiki.* Tokyo and Princeton: Tokyo University Press and Princeton University Press, 1969.

———, trans. *Norito: A Translation of the Ancient Japanese Ritual Prayers.* Princeton: Princeton University Press, 1990.

Power, John. *Introduction to Tibetan Buddhism.* Ithaca, NY: Snow Lion, 1995.

Pregadio, Fabrizio, ed. *The Encyclopedia of Taoism.* 2 vols. London: Routledge, 2008.

Puskas, Charles B., and David Crump. *An Introduction to the Gospels and Acts.* Grand Rapids, MI: Eerdmans, 2008.

Radhakrishnan, S., trans. *The Principal Upanishads.* London: Allen & Unwin, 1953.

Rakov, Jack N., ed. *The Annotated U.S. Constitution and Declaration of Independence.* Cambridge, MA: Harvard University Press, 2009.

Ravitch, Diane, and Abigail Thernstrom, eds. *The Democracy Reader: Classic and Modern Speeches, Essays, Poems, Declarations, and Documents on Freedom and Human Rights Worldwide.* New York: HarperCollins, 1992.

Rhys Davids, Caroline, trans. *Psalms of the Sisters.* London: Oxford University Press, 1909.

Rhys Davids, T. W., and Hermann Oldenberg, trans., *Vinaya Texts.* 3 vols. Oxford: Oxford University Press, 1881–1885.

Rinchen, Geshe Sonam, and Ruth Sonam, author and trans. *Atisha's Lamp for the Path to Enlightenment.* Ithaca, NY: Snow Lion, 1997.

Rippin, Andrew, ed. *The Blackwell Companion to the Qur'an*. Malden, MA: Blackwell, 2006.

Robinet, Isabelle. *Taoism: Growth of a Religion*. Translated by Phyllis Brooks. Stanford, CA: Stanford University Press, 1997.

Robinson, George. *Essential Judaism: A Complete Guide to Beliefs, Customs, and Rituals*. New York: Pocket Books, 2000.

Roebuck, Valerie J., trans. *The Dhammapada*. London: Penguin, 2010.

———, trans. *The Upanishads*. London: Penguin, 2003.

Rogerson, John, ed. *The Oxford Illustrated History of the Bible*. Oxford: Oxford University Press, 2001.

Rogerson, J. W., and Judith M. Lieu, eds. *The Oxford Handbook of Biblical Studies*. Oxford: Oxford University Press, 2006.

Rose, Jenny. *Zoroastrianism: An Introduction*. London: I. B. Tauris, 2011.

Rosenberg, David, ed. *Congregation: Contemporary Writers Read the Jewish Bible*. San Diego: Harcourt Brace Jovanovich, 1987.

Roth, Harold D. *Original Tao and the Foundations of Taoist Mysticism*. New York: Columbia University Press, 1999.

Rumi, Jalal al-Din. *The Masnavi, Book 1*. Translated by Jawid Mojaddedi. New York: Oxford University Press, 2008.

Ruthven, Malise. *Islam in the World*. 3rd ed. Oxford: Oxford University Press, 2006.

Saeed, Abdullah. *The Qur'an*. London: Routledge, 2008.

Sailey, Jay. *The Master Who Embraces Simplicity: A Study of the Philosopher Ko Hung, A.D. 283–343*. San Francisco: Chinese Materials Center, 1978. (Includes 21 of the 50 Outer Chapters.)

Sardar, Ziauddin. *Reading the Qur'an*. Oxford: Oxford University Press, 2012.

Schipper, Kristofer, and Franciscus Verellen, eds., *The Taoist Canon: A Historical Companion to the Daozang*. 3 vols. Chicago: University of Chicago Press, 2004.

Scholem, Gershom, ed. *Zohar: The Book of Splendor*. New York: Schocken Books, 1963.

Schweig, Graham M. *Dance of Divine Love: The Rasa Lila of Krishna from the Bhagavata Purana, India's Classic Sacred Love Story*. Princeton: Princeton University Press, 2005.

Sekida, Katsuki, trans. and commentator, and A. V. Grimstone, ed. *Two Zen Classics: Mumonkan and Hekiganroku*. New York and Tokyo: Weatherhill, 1977.

Sells, Michael. *Approaching the Qur'an: The Early Revelations*. 2nd ed. Ashland, OR: White Cloud Press, 2007.

Shackle, Christopher, and Arvind-pal Singh Mandair, eds. and trans. *Teachings of the Sikh Gurus: Selections from the Sikh Scriptures*. New York: Routledge, 2005.

Shaughnessy, Edward L., trans. *I Ching: The Classics of Changes*. New York: Ballantine, 1996.

Siddiqui, Mona. *How to Read the Qur'an*. New York: Norton, 2007.

Silver, Daniel Jeremy. *The Story of Scripture: From Oral Tradition to the Written Word*. New York: Basic Books, 1990.

Singh, Nikky-Gurinder Kaur. *Sikhism: An Introduction*. London: I. B. Tauris, 2011.

Skjærvø, Prods Octor, trans. and ed. *The Spirit of Zoroastrianism*. New Haven: Yale University Press, 2011.

Skousen, Royal, ed. *The Book of Mormon: The Earliest Text*. New Haven: Yale University Press, 2009.

Smart, Ninian, and Richard D. Hecht, eds. *Sacred Texts of the World: A Universal Anthology*. Bristol: Macmillan, 1982.

Smith, John D., trans. *The Mahabharata*. London: Penguin, 2009.

Smith, Peter. *An Introduction to the Baha'i Faith*. Cambridge: Cambridge University Press, 2008.

Smith, Richard J. *The I Ching: A Biography*. Princeton: Princeton University Press, 2012.

Smith, Wilfred Cantwell. *What Is Scripture? A Comparative Approach*. Minneapolis: Fortress Press, 1993.

Snellgrove, D. L. *The Hevajra Tantra: A Critical Study*. London: Oxford University Press, 1959.

Solomon, Norman, ed. and trans. *The Talmud: A Selection*. London: Penguin, 2009.

Sprong, John Shelby. *Re-Claiming the Bible for a Non-Religious World*. New York: HarperCollins, 2011.

Stausberg, Michael. *Zarathustra and Zoroastrianism: A Short Introduction*. Translated by Margaret Preisler-Weller. London: Equinox, 2008.

Steinsaltz, Adin. *The Essential Talmud*. Rev. ed. New York: Basic Books, 2006.

Strong, John S., ed. and trans., *The Experience of Buddhism: Sources and Interpretations*. 2nd ed. Belmont, CA: Wadsworth, 2002.

Tatia, Nathmal, trans. *Tattvartha Sutra: That Which Is*. New York: HarperCollins, 1994.

Taylor, John. H., ed. *Journey through the Afterlife: Ancient Egyptian Book of the Dead*. Cambridge, MA: Harvard University Press, 2010.

Tedlock, Dennis, trans. *Popol Vuh: The Definitive Edition of the Mayan Book of the Dawn of Life and the Glories of Gods and Kings*. New York: Simon & Schuster, 1985.

Teiser, Stephen F., and Jacqueline I. Stone, eds. *Readings of the Lotus Sutra*. New York: Columbia University Press, 2009.

Thompson, Laurence G. "Taoism: Classic and Canon." In *The Holy Book in Comparative Perspective*, edited by Frederick M. Denny and Rodney F. Taylor, pp. 204–223. Columbia, SC: University of South Carolina Press, 1985.

Thomsen, Harry. *The New Religions of Japan*. Rutland, VT: Charles E. Tuttle, 1963.

Throckmorton, Burton H., Jr. *Gospel Parallels: A Comparison of the Synoptic Gospels*. Nashville, TN: Thomas Nelson, 1989.

Thurman, Robert A. F. *The Holy Teaching of Vimalakirti*. University Park, PA: Pennsylvania State University Press, 1976.

Tsai, Kathryn Ann, trans. *Lives of the Nuns: Biographies of Chinese Buddhist Nuns from the Fourth to Sixth Centuries*. Honolulu: University of Hawaii Press, 1994.

Van Voorst, Robert E., ed. *Anthology of World Scriptures*. 8th ed. Boston: Wadsworth, 2013.

VanderKam, James C. *The Dead Sea Scrolls Today*. 2nd ed. Grand Rapids, MI: Eerdmans, 2010.

Venkatesananda, Swami. *The Concise Ramayana of Valmiki*. Albany, NY: State University of New York Press, 1988.

Vermes, Geza, trans. *The Complete Dead Sea Scrolls in English*. Rev. ed. London: Penguin, 2004.

Waley, Arthur, trans. *The Book of Songs: The Ancient Chinese Classic of Poetry*. New York: Grove Press, 1987 (1st ed., 1937).

Ware, James R. *Alchemy, Medicine and Religion in the China of A.D. 320: The Nei Pien of Ko Hung*. Cambridge, MA: MIT Press, 1966.

Watson, Burton, trans. *The Complete Works of Chuang Tzu*. New York: Columbia University Press, 1968.

———, trans. *The Lotus Sutra*. New York: Columbia University Press, 1993.

———, trans. *The Tso Chuan: Selections from China's Oldest Narrative History*. (*Zuo Commentary*.) New York: Columbia University Press, 1989.

West, E. W., trans. *Pahlavi Texts*. 5 vols. Oxford: Oxford University Press, 1880–1897.

Wilhelm, Richard, and Cary Baynes, trans. *The I Ching or Book of Changes*. 3rd ed. Princeton: Princeton University Press, 1967.

Williams, Paul. *Mahayana Buddhism: The Doctrinal Foundations*. London: Routledge, 1989.

Wright, N. T. *Paul in Fresh Perspective*. Minneapolis: Fortress, 2005.

Yates, Robin D. S., trans. *Five Lost Classics: Tao, Huang-lao, and Yin-yang in Han China*. New York: Ballantine, 1997.

Notes

Notes

Notes

Notes